AMERICAN DREAMS, RURAL REALITIES

STUDIES IN RURAL CULTURE

Jack Temple Kirby, Editor

American
DREAMS,
RURAL
REALITIES

FAMILY FARMS IN CRISIS

Peggy F. Barlett

The University of North Carolina Press

Chapel Hill and London

97 96 95 94 93   5 4 3 2 1

Library of Congress Cataloging-in-Publication Data
Barlett, Peggy F., 1947–
     American dreams, rural realities : family farms in crisis /
Peggy F. Barlett.
          p.   cm. — (Studies in rural culture)
     Includes bibliographical references and index.
     ISBN 0-8078-2067-9 (alk. paper). — ISBN 0-8078-4399-7
(pbk. : alk. paper)
          1. Family farms—Georgia—Dodge County.   2. Agriculture—
Economic aspects—Georgia—Dodge County.   3. Dodge
County (Ga.)—Rural conditions.   I. Title.   II. Series.
HD1476.U6G43   1993
338.1′6—dc20   92-18027
                                                                        CIP

The paper in this book meets the guidelines for permanence and
durability of the Committee on Production Guidelines for Book
Longevity of the Council on Library Resources.

To Conrad Arensberg,

for the inspiration of his scholarly vitality,

To Charles Melville,

in appreciation of all we have learned together and

the joy we have shared over the life of this project, and

To Paul Dark,

in honor of his dreams of service to the farmers

of Arkansas, Georgia, and Madagascar.

CONTENTS

TABLES, FIGURES, AND MAPS

Tables

Figures

Maps

PREFACE

When I began this study, the American farm crisis was baffling for much of the public, and with good reason. In the late 1970s, tractorcade spokespersons predicted that failure to help farmers would result in massive foreclosures and a hungry country, but years passed with neither result. By 1981, after several disastrous drought years, many Georgia farmers predicted that if the situation did not improve, they would be forced out of business. But conditions got no better and most farms continued in operation. Media coverage of the crisis told stories of bankrupt family farms and tragic suicides, but the pressing questions remained unanswered: Are family farms doomed? Did the crisis decimate the ranks of our most competent farmers? Or is it true that only inefficient farmers were weeded out, those who deserved to be forced out of business? Will the agribusiness superfarm become the way of the future and transform America's rural regions?

This book finds answers to these questions and takes a critical look at trends in American farming, their impact on rural community vitality, and the effects of federal farm legislation. Through a long-term study of Dodge County, Georgia, I have tried to take the full measure of the damage from this decade of crisis. From 1982, when the 156 farm families participating in the project were first contacted, to 1989, when the study ended, one-third of the full-time operations were forced out of business. The crisis has been baffling—for reporters and researchers—because many farms on the edge managed to hang on, struggling with their creditors and supported by suppliers, family, and friends. At the same time, some farm operators continued to make a profit throughout these difficult years. Most part-time farmers and retirement farmers cut back their reliance on the operation and avoided any threat of foreclosure or bankruptcy.

The mid-1980s saw a new federal Farm Bill that poured millions of dollars into the farm sector with disastrous effects on the national deficit. Farm incomes improved, especially for the larger farms, and some operations began to pull themselves out from under crushing debt loads. This book reveals a chastened farm sector turning away from ambitious aspirations and dreams of quick wealth. Besides acknowledging the need for a sober retrenchment in farming methods and a change in attitudes toward debt, farm families have been forced to reassess enduring values, their lifetime dreams, and their personal definition of "success."

This book is an anthropological study that connects the detailed reality and experiences in one locale to larger questions of national significance about the farm crisis. Through my long-term relationships with farm families in Dodge County, I am able to share with the reader the experiences and opinions of individuals, honoring their achievements and joining in their disappointments. As I discuss further in the Introduction and the Conclusion, much of what the farm crisis brought to the Coastal Plain of Georgia, however, is echoed in the family farming areas of the Midwest. The microcosm of one county allows us to look deeply into American rural life and to document the transformation of an agrarian culture increasingly surrounded and challenged by an industrial society and its values.

A Drive to Dodge County

Dodge County, Georgia, is a long way from the farming villages of Latin America where I conducted my previous research on changing rural life. It is also a long way from the suburbs of Washington, D.C., and Chicago where I grew up. In some ways, it is another world from Atlanta, where I currently live, and Dodge Countians celebrate that difference. But actually it is not a long drive, nor is it a long stretch in understanding from the pink-tinged marble of Emory University to the country roads where the nation's food is produced, as I hope this book demonstrates. Since Dodge County is a less familiar world to most readers than the much-pictured Iowa farm, I will paint a brief picture of the county before outlining how the project was conducted.

The drive to Dodge County from the scenic Druid Hills neighborhood where Emory is located takes about three hours, starting at the Anthropology Department on the tree-shaded Quadrangle. Driving quickly through several black and white residential neighborhoods, we enter the expressway from a soaring ramp that deposits us in the river of cars moving south. We pass tall skyscrapers, the huge municipal hospital, then the gleaming golden dome of the state capitol. Soon the stadium slips by, followed by the residential neighborhoods surrounding Spel-

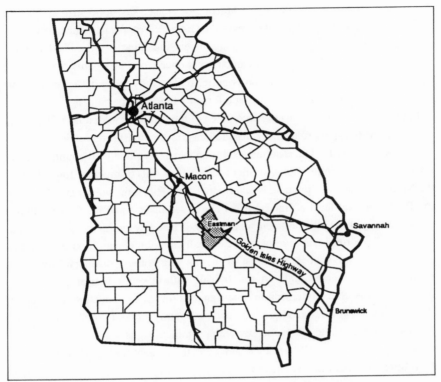

Map 1. Dodge County in the State of Georgia

man College and the rest of Atlanta University. The landscape becomes industrial, and we approach the Ford Motor Company plant. After the airport, the traffic is quieter, and we follow the interstate to our trip's midpoint in Macon.

This region is the Georgia Piedmont, home of the plantation South immortalized by *Gone With the Wind*. No longer a primary agricultural region, the Piedmont hills are too steep to be ideal farmland in this mechanized era. In the 1980s, the eroded red subsoil of the cotton heartland is covered with bustling suburbs, quiet pastures, forests, and small towns. To reach Georgia's prime rowcrop land, we drive south to the Coastal Plain, the southern half of the state that begins below Macon. As we pass through the Piedmont, the drive feels completely rural; only an occasional swingset or garage reveals the houses behind the dense pines mixed with oaks along most of the route. Though there are several good-sized towns before coming to Macon, their homes, businesses, and shopping malls are rarely seen from the interstate.

The best route through the city of Macon goes past a fast-food strip and into a quick-paced downtown expressway near the Civic Center. We pass the entrance to the Ocmulgee National Monument, a magnificent site of earth pyramids that stand as a reminder of the Native American city that once stood along this river. Then, sharply, the urban bustle of Macon is gone, replaced by swampy woodlands on both sides of the road and the wafting odors of a hidden papermill.

In this woodsy area begins the second leg of the trip, the Golden Isles Highway, a well-paved two-lane road that runs southeast to the coastal recreation areas so popular with tourists. The road moves through sparsely populated counties, flowing up and down gentle swells, similar to the rolling hills of much of Iowa. Unlike the Midwest, however, the land is mainly forested. This is the border area between the Piedmont—at least a thousand feet above sea level—and the Coastal Plain. Descending, rolling hills of green are interrupted by a few kaolin mines, small factories, and tiny rural communities. Occasionally a large, elegant house proclaims wealth from some source, but most of the housing is more ordinary. Well-kept, small brick and frame homes sit side by side with ill-kept rental properties with dirt front yards. Some intersections boast an old crossroads country store; many of these stores, however, have been replaced by brightly painted prefab convenience chains. Churches welcome passersby with prominent signs.

After passing through Bleckley County and the elegant homes of the small college town of Cochran, we enter the 500 square miles of Dodge County. Most stretches of the highway between Cochran and Eastman, the county seat of Dodge, are lined with attractive brick houses, many less than twenty years old. A few expanses of farmland, pasture, and woods hint at the rural economy, but for the most part, agriculture is not visible along such valuable real estate. After roughly a half hour's drive into Dodge County, Eastman comes into sight. Billboards, denser housing, and a grammar school announce an urban area of some 6,000 people. Soon a large modern high school appears, a water tower juts above the tall trees, and housing shifts to the sedate older homes with large porches that mark the downtowns of many small towns, North and South. Several big churches stand guard near the first traffic light, and banks and stores appear ahead.

If we follow this highway to the south, we will miss much of downtown Eastman. The Golden Isles Highway goes past several blocks of restaurants and businesses, another school, and then heads out of town, past a small industrial park and several spreading ranch houses facing lovely lakes. From Eastman, it follows the railroad line south, into farmland and woods, past an occasional house or trailer park set under large pecan trees. Perhaps fifteen minutes out of town, a lumber mill appears on the left, a remnant of the industry that brought William E. Dodge to the area. The small town of Chauncey is quiet now but once bustled with cotton gins and a turpentine still. It is the last settlement before the highway passes into the next county.

Back in Eastman, if we turn to the east, we come to a major transportation crossroads of the railroad and several highways that lead to nearby county seats and towns. A classic old railroad depot looks out over two rows of shops and businesses that line the tracks. In the next block sits the seat of county government, an impressive white-columned courthouse surrounded by modern office buildings. On the northern edge of town, we find a former cotton mill (now a hardware store) with its workers' housing still clustered around its own water tower, as if waiting still to hear the daily bell. The rest of the downtown area consists of black and white residential neighborhoods, trailer parks, and small businesses. As we drive out of town, house lots get larger and larger, their gardens bigger and bigger, until they are found on the edge of farms. Paved and dirt roads intersect, leading to the small rural communities that give a sense of identity and place to many Dodge Countians.

To visit some of the farm families in the study, we head down one of the county's dirt roads and turn at unmarked intersections, following instructions provided over the phone. Heavy summer rains often gully the road, and the car bumps its way over the rough terrain. Dust flies up, powdering the leaves. Nearing a creek, the land becomes swampy and forested, and the air feels suddenly cooler. The sides of the road close in with jumbled vines and trees; filtered sunlight dapples the dust. Soon, the roadsides open out again onto fields and pastures. A wooden frame farmhouse appears on the left, an old barn behind it. The house is shaded by an enormous oak tree, and a few shrubs and flowers decorate the front yard. Down the road sits a different kind of farmhouse: a brick ranch house with a carport. Tall metal equipment sheds face the house, marking the edge of the plowed fields. These homes are our destination; they stand in quiet tribute to the dreams and successes of the farm families who live within.

Description of the Project

Most of the information about Dodge County farms and families was gathered through formal questions and open-ended interviewing in homes, fields, and equipment sheds. Informal visits to farm families and participant-observation at farm meetings, livestock and crop sales, auctions, and church services provided further insights into Dodge County life. Other helpful sources of information were agricultural officials, lending agencies, farm suppliers, county officials, educators, and local historians. I lived in Dodge County for half of 1982 and the summer of 1983, sponsored by the National Science Foundation. After short visits in 1984 and 1985, I resided in Dodge County for nine months in 1987 and six weeks in 1989, supported by the National Science Foundation, the National Geographic Society, and the Emory University Research Fund. Emory students Barbara Sigman, Paul Dark, and Gregg Cochran assisted the work during the summer of 1983, and Alice Frye, Paul Patterson, and Marc Brooks in 1987.

Rapport with the local farm families was not easily established that first summer, especially in some areas of the county. June 1982, as it turned out, was a rather inauspicious time to begin the project. A farm equipment theft ring had just been exposed, and certain local farmers had been implicated by accepting stolen machinery. The Georgia Bureau of Investigation was continuing that inquiry, while also looking into accusations of vote buying in local elections. Ongoing marijuana surveillance throughout the Southeast had penetrated the county as well. The arrival of four researchers, supposedly to study the farm crisis, was greeted with some skepticism and suspicion. As a result, information gathering on sensitive financial issues was postponed in many cases until personal contact increased trust levels about the project. Efforts were made to share the results of the project widely and to obtain feedback from Dodge Countians. I sent copies of publications to all participants, wrote a series of columns for the local paper, and kept in touch through annual Christmas letters.

By 1987, relationships with many farm families were strong enough to permit discussion of highly confidential issues. Talks with families under severe financial stress or forced out of business were sometimes traumatic, leaving me shell-shocked and depressed by the vicarious experience of their loss. Occasionally, the pain of the crisis made us cry together. Other times, the family's anguish had resolved itself into new personal or spiritual insights, and those interviews were strengthening rather than draining.

In this intensive phase of the study, I also explored family history, personal aspirations, and attitudes toward farming and tried to interview men and women separately. Because the sample was so large and traveling across the county was so time-consuming, I was able to spend less time making casual visits than I would have liked. In all, I spent about seven hours with each of the less well studied full-time and part-time farm families and typically over twenty hours of interview and contact time with the more closely studied families. The gift of this time was precious, and I deeply appreciate the willingness of those in the study to share with me some of their most important and painful experiences.

Farm families agreed to participate in this study with the understanding that they would remain anonymous. Though I have used the actual words of individuals, I have made efforts to conceal the identities of the speakers. In many places in the text, I have said, "in one case," but actually there may be more such cases. Dodge County readers should be wary of trying to identify a particular speaker quoted here. Public perceptions of a farm's financial situation or a farmer's attitudes are often inconsistent with the details revealed to me in repeated conversations and through observation. For example, three neighbors each discussed a locally famous large scale farm, and one asserted confidently that it was about to go bankrupt, one said it was making good money all through the crisis because of the advantages it had, and the third concluded, "You know, he has to be hurting."

In describing the speakers of quotes, I have adopted the convention whereby the race of the speaker is assumed to be white unless identified as African American, though in a few cases, that identifier has been omitted to protect the anonymity of the speaker. In discussions where the age of the speaker is important, farmers who began in operation before 1960 are labeled "older," and those beginning in 1972 or after are labeled "younger." This usage reflects the three generations of farmers that are identified in chapter 2 and that figure subsequently in the analysis.

Quotations are an important part of depicting the experience and perspectives of the people I interviewed. I relied on field notes to capture people's responses and did not use a tape recorder. In presenting quotations, I have tried to use verbatim language, but in a few cases in which the original quotation was unclear, I altered the grammar to follow more standard English.

This project began and ended with the cooperation and patience of the many Dodge Countians who participated in it. It is a source of sadness to me that obligations of confidentiality keep me from thanking by name the many kind men, women, and children on Dodge County farms who made this study possible. I hope that through these pages they will hear their voices and know how grateful I am for our time together.

At every point in this study, I have received help from generous people, and I would like to thank at least some of them. In choosing Dodge County and in examining later questions about research methods and results, I was aided by

Talmadge DuVall, Director of the College of Agriculture at the University of Georgia, and by O. Cecil Smith, Gene Grimes, and many other agricultural extension faculty and administrators. I am also grateful to my colleagues in sociology, anthropology, history, and agricultural economics at the University of Georgia, Georgia State University, Abraham Baldwin Agricultural College, and Fort Valley State College.

In Dodge County, Gene Rogers, the county cooperative extension agent, was enormously helpful and considerate, as was Jeannette Cadwell, the extension home economist. I also thank Seaby Jones and the other members of the extension team. Robert Hall, Rachel Hargrove, Barbara Treece, Stacy Harrell, and the rest of the staff were endlessly patient in explaining the intricacies of the Agricultural Stabilization and Conservation Service. Jesse Bearden, George Clark, and the staff of the Soil Conservation Service went out of their way to help us with conservation issues. I appreciate the hospitable support of two county commissioners, Guy Tripp and Doyce Mullis, and their willingness to take time to answer my numerous questions. Many other courthouse workers extended kindnesses to the research team; we could not have survived without their cooperation—not to mention their maps and their photocopy machine!

For advice about Dodge County financial programs for farms, I am grateful to David Dillard, Mitch Wilcox, and Charles Atkins of the Farmers Home Administration, Tom Kite of the Production Credit Association, Al Scarborough of the Federal Land Bank, Rick Towns of the Federal Land Bank and later the Citizens and Southern Bank, and Joe Taylor of the Bank of Eastman. Johnny Johnson and Marvin Giddens of the Tri-County Peanut Company were also generous in their help in understanding Dodge County agriculture. Without the advice of Stan McDaniel of the U.S. Postal Service and his staff, we would have been unable to locate a number of farmers' rural addresses. I thank Danny Bennett for helping the project greatly in estimating the value of farm equipment, Tom Harton for sharing his atlas of Dodge County, and Julia Roberts of the *Times, Journal, Spotlight* for her generous coverage of the project.

The encouragement of state legislators Terry Coleman and Larry Walker, as well as the members of the Dodge County Chamber of Commerce and the Dodge County Rotary Club, is also appreciated. My assistants and I owe a special debt of gratitude to Buck and Lila Gilbert for providing nourishment for the body as well as the spirit. Over the years in Dodge County, I had the good fortune to rent two houses and an apartment, and I would like to thank my landlords Rick Towns, Wayne Graham, Grover Lee, and Winnie Hilton for their many kindnesses.

Experts at the Rural Development Center and the Soil Conservation Service

Preface

office in Tifton, the Agricultural Extension Research Center in Griffin, a Georgia Agrirama in Tifton all contributed to this work. Mike Hammer at the Georgia Crop Reporting Service was endlessly patient with my requests for data and queries on Dodge County and Georgia trends. I am indebted to attorney Martha Miller for thoughtful critiques of my Dodge County findings. I would also like to thank Senator Wyche Fowler, his associate Bob Redding, and Representative Roy Rowland for asking good questions and working toward a federal farm policy that may address more carefully the needs of farm families.

Rural social scientists from many disciplines have been helpful in sharpening my thinking, and I appreciate their support of an anthropologist in this project. Fred Buttel and Joe Molnar were among the earliest to open doors of cooperation; I also thank Christina Gladwin, Milt Coughenour, Jess Gilbert, Glen Elder, Patrick Mooney, Doug Bachtel, and Max Miller. Also helpful were Luther Tweeten, William Saupe, Susan Bentley, Linda Lobao, Lee Christenson, Ivery Clifton, Jan Bokemeier, Lorraine Garkovich, and Duran Bell.

A community of southern historians has been exceedingly generous in guiding me through the pine barrens wilderness, including Pete Daniel, Lu Ann Jones, and Jack Kirby. I would also like to thank Jim Roark, Jake Ward, Harvey Young, Ann Patton Malone, Mark Wetherington, Mary Odem, Allen Tullos, Kristin Mann, Jonathan Prude, Dan Carter, Elizabeth Fox-Genovese, and Cliff Kuhn.

My colleagues in anthropology have made this journey into U.S. agriculture a more pleasant process. I owe a great deal to the advice and work of Sonya Salamon, Janet Fitchen, Deborah Fink, Frank Cancian, Jane Collier, Jane Collins, Billie DeWalt, Robert Zabawa, Jane Adams, Henry Rutz, Ben Orlove, Stuart Plattner, Art Murphy, and Michael Chibnik. I am also grateful for the help I received from my Emory colleagues Carol Worthman, Fredrik Barth, Peter Brown, Bruce Knauft, Don Donham, and Mark Ridley. My work has also benefited from the stimulation provided by my students in the Gender and Feminist Anthropology seminar and the Ecological and Economic Adaptations course at Emory.

My thinking about Dodge County received important stimulation through the European research group on Multiple Job Holding among Farm Families, sponsored by the Arkleton Trust of Scotland, the European Economic Commission, the U.S. Department of Agriculture, and the Aspen Institute. I am especially grateful to Tony Fuller, John Bryden, Matteo Marini, Fernand Veuthey, Mark Shucksmith, Rudi Niessler, Lars Persson, Elena Saraceno, and Pavel Uttitz for their contribution to my understanding of European parallels to Dodge County processes.

This book is based upon research supported by the National Science Foundation under grant numbers BNS-8121459 and 8618159. Any opinions, findings, conclusions, and recommendations expressed in this publication are those of the author and do not necessarily reflect the views of the National Science Foundation. I am also grateful for support from the National Geographic Society, the Emory University Research Fund, and the Smithsonian Institution.

The Emory University Department of Statistics and Biometry and Dean Duncan and Al Shelton of the Emory Computer Center provided generous statistical and computer help. Over the years, the project has benefited from the advice of E. C. Hall, Ira Longini, Donna Brogan, and M. Elizabeth Halloran. The computer work involved in analyzing the Dodge County data profited from the efforts of Paul Dark, Marc Brooks, Elizabeth Guthrie, Maureen Eagle, Holli Levinson, Heather Dean, and Cary Hardwick. Betz Halloran provided invaluable help in carrying out the regression analyses in chapter 8, and I am grateful to Frank Cancian, Michael Chibnik, Duran Bell, Art Murphy, and Stuart Plattner for statistical advice.

The taming of my massive data into a manageable book would not have been possible without the experience and editorial encouragement of Paul Betz of the University of North Carolina Press. His wisdom, vision, and tact enabled me to produce a much better work, and I am grateful for all the help he gave me. The manuscript itself would never have seen the light of day without the endless patience and hard work of Judy Robertson. Her encouragement and enthusiasm helped lighten the burdens of this task. I am also thankful for the help of Debra Fey, Vicki Condit, Emma Dozier, Jennifer Chambers, Bobbi Patterson, and Eleanor DeBacher.

Throughout this book, readers with backgrounds in anthropology will recognize the influence of Conrad Arensberg, my doctoral adviser at Columbia University. One of the first from our discipline to resist the romance of far-off regions, he insisted that anthropology could contribute to the study of European peoples and industrial societies. His desire to make anthropology relevant not only in understanding agrarian change but also in ameliorating some of its negative effects has been an inspiration to generations of his students. My work has been profoundly affected by his persistence in seeking out the regularities in human behavior across cultural contexts, and I thank him for his generosity of spirit.

A decade-long research project is rarely a solitary effort. In addition to the experts, farmers, and students who supported me, I want to acknowledge the special help provided by Charles Melville. Beyond his patient visits to Dodge County and endless errands, his moral support made possible a journey of growth and love as well as a journey of knowledge and understanding.

AMERICAN DREAMS, RURAL REALITIES

INTRODUCTION

The farm crisis of the 1980s was a prolonged and violent thunderstorm, smashing dreams, frightening even the most economically secure farm families, and revealing in bright flashes some powerful changes in American rural life. Experts predicted that the crisis years would force out of business primarily small- and medium-sized family farms, leaving a structure of agriculture dominated by larger farms, dependent on hired wage laborers. In fact, the crisis hurt the largest farms as much or more than the others and forced a widespread reevaluation of the trend toward larger scale, ambitious expansion, and farm indebtedness.

This book draws on the stories and words of over a hundred farm families in an average county in Georgia's prime agricultural region to construct an account of the disaster years and their consequences. For social scientists whose interest in the farm crisis stems from concerns about the future of American agriculture and American rural communities, this study addresses controversies about family farming: debates about the eventual dominance of large farms, the importance of hired labor, the role of past and present government agricultural programs, and the impact of a more capitalist, entrepreneurial orientation to farm management. These debates must be located within the history of the region and the context of an agrarian way of life that is increasingly challenged by an encroaching national industrial culture. Dodge County has been the scene of tensions between an agrarian and an industrial way of life since its creation in 1870. Today, farm families face alternative visions of "success," "the good life," women's roles on the farm, proper child rearing, and prudent farm management. These dilemmas and options are reflected in decisions about farm and household management in the 1980s that in turn determine which farms survived the crisis.

Many of the dilemmas farmers face echo a wider American reality—struggles surrounding commitments to individualism versus family and community, con-

sumerism, long-term benefits versus short-term payoffs, and aspirations for upward mobility. To trace the emergence of these conflicting values, I have reconstructed aspects of social and economic life in the 1920s and 1930s and followed
the changes in rural communities from cotton tenancy in the Depression era to the
domination of owner-operated family farms in the present. After World War II,
sharp rural stratification gave way to greater economic mobility, new levels of
affluence, and a somewhat more democratic social and political order. Dodge
County and the nation saw a transformation in agriculture and industry, in markers
of social status, and in dreams of success. Its influence is seen not only in the
choices of full-time and part-time farmers and the way they run their farms, but
also in the risks they took in the 1970s boom years and the meaning of farm loss
for those now out of business.

Implications for American Communities

Unraveling the impact of the farm crisis is important not only because the farm
sector is an essential part of the American economy but also because the health
of the farm sector is linked to community welfare and the overall vitality of rural
regions. The agricultural sector (farms plus agribusinesses) employs a quarter of
the U.S. labor force and is the nation's largest industry (Lobao 1990:1). Though
farmers are only 2 percent of the population, the farming sector remains dominant
in a sixth of all U.S. counties. The *Wall Street Journal* warned in 1988: "The U.S.
has been suffering more than a farm crisis. . . . It is in the midst of a coast-to-coast,
border-to-border collapse of much of its rural economy" (August 4, 1988:1).

Of particular importance in these crisis years has been the issue of changing
farm structure; research from the 1970s suggested that large capitalist farms were
taking over U.S. agriculture (Buttel 1983; Hightower 1973; Vogeler 1981). Researchers from many fields have predicted that the number of farms will continue
to shrink until food is mainly produced on large farms, using mostly hired labor
(Goss, Rodefeld, and Buttel 1980; Tweeten and Huffman 1980). If such predictions are correct, there will be serious negative consequences for rural communities. When a multitude of farms in an area is reduced to a few large operations
(without corresponding changes in other job opportunities), community services
such as hospitals and schools are often cut back, and the vitality of community
life as measured by the number and kinds of stores, churches, and civic organizations declines as well (Fujimoto 1977; Goldschmidt 1978a; Murdock and Leistritz

1988; Sonka and Heady 1974). The cost to the nation of supporting banks and bankruptcies and of upgrading this diminished quality of life concerns legislators in Washington as well as citizens all over the country.

Large farms are usually dependent on a poorly paid class of farm workers, and thus a national farm structure based on large scale "superfarms" would necessarily be connected to higher levels of rural poverty (Goldschmidt 1978b). Recent research confirms this national pattern: farm counties heavily reliant on large operations using substantial hired labor have lower overall incomes, lower family consumption levels, and more limited life chances (Lobao 1990:70). Community life is also affected in adverse ways. Large scale farming and heavy use of wage labor are linked to less democratic political participation, lower community social participation and integration, greater unemployment, and possibly more limited future economic potential (ibid.:57, 192).

The Crisis in Dodge County

Georgia is an appropriate place for this analysis of the 1980s farm crisis because it was one of the hardest hit regions of the country. A succession of disaster-level droughts began in the late 1970s, and by the time that the early 1980s collapse of farm prices brought anguish to midwestern operators, Georgians had been in financial distress for five years. That distress continued until the middle of the decade then slowly began to lift. The impact of the crisis in Dodge County was severe but uneven. Between 1982 and 1989, one-third of the full-time farm operations were forced out of business. The two most vulnerable groups were heavily indebted large scale farms, many of whom hired full-time farm hands, and the farmers who began operation in the low-profit years. Among the bankrupt and foreclosed farms, a few were able to get back into business, but their financial condition in many cases remained precarious. At the same time that a third of full-time farmers were facing insolvency, others were making money. The unevenness of impact of the crisis has been one of the most cruel aspects of the anguish for individual families.

Farm loss is a devastating experience for those affected, wrenching marriages and tearing apart extended families. "It was a nightmare that'll never go away," admitted the former operator of a thousand-acre farm. Most farmers who looked elsewhere for work, however, were able to find adequate jobs without having to relocate, and their families now experience a new financial stability. This silver lining to the dark cloud of the farm crisis has been found in several other areas of the United States as well (Bentley et al. 1989).

Overall, farmers' management styles, investment decisions, and willingness to take financial risks were the most important determinants of survival (Bennett 1982; Mooney 1988). Some farmers benefited from more favorable opportunities to earn extra income through federal programs and others from strong skills or good soil, but the presence of such advantages could be outweighed by an ambitious farming style. Such a management orientation can be traced back in Dodge County history; it includes a desire to operate on a large scale, with sophisticated machinery, using hired labor, and with a particular concern for the family's social status and level of consumption. A view of the farmer as canny businessman, shrewd commodity dealer, supervisor of labor, and manipulator of government programs was supported in the 1970s by many sectors of the farm economy, as discussed in chapter 7. In the 1980s, unfortunately, an ambitious management style was more likely to lead to bankruptcy or foreclosure. A contrasting cautious management style reflected a different value orientation and personal aspirations. These operators avoided debt, preferred direct control over farm tasks, accepted a more modest standard of living, and expected hard manual labor and personal attention to detail to be the keystones to success. The cautious managers—both large and medium in scale—were more likely to make it through the crisis with their farm operations intact.[1]

My discussion of cautious and ambitious management styles may seem to parallel the "yeoman/entrepreneur" dichotomy described by Sonya Salamon in Illinois (Salamon 1985, 1992; Salamon, Gengenbacher, and Penas 1986). Her work, however, is based on diverse ethnic groups and the ways in which their farming and family traditions—adapted to specific European environments—were maintained under certain circumstances in the United States. Though aspects of "yeoman" farm management by Salamon's definitions are similar to my cautious management style (such as debt avoidance), her conception of the yeoman tradition involves other family goals not present in the Dodge County case (such as maintaining the farm as a generational trust). By Salamon's definitions, most Dodge Countians are "entrepreneurs" who seek family success and upward mobility, on the farm or off. Salamon's work finds that the entrepreneur tradition is more common among families of British Isles origins, and in fact most white Dodge County farmers (89%) come from Scottish, Irish, and English stock. The remaining 11 percent are African Americans, but their farming patterns show both the cautious and ambitious styles, the same as their white neighbors.[2]

In Dodge County and in parallel situations around the Midwest, the crisis brought a reassessment of the ambitious management style. Some farmers re-trenched, let go hired labor, and gave up the desire to operate such large units. A new wariness toward expansion and the use of credit became common. The cautious operators, at the same time, often felt vindicated. Their more modest living standards and medium-sized farms were more likely to survive without crippling debt loads. Researchers report similar patterns across the country (Fried-burger 1988, 1989). In Iowa the crisis spurred "a reassessment of conventional views" on good farm management and may be generating "a paradigmatic shift in rural America" (Bultena, Lasley, and Geller 1986:446). In a study of Wisconsin farmers, Patrick Mooney concludes, "Ironically . . . many of those who are sur-viving the crisis of American agriculture are those whose actions deviated from the profit-maximizing and optimizing calculations of the 1970s" (1986:54).

An analysis of the farm crisis reveals an intense ambivalence in many American farming families today as they face central unresolved questions: What consti-tutes a good farmer? What kind of life is best for my children? The rising costs of farming (and lowered profits) make entry into farming increasingly difficult. Whereas my reconstruction of the origins of current Dodge County farms shows that the post–World War II period allowed landless and small farm families to enter farming and to develop the operation successfully, farming today is a more closed occupation. Those younger farmers whose parents help them with land or capital have an edge in survival. In contrast, many parents who are not pleased with the income or security of farming urge their children to take off-farm jobs. Said one medium scale farm operator in his fifties: "I've discouraged my son from farming really; he'll be better off if he stays at the factory."

The Erosion of Agrarian Traditions

Though the crisis revealed the resilience of family farms and their ability to be competitive in an economic downturn, it paradoxically revealed certain cracks and strains in aspects of the agrarian way of life. The parents who urge their children to work off the farm are concerned with their future level of income, financial security, and other measures of success that have become dominant values in our industrial society. As the national culture surrounds the farm family, it becomes harder and harder to sustain an alternative vision of work, family, and community that values property ownership and independent production. A cautious manage-ment style must train children in relentless attention to crops and livestock, a multigenerational time frame for economic investments (with a subsequent decline in individual freedom), and an annual rhythm of effort and reward, of household scrimping and yearly payoffs. This kind of childhood socialization flies in the face of the American dream of a steady paycheck and a yearly vacation. Parents' desires for children to have "a better life," to "live comfortably," and "not to have to work as hard" may not be consistent with the survival of the farm.

The crisis also revealed tensions within the farm family and a decrease in commitment to the farm among women. Some wives of farmers were not reared on farms, and as mechanization replaced much of their field labor contributions, they became more distant from farm labor and decision making. Many women contributed essential support to the farm by working at jobs during the crisis. For a portion, such employment brought a gratifying opportunity to contribute to the family, as well as an interesting work experience. For other women, the necessity "to work off" represented the husband's failure in his breadwinner role. Pressures to reject a more agrarian value system continued on the job, as some women were ridiculed by their peers for contributing their income toward the family farm.

These strains within farm families reflect larger societal stresses stemming from an industrial economy. As business sectors rise and fall, workers must be willing to shift jobs and even location. The detachable worker must care about work quality and be responsible—but only up to a point. Monthly or weekly rewards substitute for knowledge of the overall operation, and drawing back from satisfaction with the big picture to satisfaction with the paycheck permits a different orientation to effort and reward, household consumption, credit, and risk. The farm family is in the thick of this national struggle to accommodate the demands of capitalism.

Partly because farmers are one of the few occupational groups able to resist being drawn "into the orbit of industrial and bureaucratic organization" (Starr 1982:25), they evoke an intuitive loyalty in the American psyche. Americans care about family farmers, even to the point of being willing to pay higher taxes to assure their survival (National Issues Forum 1987). There is no doubt that popular culture to some extent romanticizes family farms and minimizes the social rigidities of small towns and the hierarchies and constraints of the family enterprise (Fink 1992). Yet reverence for the farming life runs deep in our society, and it seems to reflect an appreciation for dimensions of satisfaction (Mooney 1988) that have been stripped from those of us who (in the words of a Georgia farmer) live "up there on the concrete." These dimensions include the following:

· personal empowerment and pride in meaningful work, work that clearly serves a wider societal need;

- the linkage of work and family, of long-term ties not only to kin but to a like-minded community;

- the combination of work and family with place and a sense of attachment to land and region;

- the sense that work and play, effort and leisure, flow into each other and grow out of each other; and

- a sense of daily connectedness to nature and to deeper spiritual realities embodied in the work process.

For many urbanites and suburbanites, the daily realities of supervised and secularized work, commodified leisure, frequent relocation, and fluid marriages evoke an appreciation for this alternative way of life. In assessing the outcome of a decade of drought and economic devastation for farmers, I hope to reveal aspects of America's wider transformation into an industrial society and the ways in which it affects farmers struggling not only to survive but also to "succeed."

Large Farms, Family Farms, and the Use of Hired Labor

My analysis of the farm crisis in Dodge County addresses the issue of family farm competitiveness under specific historical circumstances. In common with many economists, economic anthropologists, and other social scientists, I was primarily interested in the nature and functioning of certain forms of agricultural production when I began this study. In a market-based capitalist system, the economic performance of a particular form of production has an important role to play in its survival, and Nola Reinhardt and I have discussed a range of reasons for the competitiveness of family labor farm units (1989). Even where government policies have favored large scale bureaucratically organized farms in the Soviet Union, Cuba, and China, owner-operated agricultural units are usually more productive and more efficient (Reinhardt 1988; Rogers 1985; Rosenfeld 1985). Recent history has seen a shift of policies in many socialist countries toward smaller, family-run farms, as illustrated by Mikhail Gorbachev's call for a new Soviet farmer: "But first of all, what is needed is a person infinitely interested in the results of his work and responsible for it" (*New York Times*, July 1, 1984:4).

Alternative to this neoclassical focus on production units, competition, and efficiency is the approach that emphasizes political and economic relations between classes, and I have integrated some aspects of this perspective into the

Dodge County analysis as well. Researchers with this viewpoint argue that the survival of a particular form of production is determined by the "historical alignments of classes, manipulations of the political arena, or the interests of powerful elites" (Reinhardt and Barlett 1989:203). Analysis of agrarian class structures and governmental policies draws attention to the conditions that favor large scale production units and that have eroded family farm advantages (Bonanno 1987; Buttel and Newby 1980; Goodman and Redclift 1982; Mooney 1988).

The definition of a family farm is critical to the theoretical debate about the competitiveness or survival of this agricultural form. At issue is whether the focus will be on farm scale or the labor process; that is, whether a family farm is measured by its size and control of resources or by its reliance on hired labor. The term "industrial farm" is usually applied to farms with both of these characteristics—large factories-in-the-field, in which ownership, management, and labor are separated into distinct social classes (Barlett 1989). Such industrial farms are found in California and Arizona fruit and vegetable production but are relatively rare in the rowcrop and livestock areas of the Southeast and the Midwest. By this definition, there was one industrial farm in Dodge County at the time of this study, but it did not fall into the study sample. The neoclassical perspective labels as "capitalist" a farm that participates fully in the market, both to sell its products and to buy inputs. Though this market integration is important, I have used the phrase "capitalist farm" in this study to refer to a more industrial organization, with separation of laborers and owners and with goals and values more common to nonfarm industries.

Though researchers generally agree about the nature of industrial farms, disagreement exists over how to categorize farms that are owned and managed by families but that also use substantial hired labor (Rodefeld's "larger-than-family-farm" [1979]). Some theorists see these farms as capitalist—that is, more similar to industrial farms—while others treat them as variants of family farms (Friedmann 1978; Mann 1990). I have adopted a middle approach in which I call all the full-time farms in the study "family farms," but I have divided them into medium and large scale by combining dimensions of size and use of hired labor in a multidimensional categorization.

My ethnographic data revealed a number of problems in trying to divide these farms according to a hired labor criterion alone. Farmers who use full-time hired help often work in their fields and combine ownership, management, and family labor in ways very similar to the medium-sized farms that hire virtually no labor. Distinguishing between these two types of farms draws a line that distorts many commonalities. Although it is true that most farms that are large in size utilize the extra labor of hired hands, some are two- or three-way family partnerships that meet their needs with little paid labor. Cases also exist in which a farm lost a hired worker and subsequently shifted production strategies, adjusted for the labor loss, and otherwise continued much the same as far as the owner/operators were concerned. Another problem with the use of the labor criterion is that family members, even sons and daughters, are sometimes paid for their farm work. A farm in which a son is given a salary is often different in only minor ways from one in which the son is called a "partner" and shares access to the farm checkbook. Of course, the majority of farms in Dodge County that hire full-time hands are not employing kin but rather black and white laborers of diverse backgrounds. However, some part-time farm workers own and operate their own small farms. In sum, the multifaceted character of the labor force makes the use of hired labor form a continuum between an essentially family labor farm and a fully capitalist industrial farm. Additionally, some quite modest-sized farms tried, during the boom years of the mid-1970s, to use full-time hands in a more affluent farming style. Since in other dimensions of farm scale they could not be considered "large" or "capitalist," a labor-based definition of farm type was rejected for this study.

In light of the fact that the negative impact on rural communities of a more concentrated farm structure reflects a combination of fewer, larger farms and the creation of an agricultural proletariat, I have decided to categorize Dodge County farms by both farm size and use of hired labor. With regard to full-time farms, the distinction between large scale and medium scale farms is based on a combination of five factors: acreage, sales, capital investment, use of irrigation, and use of full-time hired labor (see chapter 4). Those farms in which the operator works full-time off the farm are categorized as part-time farms, most of which are small in scale. Those readers who are more interested in the labor process and the history of capitalist forms of production should keep in mind that though I use a more complex definition of large scale, in Dodge County most large farms do use full-time hired labor and most medium scale farms do not.[3]

Dodge County is a particularly useful place in which to study changes in farm structure because the use of hired labor and the existence of some large estates date back to the founding of the county. A diversity of farm types has existed since before the Civil War, and if large scale capitalist farms are indeed more competitive, it would be in a region with such congenial farming traditions that this form of agriculture could be expected to gain ground. However, reliance on wage labor and other forms of labor exchange declined greatly with mechanization after

World War II. The number of farms employing two or more full-time agricultural workers fell and is today a small fraction of the total in the county.

Family Farm Competitiveness: Risk, Management, Technology, and Government Policy

This study of the farm crisis of the 1980s sheds light on some of the reasons why family farms have been competitive in American agricultural history. Though the crisis was predicted to erode some of the natural advantages of moderate-sized, family-owned and -operated units, patterns of farm survival in Dodge County did not reveal this to be the case. The biological conditions of agricultural production are a key point of family farm competitiveness (Mann 1990; Reinhardt 1988). Susan Mann and James Dickinson (1978) argue that the time necessary for the growth of plants and animals—production time—is longer than the time during which human labor and capital are used, thus lowering returns to capital and making agriculture a less attractive investment. Though Dodge County farmers have become steadily more mechanized and capital-intensive since World War II, this gap between production time and labor time continues to keep expensive machinery idle for much of the year and provides a disincentive to escalation of capital investments and increasing scale.

Another dimension of the biological nature of agriculture is the need for complex manipulation of life processes, such that the desired species grow but undesirable ones do not. Weeds, diseases, and insect infestations can erupt quickly and devastate a farmer's fields. In controlling this biological risk, large scale units experience certain penalties for being unable to attend as well to scattered fields or many animals. The "biological character of agriculture impedes the development of the type of continuous flow assembly-line operation that is the hallmark of capitalist production" (Reinhardt and Barlett 1989:211).

Large scale farms also experience significant diseconomies of scale mainly from rising managerial costs as operations become more complex (Reinhardt and Barlett 1989:213). A farmer must absorb large quantities of information from many diverse field microenvironments over years of fluctuating weather. The manager of a 1,000-acre farm is therefore at a disadvantage compared to the manager of a 250-acre farm in this regard. Supervision of labor is another potential problem, causing substantial losses for several Dodge County farmers. The organization of farming tasks "in a timely manner" is also a challenge for the larger operation; some farmers who expanded to repay debts complained they could not attend properly to the acreage under production. Large scale farms can suffer from the necessity for "windshield farming," that is, too distant a connection to fields and biological processes, resulting in inadequate feedback, another potential diseconomy of scale. Farming methods can be tailored to the microenvironment of each field when the same person carries out all tasks and observes the results (ibid.:214). The linkage of effort with reward—lacking for many agricultural wage workers— is both part of the greater success of the family farmer and part of the joy that motivates the love of farming.

In other sectors of the economy, there are often substantial economies of scale (such as in auto manufacturing), but in agriculture the interactions of risk, technology, and connections to biological processes place limits on economies of scale (Friedmann 1978; Mooney 1988). John Young and Jan Newton (1980) argue that large farms have an advantage in lowering costs through bulk purchases of inputs or through special deals with agricultural service providers. Such advantages are enjoyed by large farmers in Dodge County, but they have not had a powerful effect. Medium scale farmers have been able to hold down costs in other ways— through more careful use of machinery, for instance—or they have occasionally cooperated with each other to obtain the same bulk purchases.

Technological change can erode family farm competitiveness by changing production methods to reduce risk or the effects of biological cycles, thereby making possible the industrialization of the agricultural process (Fink 1986b; Mann 1990). In Dodge County, such a process occurred in poultry production. Family farms lost the chicken and egg components of their production mix when agribusinesses developed large scale confinement systems. Other technological innovations reduce labor inputs, such as the mechanical cotton picker, the high cost of which requires a larger farm unit. Some farmers expand to support increased machinery costs; others avoid this pressure by hiring such services or sharing equipment with neighbors. Higher equipment costs in Dodge County, as in other parts of the country, have not required farm expansion to the point of using full-time hired labor (Friedmann 1978; Nikolitch 1969), and advances such as insecticides and herbicides have not been limited to the more privileged farms but have benefited a range of farm sizes.

Two recent technological developments that reduce risk have at first seemed to favor large scale farms (Goodman, Sorj, and Wilkinson 1987; Mann 1990), but their long-term effects are unclear. The first is the use of irrigation. Farmers that were able to afford the high costs of running and maintaining irrigation systems had a distinct advantage in reducing crop damage in the drought years. The second technological development is confinement systems of hog production. Increased costs and disease risk complicate the shift to such systems. Several farmers who made investments in large scale production of hogs have found profits insufficient to support the capital and operating costs. In both irrigation and hog production, then, we see examples of technological innovations that seek to raise profits by lowering risks, but their effect on the survival of medium scale family farms is yet to be seen. Both have been responsible for putting some large scale farmers in Dodge County out of business, while their medium scale neighbors breathe a sigh of relief that they resisted these innovations.

Competitiveness is also enhanced by the distinct goals and strategies of the family farm unit (Reinhardt and Barlett 1989). This organization of production can accept lower overall returns to resources since it does not have to pay wages (Chayanov [1925] 1966; Friedmann 1978). Intangible benefits of farm operation, such as property ownership and work satisfaction, balance these lower pecuniary returns (Mooney 1988). Strategies to pool resources among family members also help in farm survival. In addition to the common strategy of supplementing low farm incomes with the wife's off-farm work, in a few cases farmers received loans from other family members to help make mortgage payments. These strategies reflect a series of values embodied by the farm life that affect survival in the crisis years.

Though family farms have remained competitive, Mooney (1988) and others have drawn our attention to the ways in which they are increasingly controlled by nonfarm institutions and corporations, such as lenders, agribusiness contractors, and landlords. In Dodge County, these constraints seem to impinge on farmers' control to a lesser extent than in Mooney's Wisconsin study. Landlords are most often kin or neighbors, and their control over production processes is rarely burdensome. Relations with lenders have certainly been strained by financial hardships, but the abrupt terminations of support, pressure tactics, and arbitrary decisions found by both Mooney (ibid.) and Rosenblatt (1990) have not been typical in Dodge County.

Vulnerability to global market forces has increasingly characterized Dodge County agriculture in this century, but dependence on world commodity prices is nothing new in the South. International prices of cotton and other crops have always made fortunes or wrecked them. Dependence is much broader today, however, as Dodge County farmers buy expensive inputs, machinery, and parts and must contract for insurance, loans, and other services, all determined by markets

outside of their control. Farmers are squeezed at both ends of the production process, and as food is increasingly traded around the world, U.S. farmers complain
of "the cost-price squeeze."

A final critical issue in the competitiveness of family farms is the impact of
government policies that give special benefits to large scale farms (Barlett 1989;
Reinhardt and Barlett 1989), such as subsidized irrigation water and immigration laws permitting temporary Mexican migrants in California (Friedland 1984;
Padfield and Martin 1965; Thomas 1985). As discussed in chapter 2, New Deal
agricultural programs in the South provided subsidies to large scale farmers and
to capital-intensive production (Ford 1973; Schertz 1979). The displacement of
tenant farmers and the maintenance of large estates was due, in part, to the unequal distribution of federal resources (Daniel 1985; Kirby 1987). "The directors
of modern nation-states . . . have their hands on controls that can wipe out and
redefine social worlds within their boundaries. With very slight adjustments—
in prices, credit terms, pensions, quotas—the state can alter the panorama of
production and the quality of life in the countryside" (Harding 1984:197).

In contrast to some analyses of southern rural history, the Dodge County data
reveal that in spite of the effect of subsidies to the more affluent farmers, the post–
New Deal structure of agriculture came to be dominated by family labor farms.
Tenant farms virtually disappeared, but the large scale farms using hired labor
expanded only in size; the number of farms over 260 acres remained roughly constant. The majority of farm units after the Depression became owner operated and
used no full-time hired labor. The postwar history of the region supports theo-
ries of the competitive advantage of family farms, though large scale units have
certainly prospered and expanded their overall role in production.

A Culture in Transformation: Individual and Context

Though issues of family farm competitiveness are interesting and important, a
sufficient account of the farm crisis must go beyond the characteristics of the production unit and its economic environment to the social context of agricultural
production. Inherent in social science research is the tension between the study
of the "individual" and of the "society" or "the invisible hand" (Friedland and
Robertson 1990), that is, the different levels of analysis that produce different
kinds of understanding (Donham 1990). My approach has been to start with one
carefully selected county and then to explore in this microcosm the interconnec-

tions between the experiences of individuals and families and the wider cultural transformations on the regional and national levels.

I assume that farm men and women are rational, making choices and attempting to maximize their success in reaching certain goals (Barth 1967). The criteria of that rational maximization process are not predetermined by my analysis or limited to economic issues alone. Unlike more prescriptive studies in economics that assume that profit maximization is the proper goal of a farm firm, I have tried instead to understand farmers' own goals. In discussing the dichotomy of cautious and ambitious farming styles, I noted that they reflect different value orientations toward farming and definitions of personal success. I have also, at times, contrasted farmers' own conceptions of their behavior with my views, such as my interpretation that the ambitious and cautious farm management styles reflect the clash of industrial and agrarian economies. Combining both the diverse insiders' views and the outsider's view makes for a fuller understanding of this historical moment. Above the individual level are the small groups of people that make up households and farms. At times, these units of production and consumption are treated as the units of study, though I recognize that the interests of the individual and those of the household or farm are not unitary (Collins 1986; Fink 1992; Moore 1988).

Individual farmers today have been profoundly affected by macro-level processes, such as federal programs, changing technology, and increasing connections to international markets. Though the anthropologist's account of national policy and the world system is "necessarily partial" (Roseberry 1989:119), the study of a microcosm allows for the opportunity to measure these national and global economic processes and to discover additional dimensions in their unfolding on the local level.

For each of these levels of analysis—macro and micro—I have focused on three dimensions: economic processes, social stratification, and ideology. Economic processes are, of course, central to this study, and I have emphasized the micro-level issues of management styles and economic choices of farmers during the crisis. Connected to such choices are the historical dimensions of changing ideologies. For example, I explore the emergence of an ethic of "competitive consumerism" in Dodge County history and its links to the ambitious farming style. Unlike the situation described by Susan Harding for Ibieca, Spain, in which "villagers became captivated by secular, urban-dominated, regional and national systems of authority and belief" (1984:195), Dodge County has been for over a century the scene of conflicting views. The industrial mentality arrived in the central Georgia region with the railroads, northern investors, and merchants in the late 1800s (Malone 1981). The intrusion of new industries and deforestation altered the viability of the settlers' household economy, ushering in the era of cotton tenancy. The cultural ethos that valued "progress" through commercial development and risk-taking entrepreneurship clashed with the more cautious agrarian desire for independent landownership and avoidance of debt.

New patterns of social stratification that emerged after World War II led to greater emphasis on values of individualism and competitive consumerism. In Dodge County, the new opportunity structure of nonfarm jobs and rising family incomes broke open the rigidities of Depression-era rural communities. Farm expansion and greater affluence permitted some farmers to assert a higher social rank through the acquisition of brick homes, cars, televisions, freezers, and other consumer goods unimaginable twenty years before. Writers from Adam Smith to Alexis de Tocqueville have noted that when social status becomes more fluid within a market economy, personal achievement comes to be measured in the "style of life" that is necessary to belong to a specific "status group" (Weber 1968:932). Individuals coping with these new conditions reassess traditional values and may adopt new views or revive older ones; societal shifts "support the acceptance of new forms of consciousness, ideas, images, and worldviews" (Marchand 1985:3). These patterns are not limited to Georgia or to the South. Eric Wolf has argued that within capitalist societies in general, "success is demonstrated by the ability to acquire valued commodities; hence, inability to consume signals social defeat" (1982:390). Studies of Californians report a similar emphasis on materialist consumerism as a measure of achievement: "As the cash economy spread, money has become the dominant symbol of honor and worth" (Hochschild 1989:245; Rubin 1976).

For farmers, an acceptance of money and income as an important measure of status and success has profound implications. It can affect production decisions and family budgets, pushing farm expansion, greater indebtedness, and deferral of long-term savings or farm investments in favor of short-term standard of living. The pressures of the mass media, nonfarm neighbors, and especially children's school peers make it increasingly difficult to sustain alternative ideologies that resist the measures of personal success promoted by an industrial economy.

This example of the linkage of ideology, social stratification, and economic processes tries to draw the causal connections while at the same time providing scope for the agency of individuals. Though national and international forces can be at times overwhelming, it is important to avoid portraying farm families as victims or as helpless pawns; local cultures are capable of response and resistance to external forces (Roseberry 1989). At the same time, individuals and their motivations present an insufficient account of history. Goals and meanings are in part an adaptation to an individual's life circumstances and experiences (Barron 1990) and reflect a particular class structure and economic system (Donham 1990). Though I see on the macro level the primacy of economic and other materialist forces, on the individual level, my efforts have focused more on tracing the interactions of the economic, social, and ideological dimensions than on discovering the dominance of one over another.

One of the contributions of this study is the disaggregation of women's experience on the farm. Dodge County women's attitudes toward farming and conceptions of gender roles are another arena in which I have addressed economic change, social stratification, and values at several levels of analysis—individual, family, and national. This study has been influenced by recent research emphasizing that men and women do not necessarily experience the farm life or its demands in the same way (Fink 1986a; Haney and Knowles 1988; Fox-Genovese 1988; Rosenfeld 1985; Sachs 1983). In my attention to the diversity of women's views and expectations about the farm, marriage, and the meaning of success, I found that women's former roles in arduous field labor and the higher prestige of the role of full-time homemaker (Ryan 1981) encouraged many contemporary farm women to reject what I have called the agrarian marital model in favor of the industrial marital model. Women who hold a more agrarian model are emotionally attached to the farm, hold its success to be part of their own personal goals, and see responsibility for family livelihood as shared with their husbands. Women who adhere to an industrial marital model expect husbands to be the breadwinners and wives the homemakers. Farm women with this orientation support their husbands' farm efforts but are less personally committed to the farm.

These changing views of marital responsibilities and women's involvement with the farm constitute a shift in the "moral economy of the family" (Collier 1986; Handwerker 1986), a concept similar to the notion of the logic of production and reproduction used by many social scientists (Friedmann 1978, 1980; Gilbert and Akor 1988). Some farm women are opposed to continuing in farming, and the reasons for their antagonism reflect their gendered domains of responsibility. As the family's "consumption expert," a woman within the industrial marital model has a sense of personal success dependent on a level of income and a lifestyle that—in times of financial stringency—conflict with the need for frugality to insure farm survival. A focus on the changing moral economy of the family highlights not only dilemmas for individual Dodge County women and their choices to consume or save but also larger national shifts in gendered domains of responsibility and their implications for the survival of the family farm.

Dodge County: An Exceptional Case?

It is incumbent on anyone attempting to use a small scale unit in order to explore larger regional and national issues to discuss its representativeness. Dodge County was chosen to be as typical as possible of the agricultural areas in Georgia dependent on mixed rowcropping and livestock production.[4] Table I-1 shows that patterns of farm size, sales, and part-time farming in the Dodge County study are remarkably similar to patterns both nationwide and among the 57 counties of the Coastal Plain as well. The mean U.S. farm size was 440 acres in 1982; the same figure for the Dodge County study was 414 acres and for the Coastal Plain, 409. Though these averages conceal great diversity of farm size, the proportion of elite farms also suggests that Dodge County is not atypical. Large farms (over 1,000 acres) make up 8 percent of farms throughout the nation and 6 percent of those in Dodge County. The average U.S. farm sells nearly $59,000 worth of products a year, and in Dodge County, approximately $61,000. National statistics such as these combine full-time farmers and those who farm in addition to holding a full-time job off the farm. The proportion of part-time farmers is 36 percent in the nation and 34 percent in Dodge County. Even in the use of hired labor, the 23 percent of Dodge County farms using full-time hired labor is not far from the national level of 14 percent, a figure that combines very different areas such as the Midwest (which has little tradition of hiring full-time workers) and California (where many farms are dependent on full-time employees). The mean operator age is also similar—50.5 years nationally versus 47.3 in the Dodge study. Thus, in all of these key areas of size, scale, reliance on off-farm work, and age, Dodge County provides a useful microcosm for this study.[5]

Dodge County is located roughly in the center of Georgia, in the northern tier of Coastal Plain counties. It is one of the larger counties in the state, 500 square miles in area (1,295 square kilometers), and contains five towns and approximately twenty-five named rural communities. It is average in the receipt of federal farm benefits and less affected than many parts of the state by rural industrialization. Advice from several experts at the University of Georgia College of Agriculture helped in the selection process, during which I eliminated counties with recent

Table I-1. Comparison of Farm Characteristics:
Dodge County, Georgia Coastal Plain Counties,
and United States, 1982

	Dodge County Sample (n = 124)	Coastal Plain Counties (n = 57)	United States
Mean farm acreage	414	409	440
Farms 1,000 acres and over	6%	3%	8%
Mean gross farm sales	$61,373	$73,747	$58,858
Farms with sales $100,000 and over	19%	17%	13%
Part-time farmers[a]	34%	39%	36%
Farms with full-time hired hands[b]	23%	21%	14%
Mean age of operator	47.3	50.6	50.5

Source: U.S. Census of Agriculture, 1982.
[a]Farm operators who work 200 or more days per year off the farm.
[b]Workers employed 150 days or more per year on the farm.

extraordinary industrial growth, with unusual reliance on large peanut or tobacco program rights, with disproportionate numbers of small or large farms, and with heavy reliance on specialty crops, such as Vidalia onions or peaches. The director of the regional Agricultural Experiment Station commented in 1982 that a study of half the operators in Dodge County should provide an accurate cross-section of Coastal Plain farmers.

Although southern farms have some unique crop opportunities, Dodge County farms also have many similarities in their production mix to the more familiar family farms in the Midwest. As Gilbert Fite has said, "Within a generation after World War II . . . the modern commercial farmer in Georgia, Alabama, or Mississippi could not be distinguished from the progressive operator in Illinois, Iowa, or Nebraska, except in some of the crops he raised" (1981:207). Most are diversified rowcropping and livestock operations. Virtually all farms grow some grains: corn, wheat, millet, sorghum, and rye are common. Some of this acreage is for animal fodder, some for sale. Winter wheat and soybeans have made an important contribution to farm survival during the crisis by providing two harvests per year and generating important cash at spring planting time. Peanuts, a high-value crop due to government limitations on production, are central to earnings on most farms. Some farmers rely on cotton or tobacco for their main cash crop; others raise cattle or hogs as a specialization. Most full-time farmers sell three, four, or even six different crops a year as well as hogs and cattle.

The Diversity of Dodge County Farms

The 124 farms that make up the study were drawn from a 50 percent random sample of the 1982 list of farm operators obtained with the permission of the Agricultural Stabilization and Conservation Service.[6] Originally, 251 operators were contacted from this list, but many were found to be no longer active in the production of crops and livestock. Of 148 bona fide farm operators contacted, 94 percent or 139 eventually agreed to be interviewed. The farms of those who refused to participate covered a range of sizes and scale, and their omission does not seem to bias the sample. After those who were partners in joint operations or who operated fewer than 10 acres were eliminated, the total sample numbered 124 farms.[7]

In designing this study, I was concerned to capture the range of experiences of the farm crisis, and one of the advantages of a random sample methodology is that the full variation in human behavior can be measured and given weight according to its proportion in the population. Many dimensions of Dodge County agrarian culture cannot be discussed as "static custom" or a "homogeneous way of life" (Bennett 1982) but reflect diversity, heterogeneity, debate, and dispute. I have tried to portray not only the common themes of experience but also the variations from farm to farm and even the tensions within individuals who struggle with conflicting societal norms.

Race is one of the potential sources of diversity in the sample. African American farmers make up 11 percent (or 14 farms out of the 124 in the original sample). Found in full-time, part-time, and retired farmer groups, some are ambitious in management style but most are cautious. Because of the diversity among these fourteen cases, it is not possible to distill many generalizations about black farmers as opposed to white farmers, but such observations are made where possible in the text. Most black farmers emphasize that their problems are equally shared by other "small" farmers (though not all black operations are small). The stories and voices of black farmers are included throughout this work, but with care not to reveal details that could suggest individual identities.

There are several women farm operators in Dodge County, and four fell into the random sample. They have in all cases come to operate farms through the death of parents or spouses or through divorce, and their situations are quite different both from the other farmers and from each other. Because their numbers are so small, they are discussed in the text without identification as women in order to protect their anonymity.

A final note should clarify my definition of a farmer in deciding who would be included in the study. Not all those who claim to be "farmers" in Dodge County are actively involved in the production of crops and livestock. Such cases as a town business owner who rents out his parents' farm or a widow who keeps her land in trees were not included. But an auto mechanic with fifty acres of pasture and cows is involved in production and is considered to be a part-time farmer. Landowners who dedicate themselves to timber production alone and operators of farms under ten acres were excluded.[8]

When referring to "farmers," I have often been purposefully vague about gender, both to protect the anonymity of the women farmers in the sample and because some married couples consider both of themselves to be farmers. Relatively few farm women, however, agree that they should be labeled "operators" or "farmers," and so these terms refer mostly to men. At several points I discuss farm women and farm wives, but I do not talk about farm husbands because all of the women who are sole operators are unmarried, widowed, or divorced.

Organization of the Book

This book is divided into three groups of chapters, the first mainly historical, the second focused on the nature of farm life in the 1980s, and the third linking this context to the events and consequences of the farm crisis itself. The first three chapters trace the threads of the agrarian and industrial cultures in Dodge County from its founding to the present. Chapter 1 reviews the transition of Dodge County families from frontier settlers to sharecroppers and smallholders in the Depression era. Through the memories of living Dodge Countians, we can reconstruct the "Hoover Days" of the 1920s and 1930s and assess their impact on families today. Chapter 2 covers the transformation of agriculture in the post–World War II period and documents the transition from the world of cotton tenancy to a structure of agriculture dominated by family-owned and -operated farms. During this era, Dodge County families became more reliant upon nonfarm occupations; chapter 3 traces this change in the social world surrounding the farmer. "Good jobs" off the farm created new pressures for higher incomes on the farm, and many Dodge Countians rejected the farm life. Their assessments of "success" reflect the penetration of an industrial culture, and chapter 3 explores both the agrarian alternative to those values and the dual path of the part-time farmer.

Chapters 4 through 6 turn our attention to the farm families in the county today, beginning with the two different paths to success among full-time farms—large and medium scale. Their rates of survival through the crisis years are contrasted with those of the part-time farms and the retirement farms. The way farms are operated—the cautious and ambitious management styles—is the subject of chapter 5, and the lifestyles and consumption levels are contrasted for large, medium, and part-time farms. Chapter 6 takes up the issue of women's roles on the farm and outlines the agrarian and industrial marital models that summarize profound differences in the way women see their relationship to the farm. In each of these three chapters, I have tried to determine connections between the patterns in Dodge County life and the implications for farm survival in the disaster years.

The final group of chapters looks specifically at the 1980s farm crisis. Chapter 7 presents a review of the boom and bust years, farmers' adaptive strategies, and lenders' responses. Chapter 8 pulls together the analysis from all the chapters of the book and probes the determinants of farm survival. Its purpose is to answer the question, Who has made it through the farm crisis and why? Chapter 9 explores the implications the crisis has had for the overall structure of agriculture in the county and the ecological sustainability of the production system. It then turns to the familial level and documents the impact of farm loss in Dodge County, both in economic and in psychic domains. The Conclusion examines the larger issues in the crisis story for understanding changes in American culture and the future of our farming regions.

Often in the aftermath of a storm, the ordinary landscape is seen in a new and sharper light. It is my hope that this book will serve as a prism that refracts the light of contemporary history into the multiple hues of the many Dodge Countians— men and women, black and white, young and old—whose words (and deeds) fill its pages. In the end, the book represents only my own perspective as I seek to reconstitute the spectrum and, with it, to illuminate not only the farm crisis but also the American dreams that were brightened, shadowed, and then eclipsed.

CHAPTER

ONE

The Origins of Dodge County Farm

Culture in the Wiregrass Frontier

Along the back roads of Dodge County stand crumbling tenants' shacks, sagging old barns, and rotting mule wagons, mute testimony to the profound transformation in southern rural life over the last seventy years. The 1920s and 1930s were an era in which cotton sharecropping predominated among farming families, and sharp disparities existed between more comfortable families in town and the harsh poverty typical on small farms. Older Dodge Countians call those Depression years the "Hoover Days" and recount the specter of farm loss and dreams deferred. To understand Dodge County in the 1980s, one has to look back to life in the "Hoover Days" because the hard physical labor, the social stigma of farming, and the impoverished standard of living of that era make it a critical point of reference for many families. The cooperation within rural communities, the shared contributions of family members, and the sense of commitment to farming as a good way of life are also remembered. What today's farm families and their parents and grandparents recall of the Depression years profoundly affects how they have chosen to farm fifty years later.

The Depression era, in turn, reflects a clash of industrial and agrarian economies and values that emerged in the 1800s. The self-sufficient frontier farmers of this area of Georgia were caught up in the industries brought by northern investments in railroads and in successive booms of timber, turpentine, and tourism. Dodge County was established in 1870, and in later decades social stratification became more marked as the land filled with new migrants. Tensions emerged between an agrarian ideology, with a more egalitarian frontier tradition, and an entrepreneurial energy and orientation toward risk that brought short-lived prosperity. With the emergence of sharecropping, social rigidities increased, and a less democratic social order ensued. The early history of the county reveals an ever-greater integration with export industries, imports of manufactured products, and market forces. The ecological component of Dodge County history includes the devastation wrought by lumbering and the soil erosion of King Cotton. Through this historical background, the chapter traces the roots of the cautious and ambitious farming styles. The changing fortunes of these management orientations, and the larger value systems they represent, are a repeating pattern for Dodge County farm families from the 1800s to the present.

Settlers and Encroaching Industry in the Wiregrass Region

The early European settlers in the Dodge County area lived in an isolated frontier economy and enjoyed a more egalitarian social life than in many southern regions. At the time of first European contact, this part of Georgia was occupied by the Creeks, Native Americans living in loosely federated chiefdoms of scattered villages and towns. The Creek Secession of 1805 opened the land to settlers, who migrated mainly from North and South Carolina in the early 1800s (Owsley 1980). The region came to be thinly settled by a predominantly white population of farming families who engaged in agriculture, foraging, and livestock raising. Cut off by poor transportation from the cotton culture, several generations of inhabitants of the Dodge County area established a predominantly subsistence-oriented economy, supplemented by limited trade with coastal Savannah.

Dodge County is part of the "wiregrass" region, a belt of pine forests stretching from Norfolk, Virginia, in a crescent through Georgia to the Mississippi River.[1] The mixed soils of the region reflect a geological history of successive inundations by primordial seas. Sandy patches are interspersed with loamy and clay soils, leading to sections of oak/pine woodlands and more open grassland "prairies" (Wetherington 1985:50–61). The dominant longleaf pines created a thick canopy resulting in a relatively open forest floor, on which two-foot high wiregrass flourished.[2] Deer and other wildlife that fed on these grasses and on acorns and wild oats provided food for Indian and settler families. The settlers brought sheep, hogs, and cattle, which grazed freely, needing little protection from the mild winters. The region became a source of meat, wool, and hides for surrounding cities (ibid.:66). The tall pines and sandy soils gave early travelers doubts about the region's suitability for agriculture; some called it the "pine barrens." Once the

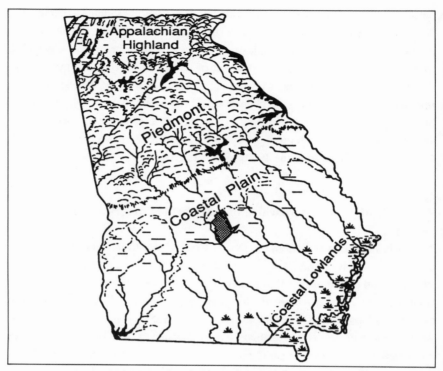

Map 2. Dodge County and the Geographic
Regions of Georgia

land was deforested, its soil variability was revealed, and some areas were found
to be ideal for agriculture. With fertilizer and lime to counteract soil acidity, much
of the wiregrass region was found to be highly desirable cotton land. Located
within what is now called the Coastal Plain region, Dodge County belongs to the
agricultural heart of Georgia.

By the 1860s, the settlers of Scottish and English origins developed a common
wiregrass culture grounded in the moral economy of small producers (McMath
1985:207). Ann Malone's study of eleven Georgia wiregrass counties finds a more
egalitarian ethic—even in race relations—than in other areas of the South. Most
settlers were landowners, owning hundreds of acres of which only a small portion was cleared for farming (Malone 1986:59). Though economic strata existed,
wealth differences were downplayed. Status was derived more from landownership and herd size than from standard of living. Neither clothing, furnishings,
nor education was highly valued in this frontier culture. "The object of work was

not social prestige based upon the accumulation of material wealth; rather . . . self-sufficiency and economic independence" (Wetherington 1985:14).

Slavery was also a part of wiregrass society, though perhaps less important in what was to become Dodge County than in some other wiregrass sections. Mark Wetherington found that for the region as a whole, one in four white men owned slaves; these slaveholders and their slaves made up about one-third of the population. Slave ownership was not necessarily evidence of affluence; it allowed some labor-scarce yeoman households "to increase their margin of self-sufficiency and, ironically, to guarantee their economic independence." For other families, slaves were a status marker, "a manifestation of individual ambition and middle class aspirations" (Wetherington 1985:16–17).

At the onset of the Civil War, many in the region were opposed to secession, but pinelanders served in disproportionate numbers in the Confederate army (Malone 1986; Wetherington 1985). The war and Reconstruction "produced little change in the subsistence-based society [of the wiregrass region] since its lands were not ravaged, and it was not dependent upon plantation agriculture or a slave labor force" (Malone 1986:55). By the 1880s, the wiregrass population included a sizable contingent of black landholders (a fifth of the population were former slaves), and they herded, farmed, and organized their homes and inheritances in ways indistinguishable from their white neighbors (Malone, personal communication). The "comparative lack of racial conflict" that characterized the region into the 1880s reflected both the relatively smaller number of black families and the "shared values and economic interests" that encompassed families of both African and European descent (Malone 1986:55).

The wiregrass settler economy was challenged in the post–Civil War era by the intrusion of railroads, extractive industries, migrants, and a new commercial ethos. "The economy, ecology, and sociology of the area [were] transformed within twenty years" (Malone 1986:73). The Macon and Brunswick Railroad, finished in 1872, cut through the wiregrass region and linked the cotton plantations of the Georgia Piedmont with coastal ports. Other rail lines followed, crisscrossing the area. The railroads served as promoters of the region, stimulating in-migration, commercial activities, and road construction.

The timber industry followed closely on the heels of improved transportation. Sawmills and lumber towns sprang up rapidly along the railroad lines to take advantage of the abundant Georgia pine forests. In the twenty years after the Civil War, the vast timber stands of the Great Lakes region and the northeastern United States were cut over, and lumber companies moved into the Southeast, Canada, and the Mississippi Gulf Coast in search of new stands (Eller 1982; Tindall 1967). One of the northern lumber barons was William E. Dodge, who established a timber colony in Georgia to replace his mills in Michigan, Pennsylvania, Wisconsin, and Canada (Wetherington 1985:220). In anticipation of the depletion of northern stocks, he formed in 1868 the Georgia Land and Lumber Company with several associates, including William Pitt Eastman from New Hampshire. The company claimed over five hundred square miles of timberland in five counties, much of it occupied by settler families (Cobb [1932] 1983).[3] Dodge was a former New York congressman, president of the New York City Chamber of Commerce, and a partner in Phelps, Dodge, and Company. In 1870, Dodge County was split off from neighboring counties and named after him. The county seat was named for William Eastman, and William Dodge donated the first courthouse (ibid.:28).

Turpentine production was another industry brought in with the railroads in the 1870s. Pine trees were tapped and the sap refined into turpentine, paint, oil, varnish, and other compounds needed by America's growing industries (Wetherington 1985:208). The forests, previously a common resource for settlers, became a resource for industrial uses as well. Settlers' sheep raising suffered as pitch-blackened fleeces brought lower prices. Also, turpentine workers were accused of poaching sheep and hogs. Labor in the turpentine industry was provided mainly by single black men brought in from Virginia and the Carolinas as forests there were played out. Living in camps provided by the company owners, this black proletariat was a source of tension with local farmers. Lumber camps were more racially mixed but were viewed as hotbeds of gambling, drinking, and violence. In later years, both turpentine and lumber workers were more often locals who tapped or cut trees for extra income or as an alternative to farming, reflecting a new pattern of wage labor less common in the wiregrass past.

These new industries brought a new scale of capitalist investment, a new organization of work life, and a new series of values that clashed with the settlers' agrarian traditions. In vertically integrated corporations, timber investors bought trees and lumber, built camps, introduced mechanical processing of the wood, and shipped it to construction sites throughout the country and abroad. Their massive investments in the 1880s dwarfed the commercial activities of previous entrepreneurs. "Crops could fail, creeks could dry up, and hogs could catch cholera, but the big mills continued to run 'smooth as oil' " (Wetherington 1985:220). For laborers, life in lumbering communities was dominated by the time-keeping whistle and new technology. In the 1880s, workers in the town of Chauncey were exposed to fancy saws, machine shops, and kilns. Although they were cut off from family and subject to the danger of injury, workers had access to better medical facilities and "electric communities" (ibid.:342, 235). The regimentation of life in these new wiregrass industries contrasted sharply with the autonomy and independence of the farming life.

The railroad and industrial growth in Dodge County established new communities, boosted local commerce, and trained a new capitalist elite. Eastman became a bustling community of engineers and businessmen led by lawyers and other political leaders (Wetherington 1985:389). The Georgia Land and Lumber Company trained a generation of successful entrepreneurs who went on to found new businesses in Dodge and nearby counties. Farmers resented the rise of wealthy merchants and bankers and wrote to local newspapers to complain of the consequent loss of their own social standing. One complained that the social order was becoming polarized into "crackers and gougers" (ibid.:410). The urban sophistication of the new industrial elites further widened the gap between them and rural farming families, whose plainer houses and homemade clothes came to be seen in a new light. "Eastman merchants, aware of an almost insatiable demand for 'Yankee notions' or anything with a European label, styled their establishments 'The New York Store' or 'the French Store' in an attempt to retain customers who were tempted to travel to larger cities" (ibid.:44).

A third industry—tourism—further spread the contact with northern industrial culture. Tourists were brought in by the railroad, attracted by the healthful, malaria-free climate of the piney woods region. Dodge County boasted two famous hotels in Eastman that brought chefs from New York City restaurants and managers from Adirondack resorts. By the early 1880s, Eastman was a "winter resort for Northern capitalists," southern elites, and convalescents, who enjoyed the mild climate and good air (Wetherington 1985:146–50).

Industrial growth had important ecological consequences for Dodge County settlers. The lumber companies clear-cut the land, and deforestation destroyed wildlife and reduced the forage for domesticated animals. "Thick shrubbery and briars" grew up where the loggers had worked, and streams filled with silt and disappeared (Wetherington 1985:242). As the timber was removed and farming expanded, soil erosion created new swamps and breeding grounds for mosquitoes. Malaria became endemic. Eastman became surrounded by "a sea of stumps," and its tourist industry declined.

From King Timber to King Cotton

By 1917, the massive stands of longleaf pines had been largely removed (Cobb [1932] 1983), and the turn of the century saw a great influx of migrants from eroded and more densely populated cotton regions to the north. From a density of only nine persons per square mile in 1885, the wiregrass counties in 1910 grew to a density of fifty (Wetherington 1985:128). At that time, 60 percent of rural families in Dodge County were landless tenants and sharecroppers, and a quarter had mortgaged property (ibid.:403). The era of the self-sufficient yeomanry had ended.

What caused the transition to cotton tenancy? Cotton prices, though fluctuating, often brought the best returns to family effort (DeCanio 1974; Mann 1990), and cotton farmers from exhausted lands in the Carolinas and north Georgia came in search of profits with which to buy their own farms. The construction of railroad lines revealed areas with ideal soil and brought in the fertilizers needed to make the land flourish. The cotton yields on the flatter Coastal Plain lands could be abundant; early settlers reported as much as two bales per acre (Wynne 1943:2). Fertilizers were often purchased on credit from town professionals and merchants who acted as agents for fertilizer companies (Wetherington 1985:281). When cotton prices fluctuated, however, a treadmill of debt left families with little choice but to continue—and even increase—their dependence on cotton (Wright 1986:110–11).

Cotton tenancy symbolized a major change in the wiregrass settlers' way of life. Sheep herding ended, and the region turned from an exporter to an importer of meat. Production of hogs, yams, and corn also declined as cotton replaced these food crops (Wetherington 1985:297). Tenancy affected both economic activities and daily life. Highly mobile sharecropper families paid little heed to land, fences, and trees and had little incentive to plant cover crops or to be concerned about soil erosion (Woofter 1936:108). Poor yields and low prices caused tenants "to be indifferent toward loan repayment" (ibid.:63). Yearly migrations diminished the desire to fix up homes or beautify them with flowers and sapped energy and "self-direction" (Raper 1936:62, 406–7).

Rural egalitarianism and racial harmony were challenged both by long-term tenancy and by new elites. Some wealthy townsfolk invested in agricultural estates, turning industrial and commercial profits toward this remaining source of income. Sharpening class lines in rural areas were also linked to new racial violence. In Eastman in the 1870s, blacks and whites drank in the same bars and their businesses were interspersed in the center of town (Wetherington 1985:415).[4] In contrast, between 1890 and 1910, a race riot in Eastman and lynchings in Eastman, Chester, Empire, and Beehive reflected rising social tensions in this transitional period (ibid.:437–40). Numan Bartley is probably correct, however, about a segment of the Dodge County rural population when he asserts, "Isolated from uptown's ceaseless struggle for status, life on the farm was less pressured, less achievement-oriented, more family-centered and, no doubt, more satisfying, provided the crop would only cash out when it came time for settling up" (1990:127).

On the eve of the 1920s, the prosperous boomtowns of the wiregrass New South were reeling, and some had been abandoned. The landscape had been transformed, and a new economy, based on cotton, had taken over. Thousands of migrants had come to this promised land, but landlessness grew steadily as the boll weevil and collapsing cotton prices took their toll. Pushed ever harder, the land eroded and produced less and less. The wiregrass region had a much shorter history of cotton production than the Black Belt counties described by Arthur Raper in *Preface to Peasantry* (1936), but by 1920 it had reached the threshold of a similar culturally and economically impoverished way of life.

The early industries of Dodge County were transformed as well. Railroad booms and busts led to several bankruptcies and northern control of many lines. Turpentine production continued only sporadically. By the 1980s, returns for turpentine labor were too low to attract workers. Though a few Dodge County farmers had turpentine workers tapping their trees when this study began, by 1989 these elderly black men had all died and no one had taken their places. The southern timber industry, however, received new life with technological advances developed between the world wars in Germany to remove resins from wood pulp (Tindall 1967). Paper companies replanted lands with fast-growing softwood varieties. Today, managed pulpwood stands, often rented from farmers or their heirs, and private timber lots provide firewood, game, and other forest products. Increases in Dodge County timber acreage began after World War II and soared abruptly with the 1950s Soil Bank program, which paid farmers to plant cropland in trees.

The Household Economy of the Depression Era

As Dodge County farmers today struggle with conflicting notions of what it means to be a good farmer and what constitutes personal success, they are influenced by their families' experiences during the reign of King Cotton. The household economy of the Depression era was bound up with world market prices, but it also was self-sufficient in important ways and was based on an interdependence of men and women. Not only did farm families cooperate in farm and domestic labor, but their organization of finances reflected, in many cases, a sense of pooled resources. This agrarian ethic of family cooperation and linkage between farm, family, work, and land emerges in the accounts of older Dodge Countians who recall their childhoods in the "Hoover Days."

Roosevelt's National Emergency Council described the rural South in 1938 as "a ravaged population living on depleted soil and suffering from inadequate diets, poor health, and unacceptable housing" (Bartley 1990:177). Though the memories of Dodge Countians have a less harsh tone, they document a way of life that had in some ways continued from the settler era but had in other ways deteriorated sharply. Low prices for cotton, the boll weevil, foreclosures, and daily hardships dominate the memories of farm families' struggles. Massive erosion and soil depletion undoubtedly exacerbated poor economic conditions, but few take note of the ecological crisis of the 1930s.

The farm economy of the 1920s and 1930s was based in part on self-sufficient agricultural production and foraging and in part on the sale of crops and livestock. Cotton was the primary cash crop, with tobacco an important supplement for some families. Livestock or milk products were also sold. Though corn was a primary staple, and beans of various kinds were important in the diet as well, Dodge County families remember eating vegetables all year round. Tomatoes, onions, cabbage, collards, okra, turnips, and Irish potatoes either survived in winter gardens or were canned. Home canning was widespread in the 1920s and 1930s among both races and all income groups. Sweet potatoes were stored for the winter in earth banks; root cellars were unknown. Wild foods such as blackberries, leaves for salads, and herbs for tea and medicines were also common. Game and fish remained an important component of the diet, as well as salted pork from the smokehouse. Beef was reported to have been eaten mostly fresh, and neighbors rotated in sharing the meat after butchering a calf. Other less fortunate families relied on a monotonous diet from the commissary or the local store.

Depression-era families purchased some items regularly. Farmers made a trip to town or to the local rural store, often on a Saturday, for wheat flour, salt, coffee, and sugar. Less frequent purchases included mayonnaise, ketchup, tea, and ice (for iced tea or lemonade). Sometimes the whole family went to town, but often the father went alone by wagon or on muleback. Children who went to town on Saturdays were often given money for candy, though one woman remembers preferring to buy bananas with her nickel. Fruit, in general, was a treat reserved for special occasions. Peddlers on regular routes also supplied rural communities with special items, such as oranges, ice, and fish. Several older farmers remember how cheap it was to live in those days. A "running bill" or credit line at the local store of $25 a month was sufficient to meet all the family's needs.[5] In the 1930s, a sharecropper who cleared $200 at the end of the year was thought to have made "a really big crop."

Most people during the "Hoover Days" lived in houses made of unpainted, rough boards and jokingly recall seeing the moon through the walls and the chickens through the floorboards. Most houses had a wood stove for cooking in the kitchen but no heat in the bedrooms. "We used quilts," said one man, and his wife added, "I feel like I get colder today than I did back then." Yards were swept bare, and one woman laughingly said that if they found a blade of grass in the yard back then, they pulled it up! With hogs, cows, and chickens scavenging through the homesteads, landscaping was impossible. Though a few people report that some families were "good livers" and had larger, white-painted houses, most who recall life in these rural communities emphasize the shared poverty and hardships: "*Nobody* had anything back then."

The house was part of the woman's domain on the family farm, and women also were responsible for the care of chickens and milk cows and had control of these products for sale. Children of tenant farmers and of all types of landholders report that their mothers sold eggs, chickens, milk, butter, buttermilk, or syrup. These products were sold to the local store or to the "rolling store," a wagon that followed a weekly route, buying, selling, and trading with rural households. Some women also sold wild berries in season.

Farm women were responsible for cooking, laundry, and other domestic work, though children were an enormous help to some. Doing the laundry, even into the 1950s, involved boiling the clothes in large pots of water, beating them on a stump with a paddle, immersing them in multiple pots of rinse water, and then wringing them by hand. Said one older woman, "My wrists were so sore, with all those boys." Women also made soap from potash, bones, and fat, though some Dodge Countians remember that a softer soap for bathing was one of the weekly purchases from the store. Women sewed most of the children's and girls' clothing; boys' and men's overalls were usually purchased. Every household had a sewing machine, asserted an older black woman. Children came home later from school than they do today and then performed daily chores such as hauling water and firewood, as well as garden work and animal care. All family members shared vegetable garden tasks.

The men's domain of crop and livestock production was labor-intensive, and women's and children's participation in field work was a necessity for all but the most elite families. Everyone picked cotton or harvested peanuts or tobacco. Even the families of some very large landholders, who hired full-time workers and had sharecropper families, were not exempt from the labor demands of harvest time. Of course, in families with many sons to help in the fields but a shortage of daughters to help with domestic chores, women might contribute less farm labor.[6] Only in a few cases were women completely spared field work out of status considerations. These were the families of the largest landowners with stores or other businesses, some of whom lived in town. Wealth did not automatically correlate with this division of labor, however; other daughters of wealthy storekeepers or large landholders reported having to pick cotton. As discussed in chapter 6, farm women rarely do field work in Dodge County today, and this pattern reflects one of many sharp divergences from the Depression-era household economy. Nor do women make soap or boil laundry—the farm life has come a long way, very quickly, from the "Hoover Days."

Women's farm production in those years offered a sphere of relative work autonomy, but women's income was often constrained by the necessities of the joint household enterprise. Unlike the reports in some areas of the country in which women's farm sales provided an independent discretionary fund and a power base within the family (Adams 1988; Fink 1986b), most Dodge Countians recall being too poor for such a luxury.[7] Only in the relatively rare cases in which basic food and clothing needs were met by the farm's production of cotton and other crops were women able to use their butter and egg proceeds as a discretionary fund under their own control. This money was commonly used to buy additional children's clothing, personal items, or products for the house and kitchen. One woman in her seventies fondly remembered her mother's "egg day." Each week, proceeds of egg sales were used to purchase clothes for a particular child, an exciting event for that girl or boy.

In more typical families, women's production was part of the weekly struggle to cover basic necessities. Such women did not feel they had any right to claim independent purchases nor, they report, did men. In this household economy, both men and women tended gardens, worked in the fields, cared for animals, and carried out some product sales. Men's work was not assigned exclusively to the market economy, nor women's to the home, and the accounts of those who lived through this period emphasize a "shared pot" philosophy in which neither husband nor wife was inherently dominant in financial decision making. This agrarian marital tradition survives today in some Dodge County farm families as does the tendency in wealthier households for women to see their money as a separate fund.

The careful use of money is often stressed as having been the ruling ethic of earlier times. A necessary virtue for landless and small farm families, frugality figures importantly in stories of wealthy families as well. One rich storekeeper and landowner was famous for saving money by collecting Coca-Cola bottles in the street and refusing to let customers take bottles out of his store. Other large land-owners talked about patching and repatching equipment, making do. The landless and landowners seem to have shared some values that softened the display of wealth and stressed the common ground among the social class groups in the rural communities.

Rural Communities and Three Social Groups

The egalitarian traditions of the wiregrass frontier survived in some aspects of Depression-era community life, but the hardships of the tenancy system created a more stratified rural world. Farming communities were relatively isolated, and transportation by mule or wagon was difficult. By the 1930s, Dodge County boasted only two paved roads, and travel between the rural communities—down dusty or muddy dirt roads—could be slow. One farmer grew up only seven miles from the community of his future wife, but "neither knew the other existed"; the distance was considered so far "it might as well have been Atlanta," he said. Every few square miles, the cluster of farm households formed a named community with a separate identity. Each community had one or more stores, a white church, and sometimes a black church as well.

These rural communities were described by many older Dodge Countians as made up of three groups of people:

• the landless, composed of tenants, sharecroppers, and wage workers ("the sharecroppers" or "the wage hands");

• the small farm owners ("the family farmers"); and

• the medium- and large-sized farm owners ("the comfortable").

The landless group was the most diverse in status, since it included some long-term tenants—who might be children of quite prosperous farming families—as well as more transient sharecroppers and full-time farm workers. Many older

Dodge Countians use the terms "tenant" and "sharecropper" interchangeably, though others are more careful to note the different combinations of land, labor, and capital exchange implied.[8] I have tended to follow Wayne Flynt (1989) in my use of the word "tenant" as a generic term for both forms of landless household producers. Dodge Countians do not emphasize status differences between tenants and sharecroppers, reflecting perhaps the fluidity both in the contractual arrangements and in the groups of families involved.

"Wage hands" were considered in some rural communities to be a step below tenants and sharecroppers, though not in others. These workers provided labor for both large and small farms and were often single men who lived with their employers. Some left the farm in certain seasons to work in sawmills or in turpentine production; others worked full-time in these industries and were provided credit and housing by their employers. Though their lives were similar in many ways to their sharecropper neighbors on large estates, these full-time industrial wage hands were seen by many farming families to be of sharply lower standing in the community. In general, however, the movement of landless individuals in and out of different kinds of work—by seasons and over the life course—militated against rigid class distinctions.

Small farm owners were the second major rural group, and their lands varied greatly in size, from twenty-five acres to several hundred. Said one man whose parents owned a hundred acres, there was as much of a social and economic gap between his family and the elite townsfolk as between his family and the black turpentine workers down the road. Informants' accounts of living standards suggest that the quality of life varied only a little with larger acreage. A 200-acre farm might be largely swamp or timber or it might need to support two or three times as many children as a smaller farm, and thus farms of 50 acres and 150 acres might yield little noticeable difference in family comfort. Some small- or medium-sized farm owners also operated a gristmill, which gave them an additional source of income. When a gristmill owner had a larger farm, the resulting income and social position might move that family to a more "comfortable" ranking above the small farmers.

"The comfortable," the wealthiest group in the rural social structure, owned large tracts of land operated by full-time hired labor, tenants, or both. The largest farmers commonly ran a "commissary" or general store, from which workers and tenants drew supplies on credit. Though some moderately large agricultural operations were limited to food and fiber production and small scale commerce, many were linked to the timber or turpentine industry or cotton processing as well.

Table 1-1. Depression-Era Farm Groups in Dodge County

| | Number of Farms* | | | | |
	1929		1934		1939
Tenants and sharecroppers	1,699	(72%)	1,673	(67%)	1,206 (59%)
Small farms	607	(26%)	717	(29%)	686 (34%)
Medium and large farms (260 acres and over)	60	(3%)	122	(5%)	141 (7%)
Total	2,366 (101%)		2,512 (101%)		2,033 (100%)

Source: U.S. Census of Agriculture, 1929–39.
*Numbers of farms are drawn from census tables of farm size, and proportions are calculated from tables of ownership categories.

Wealthy landowners in the Depression were commonly drawn from town business groups, though some were the heirs of large landowners from the settlement era.

The proportions of large farms, family farms, and landless groups varied from community to community, depending on land tenure history and the lumber and turpentine industries, but the census of agriculture reveals that sharecroppers and tenants were by far the most numerous group in Depression-era Dodge County (table 1-1). The census category of 260 acres and over is used here as a reasonable measure of the "comfortable" medium and large farms in the county. As the table shows, this group is very small, though it grows from 60 to 141 farms over the decade. In percentage terms, these farm operations are only 3 percent of the total in 1929 and rise to nearly 7 percent by 1939. During the "Hoover Days," very few families enjoyed the greater degree of comfort provided by the larger farms. Small farm owners grew from a quarter to a third of the total over this decade, and sharecroppers and tenants declined from 72 to 59 percent.[9] These figures reveal the beginnings of the major shift in southern agriculture toward the dominance of independent family farms that occurred after World War II. As the total number of farms fell in Dodge County, landless farms were being replaced slowly by larger owner-operated farms.

Though numerous, the tenant/sharecropper population of Dodge County was highly mobile and thus less able to participate in the community life of the land-owning families. Two-thirds of the landless families in 1934 had lived on their particular farm for only one year or less (U.S. Census of Agriculture). Only 16 percent of the total tenant population stayed for five years or more. If this percentage is applied to the 1929 figures in table 1-1, there were only 265 of these more permanent landless families in the county, many fewer than the small farm owners (607) at that time. This reconstruction suggests that, though numerically dominant, the mobile tenants and sharecroppers were often a less visible presence in rural communities (Raper 1936:59–60), and small farm owners often thought of themselves as the bulk of "the community." [10] Such a high rate of mobility affects the reconstruction of Dodge County history. Since only 11 percent of farm operators today are children of tenants or sharecroppers, accounts of the past may be somewhat biased by the perspectives of the landholding groups.

Economic and Political Inequalities

Although the memories of Dodge County farmers stress cooperative and egalitarian relations among wealthier and poorer families, the economic and political inequalities of the Depression era were marked. Control of land and capital resources was highly uneven (see table 1-1) and may have become more unequal as the Depression ground on. The profound insecurity of tenure, the specter of persistent debt, and the poor housing for many tenant families marked a chasm between the rich and the poor. As we shall see in chapter 2, the New Deal transformation of the southern economy and society altered many of these social class relations.

Large landowner families benefited in a variety of ways from their privileged economic position. Estate owners, especially those with stores, were described in several parts of the county as "driving people down," taking advantage of farmers in trouble to take their land.[11] One daughter of a sharecropper recounted bitterly that her parents did the work that put the landowner's two children through college. The capital accumulated from sharecroppers' efforts allowed a number of landowners to expand their farms. Political influence also enabled some to take advantage of tax sales or foreclosed property. Land was not the only property of value that was accumulated by wealthy farmers during the Depression. As New Deal agricultural programs were established, large landholders and politically well-connected individuals were able to amass the quotas and allotments that guaranteed future farm income.

Landowner families benefited from several kinds of services performed by their tenants. Many expected members of landless families "on the place" to help pick cotton or tobacco or to help with such special tasks as butchering. Large farmers also hired members of small- and medium-sized farm owner families at harvest, and some of these workers remember welcoming the opportunity for such work. Domestic work was another service available to families owning farms. Large scale farm families before World War II were surrounded by families who "helped out," and for some, these advantages continued on into the 1950s. One woman who reared a large family in the 1940s and 1950s reported having one woman come in to cook, two "nursemaids to play with the children," and a full-time "yard man." She arranged additional temporary help on a regular basis for house-cleaning and laundry and remembers these families as being "eager to find work." The workers lived in houses on or near the property and provided field labor for the farm as well. The hiring of domestic help was not limited to elite farm families, however. One woman who lived on a small farm worked by sharecroppers while her husband was employed in town received household and child care assistance from the women of the landless families.

Rural families are reported to have shared a common diet, and it is widely asserted that landholders made sure that tenants ate as well as they did. Regardless of whether this is true, the fact that there are no specific foods commonly attributed to wealthy households is significant. At the same time, some landless families were clearly at a disadvantage because owners could prohibit them from having their own hogs or cattle, thereby depriving them of this independent source of income.

Landless families were also vulnerable to the soil quality of the farm they were given. Better land meant better yields, higher profits, and a greater chance for upward mobility to buy a farm. The confidence of a large landholder also could translate into better access to loans, information about a farm for sale, or a bargain in mules or equipment. Large landholders knew the differential productivity of the farms they let out, and they made an effort to give the best land to the most able and energetic sharecroppers in order to maximize returns. Operators who were seen as "just wanting to get by" or "having less experience" could be penalized; "the harder workers were the favorites" and got the best land.

At times, landowners acted as local patrons to their sharecroppers. They were often said to be responsible for medical needs incurred by these families, were counted on to lend money in a crisis, and might intercede with authorities. Most Dodge Countians downplay these services, and perhaps they were important for only a few. But some landholders emphasize that they "looked out for" and "took care of" their tenants far beyond the simple economic transactions of farming. In such a context, tenants may have softened class resentments out of self-interest and self-protection. A landlord treated as generous and deserving might be more willing to act as a patron for a poor family. The wealthy, of course, benefited from this quieting of tensions as they benefited economically from the sharecropping system.

Politics in Dodge County both emphasized wealth differences and bound patrons to their clients. In the Depression era, powerful families often had large farms but derived much of their wealth from town businesses, real estate, or other investments. Politics was itself an important means to wealth. Said one retired large landholder, "The rich man worked on the taxpayers," meaning that more secure money was to be made from political office. Storekeepers in the small towns, with their client families dependent on credit, and local bankers were also powerful figures. Gifts and favors were the means by which many local politicians obtained office. Large landowners with political aspirations or connections gained power by being able to deliver a bloc of votes on election day. For poorer families, the gifts and favors obtained through politics meant small but important additions of comfort in hard times. Political intercession might also avoid serious legal problems or save a family from hardship. Tenants commonly followed their landlords in politics, though some interviewees remember their parents taking an independent line. Political power was not strictly limited to the wealthy; some landless people who had intermediary positions with landholders became influential. One sharecropper was also an overseer for his landowner/politician, and this role gave him considerable local power.

Rural Communities: Cooperation and Shared Poverty

Older men and women today downplay the economic differences of the past and emphasize the shared poverty of their childhood in the 1920s and 1930s (and, for some, the 1940s and 1950s as well). "We were all poor then" is a common statement. "Everyone was more or less equal, in those days—no one had fine homes, none of my friends went to college," said the daughter of one elite farm family. When I asked the son of a struggling small farmer if people he knew resented the landholder who had so much more, he replied, "No, everyone got along fine. No one was better than the other one." One farmer summarized the views of many when he said that having a large farm or a small farm was based on "luck—it was all like winning a lottery—that was just the way it was." When asked whether people were resentful of that, he replied, "No, how could you be resentful of the lottery? But they might have less sympathy for the one who inherits a farm and then loses it all." This emphasis on the "have not" days of the past reflects an implicit comparison with the abundance of the present. Today, farmers are aware of the stereotypes of the impoverished sharecropper past, and their accounts deflect attention from any internal ranking within rural communities. Such an ideology has clear continuities with the egalitarian ethos of the wiregrass settlers. More salient than wealth differences in farmers' memories is the fact that none had electricity, indoor plumbing, or window screens.

Poor health is also a part of those memories. Dodge Countians remember diseases almost mythical to urban Americans today and recall high mortality rates as well. Malaria was common in those pre-DDT days, afflicting both rich and poor. Some black families report it was less of a problem for them, and research suggests they may have had some genetic protection.[12] Although none of my informants volunteered memories of lice, hookworm, or bedbugs, when asked, older people remember them well. Men and women recall filling the house with smoke to deter mosquitoes at night, homemade "bombs" to kill chinch bugs (bedbugs), and periodic total housecleanings with lye soap to control infestations of all kinds.

High mortality rates characterized the period, and the stark reality of death intruded on many childhoods. In recounting their family histories, a number of people mentioned the early death of a parent and the severe hardships it caused. Twenty percent (51) of the individuals in the study who were born before 1930 lost a mother or father before they were sixteen. Among the 108 who were born before 1940, 12 percent experienced the death of a parent at an early age. The loss of parents to disease, accident, or homicide shows vividly the isolation, poor sanitation, poor medical care, and vulnerability to disaster that affected all rural families.

But in recollecting hard times, many Dodge Countians emphasize the cooperation among households, the church community, shared experiences in school, and other ways in which economic differences among families were deemphasized. Farm households, both owners and tenants, cooperated with each other in both agricultural and domestic tasks. "Swapping out" labor in sugar making and in stacking peanuts (for harvest) or pulling tobacco (for drying) joined together young and old from various families. Women cooperated to make quilts, and families enjoyed getting together to husk corn or boil peanuts.

Life was less hectic then, assert many today, and people had more time to socialize. Groups gathered to listen to the radio on weekend evenings and going to church was an important event. Preachers rode a circuit around the countryside and were paid with the collection that Sunday. Some families in the 1930s could count on a church service at their local church every month, but for others the worship gatherings were less frequent.[13]

Rich and poor may have paid less attention to the differences between them because ownership of property did not necessarily translate into an easy life. For example, one elite Dodge County family owned five hundred acres and had six or seven sharecropper families. A black woman helped with housework; "she practically lived there." But neither the husband nor the wife had completed six years of education, and both remember farm work as hard physical labor. In addition to helping in the fields, the wife milked cows, boarded schoolteachers, sewed her children's clothes, made soap, and prepared foods, all in ways very similar to her less fortunate neighbors. Her husband's daily farming tasks were also parallel to those of his sharecroppers. These commonalities in daily life contributed to the perceived lack of status differences among rural households.

The economic turmoil of the Depression era also undoubtedly played a role in the emphasis on shared poverty in rural Dodge County. It was a time of little optimism, and even among the affluent, many farms failed. One older man pointed out that of the half-dozen powerful or prosperous men he had known in his youth, only one had managed to hold on to his wealth. Cash and luxuries became scarce, farms were lost, and downward mobility was an ever-present reality. Under such circumstances, invidious comparisons among households may have been psychologically undesirable. The wealthy strove not to tempt fate by flaunting their affluence, and the poorer families were spared some of the ignominy of failure. The fact that some landless families were young couples awaiting a deferred inheritance may have strengthened their more egalitarian relations with surrounding parents or neighbors.

In addition, landlords with tenants did not necessarily own a large acreage; some were small- or medium-sized farm operators. To obtain extra labor, such farmers either hired a wage hand or turned a section of the farm over to a sharecropper/tenant. A number of farm families in the 200- to 300-acre range reported having made the latter choice. Some widows preferred the help of a whole tenant family to the difficulties of supervising a hired worker.

Even in the domain of landlord/tenant relations, contemporary Dodge Countians downplay inequalities and class tensions. Several who participated in the sharecropping system reported quite positive assessments: "We were lucky to have it." Though many historians emphasize the vulnerability of sharecroppers to financial chicanery on the part of landholders, few in Dodge County recall abuses of that kind. When over a dozen former sharecroppers were asked specifically about different ways landowners could manipulate store accounts or shortchange harvests, they unanimously denied that such things ever happened to them. These former sharecroppers freely discussed being victimized by other forms of cheating or dishonesty, but they did not see themselves as cheated in sharecropping. A few agreed that such abuses had been alleged but claimed that their own relationship with "Mr. ———" was not like that. "I've heard people say that," went a typical response, "but it was rare."

Many children of small landholders or tenant families emphasize the gratitude they felt for the favors and political benefits they received from local patrons. They appreciated generosity in others, and the culture downplayed resentment of the system that generated wealth inequalities to begin with. One woman who grew up on a small farm remembers with great fondness the wealthy storekeeper who commonly threw a nickel to her and her siblings as he drove by them in his car while they waited for the school bus. "He was a free-hearted man," she said in admiration.

It seems likely that the children of sharecroppers who survive in farming today represent a more fortunate group, and their experiences with the sharecropping system may have been more positive than on average. In fact, their reported frequency of moves from farm to farm is much lower than the census suggests was typical. It is also possible that much historical work, drawn as it is with greater emphasis on Black Belt plantation areas, portrays a more vicious system than was typical for the wiregrass region. Certainly, many historians note a range of experiences under sharecropping (Daniel 1985; Kirby 1987), and relationships of mutual respect and cooperation have been reported in some other areas (Flynt 1989:90). Tensions among different economic strata may also have been deemphasized out of ignorance. Since the farmers of today, whose accounts form the basis of this historical section, are primarily descendants of landholding families, they may have been less aware of the resentments and lifestyle of the tenants who needed to stay in the landholding families' good graces.

A final reason for the ideology of shared poverty is the way in which all farm families—rich and poor, tenants and landowners—were the same in the eyes of townsfolk. Rural families recount vivid experiences of town prejudice against farmers, and the image of farming as "a poor life" continues today. "Town young-uns thought they were better than we were. . . . They thought they were a grade or two higher than us," said one older man. One woman who always started school late in the fall because she had to pick cotton remembers being ashamed of her tan arms: "They looked down on you, made you feel bad." One elite woman grew up disliking farming because it meant isolation and a lower standard of living.

Her family was wealthy yet had no phone or television. When she shopped in the local town, she felt people there "looked down on country people." Being unable to walk around town on Saturdays and Sundays made her feel disconnected from a vital part of social life. One man claimed farmers had a harder time getting credit; storekeepers preferred to lend to people with a steady job. Farm families in mule-drawn wagons felt worlds away from townsfolk in cars.

Not all interviewees agreed with generalizations of prejudice against farmers. Several women from small farm families said they never felt looked down upon and could not believe anyone else experienced such treatment. A black couple concluded after considerable discussion that some people might *feel* that farming was devalued, "But people don't really look down on you." A younger white woman disagreed however, arguing that in her 1950s high school experience, a country girl was excluded from elite groups such as band or cheerleading. Leadership roles were acquired based on "who you know," and farm families were at a disadvantage.

Race and Education

In addition to inequalities deriving from access to land, rural communities were divided by race and by differences in education. As with landholder/tenant relations, the memories of Dodge Countians stress cooperation and tend to gloss over racial inequities. Blacks made up 37 percent of the county population in 1929 and 30 percent of the farm operators, as shown in table 1-2. Black farm owners lived either in predominantly black communities or in majority white neighborhoods as isolated households or as a cluster of families. Some black landowners purchased land in the pre-railroad days, and many more obtained farms as sharecroppers once the land was cleared. Table 1-2 shows that black farmers declined in number over the two decades following 1930. The proportions of nonlandowners remained high, nearly 80 percent in 1934 and 64 percent in 1949.

Landownership for blacks was aided by several federal programs in the 1940s. Even through the 1930s, however, some parents and grandparents of today's Dodge County black farmers were substantial landholders who owned and operated stores, had sharecroppers, and hired full-time workers on their farms. Contemporary black farmers in the county are drawn in disproportionate numbers from this relatively elite group.

Depression-era race relations varied around the county. In some areas, blacks encountered hostility and violence, while in others more cooperative and peaceful

Table 1-2. Black Farms and Rates of Tenancy
in Dodge County, 1929–1949

	Black Farm Operators	Percent of All Farms	Percent Tenants*
1929	790	30	—
1934	684	27	78
1939	457	22	73
1944	505	—	—
1949	445	22	64

Source: U.S. Census of Agriculture, 1929–49.
*Combines sharecroppers and tenants.

ties were common. Several black families reported balancing their fears of white resentment and retribution with their desires to improve living standards with the installation of electricity or the purchase of a car. One older woman recalled an incident of being stoned by white children as she walked to school, but she also recounted her family's successful efforts to terminate this harassment. Some blacks emphasized their relatively peaceful ties with neighbors, and it is possible that the different history of the wiregrass region permitted a moderation of the racial traditions recounted by historians of plantation areas. On the other hand, some older black farmers were unwilling to talk about this aspect of the past and may have been reluctant to share (or relive) painful memories.

Whites in Dodge County also reported a variety of different experiences and attitudes toward blacks, depending on the mix of occupations in each community. In a purely farming community, where black and white landowners and sharecroppers lived interspersed with each other, cooperation in harvests and other agricultural tasks was common. One white woman, daughter of a small landholder, remembered paying social visits with her mother and sisters to the women of the black landholder family down the road and receiving visits from them as well. A white landholder reported continued cordial ties with the black family that sharecropped part of his father's farm. One older white woman emphasized that she was brought up to think blacks "were just as good as us," but "they didn't want to mix and mingle any more than we did."

In contrast, a nearby community of small farmers had no blacks as farmers, only as turpentine workers. White children were kept apart and taught an elaborate etiquette of separation. Some white families reported growing up with a deep abhorrence of contact with blacks, and some of these attitudes survive into the present. Racial tensions seem to be less visible in Depression-era Dodge County than in the period of transition to cotton tenancy at the turn of the century, but the history of race relations and desegregation has yet to be written for this area. Both whites and blacks today assert that the county is less extreme in its racism and its resistance to integration than some other areas of the South, and many whites volunteer that their attitudes have changed since integration in schools, workplaces, and public areas has become the norm.

Education is another domain in which some rural families were disadvantaged, and race also figures prominently in differential access to schooling. Historically a strong public education system has not been a priority in Georgia (Bartley 1990), and the powerlessness of landless families was often exacerbated by poor education. In 1930, 15 percent of the population was reported by the census to be illiterate (6% of whites and 31% of blacks). In the town of Eastman, the greater proportion of black families led to a higher illiteracy rate than for the county as a whole (22%).

Most rural communities had a local white school that offered six grades in the 1920s and 1930s, though some went as far as eight or nine grades. One farmer remembered that even though he officially attended school for six years, he was not in class much. He always started late in the fall because he had to help with the harvest, and he was held out for other farm-related work during the year. He did not lament his family's decision to keep him out of high school, he said, because he knew he was going to farm. A black woman remembered being kept out of school one day a week to help with the huge chore of laundry in her grandparents' extended family. A white man estimated that he was only effectively in school for three months of the year. His wife quit school young because her father refused to buy her schoolbooks, telling her to use the other children's. Their fathers had little use for formal education beyond basic literacy, this couple said. Limited education for farm families was one important means to block upward mobility, and some landlords urged fathers to pull their children out of school to help on the farm. In contrast, one landowner proudly recounted that he counseled a tenant to let his son finish grammar school, but the father saw no reason to educate his son beyond his own level. Like this landowner, most Dodge Countians report that education was highly valued in this period, which suggests a shift in attitudes from the earlier wiregrass settler culture.

Among the families of farmers today, many children were sent on for part or all of their high school training in the 1930s and 1940s. High schools were located in the small towns around the county, and transportation presented a challenge to some families. By the mid-1930s, many white children were transported to high school by bus, but prior to the use of buses, children provided their own transportation to school by foot, horse, mule, or car.

For blacks, there was only one high school in Eastman, and there was no bus. At least one community in the southern part of the county did provide a bus for the black grammar school children, but many report that schools were a long walk from home. In some areas, black schools were held in churches because no buildings were provided. As documented by historians for other counties (Bartley 1990; Raper 1936), educational expenditures for black students in Dodge County were lower than for whites. The quality of teachers' pay and training, supplies, and facilities revealed an unwillingness on the part of the white school board to invest equally in the education of black and white children.[14]

Continuities from the 1930s and Challenges for the 1980s

From this account of Dodge County history emerges the tension and interplay of agrarian and capitalist economies and their value systems. Some settler families upheld a self-sufficient, landowning ideal and rejected the "white middle class northern industrial culture . . . [with its] powerful ideology of ambition and personal gain" (J. Jones 1985:106). Other settler families welcomed the northern investments and businesses that transformed the piney woods region as a "new, progressive element" (Malone 1986). Families were occasionally divided by the old and new ways, and enthusiastic settler sons sold their inheritances, built sawmills, or moved into town. Incoming families in the sharecropper era also brought a range of value orientations and goals, since some were former estate owners, accustomed to the affluence of having wage hands and sharecroppers, while others were displaced tenants, looking for soil strong enough to support a family (Kirby 1987:122). For the majority of Dodge County farmers who remember this era, the struggle to make it through the Depression, amid the losses all around, reinforced a cautious farm management style, with particular reluctance to expand. "I was afraid to venture out," said one older farmer. Land purchases, when attempted, were often based on substantial savings or even accomplished in cash. Caution in land rental and purchase paralleled frugality in home consumption as well. These families upheld an agrarian ethic, taking care to avoid the bondage to bank or storekeeper that could risk the loss of all the family had accumulated.

Other families were motivated by an entrepreneurial spirit that embraced debt and risk as necessary for success in business of any kind—agricultural or otherwise. Especially as farm incomes rose in the 1940s and 1950s, support for a more ambitious farming style was reinforced. Several people who went off to war in the 1940s came home with entrepreneurial ideas that clashed with the conservatism of their parents. Certain investments, such as buying a tractor, were grounds for conflict. Several farm operators today recount with bitterness their fathers' reluctance to take advantage of an opportunity to buy a prime piece of land. Younger farmers came to view the caution of the Depression era as a hesitancy to take the risks necessary for success. With the growing evidence of both the lessening impact of such risks and the increasing benefits to be gained from innovations, this conservatism was convincingly labeled backward, out of date, and unmodern. A lost opportunity for expansion was seen as a profound failure of wisdom as well as a failure of nerve. The more ambitious ethic harkened back to the successes of capitalist entrepreneurs in the 1800s and served many beginning farmers for several decades after World War II. As we shall see, the devaluation of the debt-averse caution of the Depression-bred farmer proved disastrous to some in the crisis of the 1980s.

The "Hoover Days" left a strong impact on agrarian social relations as well. Farming was linked with poverty and low status, though the widespread prejudice against farmers' children in schools slowly diminished. One older couple reported that by the 1950s and 1960s, farm children traveled more widely, dressed less distinctively, and were no longer objects of scorn. "It's a lot better now," they asserted. Though the ideology of the Depression era downplayed social stratification, the gaps between wealthy merchants and landless families were chasms, and "the lottery" placed families on one side or the other. In contrast to the more optimistic outlook of the Midwest and the Plains states where success was seen as attainable through hard work (McNall and McNall 1983:69), economic and political conditions taught many southern farmers a more sober assessment. Neither status nor success came automatically from hard work, and wealth more often came "from the taxpayer" or from money lending than from agricultural efforts. Downward mobility from debt, together with powerful external economic forces, reinforced an ethic that accepted social hierarchies and focused on shared poverty.

The structure of Dodge County politics continues to reflect the influence of aging agrarian power brokers. People with links to large agricultural estates, agribusinesses, and real estate holdings still exert considerable power. Within the small towns in the county, the willingness of powerful families to share wealth, to permit new businesses to enter, and to innovate has played a major role in determining the subsequent health or demise of these small communities. In a few communities made up of many small landowner families, a more democratic general style can be observed. Churches organize some community activities and local cooperation is more common. Families today in these historically more egalitarian communities seem to be less suspicious of the motives of outsiders, less ready to assume that all politics are based on fraud and graft, and more open to new ideas.

In Eastman, wealthy and politically powerful families continue to be mainly professional and commercial and only rarely agricultural. During the "Hoover Days," the prominent families were successful in banking, construction, candy manufacture, and agricultural processing and wholesaling (especially of cotton). Many of these industries remain, and the separation of farming families from town elites persists as a source of strain and resentment for some ambitious farmers.

Continuities from the era of King Timber can be found in contemporary Dodge County economic conditions as well. The dependence on outside investment and vulnerability to world market prices that characterized the timber boom era continue today in several modern industries. A steady infusion of support from the Reagan administration military budgets has been critical in the 1980s prosperity of middle Georgia. Other federal and state programs, as well as regional growth in industry, have fed local growth in jobs and incomes. As in the days of railroad construction and timbering, however, most new businesses are not locally controlled.

The case of Eastman's most famous industry—Stuckey's pecan candies—illustrates the vulnerability that external control can mean for local families. Begun in the late 1930s, Stuckey's expanded from the local roadside sales of candy to lucrative fast-food franchises along superhighways across the country. Several Eastman families benefited from these businesses, but as Stuckey's popularity declined, the founder's descendants sold the company to a northern conglomerate. At the time I first visited Dodge County, the candy factory in Eastman experienced major job cutbacks, and top management was moved out of state. By the end of the 1980s, however, it was again increasing its employment of Dodge County workers, and efforts were under way to regain local control.

The experiences of farm loss of the Depression years are, of course, powerfully evoked in the 1980s farm crisis, but many Dodge County families hold on to a sense of the ebb and flow of farm ownership. A number of families who lost their farms in the Depression were able to buy back the lost property in the next generation. A few recovered land as early as the 1940s or 1950s, once the farm economy became more robust. For black families, farm loss was more often permanent.

Though black farmers worked a quarter of the county's acreage in 1930, that figure fell to 4 percent by 1969.

Finally, the environmental devastation of the 1800s has now been partially remedied, but ecological challenges remain from the era of King Cotton. The reforested portions of the county have returned to timber production and again support wildlife and feed creeks. Many secondary-growth forests, however, show the effects of years of grazing. Thorny plants and jungly vines make passage difficult, and farmers often keep a few goats to clear out the undergrowth in swampy areas and along creeks. The massive loss of topsoil caused by agriculture was halted by energetic soil conservationists after the New Deal, but soil depletion and erosion continue to plague modern farming. The ecological backdrop to the drama of Dodge County families still stands, as a decade of drought created the crisis from which this study emerged. Today, after the clattering farm machinery falls silent, in the planted pulpwood stands with their careful rows of uniform tree varieties, one can hear the echoes of the quiet cathedrals of hundred-foot tall pines described by early travelers to the wiregrass region.

CHAPTER

TWO

Postwar Agricultural Transformation

and the Rise of the Family Farm

By the 1970s, farming in Dodge County was unrecognizable from farming during the Depression era. Government programs and new agricultural technology combined to transform a region dominated by cotton tenancy into one of independently owned and operated family farms. Agricultural productivity soared with new crop and livestock varieties, new machines, and the increased use of fertilizers and chemicals. Rising incomes on farms made possible an affluence undreamed of in the "Hoover Days." The majority of the Dodge County population took advantage of the advent of the automobile and new industrial job opportunities and moved away from agricultural employment. Life in rural communities was altered as well, in politics, social stratification, neighborly cooperation, and patterns of leisure.

The Franklin D. Roosevelt administration and its pivotal agricultural policies brought an end to the farm poverty of the Depression, and small farms—especially tenant farms—declined rapidly. Mechanization and federal agricultural programs pushed the typical full-time farm to become much larger. Throughout the South generally, farming opportunities declined for many landless and small farm families, but the Dodge County data reveal that the post–World War II era also allowed upward mobility for some children of these two groups who were able to enter and continue farming successfully in this period. Rising capital investments made full-time farms both more expensive and more vulnerable to economic ups and downs. These costs pushed many younger Dodge Countians to be more dependent on parental help to get started, and farming began to move toward an increasingly closed occupation.

As farming methods changed, farmers' aspirations shifted as well, and the more ambitious, risk-taking style of management gained currency. After two decades of decline, the number of young people choosing to farm soared in the 1960s, reflecting agriculture's new image. In this chapter, I identify three generations of farmers in Dodge County today and the different levels of parental support they received to enter this increasingly expensive and complex occupation. Older generations, with their caution attuned to Depression hardships, were joined by younger generations, for whom farming was a means to a comfortable lifestyle and higher social status.

Rural Communities Transformed

As New Deal programs and the second world war dragged the national economy out of the Depression, the automobile transfigured agrarian communities in Dodge County. The repercussions of motorized transportation were felt in many aspects of community life. Free-ranging hogs and cattle were one casualty, both literally and figuratively. As cars became more numerous, accidents with livestock became a growing problem, and fencing laws were enacted and enforced throughout the postwar decade.[1] As pastures were fenced, farmers for the first time were able to control animal breeding, and improved stock varieties spread rapidly. Feeding efficiency increased, and a range of innovations from soybean feeds to farrowing houses was made possible. Sales of livestock rose, as did farm income from this source.

Stock laws also changed the look of rural communities. Because cows and hogs no longer grazed up to the house, landscaping and flower gardens became possible. Urban mores of home beautification spread, and lawns, shrubbery, and flowers became more common in Dodge County yards. Once trampling and rooting animals were enclosed, the front of the house changed from being part of the farm yard to being a separate homesite, paralleling other changes in women's roles as farm producers to housewives (see chapter 6). The industrialization of chicken production led to a decline in free-ranging home flocks, and the Dodge County farmstead took on the configuration it presents today. Housing types also changed, and tenant shacks were replaced by modern brick homes (see chapter 5).

As rural housing changed, so did its furnishings, and the poverty of the "Hoover Days" was left behind for many families as the South caught up with national living standards. In 1940, Georgia per capita incomes were only 57 percent of the national average but rose to 70 percent in 1950 and 85 percent by 1970 (Bartley 1990:224). In 1930, 4 percent of all Dodge County families owned a radio, and only thirteen farm families reported owning a radio (U.S. Census of Population 1930). By 1945, radio ownership jumped to 41 percent of farm families; a third of the families owned a car, but only a quarter had electricity and a mere 8 percent had running water (U.S. Census of Agriculture 1945). By 1955, rural electrification was nearly complete—94 percent of farms had power. Indoor plumbing was more common than a decade earlier, but still only half of farm households reported running water. One Dodge County woman, daughter of a sharecropper, remembers learning to use a toilet and toilet paper for the first time in her grammar school in the early 1960s. Fewer than a fifth of farmers had a telephone in 1955, but half the farmers owned a car. By 1960, half of Dodge County as a whole had telephones. Seventy percent had televisions, and three-fourths owned a car (U.S. Census of Population 1960). Purchase of hot water heaters, freezers, refrigerators, and other household appliances showed a decreasing gap between southern and northern as well as urban and rural lifestyles (McNall and McNall 1983). Store purchases of food and clothes in the postwar era reflected new tastes, new consumer habits, and increased affluence.

Throughout this period, the revolution in transportation and lifestyles was paralleled by a medical revolution. Visits to doctors and hospitals became more common, and medical care was transformed by antibiotics, vaccines, and disease control. Malaria was eradicated, mortality rates abruptly dropped, and fertility rates were close behind. Family size changed in one generation, as families of 7, 8, and even 10 children became rare, and the 2-child family became the norm.

Rural communities were greatly affected by new employment opportunities off the farm, and private motorized transportation allowed factories and businesses to spring up away from railroad lines. New roads and private cars meant that occupation and residence were no longer linked. Expansion of government jobs, especially in growing military establishments in other counties, also provided new higher-paying employment opportunities. Labor union efforts across the country bore fruit in shorter work hours, paid vacations, and other benefits that increased the attractiveness of off-farm jobs (Kada 1980).

Table 2-1 documents the shift to a more diversified economic structure in Dodge County. In 1930, the county's 21,600 people were mostly rural and 72 percent lived on farms. War industries, agricultural mechanization, and out-migration lowered the population by 15 percent in the 1940s, but the most striking trend was toward nonfarm occupations. In 1950, only 53 percent of rural residents were

Table 2-1. Urban and Rural Population
in Dodge County, 1930–1980

	Total Population	Number of Households	Percent Rural	Percent Rural Farm
1930	21,599	4,638*	86	72
1940	21,022	4,773	84	71
1950	17,865	4,442	80	53
1960	16,483	4,427	69	27
1970	15,658	4,829	65	12
1980	16,955	5,835	69	8

Source: U.S. Census of Population, 1930–80.
*Census definitions vary from year to year and are not strictly comparable; for 1930 this figure is for families, not households.

farmers and that percentage fell to 27 percent in 1960. The rural proportion of the population, however, remained high in the postwar decades, between 70 and 80 percent.[2]

Population changes in the county were uneven and affected some rural communities more than others. In the small communities that retained enough families to feel vibrant, local churches survived and prospered, as did local stores. In other communities, population loss steadily sapped vitality and hurt neighborhood cooperation and spirit. One older couple describes lovingly the large trees that used to line the cool, though often dusty, road on which they live. Nearby small farms supported numerous houses, and the shouts of children could be heard on summer evenings up and down the road. As the farmers died off and their children moved away, the road is now empty of houses and children. The trees have been cut, little traffic passes by, and this couple is saddened by their isolation.

New employment opportunities and transportation shifted traditional rural power structures, and local politics became somewhat more democratic. Automobiles freed people from dependence on local stores for provisions, and with the decline of sharecropping, commissaries shut down. Storekeepers' power declined too, as people exercised their option to "trade" elsewhere. Shopping in town became the norm.[3] Federal programs meant local politics became increasingly connected to state and national government, and legislation affecting voting regulations and other community issues came to play a role in local political life. These trends reduced the social status rigidities of the Depression era. Arthur Raper also points out the leveling effect of automobiles. Never before in a stratified society had it been necessary to cede half the road to "a person of unknown station" or race; cars contributed to a more democratic social order (Raper 1936:175).[4]

Expanded government programs in education in the 1950s, together with declining school populations and a desire for improved facilities, led to school consolidations, and the desegregation of schools was accomplished in the 1960s with further consolidations. The rural school lost ground as the mechanism of white community cohesion. Combining black and white schools did give rise to some segregated white academies, but none survived in the county by the 1980s. Overall, desegregation in Dodge County led peacefully to mixed schools. Integration of public facilities and public jobs is rarely discussed as traumatic in Dodge County today, but the loss of control over education is another matter. A pervasive sense that school quality declined with integration marks many white conversations, and the clamor over yet another round of school consolidations in the late 1980s combined educational issues with strong feelings about the painful loss of rural community identity.

Desegregation of schools was followed by increased political participation of blacks, but the right to vote was not an issue in the county because some blacks had voted since at least the 1930s. Political representation for the approximately one-third of the population that is black, however, has been more problematic. There are blacks on the school board and on the city council, but up to the time of this writing, the county has retained the sole commissioner form of county government (which excludes minority representation), even in the face of a suit by the National Association for the Advancement of Colored People.

Community life, cooperation, and leisure were all affected by the automobile, and the changing economy brought a new ethos to rural communities. Leisure activities became more commercialized as people spent money on movies, eating in restaurants, and driving to town. Time became more scarce; commutes to off-farm jobs, more frequent shopping trips, and more distant school and church activities reduced the leisure that fostered casual relations among neighbors. People no longer have the time to stop and talk that they used to, said one older farmer: "Folks are living too fast." At the same time, cars permitted visits to more distant relatives, and the telephone allowed new levels of daily contact. Radio, television, and the decline of community activities pushed families into nuclear isolation, especially as cooperation among relatives was less needed on the farm. "The neighbor business has changed," said an elderly farmer. He used to feel secure from the threat of illness because he knew neighbors would carry out his farm tasks until he got well if he became ill. Today, he concludes, people no longer attend to each other's needs in the same way.

"The neighbor business" has also changed because of farm technology. Common tasks and implements meant a farmer helping out in the 1920s and 1930s would be less likely to harm his neighbor's mule or plow. In contrast, today an inexperienced equipment operator can do expensive damage, and variability in crop types and chemicals make stepping in to help out another farmer more difficult. Farmers with hogs try to stay away from each other's pens, in order to avoid contamination with disease. These conditions are a far cry from the days when hogs ran free and rural communities were bound together in cooperative work as well as in leisure.

The New Deal: Industry and Agriculture

The transformation of Dodge County's rural communities was made possible by New Deal agricultural programs and by the revival and expansion of the industrial economy. A key to the integration of the South into the national economy was the narrowing of the wage gap between regions (Wright 1986). Improved infrastructure in electricity, roads, and other public investments attracted businesses to the region. Industry in the North, feeling the shortage of Europeans after immigration laws were changed, sent recruiters to the South to entice migration off the farm (Raper 1936; Kirby 1987). Many Dodge Countians recall the breakup of families as siblings went North or to Florida in search of better lives off the farm. The trend toward fewer and larger farms, substitution of capital investments for labor, and increased use of science and technology had, of course, been under way in the North and Midwest prior to the Depression (Cochrane 1979; Kirby 1987). In an extraordinarily rapid series of changes, the southern agricultural economy caught up with these regions and joined a national pattern of owner-operated, mechanized, mixed rowcrop and livestock farming.

Roosevelt's agricultural policies set in motion four fundamental processes that generated the commercial agriculture that replaced cotton tenancy in the South. These processes continue to characterize the farm sector today, and each played a role in the farm crisis of the 1980s:

- the establishment of federal controls over certain crops, lowering production and raising farm incomes;

- unequal distribution of farm program benefits and the resulting subsidizing of larger farms and displacement of disadvantaged tenants and small farms;

- strengthened impetus to mechanization and capital intensification of farming; and

- encouragement of the adoption of new production technologies and scientific innovations.

To confront the massive poverty of the Depression-era South, the New Deal attempted to "curb the devastating effects of the market on traditional institutions, nature, and even the economic system itself" (Starr 1982:61). The spiral of overproduction, debt, and soil degradation fostered by cotton tenancy was reversed by government intervention in the market through production quotas, efforts to encourage diversification, and incentives to soil conservation. The cotton program was the primary focus of federal activity to raise farmers' incomes in Dodge County, but peanut and tobacco payments also came to be important. Acreage quotas and Agricultural Adjustment Act payments to farmers lowered global production levels, raised prices, and gave hope to impoverished families.

At the same time, the devastation of the boll weevil provided an impetus to pursue alternatives to cotton. By 1935, the Dodge County Agricultural Extension agent's annual report notes farmers' increasing confidence in their income levels and the resulting improvements to houses and outbuildings. In the long run, higher cotton prices led to increased competition with foreign producers and with synthetic fibers (Mann 1990; Skinner and Sanford 1990), and much U.S. cotton production shifted to the western states.

New Deal intervention in the market brought sharp gains in rural welfare but also resulted in the displacement of the poorest groups from their access to an agricultural livelihood. Throughout the region, federal programs resulted in massive evictions of tenants and sharecroppers, in a kind of southern enclosure movement (Daniel 1985). Elite landholders tended to be appointed to local boards that administered relief funds, loans, and quota allocations. Although legislation intended that tenants should receive their share of federal money, in most regions the funds were very inequitably distributed (Ford 1973; Office of Technology Assessment 1986). Some wealthy landowners received "enormous payments" and used these funds to mechanize (Wright 1986:231). Others replaced tenants with wage hands, to avoid the issue of tenants' rights to federal payments. The boll weevil, erosion, and the lure of industrial jobs led to the out-migration of millions of southerners during this period, one of the largest peacetime migrations in history (Fite 1981). Later legislation was aimed at providing tenants a greater share of New Deal payments, but these actions only had the effect of accelerating displacement (Wright 1986:232). Cutbacks in the cotton program allotments in the 1950s also resulted in the removal of tenants and lower incomes to small farmers, thereby pushing some families toward off-farm work (James 1986:171). Those remaining on the farm were encouraged to intensify production through utilizing new equipment and scientific techniques, thus climbing on the "technology treadmill" (Cochrane 1979). Federal efforts in the 1960s reduced cotton acreages still further, paid farmers a supplemental price over world market levels, and succeeded in bringing down surpluses (Skinner and Sanford 1990). However, the cost of payments to farmers was high ($847 million in 1971), and expensive subsidies to producers continue to be a problem for federal agricultural policy (ibid.:28).

The agricultural program subsidies to larger farmers "helped clear the way for the rural transformation to capital-intensive farming" (Daniel 1985:168). Wartime labor shortages pushed some farmers to mechanize; high federal subsidies encouraged others. A push and pull of both forces can be seen in the case of one large farm owner who benefited from allotments in the late 1930s but had little incentive to mechanize and was content to operate his land with the help of several tenant families. When high-paying war industries lured his most able tenant to work elsewhere, however, the owner faced a shortage of skilled labor, and his solution was to buy a tractor. Mechanizing then allowed him to evict the remaining tenant families who were forced to look elsewhere for work. The New Deal removal of tenants, sharecroppers, and agricultural workers forced a painful transition for many less fortunate families (Kirby 1987). Agricultural families who migrated north in the 1950s faced a less welcoming economic environment than those who migrated in the war years; jobs for unskilled workers were scarce and unemployment was high (Wright 1986).

Federal farm programs also encouraged an ethos of "modern agriculture" that involved technological investments to raise farm incomes. The U.S. Department of Agriculture prepared radio programs that "painted visions of tractors, implements, improved seeds, and other capital-intensive goods" (Daniel 1985:195). County agricultural extension agents and home economists supported these visions of change, though their reports do not reflect much concern for families who could not innovate for lack of money. The New Deal attempted to expand credit for farmers, and the institutions that were created in that era continue to be important to farmers today. The Federal Land Bank lent funds for farm real estate, and the Production Credit Association provided short-term loans to farmers for crops, livestock, and equipment. The Farmers Home Administration was also founded to help low-resource farmers and rural residents with credit for homes, farms, and farm-operating expenses. By the end of the 1930s, the impact of these credit agencies and the technological changes they encouraged was beginning to be felt in Dodge County. Once again, the local power structures were challenged by outside organizations, and influential farmers played (and continue to play) important roles on the boards of these credit organizations.

Roosevelt's agricultural programs brought a new level of governmental intervention in and bureaucratic control over farm production, constraining in new ways the autonomy of the household (Starr 1982:161). From the routine aerial surveillance of fields to the testing of crop quality, legions of government workers are now part of the farm's production process. Minimum wage legislation affects the costs of labor, interest rates establish the costs of capital, and regulations on chemicals and environmental hazards also restrict farm management choices. Even ideologies of "good management" and "prudent decision making" are influenced by U.S. Department of Agriculture publications, agricultural extension service activities, and the judgments of local agency boards that reward some farmers and neglect others. The legacy of New Deal programs continues to be felt in Dodge County, as farmers each year fill out stacks of forms that attest to the constraints and incentives affecting annual crop choices. At the same time, Dodge County farmers are somewhat less constrained by local and state governments than in some areas of the country. Unlike the California dairy farmers studied by Jess Gilbert and Raymond Akor (1988), their lands are not protected "agricultural preserves," nor do they receive subsidized irrigation water or benefit from special marketing orders to boost product prices. Southern peanut, cotton, and tobacco producers (as well as some corn and other grain producers), however, continue to receive a range of benefits, subject to certain constraints, that prevent the free operation of the market and provide subsidies especially to larger farmers (see chapter 4).

The effects of New Deal programs on farm numbers in Dodge County can be seen in figure 2-1. Total numbers of farms began to drop between 1934 and 1939, and this farm attrition occurred almost exclusively in tenant farms under a hundred acres, many of which were black farms (see chapter 1). Numbers of full-owner and part-owner farms remained stable until 1950.[5] Thereafter, owner farms began

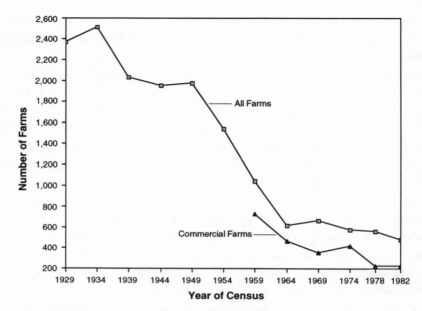

Figure 2-1. Number of Farms in Dodge County, 1929–1982

Source: U.S. Census of Agriculture, 1929–82.

to decline in number as well, though the fall in tenant farms in the 1950s was more rapid and significant. The extent of the shift in agricultural structure in the county can be seen in the raw numbers: from over 2,500 farms in the mid-1930s to 482 in 1982. The farm population began to stabilize in the mid-1960s. Beginning in 1959, the rise of small part-time farms led the Bureau of the Census to measure a separate group of operators selling at least $2,500 worth of crops or livestock. Figure 2-1 shows that these commercial farms continued to decline in numbers until 1978. This trend in Dodge County mirrors the rest of the nation, as the growing sector of part-time operators keeps total farm numbers up, while the number of full-time farm operations falls.

Agricultural Intensification in the 1950s and 1960s

The metamorphosis of Dodge County agriculture gathered speed in the two postwar decades, as advances in mechanization, higher crop yields, and the use of industrial inputs created a more capital-intensive farming system. This system brought a new affluence to the growing sector of family-owned and -operated farms, but higher incomes were accompanied by new risks and vulnerabilities and by ecological challenges. Technological sophistication became one of the joys of the modern farmer, and many in Dodge County take pride in how much farming has changed since their parents' time.

Substitution of capital investments for labor characterized all agriculture in the United States in the years following World War II (Schertz 1979:28), but mechanization in the South in particular freed families from burdensome field work and changed patterns of rural cooperation. Tractors were first used for field preparation, but equipment companies then began to develop a range of attachments that replaced harvest work teams as well. Mechanization thus affected ties among family members and with tenants and neighbors. Today, women and men alike rejoice in the resulting release of family labor from agricultural production. The sophistication of machines is also at times a source of wonder and of pride. In the place of the arduous hand labor of peanut harvests, many Dodge County families today use a peanut combine that collects the nuts, sorts them from stems and roots, and transfers them to a wagon for mechanized transport to the peanut warehouse. Of course, some wage labor continues to be important in the county, especially for the larger farmers, whose hired hands now drive the equipment as well as help out with occasional field labor.

Progress in mechanization emerged in relation to technological advances in other agricultural arenas and to the changing numbers of large farms and farm laborers. The development of a self-propelled cotton picker was encouraged by an increasing number of potential customers (thanks to 1930s agricultural program payments) and by fears of a wartime labor shortage (Cobb 1990:917). Mechanical cotton harvesters challenged university researchers and seed companies to develop cotton varieties more amenable to machine harvest. Strains were selected for uniform maturation and for heavier bolls. Row spacing was adjusted to the needs of harvest equipment, and the chemical defoliation of cotton plants was developed to cut down extraneous plant material. Mechanical harvesting still mixed stems, dead leaves, and dirt with the cotton, and cotton gins were forced to experiment with new ginning methods and cleaning machines. "Perfection of mechanization involved an all-out research effort by public agencies as well as private firms, with intense concern for the competitive position of American cotton, but little for the human consequences" (Wright 1986:247).

Capital intensification in farming proceeded rapidly in the late 1950s and 1960s, as operators invested in more equipment as well as land and buildings. In Dodge

County, farm equipment values on the average farm were only $84 in 1940. By 1969, commercial farms averaged $17,900 in the value of machinery and implements, and that figure doubled in the following decade to $35,500 per farm.[6] Capital intensification can also be seen in the long-term investments in land and buildings, the average value of which rose from the Depression-era low of $1,658 to $33,122 by the mid-1960s. In 1978, mechanization, rising land values, and inflation boosted these values to an average $155,067 per farm (U.S. Census of Agriculture 1940–78).

Rising capital costs sharply affected farm entry. Easing from sharecropping into farm ownership on the basis of profits from several good years was possible when costs of farming were low. With higher costs, family help and inheritance became increasingly important, a trend that we shall see reflected in the generations of Dodge County farmers discussed below. But when over $100,000 worth of investments are necessary to begin operations, farming is no longer an option for the average young person.

Mechanization intersected with and drew strength from a long-term process of technological change and new information on agricultural and biological processes. In the late 1800s and early 1900s, national investments in the agricultural research infrastructure of the state colleges of agriculture yielded new understandings of plant and animal functioning, growth, and genetics. This knowledge foundation was the basis for breakthroughs in agricultural techniques, feed and fertilizer efficiencies, and control of diseases. Such innovations "gathered momentum between 1920 and 1940, and poured forth after 1940" (Cochrane 1979:202). A mechanical revolution that led to the mechanization of many farming tasks was joined by both a biological revolution, which produced drought-resistant and disease-resistant varieties, and by a chemical revolution, which enhanced disease and weed control.

Astounding increases in agricultural yields were made possible in all the main crops grown in Georgia's Coastal Plain. Rising slowly prior to 1945, average yields in Dodge County are shown in figure 2-2 to grow over 100 percent in the late 1950s and early 1960s. Averages for the decade of 1965 to 1974 continued to increase; very high for corn and peanuts, they were less extreme but still substantial for soybeans, wheat, tobacco, and cotton. As we shall see, with these dramatic changes in crop productivity, accelerating through the 1950s and 1960s, the number of young people in Dodge County who chose to farm increased.

Soaring productivity per acre in Georgia is linked by Eugene Odum and Monica Turner (1988) to high rates of fertilizer use. Figure 2-3 shows rapid growth in

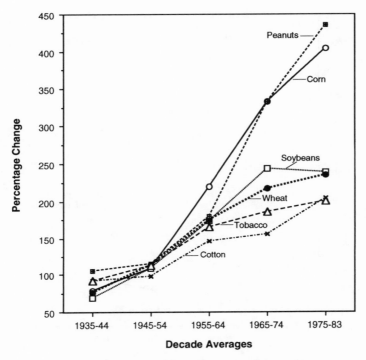

Figure 2-2. Crop Yields in Georgia, 1935–1983
(Percentage of 1945)

Source: Georgia Crop Reporting Service, 1935–83.

statewide averages of crop production based on a combined crop yield of calories produced and quantities of commercial fertilizers used in the state. Purchased nitrogen fertilizer levels rose over 1,000 percent between 1935 and 1984. Combination fertilizer (nitrogen, phosphorous, and potassium) levels used in the state increased 600 percent. This fertilizer use can be seen as an energy subsidy, generating a 300 percent increase in crop yields per acre, though more efficient plant varieties also played a role.[7]

Not only did fertilizer use increase, but chemicals such as insecticides and herbicides came to be a regular part of Georgia agriculture. By 1967, chemical use in the southeastern United States was almost double the level used in 1955 and continued to rise rapidly into the 1970s. Lyle Schertz comments that both fertilizer and chemical use contributed "to increased farm size by making production more

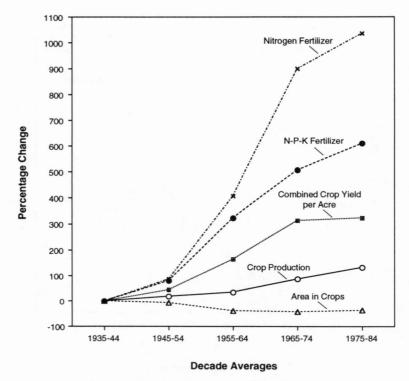

Figure 2-3. Food Production and Fertilizer Use
in Georgia, 1935–1984

Source: Odum and Turner 1988:18.

predictable" (1979:327). Some Dodge County farmers feel that higher nitrogen levels also make plants more susceptible to insect damage or disease infestations.

Each step of agricultural intensification brings its own ecological impact and conservation challenges. The high fertilizer applications common to contemporary agriculture present threats to water quality through groundwater pollution. Figure 2-4 charts the nitrogen runoff levels in the Savannah River from 1975 to 1985, and research suggests chemical runoff poses environmental dangers to rural communities as well (Odum and Turner 1988). Concerns have also been voiced about chemical contamination of Georgia's enormous underground aquifers. Data on water contamination by agricultural pesticides in Georgia are not available, but accelerating use of a range of chemicals suggests there is a need for investigation. Ecological challenges are presented by high-yield hog production as well. Disease

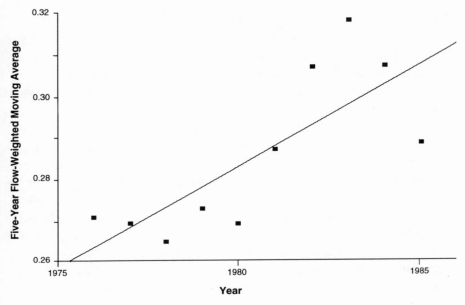

Figure 2-4. Fertilizer Runoff Levels: Nitrate and Nitrite
Levels in the Savannah River, 1975–1985

Source: Odum and Turner 1988.

contamination limits many farmers who prefer to raise hogs "on the ground," yet confinement systems are also vulnerable to disease outbreaks. Pollution of local water supplies is an additional concern with intensive hog production.

Ecological research on modern agricultural methods throughout the United States has raised cautions about the sustainability of our intensive production system (Busch and Lacey 1983; Strange 1984; Wessel 1983). Mechanization has put consistent pressure on soil structure, and problems with soil compaction and erosion have increased with each new development of heavier and larger machinery. In the 1970s, the production of a bushel of corn consumed about two bushels of topsoil, through erosion (Pimentel et al. 1976). Mechanization and capital-intensive agriculture can stimulate chains of ecological interactions whose results are not felt for decades. Just as the lumber boom of the 1800s set off an ecological transformation with powerful consequences over the long run, so too has the technological revolution in American agriculture set off ecological processes whose effects are at present only dimly perceived.

Agricultural intensification not only raises new ecological questions, but it builds new linkages to a complex nonfarm economy of agribusiness suppliers. Although the numbers of *farm* households have declined in the census, these figures are somewhat misleading when assessing the impact of agriculture. Farm tasks are now carried out in the oil refineries of Louisiana, the tractor factories of Illinois, and the peanut processors of Georgia. Salespeople earn a living today selling farmers seeds, chemicals, and crop insurance, and these white collar jobs are all dependent upon the health of the county's individual farm businesses. Though less than 10 percent of the Dodge County population lives on farms, a much higher percentage depends on agriculturally related jobs. The farm crisis of the 1980s sent shock waves through farm communities and affected agribusinesses as well.

This linkage to the agribusiness sector makes farmers into "price takers," relatively powerless in the squeeze between the prices offered by the national and international markets that buy their farm products and the prices demanded by manufacturers who sell them the seeds, chemicals, and other inputs necessary to carry out the year's production tasks. Each specialist whose services are added to farmers' expenses—from the banker to the crop duster—takes a percentage of the farmer's profit. These payments are usually due before harvest, leaving the farmer ever more vulnerable to price swings. Supply shortages also place operators in a more precarious position, whether the cause is an oil embargo or a rush on a popular seed variety. Farmers in addition face uncertainties about the quality of goods supplied.

Capital intensification creates other risks as well. Farmers who make large investments in mechanized cotton pickers (which cost over $80,000 in 1982), tobacco harvesters, or other equipment are constrained in future cropping decisions. A fall in crop prices leaves such operators unable to diversify because equipment payments remain. Some small and medium scale operators have chosen to rely on arrangements with equipment-owning neighbors to reduce their risk. Mechanization also presents new managerial challenges, as machines break down and parts are not always available. Sprayers can clog and harvesters become entangled with weeds. Many farmers have become specialists in equipment repair, and the need for such skills has come to exclude most women from agricultural production (Barron 1990). In addition, machinery can waste a percentage of the harvest—or all of it, as when cornstalks have been blown to the ground in a storm before harvesting. Some farmers with investments in fencing can manage to turn animals into such a field and recoup harvest losses in this way, but many farmers are unable to do so. The mechanical cotton picker sometimes leaves a visible white dusting of wasted cotton over the fields, and some older farmers express dismay at this unfortunate side effect of capital intensification. On the other hand, the speed of a mechanized harvest can save a crop from weather or pest damage, if the farmer has organized his or her time effectively.

A final aspect of the intensification of U.S. agriculture that affects the Dodge County story is the increasing complexity of demands on the farm manager and the resulting "speed up" in farm activities. Annual meetings with University of Georgia extension personnel introduce farmers to new recommendations, crop varieties, and production options each year. Seed and other suppliers visit farms and support these meetings, encouraging the use of their products and presenting farmers with a broad palette of production options. Chemical use demands new expertise from farmers, who must also be licensed in safe chemical application. Insurance, government programs, and operating credit all involve an array of forms, new terminology, deadlines, and regulations.

Farmers have also intensified their own labor. More acres need more attention, and increased farm scale pushes farmers to long hours. The ability to farm at night, with tractor headlights, also extends the hours farmers are able to invest in their operations. The development of new crop varieties has changed the pace of the annual round. Winters used to be a slower time, with less to be done, but winter wheat production, late harvest of some fall crops, and early spring planting have filled in much of that slack season.[8] Some farmers today report having a month or two of slower work demands, but for many, a rushed pace never lets up. The overextended, pressured farmer is now a common fixture in the county, echoing the pressures of nonfarm jobs and the faster pace brought by the automobile in the postwar era.

The greater demands on their time and their increased vulnerability within the larger economy present farmers with new opportunities and new challenges to their managerial skills. Farmers can make more money, but they can lose more as well. The complexity and cost of the new technology affects judgments of what constitutes a prudent farm manager. The wisdom of the cautious, debt-averse farmer of the "Hoover Days" has been called into question by the intensification of the production system, and conflicting visions of the good farmer have emerged (see chapter 5).

Farm Structure, Farm Labor, and the Emerging Family Farm

The postwar trends in agricultural technology, capital intensification, and government policies created a revolution in Dodge County agriculture and brought forth a new agricultural structure dominated by owner-operated units. This change in farm size and techniques reflected, as we have seen, a closer integration of the agrarian sector with the larger industrial capitalist economy. From a neoclassical economic perspective, once the wiregrass settlers abandoned their subsistence-oriented farming and became more fully integrated into the market—to sell their products as well as to purchase inputs—they could be labeled capitalist, or commercial, farmers (Paarlberg 1980; Tweeten 1984). From a political economy perspective, however, the penetration of capitalism into the countryside requires a transformation of the labor process and a separation of kin-based household units into separate classes of farm owners, managers, and laborers (Buttel and Newby 1980; Mann 1990; Vogeler 1981). This perspective on the nature of capitalism in agriculture is useful to our study of Dodge County because it asks to what extent the family labor farm (regardless of whether it is owned, rented, or share-cropped) has been replaced by a different economic organization based on wage labor. Because the transformation to an industrial society of business owners and wage laborers was occurring in the larger U.S. economy in the postwar period, the question arises to what degree these same processes were occurring within southern agricultural production. Some authors have argued that the decline of tenants and small farms was generally accompanied by the emergence of a group of landless farm workers that provided labor on large farms (Kirby 1987; Mann 1990; Wright 1986). Since most data to support this conclusion rely on the former plantation areas of the South, Dodge County with its more typical mix of farm types presents an interesting opportunity to illuminate this structural change.

The Dodge County data suggest some support for the penetration of capitalist wage relations into agriculture but predominantly show that the structure of agriculture shifted to family-owned and -operated farm units, similar to the "family farm" structure of the Midwest (Friedmann 1978; Schertz 1979). As shown in table 2-2, the numbers of owner-operated farms fell from 954 to 402 over the thirty-year period from the mid-1950s to the mid-1980s, but the overall proportion of family farm units rose from 62 percent to 83 percent.[9] These farms were operated without full-time hired workers. Farms using full-time workers declined steadily from 1959 to 1978, and their proportion of all farms in the county fluctuated between 10 and 20 percent. Responding to the agricultural boom of the early 1970s, these large farms reached a peak of 19 percent but dropped to less than half that (8%) five years later. The structure of farm units in the county, then, shows a dramatic shift *toward* the family labor farm in the thirty years after World War II.

Some large farms in Dodge County may accurately be described as capital-

Table 2-2. Farm Structure in Dodge County, 1954–1982

	Owner-operated Farms without Full-Time Workers	Tenant Farms	Farms with Full-Time Workers*
1954	954 (62%)	486 (32%)	83 (5%)
1959	723 (70%)	190 (18%)	126 (12%)
1964	438 (71%)	70 (11%)	109 (18%)
1969	553 (83%)	46 (7%)	68 (10%)
1974	472 (82%)	44 (8%)	61 (11%)
1978	398 (72%)	53 (10%)	106 (19%)
1982	402 (83%)	40 (8%)	40 (8%)

Source: U.S. Census of Agriculture, 1954–82.
*Farms reporting one or more workers hired for 150 or more days per year.

ist farms because owners do relatively little direct farm labor and concentrate on management. Farms in which owners and managers are separate people also exist in the county but are rare. Most large scale farm owners, however, work in the fields along with their hands, and it is hard to draw a sharp distinction among actual cases between family labor farms and family-owned farms that use some hired labor. In addition, some large farms are partnerships of siblings or parents and children, in which case any hired hands are usually outnumbered by owner-operators (see Barlett 1984). This diversity of labor relations among large farms demonstrates that a form of agriculture based primarily on wage labor did not emerge from the postwar years, even among the 8 percent (in 1982) that report hiring full-time labor.

Table 2-2 also shows that tenant farms declined sharply, from 32 percent to 8 percent of the farm units in the county. As we have seen, some tenants were removed, but some also died or retired, and their children had long since sought other occupations. Some of the "tenants" who continued to appear in the census figures of the 1980s could more accurately be described as renters. Others were landless families who had given up trying to accumulate enough capital to buy a farm. One woman described her sharecropper father: "He was content, I reckon. It was all he knew, just sharecropping. That was life. He said, 'I don't have the

Table 2-3. Hired Farm Labor in Dodge County, 1954–1982

	All Farm Workers	Workers over 150 Days per Year	Farms Hiring Two or More Workers over 150 Days per Year
1954	721	195	—
1959	735	218	48
1964	—	228	—
1969	859	174	—
1974	758	136	33
1978	1,566	147	37
1982	538	95*	22

Source: U.S. Census of Agriculture, 1954–82.
*The data reported for 1982 omit two categories of workers included in previous censuses and are thus not directly comparable to previous years.

money, I'll never have the money, I'll just tend what I got.' " In several tenant families, children were able in later years to buy their retired parents a house along with a small plot of land, and they ended their lives in the security of their own homes. A few other retired tenants still occupy the old houses provided to them when they were engaged in sharecropping. This housing is some of the worst in the county because owners feel no obligation to keep it maintained, and tenants have no rights to retain the value of any improvements they might make.

Though family labor farms have become the norm in Dodge County, the importance of hired labor to the new structure of agriculture should not be discounted. Full-time workers are essential to the survival of large farms, and short-term, temporary workers are important to a range of farm operators, depending on their crop mix. The sharp decline in tenant farms in the 1950s did not lead to a rise in wage workers, however. As table 2-3 shows, the total number of persons reported to work for wages in agriculture hovered between 721 and 859 from the 1950s into the mid-1970s. Echoing the pattern we saw in the previous table, the number of hired workers rose sharply with the agricultural expansion following the boom years of the mid-1970s, then fell to a postwar low in the 1980s slump. The picture for full-time farm workers (over 150 days per year) shows a more steady decline, however, from around 200 in the county in 1954 down to less than half that number in the 1980s.[10] The farms that hired two or more full-time hands have also declined, from 48 in 1959 to 22 in 1982, revealing a very small sector of farms with heavy use of regular wage labor. This group increased by only 4 in the boom years, suggesting that the rise in hired labor at that time reflected an expansion strategy of farm operators who had previously worked alone. This same pattern is found statewide in Georgia, where farms using hired labor rose in 1978 in response to the agricultural boom and then declined in 1982.

These labor statistics do reveal a greater use of paid wages, substituting for other kinds of labor exchanges in the household economy of the Depression era. Where family members or neighbors used to help out with sporadic field tasks such as peanut weeding or tobacco harvesting, workers are now more commonly paid. Temporary farm workers are hired to pick vegetables (sometimes for home freezing, more often for sale) or to harvest watermelons. The majority of agricultural workers therefore must have other sources of income and work in agriculture for only short periods in the year for extra money. In addition, many family workers, including children, are now paid, and some farmers even list their sons as full-time hands and pay them a regular salary. Thus, the figure of 538 occasional farm workers in Dodge County in 1982 combines many different kinds of people and is by no means a coherent class of agricultural proletarians.[11] The group of 95 full-time hands, however, can mostly be categorized as a distinct class of workers; their situation is discussed further in chapter 4.

Given that the postwar period saw a major transition to owner-operated, family labor farms, a second question concerning the changing structure of southern agriculture is what sizes of farms survived and to what extent smaller and less advantaged farm families were displaced by more advantaged larger farmers. The evidence from the census of agriculture suggests that large farms as a group were able to continue in operation, while most tenants and many landless farmers as a group were not. The aggregate picture seems to support an interpretation of displacement, as more elite farms seemed to be more successful in reproducing the farm in a new generation. My data from the Dodge County study, however, reveal a more diverse transition. I traced the family backgrounds of all farmers in the 1982 sample, and the results show that many children of small farm families were able to survive in farming. This second source of information lets us see the movements and decisions of actual families behind the broader measures of change in the census.

Turning first to the issue of farm size, the Dodge County data show a pattern

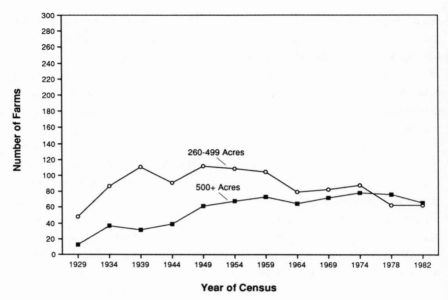

Figure 2-5. Number of Large Farms
in Dodge County, 1929–1982

Source: U.S. Census of Agriculture, 1929–82.

of decline in small farms and continuity among large farms. As we saw in figure 2-1, the overall number of farms plummeted, but as figure 2-5 reveals, the number of large farms did not greatly increase. In 1935, there were a total of 122 farms with over 260 acres, and in 1982 there were 128. Farms with over 500 acres grew from 36 in 1934 to 68 in 1954 but then remained under 80 throughout the last thirty years. The same pattern is true for the state of Georgia as a whole. Large farms can therefore be seen as a category from the Depression years that was able to reproduce itself. Small farms and tenant farms, for the most part, did not.

While the overall numbers of more elite farm families in Dodge County did not grow substantially, the amount of land controlled by each farm did rise. Average farm sizes in Dodge County more than tripled from the 1920s to the present. From an average of only 80 acres in 1929, farm sizes rose to over 200 acres in 1959 and to 274 in 1982. Because this latter figure includes a sector of small part-time farms, the average farm size for full-time farmers is considerably larger (see chapter 4). The quality of land in farming also increased, as a third of farmland from the 1930s was taken out of production. From a peak in 1949, when 82 percent

Table 2-4. Parental Backgrounds of Full-Time and
Part-Time Farm Operators in Dodge County, 1982

| | Operators from 1982 Sample | | | Farms in 1934* |
Operator's Parents	Full-Time (n = 79)	Part-Time (n = 34)	Total (n = 121)	Total (n = 2,512)
Medium or large scale farm owner**	33%	19%	28%	5%
Small scale farm owner	46	50	47	29
Tenant or sharecropper	11	10	11	67
Nonfarmer	10	21	14	—

*Repeated from table 1-1; proportions of types of all farms in Dodge County in 1934
(U.S. Census of Agriculture, 1934).
**Farm size 260 acres and over.

of the county's total land area was farmed, the percentage fell to only 41 percent
in 1982 (263,264 acres to 132,166 acres). Much of this land went into timber
production—some of it induced by the Soil Bank programs in the 1950s—leaving
the best land in farms. Hilly areas, sandy soils, and heavily eroded lands tended to
be taken out of production, and the rise in overall farmland quality played a part
in the soaring yields and higher per farm profits discussed previously.

Turning now to the data from the Dodge County sample, we can see that the
changing structure of agriculture did not result in the complete exclusion of landless and small farm owners from continued production. The larger farms with
better soils that characterize the county today are owned by descendants of all
rural groups, though more affluent farm families have been disproportionately successful in passing on farms. Farmers in the study were asked about their parents'
farm size and ownership for the period when the future operators were in high
school, thereby measuring not their parents' ultimate farm size or ownership, but
the reality at the point when the young person was deciding whether or not to take
up farming.[12] Table 2-4 divides the families of the 121 operators in the study in
1982 into full-time and part-time groups and shows the percentages from each
of four parental backgrounds. For comparison, the table includes the proportions
of medium or large, small, and tenant farms in the county in 1934 from census

figures. To be consistent with the 1934 groupings, medium or large farms were defined as 260 acres and over.

Although only a third of farm units in 1934 were small farms, almost a half of all operators today are children of small farm families. A tenth of farmers today are children of sharecroppers, and 14 percent are children of nonfarmers (these are usually operators whose grandparents, uncles, or other close relatives encouraged them to farm). The presumably more disadvantaged landless and small farm groups nevertheless provided the offspring who make up nearly three-fourths of all farmers today (and 67 percent of full-time farmers).

Large and medium scale farm owners, however, were somewhat more successful in passing the occupation on to their children and, not surprisingly, make up a much larger proportion of the farm population today. Although such farms were only 5 percent of the total in 1934, descendants of these more affluent families are now 28 percent of the total and a third of full-time farmers. Consequently, generalizations about the postwar structure of southern agriculture are correct in showing a proportional increase in large farms and reliance on wage labor but have tended to overemphasize the exclusion of non-elite families from farming. Although this pattern must be verified by further research, it does suggest that an overemphasis on plantation areas of the South has hidden some more democratic aspects of the structural change in which the children of small family farms have been able to enter the more expensive, mechanized farming profession we see today.

Generations of Young Farmers

Although many sizes of farms were able successfully to transmit the farm to the present generation, farming in the postwar era became an increasingly closed occupation. As we shall see in chapter 3, alternative jobs in other economic sectors became more attractive, and fewer and fewer young people attempted to take up farming. The greater cost and new skills required also deterred some young people, while children of landless families were often deprived of a choice in the matter. Table 2-5 shows a sharp drop in the numbers of young farmers, from 475 in 1945 to 97 fifteen years later. By 1964, there were only 35 young farm operators reported by the census. We saw earlier in this chapter (see table 2-1) that the county population remained relatively stable in the 1950s and 1960s, so this decline in young farmers reflects economic change and personal decisions (Easterlin 1980).

The same collapse of numbers in farming can be seen in the data on current Dodge County farmers and when they entered farming, but an interesting re-

Table 2-5. Farm Operators under Age 35
in Dodge County, 1945–1982

| | Full-Time and Part-Time Operators | |
	Number	Percent of Total under Age 65
1945	475	27
1959	97	9
1964	35	6
1969	79	12
1974	64	21
1978	91	16
1982	70	15

Source: U.S. Census of Agriculture, 1945–82.
Note: Data not available for 1949 and 1955.

surgence of interest in farming appears in later cohorts. Figure 2-6 graphs the numbers of operators entering farming in five-year cohorts and divides the entire sample into three generations, those entering prior to 1960 (Generation 1), those entering between 1960 and the beginning of the agricultural boom in 1972 (Generation 2), and those entering in 1972 and later (Generation 3). Young men joining their parents or siblings in partnerships were counted as equal to those who started farming on their own.

Generation 1 farmers began farming before 1960. The group shows the same decline of interest in farming as revealed in table 2-5, as cohorts gently decline in size.[13] Figure 2-6 does not show the same large number of farmers in 1945 as the census figures in table 2-5 because many of these farmers had died or retired by 1982, when the study began.

Most of the farmers of this generation were modest in their goals and were proud to have succeeded as farm owners. The majority were children of small farm owners or sharecroppers, and their farm management style was cautious, reflecting the powerful memories of Depression-era hard times. Exulting in the affluence brought by the revolution in agricultural production, they were proud to be part of a new, more comfortable life on the farm. A small group of Generation 1 farmers were returning veterans, and they were dissatisfied with the traditional technology of mule farming. Using their military severance pay (or family profits from the

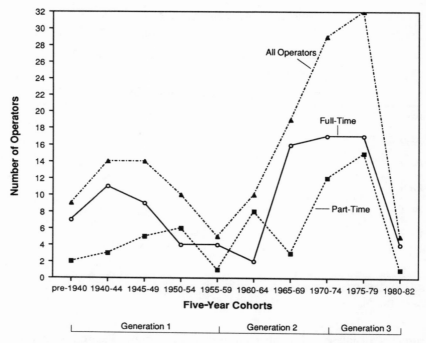

Figure 2-6. Operators' Year of Entry into Farming,
Dodge County Sample

war years) to buy land and equipment, some members of this 1940s generation spearheaded the technological revolution of tractors and other innovations.

Parents of Generation 1 farmers rarely provided many resources to set them up in farming. Only a third of families were able to lend some land to their children, and, interestingly, these generous parents were no more likely to be large landholders than small. About half of Generation 1 operators benefited from the loan of equipment, and a fifth were given some livestock to begin farming, but most parents were too poor to help much. One older woman recalled that all her parents gave her to help start her new life in farming were two pillows at marriage. When asked if parents helped out with land, machinery, capital, or other help, most Generation 1 Dodge Countians shook their heads, claiming that "they weren't able."

Generation 2 farmers began to farm during the transitional period when yields were skyrocketing and farm incomes were rising. A new image of the farmer, not behind "a dirty old mule," but atop a tractor that cost more than a fine car began to emerge. The Census of Agriculture records a doubling of the number of young farmers by 1969, from 35 to 79, and figure 2-6 illustrates the rise in the number of full-time operators during the 1960s. It might be expected that the cohort entering farming grew in 1969 because of the postwar baby boom, but the population figures for Dodge County do not show a postwar birth increase. Young people make up approximately the same proportion of the total population as in the decades before and after the 1960s. The surge in the number of young farmers is therefore not demographic but reflects the greater desirability of farming.

Generation 2 farmers were a new breed who recognized the greater challenges of farming, the need for greater resources in order to farm, and the potentially higher incomes. Although they were aware of the hard times of the 1940s and 1950s, most were the children of farmers who had done well, having expanded the farm operation. Some were motivated to continue an independent way of life, appreciating the freedoms of farming, and not expecting great increases in standard of living. Others looked to farming as a way to become more affluent. They aspired to a larger, middle class house, a nice car, and other measures of success. Some inherited large estates from a prewar generation and adopted a philosophy of expansion and farm improvement through capital investments. As farm profits rose in this period, new equipment and new farm facilities were financed mainly through savings, though some operators also turned to modest borrowing. New machines, crop varieties, and chemicals made large scale farming seem within closer reach, and aspirations to "make money" in farming took hold. The majority of the young men in this generation were aiming much higher than the majority in Generation 1.

For Generation 2, substantial parental help with land and equipment was the norm. Two-thirds benefited from the use of land without rent in their early years, nearly three-fourths received the loan of equipment, and half were given some livestock. For Generation 2, another important aid to establishing a farm was access to federal agricultural programs. Forty percent obtained allotments from their parents—either sold, rented, or loaned—in their initial years of farming. Such government assistance was more common for this group than for both the succeeding and preceding generations.

These Generation 2 farmers also had a different relationship with their fathers. Generation 1 farmers were commonly independent from the parental farms. Parents either had no resources to offer the young couple, had no way to encourage a young man to join the farm as a partner, or had too many sons to think about joint operations. Also, joint operations seem to have conferred relatively little

advantage, beyond an apprenticeship period. Many sons preferred greater independence, wanting to try new technologies and ideas that were resisted by their
fathers. Land was relatively cheap in this period, and as tenants died or left, farms
became available quite readily. Larger families and lower life expectancies also
meant more Generation 1 farmers began farming after their fathers had died.

Most Generation 2 farmers had younger, more vigorous fathers, who wanted
their sons to join the operation. Two men working the farm provided advantages
in additional labor and management skills to allow further consolidation of profits
and expansion. In several cases, a father had suddenly lost a good hired hand,
making him desperate for his son's skilled help. Sons were occasionally "called
home" from school or jobs to help out "temporarily," but the situation became
permanent. In this way, some older operators faced the changing availability of
farm laborers and tenants by becoming partners with their sons. Also, the need for
new skills in farm labor, due to the increased sophistication of crop and livestock
care, meant the traditional skills of some farm laborers were no longer adequate
for the new farm demands.

Fathers who could work well with their sons and who had amassed sufficient
resources to provide an attractive income were more likely to be successful in
transmitting the farm in this period. Among those families whose operations had
not expanded or utilized new machines and technology, the farm was evaluated
less positively. Fewer of these families encouraged their children to farm, and they
had fewer advantages to offer the ones who were inclined to try. Several Generation 1 fathers talked about the limits on their own farm expansion because their
sons had chosen not to join them. Cases of brothers in which one farmed with a
son and one did not are powerfully illustrative that joint management, in a time of
capital-intensive farming, can be highly beneficial. One struggling Generation 2
farmer with no sons said wistfully, "It would have made a world of difference if
I'd had a son."

Generation 3 farmers were drawn to this occupation after the boom years of
the early 1970s. They are the largest group; 91 young farmers are recorded in the
1978 census, as opposed to only 64 four years earlier (see table 2-5). Figure 2-6
shows that part-time farming rose sharply in this generation, also in response to
the boom, while full-time farming continued to attract young men. In Generation 3, there seems to be a brief opening in the otherwise closing door of farm
occupations.

Generation 3 farmers represent a diverse group in terms of family background
and parental help. Some from elite farm families continued the pattern of significant parental assistance found in Generation 2. The proportion of farm operators

from medium and large farm backgrounds fell, however, from 38 percent in Generation 2 to 19 percent in Generation 3. The falling percentage reflects two trends: a rise in the number of young farmers from modest backgrounds and a new group of second career farmers, whose first career had been in a nonagricultural line of work and who chose to give up their "good jobs" elsewhere for a try at farming. The majority of those in Generation 3 either left their work in factories and skilled blue collar jobs or opted not to pursue them in the first place, motivated by the high farm profits of the boom years. Young men from landless, small farm, and even nonfarm backgrounds were drawn to farming in greater numbers than in previous decades. Many of these less-privileged young farmers began with little or no parental help, often with considerable financing from farm lenders and banks. This trend was supported, as discussed in chapter 7, by the inflation of the early 1970s and the generous policies of many lenders. Because of soaring land values, many were forced to rent and wait until they were able to buy land. A few from larger farms joined in family partnerships and benefited from free land, equipment, and allotments. Others were able to ease into purchasing the family estate, but fewer than half of this generation received family help with access to land.

Expectations were high for this generation, as farming "caught fire." Not only were the children of affluent farmers hoping to live well, but many from more modest backgrounds had similar aspirations. Especially for some second career farmers, agriculture was an almost glamorous opportunity to mix independent business ownership and entrepreneurial savvy with deep roots in the rural community. Rising standards of living among farmers challenged the older image of the impoverished farm family. Not all Generation 3 farmers were ambitious and oriented toward a higher-risk management style, however. Some were children of cautious operators—medium scale or even large scale—and they chose farming because they loved the occupation, not because they hoped to get rich.

The numbers of young farmers show a dramatic collapse after the crisis years of the late 1970s and early 1980s. Successive droughts and declining profits dampened interest in farming. A very small number of young people tried farming but few stayed with it; only four full-time farmers and one part-time farmer in the study sample entered this occupation after 1980, reflecting the "bust" of farming conditions. My efforts in 1987 to locate new farmers who entered after 1982 were largely unsuccessful. It is a source of dismay and some loneliness for the younger farmers in the county as they mature that no one is coming along behind them. The brief period in which farming became a more democratic opportunity was soon over, and the ebullient optimism with which some entered a farm career was short-lived.

THREE

The Clash of Agrarian and Industrial

Values and the Part-Time Farm Solution

The postwar family farms in Dodge County are now surrounded by people who live in rural areas but work at jobs. The nonfarm world of work brings with it values from an industrial economy that challenge older agrarian traditions. Rising incomes and steady pay from jobs create expectations about family lifestyles that have moved Dodge County toward a consumer society, and assessments of the "good life" now increasingly emphasize individualism and materialist accumulation. The American dream of affluence, based on income and lifestyle, challenges the agrarian definition of "success" that encompasses independent livelihood, property ownership, and nonmonetary work satisfactions.

"You can't blame the children for going off to get good jobs," remarked an older woman from a medium scale farm. Her comment reveals a profound ambivalence that is the legacy of the economic transformation that we saw in the last chapter. As job opportunities have expanded, most farm children have sought out higher incomes and entered a work world unknown to their parents. Remaining farm families experience these value clashes and seek ways to uphold their own agrarian beliefs and to find compromises with social status pressures for consumption. This chapter will describe the changing social world of Dodge County, the breakdown of the old agricultural hierarchies, and the emergence of lifestyle as a primary measure of personal success. This same transition to a consumer ethic has been described in other cultures at a similar historical moment—when an industrializing economy combines rising affluence, blurred social ranking, and ambiguous measures of prestige. One group that has found a way to reconcile these divergent value systems are the part-time farmers, who combine the security and higher income of off-farm work with the agrarian satisfactions of an agricultural enterprise.

The Agrarian Definition of Personal Success

In Dodge County today, farmers express an agrarian ethic when they talk about farming and why they love it. For many, the occupation of farming is more than a particular job; it is a meaningful way of life that incorporates "a sense of purpose, spiritual values, a sense that what one is doing is the right way to live and that alternative ways are inferior" (Rosenblatt 1990:73). "The farmer is the most important one, even if town people don't recognize it," said one Dodge County woman. Though farm families enjoy a rising standard of living, their sense of success is less based on consumption levels (Mooney 1988). Instead, they talk about dimensions of satisfaction in the farming way of life.

Primary among these agrarian values are aspects of the work process itself: freedom from supervision, flexibility of work pace, and daily independence from supervision (Brooks, Stucker, and Bailey 1986; Schroeder, Fliegel, and van Es 1985). One woman farmer who has worked in a factory said, "I enjoy it; I like to see things grow—that's why I like to mess around with hogs." For her, indoor jobs are unacceptable because "you're shut up" and "you have to punch a time clock." "Farming, if you're hot and tired, you can stop. When you're working for yourself, you can set down if you want; you can work when you want to." On the job, you've "got to do what *they* say." Many farmers echo this emphasis on independence in their daily work lives. "You can't just do whatever you feel like," they emphasize, but the farmer *is* able to take an afternoon off to be with a child or go to a school or church function. "You only have to get up early by seasons," pointed out one older woman.

A sense of accomplishment is important to Dodge County farmers. Unlike many employees, they can make plans and experience personal efficacy (Cobb 1984). They report "a special feeling in the spring when you get out and prepare the land and then plant, and when the trees begin to turn green and the crops begin to grow, you feel like you really accomplished something." "There's a sense of responsibility involved. You hatch the egg—and even create the egg—then hatch it, raise it, and put it in the marketplace. It's a creative process." A farmer feels satisfaction after solving a problem or figuring out a way to save money: "He pokes out his chest and is proud of it." For some, farming is an opportunity for achievement, "to handle money," "to have a big farm, big barns, and plenty of equipment." For others, it is important to feel needed, to be providing the basic necessities for the country.

Farming becomes more than an occupational identity; the work creates a compelling emotional attachment that many men and women allude to. "Farming gets in your blood" is a common way of putting it. "Farming is a disease—once you catch it you never get rid of it." One wife said, "You can't separate [my husband] from farming any more than you can separate him from his *skin*." This tenacity of the satisfaction of farming is usually described with a smile. But a young farmer forced out of business during the crisis described his thwarted love for farming with a deep, wrenching pain: "I always wanted to farm. It's in your blood. . . . It's like a mean dog—there's nothing you can do but kill it. Nothing'll change its meanness."

Part of the addiction of farming is the uncertainty of the reward: "I enjoy the challenge of the gamble." "The farm is a dream, and either it comes true or it doesn't. When it comes true, you want it over and over." The farmer matches human wit, skill, and experience against nature, the experts, and the multinational corporations, and sometimes wins a good annual return. In the boom years, the experience of successful farmers and the upbeat advice of the agricultural experts whetted the appetite. Some men and women dislike the gambling part of farming, but even they volunteer, "It *is* a good feeling when it turns out good."

Another powerful attraction to farming is the connection to nature. All ages of farmers greatly value "being outdoors," "seeing things grow." One man worked for several years after college in Atlanta in an office without a window. Today, he is outdoors every day in all weather. He, like others, values a workday that lets him hear birds sing, see "the wonders of nature," and smell the soil. Even those who use hired labor value many of the same sensory stimuli. One large scale farmer claimed, "You are not really living until you walk across a field in late October, hearing the combine harvesting the corn, seeing the leaves turn color, and feeling the cool air." The smell of newly plowed land in the spring is recalled reverently as much by those who no longer farm as by those who still do.

The connection with nature involves a connection with deep religious beliefs as well. "You look at nature all day long—God is all around you." "There has to be a higher power. . . . Take a baby—how can anybody look at a baby and not know there's a higher power? It's like looking at crops grow. There's a baby there, all innocent." Said a woman whose husband's desire to farm drove the family deeply into debt, "It has to do with deep morals—a force stronger than you that keeps you there." These connections with life, with production, with the rhythms of nature are more potent than the satisfactions of other jobs. Some farmers agree that their work keeps them connected with God and deeper life forces in the same way that women come to feel connected through the mysteries of birth. Farming brings a person "to depend more on a higher power—you're closer to nature, see the growth and reproductive powers of nature." "You have to have faith, to be a farmer," say many in Dodge County. "A person on the outside can't comprehend a person's feeling for the *land*. It's not *like* a piece of equipment." These deep connections plus the preference for outdoor work and independence led one retired farmer to assert his love for the beauty of fields when viewed from the top of a combine, the peace of working with cows. "When I die, I will know I spent the last years of my life doing exactly what I want to do—exactly what I love."

Some farmers emphasize many of these same criteria in claiming that off-farm employment is less desirable. Daily life in a factory, store, or other indoor job is very different from farming, and being cut off from nature, fresh air, and the varieties of weather is very unpleasant for some Dodge Countians. "I didn't like that closed-in feeling," said one farmer who worked for a while in a store. Loss of control over work time and pace are also cited as disadvantages to taking off-farm work: "I hated to have my life controlled by the clock—being there at 7:00 and knowing I couldn't leave till 3:30. . . . It nearly killed me!"

Farming is not a "push-push thing with a time schedule on you," said one black woman who reluctantly works off the farm. Pressures to produce on the job are most obvious in the shirt factories, where inability to "keep up with the production" can lead a woman to be "timed out." Older employees who are unable to sew at the required speed often have few other job alternatives, and the loss of this income can be a real blow to family finances. In other factories as well as some offices, machines set the pace, and humans conform to the machines' initiative. "And a person can't go to the house when they want to."

Unlike the farmer, whose work can often be independent and solitary, most jobs involve complex relations with coworkers, supervisors, and subordinates. Many workers talk about the "pressure," "stress," and "hassle" of their jobs. "It gets on your nerves, working there." Though farming has its own aggravations, they have less to do with the foibles or ill will of other humans. Petty harassments rankle, such as denial of a vacation request or criticism from a supervisor who has not come up through the ranks. Said one young man who tried factory work briefly before coming back to farming, "Everyone there was afraid to do any more work than the other one."

Finally, there is a sense that off-farm work is less meaningful, less important work, though few Dodge Countians will say so outright. Said one farmer who stressed the pride he feels in his work, "Now, I don't want to badmouth putting tires on a car; somebody's got to do it. But the auto worker has to feel less pride, seeing a car go down the street." Jobs less often continue a family tradition, and they can leave the worker feeling both more independent and more disconnected. For those who value the farm as an effort of an extended family, off-farm work is painfully isolated.

In their efforts to retain many of these values, farm families feel beleaguered. These noneconomic aspects of "success" are rarely articulated in an industrial society or expounded by opinion leaders, teachers, or the media. Their invisibility in the public domain weakens their power. Farmers assert these values with a truculence and defensiveness that reveals their awareness that such orienting values are not shared by many people. Farmers know that some see such values as a rationalization for an inferior life's work.

Some nonfarmers also deny the validity of farmers' claims. The purported independence of farming is dismissed by those who point to the squeeze of rising costs and falling prices. Embargoes and shifting federal programs pull the rug out from under prudent farm planning. Lenders and farm experts seemingly converge on the producer, each trying to tell the farmer what to do. For many outside farming (and some inside, as well), the freedoms of farming are an illusion. Even the sacred connections of farming are denied by some. One young farmer rejects any idea of farming as a special or more spiritual calling: "You can feel as close to God as a research scientist in a laboratory as being a farmer."

Farming Becomes a Minority Way of Life

In the years since World War II, job opportunities outside farming expanded rapidly, and with this new economic base came a shift in values and definitions of success (Gallaher 1961). "*Having* something" became the marker of success, and many young people, encouraged by their parents, have abandoned the farm life to "have more." "Farming just couldn't support the lifestyle we wanted," said one couple. Adoption of these industrial values was a response to the dire poverty of the Depression years and offered hope for a rise in social status by abandoning the agrarian desire to own property and sustain an independent livelihood.

Census figures as shown in table 3-1 reveal the decline in the number of adult

Table 3-1. Occupations of Men in Dodge County, 1930–1980

	Percent of Total Employed*					
	1930	1940	1950	1960	1970	1980
	(n = 6,349)	(n = 5,519)	(n = 4,913)	(n = 3,771)	(n = 3,308)	(n = 3,418)
Total agricultural occupations	71	56	43	24	15	9
Farm operators	39	34	35	15	8	7
Farm laborers	32	22	9	9	8	3
Other occupations	29	44	57	76	85	91

Source: U.S. Census of Population, 1930–80.
*Employed population aged from 10 to 16 and over, depending on the year.

men in agricultural occupations in Dodge County over the last fifty years. At the height of the Depression in 1930, 71 percent of all adult men were employed in agriculture as farm owners, tenants, or laborers.[1] Other jobs in timbering, retail, public service, professions, construction, and manufacturing totaled only 29 percent of male occupations. By 1950, fewer than half of men worked in agriculture, and ten years later the figure was again halved. Though Dodge County is considered a rural and agricultural county, fewer than 10 percent of men were farm operators or farm laborers in 1980.

Class background plays a role in determining what kinds of work farm children move toward when they leave agriculture. In tracing family histories, I found that men from small farms generally take skilled blue collar jobs such as trucking, electronics, sheet metal work, or "mechanicking." Women from these families commonly work in the candy factory, in the shirt factory, or as cooks. The children from medium- or large-sized farms tend toward clerical, sales, and other white collar jobs. Large scale farmers' sons and daughters are more likely to be teachers or some other type of professional, have civil service jobs, or operate their own businesses. The children of sharecroppers usually move on to blue collar and skilled trades; in previous generations, work in timbering, lumberyards, and construction were the main occupations available. Such work is also common among children of agricultural laborers, though many today also work in factories.

Table 3-2 shows that job opportunities for African American Dodge Countians changed more slowly than for whites. Conversations with black farmers confirm

Table 3-2. Occupations of Black Men and Women
in Dodge County, 1930–1970

	Percent of Total Employed*					
	1930		1950		1970	
	Men	Women	Men	Women	Men	Women
	(n = 2,507)	(n = 705)	(n = 1,308)	(n = 556)	(n = 585)	(n = 572)
Farm operators	29	9	31	5	6	0
Farm laborers	37	40	8	13	23	4
Domestic service	1	45	1	49	0	39
Other occupations	34	7	61	33	72	58

Source: U.S. Census of Population, 1930, 1950, 1970.
*Employed population aged 10 and over in 1930, 14 and over in 1950, and 16 and over in 1970.

that many of their relatives found broader occupational opportunities available in northern cities. Agricultural work as farm owners, tenants, or laborers was the predominant occupation in the Depression years, but by 1950 the majority of black men had found nonfarm jobs. For black women, the most common occupation in both eras was domestic service, and not until 1970 did other occupations employ the majority of black women. In that year, 72 percent of black men and 58 percent of black women had found jobs outside of agriculture, though employment trends over the subsequent twenty years continue to show few blacks in sales, clerical, professional, or managerial positions. These more limited employment opportunities affect African American farm families by reducing sources of off-farm income during the crisis years, as we shall see in chapter 6.

Blacks' career decisions are affected by their limited job alternatives as well as by declining access to land resources. They therefore experience a different context from which to evaluate the farming occupation. One older black man said he always believed that if you are "honest and straight and pay your bills, you can be *somebody* as a farmer. A man can take care of his family and pay bills and be a *man*, and that feels good. But he don't feel as good as he used to," he added, noting the deterioration of farming conditions in recent years. Because of limits to alternative opportunities for respect, those African American families who enjoy agricultural work are proud to be able to continue a farming tradition. For them, as for some white families, upward mobility can be achieved by embracing a farm career. As for access to resources, all the current black farmers in the study are either children of relatively fortunate black farm owners or the beneficiaries of federal programs that made possible the purchases of farms by black families.

In deciding whether to continue an agrarian way of life, Dodge Countians benefit from having the option to plant pulpwood trees on family lands instead of farming. The decision to discontinue farming, therefore, is not inevitably bound to the choice to sell the farm, though many heirs do choose to sell all or most of the land. Children who opt for other occupations often want to continue rural life, and they build a house on family land or nearby, maintain rural shopping and visiting patterns, and attend church in the rural neighborhood.

The Industrial Definition of Success

The reasons people express to explain their choice to farm or to reject farming reveal the transition from a dominant agrarian perspective in which off-farm work is somewhat stigmatized to a more complex reality in which off-farm work has a number of more desirable characteristics. Many older Dodge Countians recounted that they felt little sense of occupational choice. "Farming was all there was." One older man who began farming in the mid-1940s reflected that he had few other lifetime goals: "I just wanted to make a living—didn't look that far ahead. Didn't care that much about accumulating a whole lot."

Among this generation, there are still echoes of an agrarian worldview that sees only two work domains: farming and "public work." Public work included a broad range of jobs in logging, construction, and factories, as well as a few positions in teaching, clerical work, and civil service jobs. Owning one's own business was not usually labeled public work. Through the postwar decades, the negative connotation that the phrase may have once had has now faded. Today it is a commonly heard neutral description that sums up a range of nonfarm occupations.

As new job opportunities became a reality in Dodge County and young men and women embraced the higher and more secure incomes they offered, their views of farming changed. Over and over, I heard repeated: "You can make a living in farming, but you can't make any money." Making money moved to center stage in many farm families whose children in the 1940s, 1950s, and 1960s opted for a more affluent life. Said one: "I didn't want to continue the farm life I grew up with; those were the bad old days!" The steady and reliable income from jobs came to be seen as a more solid and respectable way to support a family. "Farming is a terrible way to make a living," said one woman. A middle-aged man remembers his father's small farm not for its remarkable survival through the Depression and even expansion in postwar years but for the inadequacy of the living standard it provided: "We were *poor*. We didn't *have* anything." Like what? "The luxuries of life—going to town—we stayed home. Going to the show. Now we went to the show, but it was rare. And we had to do things on our own to make money."

The dreams of farm children in the postwar decades were increasingly focused off the farm, toward a definition of personal success based on lifestyle and consumer goods. Status markers such as a "nice brick house," a new-model car or pickup truck, and perhaps a boat are discussed by many Dodge Countians. College education for children is important to many parents, and to meet these goals, a higher salary or some other reliable income source is essential. Farmers are famous for having to scrimp: "I wanted to give my family more than I could farming," said one man who went to work for a utility company.

The uncertainty of income from farming was another drawback that led farm children to seek the security of a paycheck. One part-time farmer said, "I *might* have made it, but it would have been a poor risk. The thing is, you might get ahead [through farming] but you might lose everything and have to start completely over." This man, like others, was not willing to take up a line of work in which such losses were more likely. For him, the standard of living from farming was acceptable, but the risk of losing everything was not.

Jobs also encouraged new values about working conditions and benefits; pensions and medical insurance are mentioned frequently. As these financial safety nets became more common, agrarian "independence" in these respects became a drawback. Of course, not all Dodge Countians have access to jobs that pay well. "The bad thing about small towns is that women don't make any money," said a woman who grew up in a big city. But even in jobs where wages are low, the fringe benefits provide important security.

Rejection of values based on agrarian dimensions of satisfaction is also connected to the nature of agricultural work in the past. Hard field work is not remembered fondly by many men and women interviewed; plowing with mules, milking cows, and the daily chores after school were sometimes dreaded. Picking cotton in the hot sun, hoeing peanuts, and other field work left many "glad to get away." Being outdoors in all weather is also seen by some farm children as a minus, not a plus. Jobs in other sectors, whether public safety, highway construction, factory work, or skilled trades, were more appealing. "I didn't want to work that hard," said many men who opted for other jobs. "When I was young, I wouldn't have done it for nothing!"

Escape from the discipline of parents was also mentioned by several Dodge Countians who like off-farm work. "My parents wanted me to work all the time so I was glad to take a job off," said one son of a small farm family. He recognized that "staying with the farm all the time" is necessary to make money on the farm, but he rejected that lifestyle. Some people enjoy the social life on the job and the opportunity for contact with nonrelatives, though the opportunity to establish supportive relationships varies greatly with the type of work. Rejection of farming for some couples means "freedom from personalistic power relations of small communities and interdependent households" (Schneider 1987:755).

The emphasis on greater individual freedom is another way in which industrial values differ from agrarian ones. Such a desire for personal autonomy conflicts with the farm's need for multigenerational cooperation and planning. Parental help, as we saw in chapter 2, can be critical in enabling children to farm or to operate at an affluent level. As farming has become more capital-intensive, investments are more often planned for the long term. Farm children learn that the optimal piece of land may only be available for purchase once in a lifetime. Some children share in the family decision to buy such property, but this norm of intergenerational coordination conflicts with a norm to allow children free choice to seek another occupation or to farm. There are several cases in Dodge County of fathers who developed their farms in the expectation that sons would succeed them, only to be bitterly disappointed.

The relentless attention to crops and livestock demanded by careful farming is also a way in which personal liberty is constrained by the agrarian way of life. As employees off the farm have won shorter workdays and work weeks, the hours of farming that once seemed "normal," now seem long. With the spread of an entitlement to a paid vacation, this aspect of the industrial sphere is frequently seen as necessary to a satisfactory life. But the farmer "cannot have a vacation like regular folks." Many farm families report canceled vacations and disappointed recreation plans because of emergencies on the farm.

Flows of income and patterns of savings are an especially critical point of contrast between these ways of life. Most farm activities generate an income only once a year, and with yearly mortgage payments, farm families have an annual rhythm of savings and expenditures. A big check in the fall or spring must be spent slowly so that the money will cover months in which there is no income. Household expenditures require long-term planning in a way very different from budgeting the steady flow of money from a regular paycheck. In addition, farmers face droughts and slumps and, if cautious, must save over the long run to build up a cushion for such years. Said one farmer, the key to success was "use what you need and put the rest back." It is not always easy to defer household expenses, "using a tight belt," and it is more difficult for families surrounded by wage workers. Research shows that personal savings decline in proportion to the amount of time "spent in the presence of persons who consume more" (Friedland and Robertson 1990:80). As Dodge County farm families are influenced by the mores of a consumer society—and parents desire to provide advantages to their children similar to those provided by nonfarming parents—aspects of the agrarian way of life become harder to sustain.

Shifting parental values in Dodge County can be seen in different families' child-rearing patterns. Including children in farm work is the first step in teaching a nonindustrial orientation to life and work. Said one mother: "People would say we are cruel for making the children work after school, but we feel it's important to make them feel a *part* of the farm." One son is interested in rowcropping and his parents plan to buy him an old tractor that will be his responsibility when he reaches age thirteen. It will make him feel that he has "a *purpose* here," his mother said. The other son is interested in hogs, so they plan to expand in livestock, giving him some females to raise. When he sells the hogs, she said, he'll have to "pay his bills" to his parents for the costs, but he can keep the profit. "You have to let them make money when they're eleven, so they'll have enthusiasm [for farming] when they get older." "You have to start them at birth, practically, to raise 'em to be what you are."

Parents who are trying to teach their children to be farmers usually share financial realities with their children. One woman stressed to her children that "they can't look at their grandparents' house and think that's how farmers live." The new brick house of the grandparents was built late in their married years and reflects the accumulated affluence of a lifetime. Some farm families restrict treats in certain seasons because the family is "saving up to pay the note." One woman said she tells the children that "there isn't money for extras." In this way, children learn to adapt their expectations to the reality of the farming cycle and to understand that farm responsibilities come first.

In families in which treats for children come year-round, no such priority of values is expressed. Some farm parents are more concerned to provide children with a lifestyle like that of their school peers. These parents want children to "be happy" and have no desire to urge them to farm. In one such family, the teenage son has no regular chores on the farm. "I don't want him to feel locked into farming," explained the father. Sometimes the boy wants to help, but the father said, "I can't rearrange my own work schedule or the hand's for my son's convenience." In such families, children are given an allowance or spending money regardless of their contribution to the farm. Many teenagers hold jobs in town, which helps cut down their expenses to the family but also reduces the time available for farm chores.[2] In each of these domains—children's farm work, family financial rhythms, intergenerational coordination, and emphasis on individual freedom—the transmission of farm values is increasingly difficult as farming becomes a minority way of life.

The Consumer Society in Historical Perspective

The southern shift to an industrial worldview recapitulates a historical process that has occurred before in other parts of the world. In *The Good Life: The Meaning of Success for the American Middle Class* (1989), Loren Baritz argues that the same lifestyle preferences that are expressed today by Dodge County families are part of a national middle class ethic that emerged in the northern states in the 1800s. Personal progress in this ethic is measured by the ownership of goods and property "on an ascending scale of expense: first, clothing and cosmetics required by the community for the mate hunt, then a car, a house, its appropriate furnishing and accouterments, then college for the kids, and finally surplus cash. At each step, ownership of property reveal[s] a successful personality to oneself and others" (Baritz 1989:106).

Though "the almighty dollar" is an aspiration with deep roots in American history, the increasing affluence of the southern economy brought such concerns into greater focus in the postwar era. Historians note that isolated rural areas, both North and South, were brought more into the national mainstream and adopted the values of "the metropolitan middle class . . . [that emphasized] atomistic individualism, consumer materialism, upward mobility, and unfettered economic development" (Bartley 1990:182; Gallaher 1961). This new system built on the traditional frontier and immigrant American values of achievement, self-improvement, and progress but shifted the focus from production, "respectability, hard work, and discipline" to consumption and "purchased status symbols" (McNall and McNall 1983:78–79).

This transition in the definition of personal success reached Dodge County through the mass media and through the forces of reform and "progress" reflected

in the New Deal. Radio and movie theaters brought these more urban and cosmo-
politan values into small towns, "depicting new ways of life and new moral standards" (McNall and McNall 1983:191). Reports of the Dodge County Agricultural
Extension Service and the home demonstration agent, forerunner of today's home
economist, reflect the linkage of rising incomes, new skills, and changing values.
In 1938, the home demonstration agent proudly quoted one woman's account of
the highly popular mattress-making program: "It's this way, you make a mattress,
your bed looks old so you work on that, then that calls for a new spread and you
begin on maybe a tufted one. Then that perks up a room so that you need rugs,
pictures, and maybe a new window cut in so that the whole family can enjoy the
change" (USDA 1938:18). Girls in 4-H clubs were shown how to raise fruits and
vegetables for their lunches in order to save their money for "permanents and
trips." Decoration of the home and yard came to be seen as an expression of self-
worth (Archibold 1989; L. Jones 1985). One letter to the agent demanded, "Tell
me how to get a lawn under trees, now that you have my wife thinking that she
must have a lawn" (USDA 1938:19).[3]

This transition to a "consumer society" is not unique to the United States; similar changes in values have also been described in the rise of industrial society
in England, France, Germany, and Spain. As the emphasis on family production
declines, lifestyle takes center stage (Collier 1986; Harding 1984). Social stratification becomes more fluid, and local markers of success become more varied.
In and around London in the late 1700s, expanding industries and wealth from
England's colonies raised the disposable family income for many groups (McKendrick, Brewer, and Plumb 1982). New industries served demands for the rising
household consumption of clothes, pottery, new foods, books, and the arts. Involvement in clubs, political organizations, and self-improvement was part of this
"consumer society." Unlike many other European countries, England was characterized at that time by "closely packed social strata" without the large gaps
between classes found in France and elsewhere. "In England . . . there was a
constant restless striving to clamber from one rank to the next, and . . . possessions, and especially clothes, both symbolized and signalled each step in the social
promotion" (ibid.:20–21).

Alexis de Tocqueville, in his travels through America in the early 1800s, commented on a similar consumption emphasis and attributed it also to a fluid stratification system, especially in the North. His comments about his native France
might also describe Depression-era Dodge County; he claimed that in a static aris-
tocratic society, "the people in the end get as much accustomed to poverty as the

rich to their opulence. . . . The former do not think of things which they despair obtaining" ([1840] 1958, 3:263).

Rosalind Williams describes the emergence of consumer society in urban France in the years between 1850 and 1912. Rising industrial productivity, growing consumer purchasing power, and lenient credit from banks led to rapid changes in diet, dress, and the purchase of other consumer goods. Merchandise became "a means of personal and social self-definition" (Williams 1982:13; Barnett and Magdoff 1986). Even in China in the nineteenth century, rising incomes from the development of a textile cottage industry made social strata more fluid. Though China certainly had no traditional emphasis on equality or democracy, it was characterized not by a rigid aristocracy but by gradations of wealth. Local measures of success became more ambiguous, thus "one of the best ways to demonstrate success or a claim of success was to practice a style of life . . . that revealed high social status" (Hamilton 1977:886–87). Max Weber's work on lifestyle and consumption patterns also noted the role of fashion in marking social status among competing groups. This pattern exists in America "to a degree unknown in Germany" (Weber 1968:933).

The linkage between consumerism and more fluid social stratification was true of postwar Dodge County as well. As occupational diversity grew, class rigidities were loosened and social status became more ambiguous. When farming dominated the economy, the size of farm one owned or the number of tenants one retained could serve as an indicator of prestige, although we have seen that these rankings were downplayed in accounts of daily life. In an industrial economy, however, productive resources no longer serve as a uniform marker of status. Differential prestige is accorded to certain jobs and working conditions, but when workplaces are out of the public view, it is difficult to assess. Even the distinction between manual labor and mental labor becomes blurred in Dodge County when many skilled technical workers in civil service jobs receive better pay and benefits than local white collar workers. Claims to status and rank are thus made increasingly through lifestyle, and consumption becomes the means by which diverse gradations of waged and salaried jobs are marked in the community.

Faced with the growing dominance of this new status system, farm families seek to counteract the Depression image of rural poverty that grants nonfarmers social superiority. One wealthy Dodge County farmer complained that farmers are still treated as though they "live in a shack, have one old pair of overalls and a broken-down pickup truck." This farmer's large brick home and expensive cars, in turn, mark his claim to a higher status ranking. Several teachers reported that children as young as five engage in verbal duels of competitive consumerism: "What! You don't have a satellite [dish]?!" Pressures for status consumption can also be seen in farmers' expensive farm equipment. Young farmers who aspire to higher social status are seen as valuing their four-wheel drive pickups, hunting dogs, and fancy guns. These items give them "a tough image," said one young farmer who shared an appreciation for these prestige markers.

Some theorists see the penetration of consumer materialism in a less positive light, as downward mobility from farm owner to laborer (Davis 1980; Mooney 1988; Bonanno 1987). Vulnerable to the employer's power, such workers have given up a secure and independent base in agricultural production. David Gartman argues that this emphasis on lifestyle serves the interests of industry both through the expansion of a domestic market for manufactured products and also through a dulling of the power relations between workers and owners. The emphasis on consumption obscures "the qualitative differences of economic power and ownership in production. The privileged are distinguished . . . by their objects" (Gartman 1986:172).

There is no doubt that industry is served by expanding consumer aspirations among workers and that it seeks through advertising to link certain products to personal success.[4] The analysis of proletarianization needs, however, to be balanced with the perspectives of the actors on the local level. When seen in light of Dodge County history, the devaluation of the farm is a celebration of greater affluence and a rejection of the hardships of the Depression and cotton tenancy. It is true that many Dodge Countians have turned away from an independent agrarian work life that offers control over productive resources. Unlike rural families in developing countries who see land ownership as salvation and security, these U.S. farm families emphasize the opposite—that security lies in selling their labor, not in producing food. The past forty years supports their judgment: jobs for the families I interviewed have for the most part been secure (Barlett 1986a). The emphasis on consumption as a marker of self-worth and social status may deflect attention from the power of giant corporations, but it is also a marker of a more fluid and somewhat more democratic social order. It is instructive that such a concern with lifestyle has emerged not only in Dodge County but also amid economic circumstances in Europe and China that were not dominated by large corporations.

These new values and expectations embedded in the shift to an industrial society create stresses for the family farm. The shifting values that support an industrial economy undermine "the cultural autonomy" of agrarian sectors. Small towns and farmers feel "the pressures of consumerism" (McNall and McNall 1983:254).

As Jane Collier reports for Spain, "Parents who refuse to replace old furniture or to buy modern appliances appear to be depriving their children of material comforts and social advantages the family can afford" (1989:24). As farming and farm neighbors are no longer the main sources of good jobs, young people look toward other styles and values that orient them toward the dominant culture (Barron 1990). Even in Saskatchewan, Canada, John Bennett reported the penetration of these values, as some farm families used money "to keep up with the Joneses . . . [and] to prove that one is 'making it' " (1982:419). The agrarian and industrial worldviews have been presented here as opposite views held by different groups, but in fact these value systems often war within the same individual. Some families seem to have made their peace with the path they have chosen, but others express great ambivalence about the pros and cons of the farm life.

Part-Time Farming: Combining Job and Farm

One solution to struggling between these alternative cultural definitions of success is to embrace them both by farming part-time. The combination of a farm and nonfarm career was described for Illinois farmers as "the best of two worlds" (van Es et al., 1982). In Dodge County, part-time farmers are able to conform to the dominant industrial values concerning affluence and the meaning of personal success, while also gaining some of the satisfactions of the agrarian ethic. Part-time farmers emerged as a significant group in the 1950s (see figure 2-1), and by 1982, they numbered over a third of the farm operators in the study (38%).[5] Most of these farm operators made career decisions in their youths to pursue full-time off-farm work, but at some point later in their lives, they began to farm as well. A national and even international phenomenon, part-time farms in 1982 made up 36 percent of all farms in the country and are a growing sector in other industrial countries as well (Barlett 1986a).

Part-time farming became possible because of the rural transformation described in chapter 2. Good roads and private automobiles provide the mobility to live on a farm and work elsewhere. Mechanization enables the cultivation of a small farm fairly rapidly, making it feasible to tend a farm primarily on evenings and weekends. Tractor headlights, as well as the tractors themselves, allow the part-time farmer to use after-job hours for farming. The rising productivity and profitability of agriculture in Georgia also play a role. Small acreages can now produce a sufficient income to pay for a tractor and other equipment, with a profit left over (at least in good years) that gives an incentive to the part-time farmer. Finally, the availability of jobs with some flexibility in time off is essential. Most part-time farmers cite a particularly cooperative supervisor as one of the reasons that they stay with a certain job. Though it might seem desirable to find nearby jobs and save time commuting, part-time farmers often travel considerable distances. A quarter of such operators in the county commute over a hundred miles a day, round trip, sacrificing travel time to be able to remain in the rural setting while holding a job that will let them "have something."

There is no doubt that part-time farming demands an intensified use of resources and labor in agriculture. Balancing these "two worlds" means that time is at a premium, and the part-time farmer must scramble in certain seasons to fit all tasks into the day. This pressure makes investment in equipment mandatory, and because equipment breakdowns can be less easily absorbed by a farmer who must be at a job all day, part-time farmers tend to invest more heavily in equipment, per acre and per unit of output. Though some experts argue that the efficiency of this capital intensification through purchases of farm machinery is less than ideal, most observers are persuaded that part-time farming is good for equipment dealers and farm supply companies. Without the purchases of farm inputs by part-time farmers, who operate one-third of all farms, suppliers and dealers would face a much less favorable economic environment. Since loss of these local services would hurt full-time farmers as well, most policymakers have come to value the stability part-time farming brings to agricultural structure.

In addition to the intensification of capital on these farms and a kind of labor "speedup" that makes for long hours in some seasons, the part-time farm family combines more resources toward their livelihood than was common in the past. In the Depression era, either a job or a farm supported a family, but today these part-time farming families take the land that used to be sufficient to provide a living for a family and add on at least one full-time job and sometimes two. This combination is chosen to give them the lifestyle and consumption standard they desire, but it can also be seen as its own kind of resource concentration. Just as full-time farms have grown larger since the "Hoover Days," small farms also persist, but usually with off-farm work to subsidize them.

Family incomes most commonly include both a husband's and a wife's salary and averaged $33,000 in 1986. This figure illustrates that part-time farmers are certainly not an impoverished group, nor can they be said to provide cheap labor for local businesses.[6] Though farm incomes themselves may be low, part-time farm families on the whole in Dodge County are a relatively affluent group. About half the men on part-time farms in the study were white collar workers or professionals in fields such as education, law, government, or retail business. Common skilled blue collar occupations include mechanics, electricians, and public safety officers. Women on part-time farms who have jobs are mainly secretarial or clerical workers, though some are teachers or teachers' aides (see chapter 6).

The Decision to Farm Part-Time

Men and women on part-time farms say that they attempt the heavy workload and risk of farming along with commitments to jobs primarily for economic reasons. Eighty-five percent see the farm as a second job, as an effort to earn more money and therefore further the family's pursuit of affluence and a rising standard of living. The annual rhythms of farm income act as a kind of forced savings, producing a fall bonus of $10,000 or so. When invested in land, such bonuses not only result in added income but help the farmer increase property to a level some admit they would not have achieved otherwise. The tax benefits of part-time farming are noted by a few farmers, but most families are disdainful of the notion that they farm for tax reasons. A small, stratified sample of part-time farms in Dodge County allowed me to consult their accountants on this matter, and their tax forms upheld the farmers' statements. Tax savings are usually not large and for many, farming costs are high.

Part-time farms are often part of a retirement plan. As one man said, making $2,000–3,000 on the farm today "isn't making *anything*. But it *would* be, if we were retired." Farming also provides security, "something to fall back on if anything should happen to my job." Both men and women make such comments, and not only the older people who remember the hardships of the Depression, but also younger people who fear that a second Great Depression is imminent. Land is also desired as an inheritance to children. The opportunity to bequeath a potential source of earnings, plus hunting and fishing recreation, to one's children, is for some families a status marker.

In contrast to the ways part-time farmers see the farm as part of a quest for affluence and a rising standard of living, they also articulate agrarian values. Men, especially, point to the satisfactions of physical labor, to greater satisfaction in farming than in their weekday jobs. They also talk about the excitement of the gamble and the freedom from job supervision that attract them to farming "on the side." Women are more likely to emphasize their satisfaction with living in the country, with its more wholesome environment for rearing children and the opportunity to grow more of the family's own food. Both men and women value farming for the opportunity to continue aspects of a family agrarian tradition.

At the same time, there are ways in which the industrial society's emphasis on individual choice can be seen in the typical part-time farm family. Only 10 percent of husbands say that the farm is a "family project." Instead, most see it as a personal hobby or a second job. Women, even on full-time farms, are not usually full partners in the decision to farm but rather are consulted as the husband makes the ultimate decision. This is especially true for the decision to add a part-time farm. One part-time farmer who was distressed that his wife's salary was helping to compensate for drought losses on the farm explained, "She didn't take on the farm—I did."

Almost four in ten wives on part-time farms expressed negative attitudes toward farming: "I'd rather he not do none of it," said one woman. "Farming bugs me; I like sure things." As for shared labor on the farm, most part-time farms depend little on the work contributions of women or children. In these ways, the agrarian linkage between farm and family has been eroded, and the part-time farm in many cases is not a joint household endeavor.

A part-time farm can be, nevertheless, a source of pride and accomplishment for some men and women. Dreams of success are made possible by combining job and farm, as illustrated by the case of the Bennings (a pseudonym). Both have held full-time jobs all their lives and are proud that the farm provided both extra income for their children's college education and a safe and attractive home. Bill Benning enjoys hunting and fishing on his family's land and finds the work with livestock and crops a therapeutic change from his job. Barbara Benning appreciates the high-quality food from their garden and the "extras" made possible from farm income. The Bennings enjoy good health and are proud of their two married children who live nearby. The three families all attend church together. In discussing their satisfaction with their life choices, the Bennings conclude: ". . . and we've got the income to buy anything we want!"

The rise of the part-time farm brings into focus the transformation of the Dodge County economy and culture. Beginning with the first intrusion of industrial values into the agrarian world of the wiregrass settlers, new patterns of employment have strengthened an emphasis on individualism and material success. The organic connections between work, farm, and family that characterized the agrarian past have lost ground and are less valued among recent generations. As social status and ranking have become more fluid, a consumer ethic has permeated the fabric of rural life. Many families have come to reject farming and to embrace a less risky, more affluent life in other occupations. This perspective provides a complementary view to the analysis of economic change in the South that emphasizes the ways in which farm families were "squeezed out" by the transformations of agricultural mechanization, technology, and the New Deal.

Some Dodge County families struggle to uphold an agrarian ethic that values nonmonetary dimensions of success, including daily work autonomy, opportunities for achievement and reward, and spiritual connections to nature and to the work of farming. Their challenge is shared by many Americans who are dissatisfied with the rewards of a consumer culture. Agrarian and industrial values war not only within individuals on Dodge County farms but within the wider American society. This tension between definitions of success also has implications for how farms are run and households managed, choices that, in turn, have profound effects on farm survival through the crisis years.

CHAPTER

FOUR

Large and Medium Scale Farms:

Privilege, Skill, and Survival

The changing economic conditions of the postwar era have produced many different kinds of farms in Dodge County, including full-time, part-time, and retirement farms. This chapter will focus its attention primarily on full-time farms, using the cases of the McClintocks and the Graingers to illustrate the large and medium scale groups. These two clusterings of farms share a common commitment to an agrarian way of life but also reflect two distinct paths to success. The rates of survival of the different types of farms through the 1980s crisis will be compared, revealing that the smallest farms—both part-time and retirement—show the greatest resilience and have been the least vulnerable to financial disaster through the 1980s.

This chapter also seeks to understand the origins of the large scale farms in Dodge County. As described in the Introduction, the growing dominance of large farms in American agriculture has important consequences for the health of rural communities. As Dodge County moved away from its highly stratified structure of the 1930s, it came to look more like the Midwest with its rowcrop- and livestock-producing family farms. Nevertheless, the South has maintained a group of large farms based on hired labor, unlike the midwestern family farms that tend to be operated by one family alone. Are large scale farmers the recipients of privileges and of access to superior resources transmitted from generation to generation? Or are they the entrepreneurial result of superior farming skills and managerial energy, given the ready availability of cheap land, capital, and federal support in the South? Contrasting the large and medium farms in Dodge County on a range of dimensions will reveal both the origins of large scale operations and the likely consequences of such a structure for the future.

We can begin to understand the diversity of Dodge County farms through the portraits of two Generation 1 couples. The McClintocks and the Graingers have different farming goals and definitions of "success," and though each family emerged from different origins in the "Hoover Days," both have survived the current crisis of the 1980s. Each family description is a composite of several similar couples (to protect the identity of families in the study).

The McClintocks: A Medium Scale Farm Couple

Sitting in the living room of their small wooden house in 1987, reclining on Naugahyde recliners, Mac and Martha McClintock reflect on their accomplishments. Operators of a middle-sized farm (three hundred acres owned "free and clear!"), the couple is in their late fifties, and their lives are abundant beyond anything they could have imagined when young. His parents were sharecroppers and hers owned a small farm. As a young couple, they sharecropped for many years. "I couldn't get no start when I was young—I would have loved to have bought land before, but I was just a poor boy," said Mac. "What we got, we *dug* up—we slaved for it. If you've got a job today, you've got nothing. If you have a farm, you've got *something*; and we've still got it!" he concluded triumphantly.

The McClintocks' living room boasts a sofa and doily-covered formica tables, with pictures of family members on the walls and a large television in one corner. Passing through the dining room with its formal, dark table and past the piano, one comes to the kitchen where they normally eat. On a side porch stand the freezers, storing a year's supply of meat and vegetables. Married children live nearby, and though Martha's full-time job in town and Mac's occasional part-time work as well as full-time farming keep the senior McClintocks busy, they enjoy the closeness of seeing grandchildren regularly.

Mac and Martha deeply appreciate the things that make their lives more comfortable today: running—even hot—water, electric light, a refrigerator, freezers, a clothes washer and dryer, and screens on the windows. None of these were available to them growing up or in their early married years. "Young folks nowadays don't know what hard times is. . . . They don't know what it is to do without."

Farmers like the McClintocks are reluctant to borrow money and have built up their farms through savings. "Debts always worry me," said Mac. Martha is relieved as well that they can face these severe drought years with no debts or interest to pay, a steady income from hogs, cattle, and crops, plus the cushion of their off-farm income to help out with bills and groceries. They feel financially secure in spite of the droughts, and their diverse production mix allows them to weather the slump in farm prices. The low-profit years have meant some painful cutbacks in luxuries, but their basic needs have been met.

Operating a farm was not really a choice for the McClintocks—"it was all there was." But it has been a good and satisfying life, says Mac: "I just love it." None of their children has taken up farming, and they are glad: "I wouldn't want my children to take that line of work." For both husband and wife, nonfarm occupations are thought to provide better incomes and opportunities for happiness for their children.

The Graingers: A Large Scale Farm Couple

George and Gerry Grainger also approach their sixties and retirement with considerable satisfaction, but theirs is a large scale farm of over a thousand acres. Comprising some of the best land in the county, the farm is highly diversified and has been profitable all through the crisis years with minimal debt. Expensive investments in equipment, irrigation, and animal facilities were paid off before the droughts hit, leaving the farm better prepared to withstand reduced prices. George jumped on the technology treadmill early and now benefits from high yields.

Both George and Gerry value hard work and admire it. George sees the farm as primarily his business and has managed it with intense energy, long hours, and "blood, sweat, and tears." He says he substituted labor for cash whenever possible, never hired services he could do himself, and avoided debt. He cares for his animals and crops with the help of a full-time hired hand and with occasional additional workers.

George and Gerry both came from better-off farm families, and George was college educated. His father had a large farm that was worked with mules and half a dozen black and white sharecroppers. After World War II, his father bought a tractor and cut his labor force in half. George worked a tract for his father on halves briefly then amassed sufficient capital to begin to buy land. The two farms shared some machinery and coordinated purchases of additional equipment. When his father retired, George continued to expand and buy more land and equipment, benefiting from his considerable skill, his family's larger than average peanut allotments, and some of the best soil in the county.

Gerry identifies herself as a "farm wife and homemaker." The yard is well landscaped, healthy houseplants decorate several windows, and the house is filled with finished wood and upholstered furniture and some antiques. Although maintaining the house "clean and well kept" is important to her, she would also like to add a satellite dish and redo some of the furnishings. She loves country living and marrying a farmer seemed "second nature." She is glad she never had "to work out" (meaning off the farm). She knows many women who want to have jobs and who believe the work is necessary and important for them, but she feels fortunate to have stayed at home.

Both of the Graingers emphasize that their primary goals in life were to educate their children and to see them happy. All of their children attended college and all but one currently live in other Georgia cities, enjoying white collar or managerial jobs. The remaining son is planning to stay on the farm when he finishes college. Passing the farm on to his son is a joy to George, and he is already working out the financial arrangements, to go into effect once the son has worked his way into becoming a true partner. Gerry is more ambivalent about a farm career for her son: "It's such hard work, and I don't really want that for him." "The important thing is for our children to be happy and satisfied with their work," they both agree.

Overview of Farm Types

These two families are part of the *full-time farm group* that makes up almost half of the operations in the county. Table 4-1 shows that this 47 percent of operations controls three-quarters of the county's farmland. On full-time farms, families try to make a living from the sale of crops and livestock (and occasionally timber), though off-farm income has come to play an important role in recent years. Off-farm jobs are commonly held by wives, though a few husbands also take occasional part-time work. The median age of full-time farmers was thirty-eight in 1982.

Some full-time farms are dedicated just to livestock and some just to crops, but a mix of both is more typical. Farm facilities, soils, and the lay of the land all play a role in determining the optimal crop and livestock mix for a farm. The vast majority of full-time farms grow corn, soybeans, wheat, and peanuts. Peanuts must be rotated with other crops to avoid pest problems, and corn and soybeans are the usual alternatives. Corn is used for feed as well as for sale. As noted in chapter 2, soybean production today is often rotated with winter wheat, allowing two harvests a year on the same acreage. Only a quarter of full-time farms plant cotton, mostly large operations, and a few producers specialize in tobacco and watermelons. Most farms have some cattle, and about half keep hogs. Overall in the county, income from livestock roughly equals income from crops.

Most full-time farmers own part of the land they operate and rent additional

Table 4-1. Farm Types in Dodge County, 1982

Farm Type	Number	Median Acreage Operated*
Full-time**	58 (47%)	464 (75%)
Part-time	40 (32%)	122 (18%)
Retirement	26 (21%)	102 (8%)

*Significant at the .00 level by Kruskal-Wallis test (chi-square = 47.6).
**Includes operators who took jobs in response to the crisis after 1978.

acreage. Many are still paying off the land they have purchased. A few farm operators are entirely renters, but they do not form a distinguishable or disadvantaged
group. Some are newer to farming, and with the poor profits and high interest
rates of the crisis years, they have preferred to wait to undertake the investment
of land purchase. Many farm renters have access to family land and are free to
make conservation or irrigation investments on it. In some cases, the failure to
purchase land is more determined by long-lived kin or neighbors who prefer the
rental income and do not want to sell. Land becomes available rarely in particular
farm communities, and operators cannot always find suitable property when they
are ready to buy. Some fortunate farmers have purchased all the land they operate
and benefited greatly in the drought years from their lower fixed costs. Part-time
and retired farmers are particularly likely to have paid off their farms and are thus
freer of risk.

Part-time farms are also an important part of the rural economy, making up a
third of farms and almost a fifth of the land operated. Most part-time farms are
under 200 acres, with a median of 122 acres. In operation, they are usually minia-
ture full-time farms, with a full range of crop and livestock activities. Farm product
sales tend to be between $10,000 and $20,000 per year. Part-time farmers' median age is forty-five, making them only slightly older, on average, than full-time
farmers.

The smallest farms in Dodge County are the *retirement farms*, which constitute
a fifth of all operating units. Their median size is 102 acres, though a few operate as many as 200 acres. Commonly, only half this land is in crops and pasture;
the remainder is timber or fallow. This group is made up of operators who label
themselves "retired" or who receive social security. Some are older versions of
the McClintocks who want to hold on to their property but who plant fewer row-

crops than a full-time farm family. Other retired farmers are older versions of the Graingers, and they rent out, sell, or plant to trees a substantial portion of their acreage.[1] A few Dodge County farmers who are disabled, though under sixty-five, are included in this group. Together, these retirement farms make up only 8 percent of the farm acreage in the county. Their sales are usually low—the median is under $5,000 gross sales per year.

Retirement farmers view their operations as either recreation or a livelihood depending on their economic circumstances. For those former employees whose retirement provides them a comfortable pension (about a third of retirement farmers), the farm is an enjoyable "hobby," a way to keep active and healthy. For the majority of elderly who are less well-off, farm income and farm products are essential to their survival free of public assistance. The farm makes the difference between comfort and poverty. The vegetables and meat from the farm are cheaper than purchased food, and sales of hogs, cattle, and some crops bring in the money to pay bills and buy groceries. These couples appreciate homegrown food's higher quality as well. Most retired farmers own their land and homes without debt. Their cash income may be low, but thanks to past investments in the farm, they live comfortably. The lifestyle of retired farmers often contrasts sharply with nearby rural residents who own no property and must rent housing. Retired farmers thus represent an important component of rural welfare, though their overall role in national farm production is small.

Partnerships between fathers and sons and between brothers are an important variant of the farm types.[2] Brother-brother farms can be part-time but more commonly are full-time operations. For father-son partnerships, it has happened that a father with a part-time farm took on a son who wanted to operate the farm full-time, necessitating considerable expansion of acreage and machinery. The reverse also occurs, in which a son is glad to help out his full-time farmer father but also wants a job to provide a more secure income for his own family. Most often, partnerships involve two or three households, all of which are dedicated full-time to the farm.

To establish a new generation on the farm, there is no fixed rule of inheritance, parental help, or partnership in Dodge County. Individual circumstances, personalities, and opportunities determine whether a young man becomes a helper on his parents' farm, a paid employee, a partner, or an independent operator. Most men live at home until marriage, but the extent to which they pool finances with their parents or operate quite independent budgets varies greatly. Once married, sons negotiate with their fathers for access to resources and aid. Some families expect aid to be limited to a transitional period; others expect close cooperation to continue lifelong.[3]

Such inheritance and partnership decisions, however, affect greatly the operation of the farm. As we shall see, partnerships in which sons forced fathers to overexpand are an important sector of the Dodge County farms that faced bankruptcy and foreclosure. On the other hand, fathers whose sons chose not to farm are themselves handicapped in their ability to invest in new technology. Some of the most rapidly growing and financially sound full-time farms are partnerships, which shows that successful multihousehold cooperation can be critical for survival in the current crisis.

The fourteen black farms that fell into my random sample exhibit all three farm types (full-time, part-time, and retired), but there are no partnerships. The black part-time and retired farms cannot be distinguished from the white farms on the basis of commodity mix. The full-time farms of African Americans are smaller than the median white farms and therefore emphasize some higher-value vegetable crops and livestock enterprises, though all produce the typical corn, soybeans, and peanuts of full-time farms. As property owners, these farmers are of relatively high rank among black Dodge Countians. Few, unfortunately, will be able to transmit the farm to a son or daughter who will continue the operation. As befitting their more elite status, many of these children complete college and choose jobs instead of farming. Black operators are mostly over fifty-five, and because of the difficulties in recruiting a new generation to farming, they represent a vanishing group in the county. Their property, however, may remain as family investments in timber or rented farmland.[4]

Contrasts between Large and Medium Scale Farms

The cases of the McClintocks and Graingers illustrate the bimodal distribution of full-time farms in Dodge County. Unlike the pattern found in Illinois (Rogers 1987), the sizes of full-time farms are not clustered around a mean, as shown in figure 4-1.[5] The farms under 500 acres make up 64 percent of full-time farms, and those over 500 acres (36%) show a small cluster around 600 acres and then are dispersed over a broad range of sizes. This bimodal pattern is echoed in farm sales as well. A substantial group of farms sells less than $100,000 gross per year; a second, smaller group of farms typically grosses more than $200,000 a year in sales.

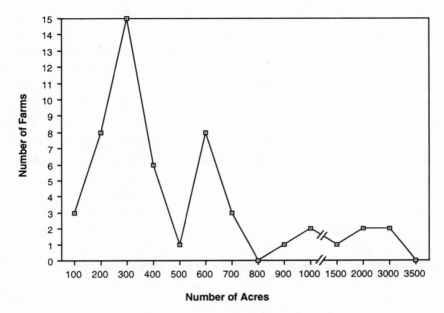

Figure 4-1. Farm Sizes of Full-Time Operations
in Dodge County, 1986

For the purposes of dividing the farms in the study into large scale and medium scale groups, I found that a simple acreage definition of scale did not produce coherent or homogeneous farm groups because of variations in wasteland and crop and livestock specializations. The definition of a large or medium farm that I used in previous chapters—the census category of 260 acres and over—is no longer appropriate in this era of mechanization. The most accurate way to create a measure of large scale, I found, was to combine the following five criteria:

· size (over 500 acres operated or over 200 acres of rowcrops per operator);

· sales ($100,000 or over in annual gross farm sales);

· capital investment in machinery and equipment over $70,000 in assessed value;

· use of irrigation prior to 1982; and

· use of full-time hired labor.

I coded farms with either four or five of these characteristics as large scale, and farms with two or fewer as medium scale. There were five farms with three of these characteristics, and I assigned them to one group or the other based on my judgment of the overall farming operation. In addition to producing quite consistent groupings, this measure of scale also reflects farmers' own views. Many Dodge Countians divide the world of full-time farmers into two general scale groups. One woman ticked off four characteristics that for her define large scale farmers: they own more land, rent more land, use large, expensive equipment, and receive big government payments.[6]

In the culture of the county, these farm types are not automatically considered as more or less successful, however, because depending on the class backgrounds of the families involved, each can be seen as resulting from upward or downward mobility. As we saw with the McClintocks, some medium scale farmers consider themselves to be highly fortunate, and not all large farm families like the Graingers are satisfied with their accomplishments. These subjective assessments of success will be discussed in chapter 5. In addition, the types do not represent a developmental cycle, in which many families begin at medium scale and expand to large; farmers from Generations 1, 2, and 3 are found in both groups.

The contrast between large and medium scale farms is substantial, as shown in table 4-2. Medium-sized farms substantially outnumber large farms, 37 to 21. However, with the greater number of partnerships among larger farms, the numbers of operators are closer—41 medium scale operators versus 36 large scale operators. Some medium scale farms are as large as 500–600 acres, though most are in the 200–350-acre range. The typical larger farm is nearly five times bigger in acreage, by the mean and the median, both in total size and in rowcropped land. Farms of several thousand acres are not rare. Livestock volume is proportionately larger as well, though harder to measure since hogs and cattle are sold at various times of the year (and also fluctuate more from year to year). Sales figures show that three-quarters of farm product sales (from full-time farms) come from the large scale farms and only a quarter from medium scale farms, though these figures also reflect low sales from drought losses, which disproportionately affect the unirrigated medium scale farms. Sales figures say nothing about farm profits but rather indicate a general level of farm production.

The medium scale farms are less likely to have expensive machinery, and their farms show fewer capital-intensive investments such as wells, drainage pipes, irrigation equipment, silos, or hog facilities. Large scale farms boast a median value of $246,733 in these investments compared to a median of $22,234 for the medium scale farms. This figure represents the resale value of these investments— vastly lower than the actual cost to farmers, given the deflated market of 1987 in

Table 4-2. Large Scale and Medium Scale
Full-Time Farms, 1986

	Large Scale	Medium Scale
Number of farms	21 (36%)	37 (64%)
Number of operators*	36 (47%)	41 (53%)
Median acres operated**	1,042 (73%)	258 (27%)
Median gross farm sales**	$255,250 (78%)	$39,000 (22%)
Median equipment and facilities resale value**	$246,733 (82%)	$22,234 (18%)

*Includes all operators entering and leaving farming between 1982 and 1989.
**Significant at .00 level by Kruskal-Wallis test.

which the calculation was made. Medium scale farms are also more likely to purchase secondhand equipment, which further lowers the estimate of their capital investments.

Medium scale farms, when compared as a group to the large scale farms, are therefore more efficient in their use of capital but slightly less efficient in their use of land. The figures show that large farms use 4.8 times as much land as medium-sized farms to generate 5.8 times as much product (by value) with 8.1 times as much capital investment. Of course, there is great variation from farm to farm, and this efficiency comparison cannot be generalized to individual cases. Unfortunately, it is too difficult to collect data on days of labor and labor intensity on Dodge County farms to be able to make these same efficiency comparisons by work input.

Use of Hired Hands

George Grainger's farm relies on the labor of a full-time hand, but Mac McClintock does all his own work, with only occasional volunteered help from his brother who lives nearby. This contrast in the use of hired labor is typical of the two scale groups; all the large scale farms use hired hands on a full-time basis, with the exception of a few family partnerships. Though most medium scale farms use no regular help, the boom years of the 1970s led one in six medium scale farmers to use a full-time worker. These hands either supplemented an ailing farmer's inadequate strength or represented a desire on the part of the operator to enjoy the status and convenience of operating the farm in a more affluent manner.

Changes in job opportunities described in chapter 3 affect the supply of wage labor for farmers. Throughout the study years, some farmers complained that the quality of hired help had deteriorated, and as old workers died, young replacements were harder to find. This scarcity may reflect rising education levels among the poorer black and white families and the existence of other jobs in an expanded economy. The long hours and low pay of agricultural work are less desirable as better alternatives have become available. Part-time help can be found for harvesting watermelons and tobacco, but many operators report that the supply is increasingly unreliable. As this research was ending, Hispanic farm workers were beginning to be more common in Georgia and other states of the Southeast. This trend may have an impact on the future use of hired farm labor.

The use of hired workers involves a degree of risk. Modern crop species and farming methods require careful timing, and a worker who does not show up can have a more significant impact on a harvest today than was true fifty years ago. Farming with hired help is frustrating for most Dodge County farmers who employ laborers. Though they acknowledge a few exceptions—who are usually more highly paid—the majority of large landholders feel their hired hands hurt farm productivity in various ways. Chemicals may be mixed and applied with less care, gauges on equipment are less likely to be monitored, and if a nozzle becomes clogged during spraying, the hand may not stop to fix it, since "the bossman will never know." Crop damage somewhere in the county from worker inattention to chemical labeling was reported in every year of study. Machinery may be driven more roughly by hired help, and repair bills may be higher. Some operators complain that workers do not learn the machines as well as owners and may be slower to make minor repairs in the field. This litany of complaints is not meant to suggest that most workers are unreliable or unskilled but to emphasize that the use of relatively poorly paid hired hands does present a risk. Joining with a family member in partnership does not guarantee that farm work will be performed more reliably or better, but chances are greatly improved.

Research in 1983 showed that pay scales are generally low for farm hands, and thus the comfort enjoyed by a large scale farm family is often linked to the poverty of one or more worker families. Median pay for a full-time hand in 1983 was $135 a week or $26 a day, and most hands are paid uniformly throughout the year, though hours vary by season. Over eleven hours of work a day is common in the summers, but other seasons permit a shorter workday. Roughly two-thirds of the farm hands interviewed in 1983 were black and one-third were white. Most were children of farm workers (one-third), sharecroppers (one-fourth), or farm owners (one-fourth) (see Barlett 1986b).

In addition to a salary, a farm worker usually receives a range of in-kind benefits. Housing is commonly provided—usually a wood frame house or a trailer, often without central heat or air conditioning. If it has a wood-burning stove, wood is usually available from the landowner. Meat and vegetables are provided on some farms—a holdover from large communal butchering, after which meat was preserved in the smokehouse. The "free" vegetables have to be picked and processed by the worker, but food costs are substantially lowered by this addition to the diet. Some workers have the full-time use of a truck, with gas provided, which makes the low pay more palatable, especially for younger laborers who have no other means of transportation. Some owners pay electricity bills as well, but one explained that this was mainly to avoid the aggravation of having service cut off and the meter taken out when workers fall behind in payments. Some employers deduct the total electricity cost from wages, some deduct a portion, and some do not charge workers for power or water. Depending on the value given to such benefits, wages can be made to look much better or much worse. One man who worked for $175 a week ($9,100 a year) calculated his total housing and food benefits package to be worth $1,550, raising his annual income to $10,650. Echoes of the dependence of Depression-era tenants on their landlords remain in these ties between farm hands and farm owners.

It should not be assumed, however, that the low pay leads most farm workers to see their jobs as undesirable or degrading. Interviews with twenty-three full-time hands in the study found that workers were very similar to owners in their statements about the farm life (Barlett 1986b). "Farming is my greatest love—it's the best way of life," said one. "Some people see this work as just a job, but to me, it's an occupation, a way of life—I always wanted to farm." Workers say they value the opportunity to be outdoors and the freedom from constant supervision. A few feel farm work is healthier than alternative jobs. Though many farm workers are frustrated by the low pay and the long hours, fewer than half expressed negative attitudes toward the possibility of their sons going into the same occupation.

Dimensions of Privilege and the
Origins of Large Scale Farms

The detailed information from Dodge County farmers helps us to explore the role of different kinds of advantages in creating the substantial sector of large scale farms found in the county today. It also shows that medium scale farms are not different from large scale farms in a surprising number of dimensions. This section looks at family background, education, access to family resources, skill, experience, quality of soil, and off-farm income for evidence of advantages enjoyed by larger units. The next section explores the patterns of federal agricultural program subsidies.

The large scale and medium scale farm types reflect different family backgrounds. As chapter 2 would lead us to expect, medium scale farmers today are more likely to. be from modest farm backgrounds; their parents were tenants, renters, or small farm owners in 76 percent of the cases.[7] In contrast, only 38 percent of large scale operators have similar backgrounds. The fact, however, that nearly four in ten large scale operators came from small farm or nonfarm backgrounds suggests that there has been considerable opportunity for upward mobility over the last several decades.

As might be expected from the medium scale farmers' more modest backgrounds, they tend to be less well educated, as shown in table 4-3. Higher education is assumed by many researchers to enable a farmer to use more sophisticated technology, keep up with scientific reports, and have the skills to get expert help when needed. Less-educated farmers might be expected to be at a disadvantage for the same reason. It is possible, however, to argue the reverse: that college-educated operators learn a higher-risk expansion-oriented farming style that may make them more vulnerable. The majority of large scale farm operators have had some college (for an average of 13.5 years of education). Many medium scale farmers were not able to complete high school because their families needed them to work. In fact, nine of the older medium scale farmers attended school for only eight or fewer years. For younger, Generation 3 medium scale farmers, high school graduation is the norm, and college is not rare. For the group as a whole, the average completed education is 10.4 years, significantly lower than for the large scale farmers. As we shall see in chapter 8, educational attainment does not seem to affect farm survival.

Parental assets also do not account for the existence of the large scale farm group in Dodge County. The self-made man—as Mac McClintock claims to be—

Table 4-3. Contrasts between Large Scale and
Medium Scale Operators, 1986

	Large Scale	Medium Scale
Average years education*	13.5	10.4
Access to family land	38%	46%
Access to family equipment	24%	32%
Average overall skill score* (possible range = −10 to +10)	3.4	0.2
Average crop skill score* (possible range = −4 to +4)	0.8	0.1
Average years farming experience	21.5	23.2
Average acreage good soil	52%	49%
Average off-farm income	$18,031	$14,072

*Significant at .01 level using the Kruskal-Wallis or chi-square test (all other variables shown are not significant at .10 level).

in fact is more the county norm. Access to family land—for free or for rent—is an important advantage to some individual operators, but large and medium scale groups both enjoyed this advantage (38% and 46%, respectively). Access to equipment or capital was also important on many farms, but both large scale and medium scale farms also benefited from these resources. Wealthier families undoubtedly had more resources to pass on, but it is interesting to note that six in ten large scale farms received no family aid with land, and nearly eight in ten had no aid with equipment.

Good management, energetic work, and farm skill seem to play a more important role in determining larger farm scale. Some Dodge Countians feel that superior farming skills, leading to higher sales and higher net income, are the primary determinant of larger farm size. Farmers respect the knowledge and dedication needed to master the intricacies of agricultural production—matching seed varieties, soil types, fertilizer formulas, and chemical usage recommendations to the particular character of individual plots and the annual roulette of weather conditions. Energy spent to discover the latest information about soil conservation, machinery, or inputs is not hampered by farm scale. Though older farmers with poorer education may have some handicaps, there are enough cases of considerable farming sophistication among them to illustrate that the handicaps can be overcome. The combination of hard work, attention to detail, intelligence, education, personal knowledge, and good sense all combine to allow a farmer to create a profitable business against formidable odds.

Farm skill does correlate with farm scale. Though it is difficult to find a valid measure of skill across different types of farms, with the help of farmers and county experts, I created a composite score of ten different variables of farming skill (see appendix 1). Information was drawn from interviews and crop records to assess skills in producing peanuts, corn, wheat, soybeans, and hogs; information gathering; marketing; government program participation; and the use of soil conservation measures and soil testing. Irrigated and nonirrigated crops were treated separately. For each measure, a farm earned -1, $+1$, or 0 points, for a maximum of ten possible points.

Large farms are much more likely to score higher than medium scale farms on these measures, with an average score of 3.4 versus 0.2. Three-fourths of the larger farms score three or over, but fewer than one in five of the medium scale farms reaches that level. Skill in crop production alone also varies by scale. After considering the five-year average production of peanuts together with 1986 yields of corn, soybeans, and wheat (see appendix 1), I found that large farms typically scored high in at least one of these crops with an average score of .81 versus .05 for medium scale farms.

While these measures of skill are quite elaborate and tend to be generous in evaluating individual farmers, they still have several flaws that should be noted. Farms oriented toward livestock production earn lower scores because they grow fewer crops and are more likely to find the changing regulations of government programs burdensome. They may also find it more efficient to put less energy into high crop yields, and thus an assessment of production skill is skewed against them. Chance factors in 1986 may also lower skill measures inappropriately: an outbreak of hog disease may remove that indicator of higher skill for an otherwise strong livestock producer. An alternative reason for lower scores is that some farmers may choose to accept modest yields but seek to lower costs and use resources efficiently. For farmers with substantial interest in crops, however (and this is the majority of both large and medium scale farmers), the measures are useful and in general conform to other indicators and my own subjective assessments of overall farming skill.

Another dimension of skill is experience. One farmer who started well before the crisis years had great sympathy for young farmers: "No one can make money in the first three to four years," he said. "You need that OJT—on the job training." A farmer who has seen many seasons will know how much soil moisture is enough to make seeds germinate in a dry spring. Such a judgment about when to plant cannot be made as easily by an outside expert because the soil of each field holds moisture differently. Likewise, an experienced farmer knows when a crop must be sprayed or harvested and when the work can be deferred ("treated like a stepchild").

Large scale and medium scale farms are not different in the years of experience of their operators, nor are the two groups significantly different in the extent to which they have lured second career farmers from other occupations. Three in ten medium scale farms have this disadvantage in experience, and the figures for large scale farms, taking all partners into account, is only slightly lower.

Good quality soil is an important farming resource that can be expected to boost farm performance. It might be expected that with higher profits, large scale farms have had an advantage over time in buying better land. Good soil helps a farmer in two ways: it boosts yields by requiring less fertilizer, and it also holds moisture better in droughts. Land quality was measured in a painstaking process in which the total acreage of good, fair, and poor land on each farm in the sample was calculated using soil maps (see appendix 1). Table 4-3 shows that large and medium scale farms are very similar in their soil qualities, showing the average acreage of better soil to be 52 percent and 49 percent, respectively.

A simple percentage of good or poor land can be a distorted measure of resource quality, however, because some farmers with considerable poor-quality land put it into pasture or trees and still have plenty of the best land for their rowcropping needs. A better measure assesses the availability of good quality land to meet rowcrop acreage in 1986. Large farms can meet an average of 67 percent of their rowcrop needs with good soil; medium scale farms show an average of 69 percent. Variation around these averages shows both groups benefit from good soil resources. Thus, the power of larger scale and higher sales has in general not been translated into control over the better land in the county.

In chapter 1, we saw that many large scale farms in the Depression era were aided by (or were actually the products of) substantial off-farm income from town jobs or businesses. Some wealthy farmers today receive substantial income from investments or savings. Many farm families of all sizes benefit from the wife's salary income. Since the more educated and well-to-do the family background, the more likely an individual is to obtain a higher-paying job, privileges of past generations may show up in the families' off-farm income. In turn, this income may support larger farm scale.

The Dodge County data, however, do not support the notion that off-farm subsidy is substantially higher on large farms. Though their average is $18,000, compared to $14,000 on medium scale farms, this difference is not statistically significant. Most farms receive some outside income—a full-time or part-time job or some interest income from savings—and this support does not vary by class background. In part, this surprising finding reflects the relatively narrow range of salaries for women in the county. It is also testimony to the upward mobility of poorer farm families and the availability of a new opportunity structure of nonfarm jobs.

Federal Farm Program Benefits

The contrast between large scale and medium scale farms is perhaps most dramatic in the difference between their access to federal farm program benefits. Table 4-4 shows that the median amount received in 1986 was under $1,000 a year for medium scale farms, while large scale farms received over $20,000. Larger payments to larger farms reflects the organization of these programs, in which payments are tied to the volume of production. Both farmers and researchers assert that these subsidies are critical to the maintenance of larger scale. In fact, as new ceilings on payments per farm were enforced in Dodge County in the later 1980s, some large scale operators responded by cutting back rented acreage. In addition to promoting concentration of land and capital on large farms, agricultural programs also give the more favored farms higher and more secure profits.

The peanut program is the primary example and constitutes one of the most important resources a farmer of any size can obtain in Dodge County. In 1986, a year in which alternative crops looked particularly unprofitable, peanut sales made up 80–90 percent of crop sales, for both medium and large scale farmers. When livestock sales are included, peanut sales in Dodge County in 1986 came to 45 percent of total gross sales. A decision to grow peanuts is constrained by the current version of the New Deal federal price and acreage controls that allocates a "quota" of peanuts to certain fields. Owning land that has a peanut quota gives farmers rights to sell a fixed number of tons of peanuts, at a price that has been quite favorable. Over the decades, land sold can carry this profitable quota to its subsequent owner, or the peanut allotment can be sold separately. It can also be rented, and for heirs and widows of farmers, renting land and/or its allotment pro-

Table 4-4. Peanut Acreage and Allotment and Other Federal
Program Payments by Farm Scale, 1986

	Large Scale	Medium Scale
Median acres of peanuts planted*	98	21
Median tons of peanut allotment owned**	16.3	9.0
Median other federal program payments*	$22,500	$883

*Significant at .00 level by Kruskal-Wallis test.
**Significant at .04 level by Kruskal-Wallis test.

vides crucial income. Table 4-4 shows that access to peanut allotments is much higher on large scale farms and thus generates considerable farm income.

The advantages of larger allotments have been inherited by some farmers. In a few cases, substantial allotments date back to political connections during the New Deal. More commonly, both large and medium scale farmers seek to enlarge their participation in the programs by purchasing lands with good allotments or by buying the allotments separately. Powerful farmers may have an advantage through their information networks to know who is selling an allotment; they also may have the ready capital to buy. Other inducements offered by large scale farmers can be important as well. One large landholder was able to convince a widow to shift her allotment rental to him and away from a medium scale farmer who had rented it for years. In this case, the large scale farmer offered to help out the widow with certain equipment and services that she needed, but the medium scale farmer had no excess capacity in either his equipment or his time and had no hired hands to carry out such favors. In these and other ways, peanut allotments have come to be highly concentrated among large scale farms in Dodge County. The peanut program, as amended in the 1980s, maintains farmers' incomes considerably above what they would be without the program, but it does so by restricted supply not by any direct subsidy to the grower (Schaub 1990).

The high profits in peanuts fuels the technology treadmill, boosting capital intensification, which sometimes in turn lowers risk for the larger farmer (Cochrane 1979). To protect their investments in peanut fields (whose inputs are costly and represent a major outlay), big peanut growers were among the first to buy irrigation systems. Once under irrigation, fields are much less susceptible to drought, which thereby guarantees some profits to the large farmer in dry years. Meanwhile, medium scale farmers who cannot afford the outlay required for irrigation watch their peanuts burn up in a drought. These medium scale farmers praise the federal crop insurance program that at least protects them from total loss by covering their costs.

The federal cotton program has a very different history, but large scale farmers enjoy a substantial advantage in this domain as well. In the decade before the late 1970s, Dodge County cotton profits had fallen due to competition with new international producers and the banning of DDT, which lowered yields. Only a few large farm operators stayed on in cotton to recoup their investment in expensive cotton machinery. Costs of hiring neighbors with equipment to harvest the cotton and difficulties in finding someone free to do the work deterred many small and medium scale farmers from continuing cotton production. Federal cotton programs in the late 1970s responded to increased global demand and shifted the basis for determining allotments away from each farm's long-term production history. Farmers were now free to "build up a base" and obtain program support, even though they had never before been entitled to cotton allotments (Skinner and Sanford 1990). Cotton became highly lucrative again in the South, due also in part to new chemicals to replace DDT.

Large farms in Dodge County had an immediate advantage in responding to the new provisions of the cotton program because they already had a production history. Medium-sized farms were again deterred, this time from both the high cost of machinery and the lower profits without federal program assistance. Eligibility is based on the average of the previous five years' production; until that base is built up and benefits are received, cotton is usually produced at a loss. Thus, entrance to the cotton program is possible through planting the crop at a loss for several years, but few medium scale farmers can afford that investment. Provisions of the 1985 Farm Bill and fluctuating world market conditions brought virtually all U.S. cotton under the federal program, and payments to producers averaged 22 percent of total cotton income in the late 1980s (Skinner and Sanford 1990:29). In Dodge County, these changes mostly benefited large scale producers.

The tobacco program used to be an important exception to the trends in the peanut and cotton programs because it supported a range of small and medium scale farmers (Daniel 1985). Allotments historically could not be moved off the farm, thus preventing the development of economies of scale (Wright 1986:248). Tobacco families overcame the labor bottleneck at harvest by swapping work with other producers and hiring neighbor children. When federal regulations allowed allotments to be rented and moved to the renter's own fields, a few large farms in the county bought expensive labor-reducing equipment. In addition, by offering steady work to pickers, they were able to attract labor in the shrinking labor market. Greater rural affluence and declining family size reduced the number of children available for harvest work. When the program also cut the size of individual tobacco allotments in the 1970s and 1980s, to lower supply and costs, many smaller producers retired or gave up tobacco. Today, perhaps a dozen producers in the county continue the crop, most using capital-intensive harvest and drying technology. Tobacco no longer provides a basis to sustain a substantial sector of medium scale farmers.

In addition to income received from the peanut, cotton, or tobacco programs, many farmers receive federal payments for drought losses, land placed in the Conservation Reserve Program, construction of soil conservation terraces and waterways, and other activities. Large scale farmers have advantages in qualifying for many of these programs. For example, to "set aside" a percentage of crop acreage in order to qualify for federal programs, the large farm operator can choose a boggy corner of a field or some less productive acres and continue production without difficulty. The medium scale farmer, on the other hand, may need the production of the total acreage, especially if it is a feed crop for animals.

To receive payment for acreage set aside, a farmer must have a production history on record with the Agricultural Stabilization and Conservation Service (ASCS) office. To verify yields, an inspector must come to the farm; if grain is to be measured in a bin, two visits are necessary—one to check the empty bin and one to verify the new production. The expense for these visits must be paid by the farmer, and more importantly, there is often considerable waiting time involved. Many smaller operations cannot afford to give up a morning's work to arrange verification when there is no current government program of interest to them anyway. The larger farmer may have more equipment repair or labor supervision to do at the farm base and thus be less inconvenienced by the wait.

Incomplete ASCS record keeping hampered the medium scale farmer in receiving disaster payments as well. Several farmers produced higher than average yields on crops used for feed. Since these crops were not sold, they had no records of the harvest and no need for such records until the drought years hit. Disaster payments were based on ASCS records of a farm's three-year average production or, if those figures were not available, the county's average production of that crop. For some crops, the county average was sufficiently low to make payments laughable to the farmer who had just experienced a major drought. All of these procedures are eminently sensible from the point of view of verifying fair payments to farmers with losses, but they have resulted in continuing disadvantages to the medium-sized farms in the county.

Some medium scale farmers say they purposely avoid participation in federal agricultural programs. Their resistance represents a desire to remain independent from federal control and from the bureaucratic intrusion into operators' plans, budgets, and time. The difference in total federal payments received by large and medium scale farms thus reflects an interaction between disadvantages to medium scale and avoidance of governmental intervention. The operation of a large farm, however, receives a significant annual infusion of support.

In attempting to understand the origins of Dodge County's large farms, this review of the characteristics of large and medium scale farms suggests that large farms have not emerged primarily from the inheritance of large tracts of family land, from family privileges in access to cheap (or free) land or borrowed equipment, or from access to better soil. Large farm operators do not, on the average, have more experience or higher off-farm incomes. Though advantages of these sorts do favor particular individuals, as a whole, the large scale farmers have mostly built up their operations over their own lifetimes, purchasing land from neighbors and kin. The profits with which to expand have come mainly from strong farming skills and also from access to federal payments. Agricultural commodity programs have played a key role in sustaining the sector of large farms in Dodge County—a contribution that is particularly vivid in these crisis years with low overall profits. In addition, it is important to consider the farmer's desire to operate a large farm. The issue of personal aspirations and management style will be the subject of chapter 5.

Farm Survival

Though large scale farms have been shown to have substantial advantages in some domains, they are not more likely to stay in business through the recent crisis years. Table 4-5 shows that approximately a third of both full-time groups have been forced out of business by financial difficulties. In contrast, the part-time and retirement farmers have, to a much greater extent, been able to remain in operation. Their higher survival rates reflect both great caution in taking on expenses and debts and the ability to absorb low farm returns through income from social security, pensions, or jobs.

The figures on farm loss in the crisis suggest that large and medium scale farms represent not simply more and less privileged farms, but two distinct paths to farm success. The medium scale farms may produce less income, be operated at a lower overall skill level, and receive smaller government payments, but they are

Table 4-5. Farm Survival by Farm Type, 1989

		Total	Out of Farming, 1989[a]
Full-time:[b]	Large scale	21	29%
	Medium scale	37	35%
Part-time		40	13%
Retirement		26	4%

[a]Includes farms declaring bankruptcy (though some were temporarily back in business through debt reorganization), foreclosed by a lender, or voluntarily out of farming; deceased and retired farmers not included. Rates of survival for full-time, part-time, and retirement groups are significant at .00 level (chi-square = 11.48).
[b]Large scale and medium scale groups not significantly different by chi-square test (p = .83).

not handicapped by these disadvantages. The risky nature of farming has allowed medium scale farmers to fill a niche that resists the trend toward concentration in farm size. Comprising a majority of farms in the county, modest scale operations are equally successful in obtaining good land and are aided by similar cash infusions from wives' jobs and savings. They are highly efficient in their use of capital and may seem "less skillful" in part because they emphasize a diversified, one-man operation with lower costs and lower risks. Because medium scale farms are so numerous, they help to support local businesses—both agricultural and retail. They are, in fact, a solid small-business sector in the county, helping to support not only grain warehouses and supply companies but also auto dealers and furniture stores.

Large scale farms can be seen as capital-intensive operations that support a more affluent standard of living. Most of these operators maintain their scale and use of hired hands with energetic commitment to high yields and aggressive use of federal programs. Their choices limit the number of people who can live by farming in Dodge County, and their household expenses support different kinds of retail businesses. That the privileges enjoyed by many large scale farms have not translated into higher rates of survival is a surprising finding, and one that deserves further exploration. Each of the next three chapters will add to our understanding of farm survival, and we will return to the determinants of farm loss in chapter 8.

FIVE

Management Styles and Consumption Standards:

Dimensions of Success

Among full-time farm operations in Dodge County, two distinct farm management styles reflect the tensions between agrarian and industrial values, modest and affluent farm backgrounds, and older and younger generations. The agricultural transformations that have unfolded over three generations of farmers—technological changes as well as social status changes—are revealed in farmers' goals and in their notions of success, of having "made it." This chapter will explore contrasting ideologies of "good farming" as embodied in the cautious and ambitious farm management styles.

Success, as we have seen in chapter 3, is also linked to lifestyle, and the different farm groups in the county can be distinguished by houses, cars, and other aspects of their lifestyles. Some individuals desire a level of consumption comparable to suburban living standards, while others have more modest aspirations based on their family's background and memories of past poverty. These dimensions of social status are different for large and medium scale farmers and for part-time farmers as well. In my analysis, I have tried to describe the central trends for the whole county, while attending also to the diversity by farm scale. These issues of management style and lifestyle are critical in the struggle for survival in the 1980s slump, and this chapter will provide the background to understand the effect of the crisis on the dreams of different kinds of Dodge County farmers.

Pride in farming and in the farmer's "craft" (Mooney 1988) is one of the satisfactions that draws people to this way of life throughout the country. In the South, however, the poverty and lack of managerial control from the sharecropper past created a more clouded sense of farming craft. Writing of his Iowa father, Douglas Bauer talks of the skill that is assessed by neighbors and even by the grain dealer who buys the farmer's product: "I raise the tail gate . . . and my father's corn . . . flies past me. My father's labor is swirling liquidly about me . . . and it seems the purest corn I've seen, dustless and immaculately made. I see no broken kernels, no rotting teeth, not a stalk" (1979:75–76). In Dodge County, there is less of a shared consensus about farm skill. Standards of expertise and of product and community support for the farmer's craft are not as developed, reflecting the multiple traditions of industrial entrepreneurship and agrarian independence in wiregrass history. Perhaps the notion of craft has less power where large landowners in the past did no field work themselves and where indebted tenants felt trapped by world market swings in cotton prices and by insecure tenure on eroded, depleted soils. Certainly, the ups and downs of the farm economy from the 1920s through the 1960s taught diverse lessons to Dodge County families.

I have come to understand the complex decisions of developing and running a farm enterprise as reflecting two ideal farm management styles: cautious and ambitious. Cautious managers prefer to avoid debt, respect attention to detail and hard physical labor, and aspire to a modest but comfortable lifestyle. At the other extreme are the more ambitious farm managers who use the farm to attain different social status and personal achievement goals. These operators seek to farm on a large scale, with hired hands, and are willing to take significant risks. They want their farm size, sophisticated equipment, and family lifestyle to proclaim a different kind of success. The ambitious style, through its desire for large scale and the use of hired labor, can be seen to exacerbate the disadvantages that stem from the difficulties in careful attention to biological cycles, timing of farm tasks, and feedback and information flow on large units (as discussed in the Introduction). As we will see, however, scale and management style are separate dimensions of farm operation, and both scale groups exhibit both management orientations, though to differing degrees.

Although some farmers talk about their dreams and run their farms in a way highly consistent with one of these two ideal constructs, many farmers show a mix of these cautious and ambitious traits. In the discussion that follows, I have tried to draw out examples that best clarify the two management styles, but I do not mean to imply that all farmers fall neatly into one group or another.

The distinction between a more entrepreneurial management style and an alternative cautious style is echoed in many parts of the country. In 1885, a Wisconsin state agricultural convention speaker spoke of the "craze for sudden wealth [that] is a sort of contagious and popular insanity . . . [from which] the farmers have not wholly escaped" (Adams 1885:387). He reminded his listeners that "the average farmer can expect to reach a comfortable financial condition, but he can no more become rich than he can reach heaven by being elected to the legislature" (ibid.:386). Caution in accepting debt was a major theme in this speaker's advice to the prudent farmer. Jack Kirby also contrasts the family farm homesteaders of the frontier West with the entrepreneurial "bonanza farmers." The "ultimate corporate bonanza farmer was Thomas D. Campbell . . . [whose] maxims were borrow big, buy every piece of labor-saving machinery available, hire labor, and plant big" (1987:6). These same distinctions were noted in South Dakota, where Scott McNall and Sally Ann McNall in the 1950s differentiated large farmers (over a thousand acres) "who saw themselves as business persons" from traditional farmers who saw farming as a way of life rather than a business and who avoided going into debt (1983:264–65).

Different management styles not only are found in different groups of people but also are philosophies responding to different conditions. Many authors see the entrepreneurial approach as the historical penetration of capitalism into the countryside (Danbom 1979). For those families who held on to a more cautious management style, their "agrarian values came into conflict with the larger thrust of American society" (Barron 1990:17; Mooney 1988). For farmers, these different ideologies represent distinct notions of proper management. John Bennett described the Canadian farmer as well aware of the economic "rationality" and business ethic expected by economists and promoted by the extension service; however, "he knows the process does not work that way" and does not try to conform totally to the capitalist outlook and goals (1982:22). This caution responds to the lessons of arid agriculture in Saskatchewan and the multiple goals of families beyond farm profitability.

Turning to the other dimension of success treated in this chapter, household consumption can be seen as a marker of status in other farming areas around the country as well (Salamon and Davis-Brown 1986). The greater penetration of an industrial culture into the South, however, may account for the greater emphasis on consumerism in Dodge County when compared to farmers in Iowa or in Canada (Bennett 1982; Friedburger 1988, 1989). In Bennett's study of Canadian farmers, he found that about half of the wealthiest operators had the most modest lifestyles among farmers as measured by household and personal possessions. The local culture incorporated "a kind of reverse snobbery . . . a pride in living simply, whatever one's resources and income" (1982:418–19). In general, this value stance contrasts sharply with Dodge County where there is a stronger need to mark a family's transition away from the "Hoover Days." Said one wealthy farmer, "Consumers resent seeing farmers do well—they don't like to see farmers in four-wheel-drive vehicles, in town eating breakfast, eating dinner in a restaurant. You're supposed to stay on the farm from sunup to sundown and wear holey overalls and no shoes, so the price of food will stay low." Another large scale operator echoed, "Farmers used to be second class citizens and people in town would look down on us—as peasants, as people who don't have air conditioning in their homes. But today, homes in the country are furnished the same, and we eat the same or maybe even better."

Despite these cultural pressures in Dodge County to use household consumption as a marker of success, there are some families who reject consumerist values and uphold an alternative pride in frugal money management. Several women said, for instance, "I know what to want." "I've never been one to want, want, want," explained another, careful not to desire things she cannot afford. This attitude reflects an agrarian commitment to farm survival over consumption and puts farm survival and freedom from debt ahead of success as measured by lifestyle. The existence of farm families that live by these agrarian values supports theorists who hold that family farms can outcompete large, industrial-type farms because of their willingness to accept lower incomes. Such an agrarian conception of personal success seems to receive somewhat more community support in the Canadian and Iowan cases, whereas in Dodge County, there is some ambivalence and tension within families and within individuals with regard to these issues.

Cautious and Ambitious Farm Management Styles

In his study of Saskatchewan farmers, John Bennett developed the term "management style" to describe the ways operators handle their resources and earn "social credit" (1982:413). He found that management style was more important than either affluence or lineage in determining a farmer's reputation in the community. In Dodge County, however, there is no community agreement on what management activities make a farmer "a good feller" (Bennett 1980) or constitute "prudent management." Especially as the boom and bust conditions of the 1970s left farmers reeling, there remains no moral consensus on the right way to farm. As individual farmers make money or go under in bankruptcy, the community weighs its judgments, and individuals reevaluate their personal aspirations. Both styles, then, are considered "good" and "successful," though usually by different persons in the county.

Several characteristics distinguish the ambitious style:

- a desire for larger farm scale;
- a desire to supervise hired labor;

• a desire to avoid considerable manual labor and physical exertion;

• a shift from a desire to attend personally to details of crop and livestock production to a desire to attend to financial details;

• a greater willingness to accept debt as a necessary part of farming;

• a desire to use farming as a means to establish a higher social status; and

• a desire to demonstrate this status through a more affluent lifestyle.

Farm scale is one goal that farmers talk about frequently. Said an older medium scale farmer, "Wanting to be big never crossed my mind—all I wanted was to have something for the younguns." In contrast, one young farmer from a medium scale farm family began farming with the goal to buy a thousand acres and work it with three hired hands. An ambitious older farmer reported his lifetime goal as a young man had been "to make a million dollars and retire by fifty."

Desired farm scale is linked to a farmer's attitude toward using hired hands. Those who prefer to avoid hired labor and to keep a farm to a size that can be personally managed stress their satisfaction at "doing it right." A young man in partnership with his father said, "I never wanted to have it real big because you can't get good hired help. One of a hundred will do a good job." Disdainful of large scale farmers, another operator said he had never wanted to use hired labor: "It wouldn't work—I've watched it break farmers." Said one man who refused to expand, "You can't get it done like it should be." In contrast, the ambitious farmers welcome the role of supervisor and find it preferable to delegate the difficult and tedious farm tasks. Their sense of place in the social system is linked to employing hired hands.

Connected to desired scale and use of hired labor is a different orientation to hard work, attention to detail, and pride in farm craft. Though all farmers stress that they work hard, for the cautious, this work ethic is connected to the honor and virtue of the farm life. Pride in high production was expressed by a hog farmer who claimed, "I live with 'em," meaning he watches his animals' progress daily and often stays up nights to be sure they farrow safely. This level of care yields a maximum number of pigs per litter and makes a significant financial difference over a year. Another farmer who relies on hired help for the majority of his farm work still feels that his own efforts are the key to his success. Up at five o'clock, at work by six, he expected the same of his hands. "We went twenty-five to thirty years without a vacation," he stated proudly.

In contrast, an ambitious young large scale farmer discussed an older neighbor,

noting that "he thinks nothing of hoeing peanuts or watermelon all day. Not me—
I want some kind of chemical." We laughed and I suggested that such an attitude
is what makes older farmers say younger ones do not know how to work. "That's
not work," he replied. "That's killing yourself." On the other side of the coin,
one overextended large scale farmer expressed frustration that his farm work "gets
done a bit slapdash." His emotion reveals some regard for the work ethic, but he
has not changed his operation to pursue it.

Attention to detail varies from farmer to farmer. Particularly in the use of irrigation, some farmers are cautious to avoid malfunctions. They take pride in the fact
that they get up at regular intervals during the night to check the water flow and
machinery. At the other extreme are farmers who let irrigation run all night and
hope that it will not malfunction. Some farmers are more careful to check farm
machinery while in operation and stay busy in slack seasons keeping equipment in
top condition. They are diligent in observing fields for insect or disease damage;
some even pull weeds by hand to keep seeds from spreading. Part of the difference
in these two management styles is simply energy level, but there is also a distinct
value difference between a farmer for whom such diligence is tied to self-respect
and the self-image of a "good farmer" and an operator who carries out these tasks,
knowing they are essential, but who hopes someday to be free of such tedium.
Another determinant of differences in attention to detail is farm size; of course, all
of these ways of attending to the needs of crops and livestock are more difficult on
a larger scale farm.

Attention to detail and respect for manual labor are not necessarily combined
with soil stewardship in Dodge County. Gullies in fields, "balds" where topsoil
has been washed away, and sediment along roads are accepted as ordinary facts of
life. It is not uncommon for an otherwise cautious farmer to fail to acknowledge
that past land use is a part of present farming conditions. For example, one farmer
pointed out that a particular field always suffered drought stress first but did not
link that fact to erosion and a thinner topsoil layer. Some farmers take pride in
building up terraces and using new methods such as no-till. Soil conservation has
been actively encouraged by a series of strong Soil Conservation Service agents in
the county, and some operators regard care for soil resources as a component of
good farming and a cautious management style. But a disregard for soil resources
has deep roots in southern history and is fed by the mechanization of agriculture,
the chemical revolution, and the removal of much diversity of soil organisms.
There is no shared philosophy of the land as a living ecosystem and farming as
a partnership with nature. Soil stewardship is a concern that varies from farm to
farm and is not automatically linked with either a cautious or ambitious style.

The "craft" of farming for the more ambitious operator has shifted somewhat from an emphasis on the rhythms of nature and the nurturance of productivity through hard physical labor to the art of money management. Ambitious farmers take pride in canny marketing, bulk purchases of inputs, and special deals with suppliers. They "farm the programs," paying careful attention to changing federal regulations for new opportunities to maximize profits. The farmer who has as much interest in his loan portfolio as in his crops embodies a different notion of success.

Orientation to debt is another dimension of management style. One large scale farmer said: "I've had the initiative, ambition, and guts to tackle things. And I'm not afraid of debt." Some operators support their ambitious style with tales of relatives who took risks during the Depression era. One farmer recounted his desire to imitate the more daring of two uncles: "He took chances—he went broke a lot—but he always bounced back." The other, more financially conservative uncle was appalled at this behavior: "He didn't believe in spreading out too much— he thought debt was going to ruin the whole family." Cautious farmers today, both large and medium scale, echo the latter philosophy. "Do without and do the best we can; don't buy more than we can pay for," said one young farmer. "We don't buy new [equipment]; that's how we stayed in business." One black farmer bragged that he had never been able to buy a new car or a new tractor, but he has stayed "out of trouble" on the farm "with a tight belt." One large scale farmer who retired and turned the farm over to his son found the young man following a more expensive style of farming: "He did it like he wanted, and he didn't cut corners." In another case, an ambitious son of cautious parents claimed borrowing was more "modern." His farm now faces foreclosure, and his mother concluded, shaking her head with sadness, "Sometimes you have to learn the hard way." Ambitious farmers see taking risks and going into debt as necessary. They look down on cautious farmers as old-fashioned, unskilled, or insufficiently entrepreneurial to be a success. Upward mobility, for them, results from taking risks and expanding the operation.

Ambitious style is connected to a desire for higher social status, which is of less concern to the cautious manager. Said one older medium scale farmer, sitting in a lawn chair under the carport of his small white frame house, "I never wanted much, never had much, neither. But I don't want no pots of money. Nowadays, some people farm to get rich!" Another medium scale farmer who lives in a run-down wooden house with old, battered furniture says he does not want anything in particular for his home: "Wouldn't do to have too much—would get too big-headed." Many of the cautious medium scale farmers see the more ambitious medium scale farmers as pursuing status goals at the expense of prudence: "They want to be big shots."

Both cautious and ambitious operators resent the stereotype of the farmer as an unshaven hick "with tobacco dribbling down his chin," but the status ambiguity is particularly troubling to the more ambitious farmers. They want to be seen as sophisticated business people, managing intricate machinery with technical know-how. Farming is their choice to fulfill a series of personal goals, and though they may express love for it, they can more readily imagine giving it up.

It is telling that when asked, "How important is it to you to think of yourself as a farmer?" cautious farmers, large and medium scale, often said, "very important," with emphasis. However, ambitious large scale operators were more likely to say, "Well, I don't mind admitting it—I don't have anything to hide."

The goals of ambitious farmers are connected to a certain level of affluence. Farming must provide them with a standard of living comparable to professionals or middle management employees. "If I got a job," said one college-educated young farmer, "I could make $30,000 and have a moderate lifestyle and money in the bank. If I can't do that with farming I don't want it." He went on to say that there is the potential to make more than that in farming, though not at present. "There's no reason," he asserted, "why a person can't be successful and work an average of forty hours a week in farming. I would like to have plenty of money and go winters to Acapulco—my dream is a jet set lifestyle." Though such grand dreams of wealth through farming are mainly characteristic of younger, Generation 3 farmers, all ages of farmers with an ambitious management style put a certain level of living ahead of continuing the farm. One couple remarked, "There's no point in keeping at it unless you can be comfortable." Said another woman, "I've always wanted a *lot*, though I'm willing to work for it. I've never had a vision of being rich—having maids—but wanted to be comfortable." For her, being "comfortable" means "not having to work as hard as my parents did" and "to avoid the kind of penny-pinching I grew up with."

Although many Dodge Countians desire to be "comfortable," their family backgrounds lead to very different aspirations and meanings for that word. One cautious farmer had "no plans to make a pile of money," and he and his wife are satisfied with their small brick home and medium scale farm. Their neighbor seems to echo these aspirations, saying he wanted to live "not fancy, just comfortable," but his large home (3,500 square feet), expensive vehicles, and nearly 1,000-acre farm show he has a different definition of "comfortable." One elite woman said, "I don't want my children to be wealthy, but make a living and have enough." Her standards of what constitutes "enough" are revealed by her own ample and well-furnished house, the family's two trucks and three cars, and their swimming pool. When her medium scale neighbor says, "I never wanted much," he refers to a very different lifestyle.

The cautious and ambitious styles, agrarian and industrial worlds, and alternative evaluations of success and status struggle against each other in daily Dodge County reality. Farmers are influenced by the agricultural extension service, farm magazines, agribusiness representatives, and formal education that pushes a more ambitious management style. Those who embrace such values see themselves as participating effectively in the national culture of a competitive capitalist society. In contrast, the cautious farm managers see themselves as continuing a tradition of careful commonsense farming. Some shared meanings of "good management" can be heard in farmers' conversations, but contested interpretations of success are often expressed.

Though in many dimensions, it is agreed that the ambitious farmer is more progressive and more modern, the cautious management style continues to have some moral power. Several large scale farmers who use an aggressive, entrepreneurial style claim they are actually conservative cost-cutters. One affluent and politically well-connected farmer explains his success as due to the frugality he learned from his parents. Open celebration of affluence is rare and seems to reflect a hesitancy to proclaim oneself a winner because of an awareness that, within our competitive system, to do so means that many must then be labeled losers. The modesty of the cautious style is echoed in Christian values that also generally militate against flaunting a desire for accumulation of wealth and an ambition for upward mobility. More fortunate farm families seek to reconcile these divergent ethics by redefining "affluence" as the more acceptable "being comfortable." Said one farmer, "I just want to live mediocre," but his two diamond rings flash a different message.

Influences on Management Style

Cautious and ambitious management styles are found among both large and medium scale farms, as shown in table 5-1, but there are some interesting trends through the three generations. For this table, I coded the operation of each farm in terms of greater or lesser conformity to one of the two styles. The figures show that operators of large farms as a group are split evenly into cautious and ambitious styles. In Generation 2, however, the ambitious style is more common, and

Table 5-1. Ambitious and Cautious Management Styles
by Farm Scale and Generation

Full-Time Farms	Percent Ambitious	Percent Cautious
Large scale		
Generation 1 (n = 6)	50	50
Generation 2 (n = 7)	71	29
Generation 3 (n = 8)	38	63
Total[a]	52	48
Medium scale		
Generation 1 (n = 14)	7	93
Generation 2 (n = 6)	14	86
Generation 3 (n = 17)	65	35
Total[b]	32	68
All farms[c]	40	60

[a]Chi-square = 17.82, d.f. = 5, p < .01.
[b]Chi-square = 1.74, d.f. = 2, p = .42.
[c]Chi-square = 15.05, d.f. = 2, p < .01.

in Generation 3, somewhat less so, though the numbers involved are small. The majority of ambitious Generation 2 operators are individuals who seem to be more anxious to assert higher social status to offset their lower-status career choice, while the majority of Generation 3 operators seem more secure in their elite status and do not strive to manage the farm in the more affluent style. This shift between the two generations seems to reflect the increasing economic value of farms since the 1950s and the waning of the negative image of a farmer.

Medium scale farmers are substantially more likely to be cautious (68%), but here, too, there is variation. More Generation 3 farmers operate in the ambitious style, seeking to use hired hands, debts, and expanded scale to be upwardly mobile. Their use of debts, especially fat disaster loans, to finance family consumption reflects an orientation toward proclaiming upward social mobility. Several built a new house or bought a new car or truck with such payments—financial decisions that were often greatly regretted when the droughts continued and crop prices remained low. The older two generations of medium scale farmers tend to be more cautious, remembering Depression-era hardships and valuing the accomplishment and security of a debt-free farm.

What determines farm management style? Though I expected family background to play a major role, statistical analysis shows no relationship between class background and management style. Clearly, elite farm background is crucial in some cases by setting a standard of affluence and consumption. For those who grow up in a comfortable home, on a farm operated by hired workers or tenants, such a farming style comes to be taken for granted. Ambitious farmers, however, are also found among those with modest farm backgrounds. They wanted to be wealthy—or "comfortable"—in reaction to the difficult years they experienced growing up. "I had a crazy ambition to be a successful farmer . . . coming from nowhere, from the bottom of the barrel. The rest of my family didn't *suffer*, but they never *had* anything." Others perceived their parents as downwardly mobile from a more prosperous family past. A few were disappointed in their fathers' failure of courage to "reach out," take risks, and be successful at a larger farm, and they were committed to avoiding these errors themselves.

In another way, parental guidance—or the lack of it—seems to have had a role in the adoption of the ambitious style. Among the ambitious large scale operators, almost half had fathers whose primary occupation was a nonfarm career. These families owned land, but the bulk of the work was carried out by renters or hired laborers. Sons in these families were not involved to the same degree in the yearly rhythms of farming. Nor was caution in financial planning transmitted, because the family lived primarily on the more predictable off-farm income sources. In contrast, all but two of the cautious large scale operators (out of a total of sixteen such operators on ten farms) had worked regularly in the fields at their fathers' sides.

The interactions of husbands and wives also seem to influence management style. A desire to provide an affluent lifestyle for their wives and families is one attraction of the ambitious style for some men. In a few cases, a wife was opposed to the farm life, and her support had to be won through meeting certain household consumption goals. The reverse situation can also be found, in which the husband is more ambitious and the wife, cautious. Said one woman, "I'm a conservative. He'll take a risk and I'll do the worrying." As we shall see in chapter 6, family consumption is intimately bound up with some women's attitudes toward farming, and the penetration of industrial values changes expectations of marital roles as well as the role of the farm for some families.

Dimensions of personality and individual preferences also play a role in explaining management style, as shown in the case of two brothers. Their father, an elite farmer in the 1920s and 1930s, operated seven hundred acres together with his two sons and several hired hands. The younger son served as the foreman and "bossed the hands," and the older son simply worked on the farm. This latter son bought land with his share of the inheritance after the father died and continued to farm conservatively all his life, never relying on hired hands. He avoided debt, lived modestly, and reached retirement age at the time of this study. The other son continued his father's more entrepreneurial style. Purchasing land that he operated with hired workers, he also expanded into business. Though highly indebted by the 1980s, he also had high assets and thousands of acres in operation, both owned and rented. His income from other businesses subsidized the farm.

The same divergence of management styles can be seen among part-time farmers, and a small group of more ambitious investors can be distinguished from the majority of part-time farmers who tend to be cautious. Investors enjoy owning farmland, and some do a minimum of supervision and work, but the bulk of the farm labor is carried out by a hired worker. Out of forty part-time farmers in the 1982 survey, there were six investors, most of whom received their land as an inheritance. One investor summed up his philosophy: "The best life is to own a farm, have a good job, and have a good person to take care of your farm."

The majority of part-time farmers—whom I have labeled standard part-time farmers (Barlett 1986a)—enjoy the challenge of farm management and take pride in close attention to crop and animal cycles. They are usually debt-free and follow a strategy of building up their farms slowly and cautiously, fixing fences and adding hog facilities or grain storage a step at a time. "Making big changes overnight" got some farmers in trouble, they say. One standard part-time farming couple stressed their aversion to any form of debt on the farm. "I was raised poor as dirt," said the wife, "and don't like to owe anything." "As long as she owes $2, she'll worry," confirmed her husband.

A few part-time farmers hold a more entrepreneurial view that "saving is fine, but you can't take it with you." Said one, "I'm not the type to save—spend now, enjoy life now." A few such part-timers took risks with disaster loans and farm debts; the consequences of their more ambitious farming aspirations will be explored in chapter 8.

Lifestyle and Success

Household consumption provides a marker of success for both cautious and ambitious farmers, but the content of those aspirations differs and there is a greater emphasis on lifestyle embodied in the ambitious management orientation. In Dodge

County, types of homes and furnishings, vehicles, appliances and entertainment items, and other elements of lifestyle vary by farm size and generation and verify the family's ability to transcend the stereotypes of the impoverished "dirt farmer."

The quality of *housing* is one of the most dramatic changes in rural Dodge County. In T. J. Woofter's study of the Depression-era South (1936), there appears a photograph of a brick overseer's home on a large Mississippi plantation. Such a home contrasted sharply with the run-down shacks that provided shelter for the bulk of the population. Today, the most typical house for Dodge County farm families is a brick home virtually identical to that overseer's house. I have labeled such a house "Type 2," one of the following four general types of farmhouses found among families in the study: 1) small wood frame or cinder block homes, 2) modest brick homes, 3) larger brick homes, and 4) elite houses of several kinds. Each of these four types is associated with a different style of interior decoration and taste.

Only 5 out of 106 full-time and part-time farm families surveyed do not own a house but instead rent or own a mobile home. The costs of housing are substantially less in Dodge County than elsewhere in the country. A fairly large house, built partially by the occupants, can cost as little as $30,000 and often is purchased by farm families without a mortgage. In contrast, a new harvester for the farm costs at least twice that much. One young farmer acknowledged that he lives well: "I don't have no fancy house, but I'd have to have a fancy job to have this." [1]

A quarter of farm families—like the McClintocks in chapter 4—live in Type 1 wood frame or cinder block homes. Space is moderate, commonly 1,500–1,800 square feet. Such houses have one or two bathrooms and rarely have central heat or central air conditioning. Heat in winter is provided by gas or electric space heaters or by wood-burning stoves. Many such families have no air conditioning, though some have one or two window units. Living room furniture commonly includes vinyl-covered recliners, perhaps a sofa, and a formica table. A few older, polished wood tables or cupboards are also typical. Plastic-covered furniture is convenient since it allows a farmer to come in dirty at mealtimes and rest a bit before returning to work. A plastic tablecloth covering the kitchen table, where the family eats most meals, serves the same purpose. Flooring is usually vinyl with throw rugs—often homemade—in the primary living area. Walls are often covered with sheets of wood-grain paneling and are decorated with photographs and diplomas or occasionally religious pictures. Landscaping varies greatly. Some yards are simply grass, with no trees or shrubs, but other families are avid gardeners and the yard boasts an accumulation of blooming plants. This variation in yard care is true of all housing types, with the exception of the most elite homes, which are more likely to look professionally landscaped.

A brick home is a marker of success to many couples, and four in ten farm families live in Type 2 modest brick homes. Houses in this second category often approach 2,000 square feet in size and usually have one and a half or two baths (the median among farm families). A typical kitchen has formica counters on two sides, a wall oven, a dishwasher, and a large freezer just outside the door. The dining room may boast older wooden chairs and a table covered in a plastic lace tablecloth. Living room furniture is commonly upholstered in either fabric or Naugahyde, and the floor may have indoor-outdoor carpet or throw rugs. A few of the smaller brick houses have central heat or air conditioning, though some heat with a space heater, wood-burning stove, or fireplace and have only a window air conditioning unit in the bedroom.

The larger, more ranch-style Type 3 brick house often combines brick with some wood or vinyl siding. Though there may be a front door, access through a garage or carport on the side is the usual entrance for family and friends. Rooms are larger, and there are more bedrooms in these middle class brick houses; square footage rises to 2,000–2,500. More than two baths is typical, and though there may be some vinyl furnishings, there will likely be a formal living room and dining room with finished wood and upholstered furniture, plasterboard walls, broadloom carpet, and framed pictures, baskets, plants, and other decorations. Two in ten farm families, including the Graingers, live in this type of housing.

The top 12 percent of farm families in Dodge County live in Type 4 homes that represent a more affluent lifestyle than those in the Type 3 larger brick houses. Some have renovated large, older wood frame houses, covering them in expensive siding. Others have built architecturally unusual, multilevel houses with large windows and sliding glass doors, perhaps facing an attractive pasture or pond view. Some of these elite houses are larger versions of the Type 3 brick house but with considerably more space. Type 4 houses usually exceed 2,500 square feet and may reach 5,000 in some cases. Three or more bathrooms, a large well-equipped kitchen, a substantial family room, and a deck, porch, or patio make these houses very similar to elite suburban homes in any metropolitan area. They may have such features as an attractive fireplace, and the floor may be carpeted or covered with fine rugs. Furniture often shows a distinctive style—modern, country, or traditional. A number of these elite houses also boast a swimming pool. They are commonly landscaped with sculptured beds of ornamental shrubs and flowers.

Cars and trucks are the second most important status marker. How many vehicles a family has, what year or model they are, and whether they were purchased new or used all contribute to the status statement they make. Several older, medium scale farm couples have no automobile and get by with one ancient pickup truck. More typically, families have both a pickup for the farm hauling and an automobile for the family's use. This car is sometimes designated as the wife's vehicle.

American makes of automobile are most commonly purchased, ranging from Buicks and Chryslers to Fords and Chevrolets. In general, farm families own middle-priced models, and differences in income are reflected in whether the cars are bought new or used. A few large scale farmers express claims to status with high-prestige cars such as Cadillacs or Mercedes or with powerful trucks. Others can afford to do so but drive a more middle range car instead. Sporty models of American cars like Thunderbirds or Camaros are occasionally chosen by younger men. A few Japanese trucks or cars—Hondas or Toyotas—appeared in the later years of my study, usually owned by younger couples or by mileage-conscious older farmers. Expensive pickups and cars tend to be the province of large scale farmers; medium scale farmers rarely buy such cars, even used. For them, the more modest Buick, Chrysler, or Oldsmobile is status marker enough. The same pattern holds for owning large numbers of trucks and cars. The typical large scale farmer owns five farm trucks of various types, but the medium scale farmer owns only one or two.

Cars for children are an important domain of status-oriented consumption. A few elite farm families boast expensive vehicles for all their children. In less well-off families, a child may own a car or truck (often seen as necessary to get to and from school and an after-school job) but will pay for the vehicle himself or herself. Some parents who have given their children a new pickup truck or sports car value the opportunity to demonstrate their success to the child's peers. Several parents who experienced farm loss or high debts later admitted, however, that such an expenditure for children's vehicles was one of their biggest mistakes.

Appliances and entertainment items are a third component of an affluent lifestyle (Bennett 1982:421). Refrigerators, freezers, stoves, and ovens are now considered so essential that they are present in all farm homes. Among full-time farmers, all but one household have an automatic clothes washer, but a few less well-off families do not have a clothes dryer. After a washer and a dryer (which 93% own), families generally add a dishwasher and then a microwave oven[2] (both owned by roughly 75% of families). Among entertainment items, virtually all families have a television and a radio, and about half have a piano and a VCR as well. These items are found in different generations, however; pianos are common among

Generation 1 and 2 large scale farmers and among part-time farmers. VCRs are more characteristic of younger families. Almost a fifth of families boast a recreational vehicle—usually a camper—or a motorboat. In general, farmers have small fishing boats and are not caught up in the competition to have fancy boats as seen among some nonfarm families. Computers are rare (11%), though growing in numbers, and in 1987 were used much more for children's games than for farm accounts. A satellite dish was found in 18 percent of households, almost all of them Generation 1, large scale farm families.

Eating in restaurants and taking vacations are two other ways of living a more affluent lifestyle. In 1986, almost half of Dodge County farm families took no formal family vacation. Of those who did, some drove to campgrounds or beaches in Georgia, but most went out of state. A few went to Walt Disney World or joined charter trips to Las Vegas or other vacation spots. Eating in restaurants is seen by many families as a sure way to spend money fast, but such activities vary greatly by season and are hard to measure. Other markers of a more affluent lifestyle among Dodge County farmers are sending one's children to private school (9%), owning a vacation home (6%), and hiring domestic help (26%). Employing a maid is more common among large scale families, but a few medium scale families hire domestic help out of necessity because of injury or ill health. Some men and women expressed the importance they attach to owning a diamond ring.

Patterns in Household Consumption
by Scale and Generation

This description of farm housing, vehicles, and appliances documents that Dodge County farmers have come a long way from Tobacco Road images of rural poverty. Table 5-2 shows that large scale farms are more likely to support Type 3 and 4 houses and fancier cars. On average, these farms have more appliances as well. As we saw in chapter 3, however, a Type 2 house, a car, and a truck represent significant upward mobility and personal success for many medium scale farmers.

Some farmers worry that younger generations have strayed too far away from their frugal roots. Older farmers frequently express their surprise at the speed with which younger couples expect to accumulate goods. "Young folks nowadays want a higher standard of living; they won't take it slow." Said another older farmer, "Young people are just living too high for farming." A wealthy farm woman remembered being satisfied in the 1940s with "plastic and cast iron." She had no

Table 5-2. Household Consumption
by Farm Type and Generation

	Percent Housing Types 3 or 4[a]	Percent More Affluent Car Ownership[b]	Average Number of Appliances[c]
Large scale			
Generation 1 (n = 8)	75	63	5.5
Generation 2 (n = 9)	44	50	5.9
Generation 3 (n = 13)	46	64	5.0
Medium scale			
Generation 1 (n = 14)	7	7	3.0
Generation 2 (n = 6)	0	0	4.3
Generation 3 (n = 18)	22	40	4.2
Part-time			
Investors (n = 6)	50	—	4.6
Standard (n = 31)	23	—	5.2

[a]Chi-square = 50.18, d.f. = 28, p = .01.
[b]Top two quartiles of vehicle ownership as coded by make, age, and number. Chi-square = 23.65, d.f. = 15, p = .07.
[c]Includes appliances and entertainment items; the 9 items surveyed are clothes washer, clothes dryer, dishwasher, microwave oven, VCR, satellite dish, piano, recreational vehicle or motorboat, and computer. Chi-square = 22.72, p < .01, by Kruskal-Wallis test.

carpet until her children were older, and her sofa was covered with Naugahyde. "But our children's wants are different from ours," she said; they want a fabric sofa, carpet, and a clothes dryer.

The increasing cultural emphasis on household consumption can be seen by contrasting the generations of medium and large scale farmers. Table 5-2 shows that Generation 3 families in the medium scale group tend to have more affluent housing and cars than Generations 1 and 2.[3] Some of these Generation 3 medium scale families have benefited from the extra income of wives' jobs. The youngest generation on large scale farms do not show a tendency to consume above the level of older generations, but they are not far behind, either. They are, as suggested above, relatively secure in their social standing and have been content to try to reproduce the consumption standards of their parents.

The levels of household consumption shown in the table also illustrate how part-time farming generally supports greater affluence than a full-time medium scale farm. Through higher numbers of appliances, more frequent Type 3 and 4 houses, and more regular vacations and meals in restaurants, the part-time farm family can assert a lifestyle more similar to a large scale farm than to the bulk of medium scale farms.

It should be reiterated that these numerical measures of household consumption patterns do not represent a ranking of goals shared by all farm families. One Generation 2 farmer eloquently contrasted his conception of "success" (which means to him "doing what one does well") with "accumulation." He holds television partly responsible for making his children feel like they have to have a "house and a car and a boat. . . . We have moved too far in the direction of worshipping money." He stressed that "some parents have gotten needs, wants, and gifts confused." One older woman on a full-time farm has only one appliance—a washing machine—and says she is not particularly interested in a clothes dryer, air conditioning, or central heat. The split upholstery on her vinyl-covered armchairs in the living room does bother her, and even though she says, "Naturally I'd like to have more and nicer things," she and her husband "try to save everything we can" to support the farm and pay off debts from the drought years.

In contrast, a part-time farmer who is less ambivalent about accepting such consumerist values boasted of the fact that he gave cars to all his children when they were sixteen, and "if they want $300 to spend on clothes, my wife and I give it to them." This consumer pressure also affects the more ambitious full-time farm families, for whom the inability to afford more appliances or fancier cars may promote a sense of frustration, even failure, despite the reality that their living standards are far above the norm.

In sum, we have seen how farm families in Dodge County uphold diverse views of success on the farm and in the home. There are no heroes or villains in these management styles, only alternate paths, alternate choices. Individual men and women bring together their personal backgrounds, temperaments, peer and family pressures, and opportunities and fashion a life on the farm to try to achieve their own visions of success. As the generations have passed, farm life in Dodge County has become more affluent, more capital-intensive, and more risky. As we shall see in chapter 7, the farm crisis pulled these gradual changes onto center stage, and it raised questions about the viability of the ambitious style in an economic slump. Questions emerged also about desired living standards and the ability of the farm to keep up with nonfarm lifestyles. For some farm families, declining incomes and rising debts forced a painful reconsideration of their dreams of success and the ability of farming as a means to achieve them.

Behind these dreams are the ebbing agrarian values and the governing images of success in mainstream U.S. society. Many Dodge Countians express clearly the unease they feel at the rapid value changes that surround them, but they have no leaders and no forum in which to publicly articulate an agrarian alternative. The increasing invisibility of frugal family farmers is articulated by one town woman who asserted, "That way of life is *gone*." Yet the data from Dodge County show that both medium scale farms and the cautious management style exist and thrive. Against the odds, some farm families have been able to transmit these values to their children and have made them the basis for a fulfilling life. Multiple paths to success in Dodge County are alive and well, and ironically, the crisis seems to have acted against experts' predictions to support that diversity.

CHAPTER

SIX

Inside the Farm Family:

Transformations in Women's Marital Roles

I became aware of the diversity of women's attitudes toward the farm in the first week of my fieldwork in Dodge County. As I traveled with three student assistants to become more familiar with the county roads and crops, we paused by a field with newly emerging green leaves, unsure whether we were facing a peanut or soybean field. Fortuitously, a young farm woman drove up to the field in a pickup truck. She came to pick up her preschool son who had been riding with his father in the tractor while she went to a funeral. When asked to identify the crop, she protested: "Don't ask *me*—I just do the cooking!" Her comment reflected both her distance from farm operations and her identity as a homemaker, not a farmer. The next day, I met a woman on a part-time farm who talked about "our farm" and "my hogs." She was clearly the primary animal caretaker, and her identification with the operation conformed more closely to my stereotype of the active farm woman.

Dodge County farm women thus show a range of involvement with and commitment to the farm, and some simply chose to marry a man who happened to farm. Some talk passionately of their love for farming, but others would sooner leave it. The hostility that some women express toward farming was one of the surprises of the study. Popular accounts of farm stress and movies of the crisis portray couples united in their goals and commitment to save the farm, but in roughly a third of the families interviewed, women's negativity toward the farm created a tension that was palpable.

This chapter will explore the changes over the last three generations in women's conceptions of marital roles and their sense of connection to farming as a way of life. Women's work on the farm has greatly decreased, work for pay off the farm has increased, and couples' expectations about pooling family income have also changed. The financial crisis faced by some farm families has thrown a new light on issues of women's legal rights to the farm and legal responsibilities for farm debts. In each of these domains, we will trace an agrarian way of life increasingly surrounded and challenged by pressures and values from an industrial society.

In conversations with nearly a hundred Dodge County farm women, it became clear that there are two different conceptions of ideal marital roles, which I have called marital models. Jane Collier has described a similar contrast among women in Spain (1986), and I have used her labels, agrarian and industrial, to identify the two different models. These conceptions of gendered responsibilities and work roles have been called "the moral economy of the family," and many studies show that industrialization brings increasing individualism into expectations about rights and responsibilities between husbands and wives (Adams 1988; Fink 1986b; Handwerker 1986). The farm crisis highlights the changing moral economy of the family in Dodge County as financial tensions reveal disagreements about spending priorities. These financial disagreements reflect, in turn, women's and men's personal dreams of success and their responses to their own failures to live up to certain ideals.

Women's marital models are part of larger family orientations to debt, social status, consumption, frugality, and management style, factors that are critical to getting through the drought years.[1] This chapter will first explore the dimensions of contrast between the agrarian and industrial marital models, present the historical context for the change in ideal gender roles, and then turn to actual patterns of financial management, employment, farm and household work to explore how differing value systems take form in daily life.

Contrasting Moral Economies

The agrarian and industrial marital models can be seen by the outsider as contested ideological systems, but Dodge County farm women do not articulate them as distinct alternatives. Instead, they perceive themselves to be in a world of conflicting expectations about marital roles and struggle to find a path through these values and demands. Many are aware of a historical trend away from popular respect for the agrarian model. For most of the women I talked to, their own perspectives on work, money, and family seem to have remained stable for much of their lives.

For some, beliefs have changed from exposure to new ideas, changes in economic or family circumstances, or negotiations with their husbands. More often, however, I saw a clash between a woman's marital model and her daughter's. In her work with California families, Arlie Hochschild found that rapid societal change can leave ideas about gender "fractured and incoherent." An individual's beliefs, daily behavior, and emotions about gender roles are often inconsistent (1989:190). In this study, I have not tried to explore all of the complexities of family dynamics and changes within individuals but have instead searched for the larger connections between the economic and cultural context of Dodge County farms and the central, orienting values in people's lives. In some ways, these marital models reflect a distinct southern heritage, but they also reflect processes found in other areas of the United States and in other industrializing countries as well.

The key contrasts in ideal marital roles between the agrarian and industrial models are summarized in table 6-1. The agrarian perspective sees both spouses as partners in a joint family enterprise oriented around the farm. Though there is a gendered division of labor, its spheres are seen as interdependent, and both spouses have financial responsibilities to the family. Women with an agrarian perspective identify with the farm and are committed to its success. The industrial model is not, of course, limited to people who work in industries but rather is the gender ideal that emerged among middle class urban women in the Northeast during the early 1800s (Ryan 1981). Women's roles were redefined away from production and toward consumption, domesticity, and responsibility for the family (Adams 1988:466). The husband is expected to be the breadwinner, and the farm is seen as his occupational choice, not necessarily a family project. The woman with an industrial orientation is less likely to identify with the farm or to embrace it as a personal commitment.

The agrarian perspective reflects a continuity between work, home, family, and farm. The farm is a joint commitment by husband and wife, and responsibility for family welfare is also shared.[2] The agrarian household is seen as a working partnership in which the individual goals of husband and wife are subordinated to farm and family success and to joint ownership of property (Collier 1989). One younger Dodge County farm woman said, gesturing at the fields outside the kitchen window, "Looking out, we can say we did this. Looking at it, be proud of it. It's a good feeling, seeing that you have accomplished what you set out to do." "It's our livelihood," said another woman, stressing her involvement; "*we* farm."

This shared commitment to the farm and integration of the enterprise with the family does not prevent a distinctly gendered division of labor (Sachs 1983).

Table 6-1. Contrasts between Women's Marital Models

Agrarian Marital Model

Husband and wife are partners in the family farm enterprise and both share financial responsibilities.

Wife's personal aspirations are linked to farm success.

Wife has emotional attachment to the farm and farm life.

Leisure and companionship goals reflect a unity of farm and family.

When wife has job, incomes are pooled, reflecting joint responsibility.

Industrial Marital Model

Husband has primary financial responsibility as breadwinner; wife has primary responsibility as homemaker.

Wife's personal aspirations emphasize family consumption, caretaking, and children's achievements.

Wife has little emotional attachment to farming except from a desire to support her husband.

Desired leisure activities and companionship with husband may conflict with farm responsibilities.

When wife has job, earnings are her discretionary fund, reflecting husband's primary responsibility for finances.

One older woman describes her marriage as the union of "two specialists." Her husband is responsible for the crops and livestock, though she helps, and she is responsible for the family, house, garden, and the yard, with his help. Some agrarian women express strong positive feelings about the farm work they do: "I just *love* farming." Others do relatively little of the farm labor but think of themselves as integrally part of the farm operation: "I don't do much, but what I do is *important*." One woman works at a full-time job, and her domestic work fills her remaining time, but she says, "Even while cooking, I'm helping us all out on the farm. . . . We're all fighting a common battle." Many children pay tribute to their mothers' long hours in the fields and care for animals. "She worked really hard," said one son from an agrarian family. An elite woman stressed with some righteousness that she had done field work when younger, "for the family, to try to pay for the place."

For a woman with an agrarian marital model, shared responsibility and identification with the farm is often joined with a strong emotional attachment to the farm life. One woman from a large scale farm contrasted the "peace of mind" it creates with the "hustle and bustle" of her job. Said another from a small family farm, "I really have always liked it." A mother of teenage children stressed, "Farming teaches children you get out of it what you put into it; it's a reap-what-you-sow kind of thing." An older woman summed up, "There's not a lot of money in farming but there's a lot of pleasures."

Dodge Countians who share the agrarian perspective emphasize the interdependence of male and female spheres of work and resist the societal tendencies to rank men's work above women's. One black farmer stressed that domestic and farming roles are not arranged hierarchically: "It's like the parts of a car; it takes all the parts of a car to make the car go. We all do our part and no part is more important." Men and women are influenced, of course, by the mainstream culture's devaluation of domestic work and the power that accrues to the farm operator from his experience with outside institutions and greater control over financial affairs. An ideal of husbands' dominance over wives is also reaffirmed in church, through Baptist attention to scripture. But though many women are reluctant to verbalize contradictions to these norms, daily reality on many agrarian farms seems to be construed by both husbands and wives as a less hierarchical partnership. Said one woman, "The man is the provider, but not the boss." This perspective seems to reflect that the work women do is central to the quality of life that agrarian families cherish. Though my evidence suggests that the agrarian marital model downplays marital hierarchy, it is possible to argue that hierarchy is a separate dimension from the agrarian model of interdependence and shared financial responsibility for the family. Couples may vary in the extent to which they expect shared power or male dominance. My own data are not adequate to measure this aspect of farm family life, but it is clear that it would be incorrect to assume that all rural American families are patriarchal (Adams 1988; Fink 1992; Mann 1990). In general, women with an agrarian model expect a degree of shared decision making, especially with regard to family finances. Even when women have independent incomes from their jobs, money should be pooled and jointly allocated. This "shared pot" ideology of family finances reflects the agrarian perspective's less individualistic emphasis. Expectations of shared decision making with regard to other farm and home tasks, however, are balanced by the considerable autonomy in men's and women's separate spheres of work.

The industrial marital model emerges from a society of individual workers for whom labor and family are no longer embedded in a shared farm enterprise (Collier 1989). Ideally, the husband is the sole provider, and the wife is a full-time homemaker.[3] For farm families in Dodge County, the industrial perspective means that the husband has chosen farming as his life's work, but the wife may not share his personal commitment to the farm. "I have nothing to do with the farm; don't know nothing about it—I just live on it," said the wife of one young full-time farmer. Echoed another woman on a part-time farm, "I don't fool with the farm at all—housework is my job." Part of this distance from the farm is the wife's respect for her husband's autonomy in choosing his own work. As the family's "producer," the husband creates the opportunity for the wife to be the "consumption" expert. The woman's sphere of household consumption, especially in the context of rising incomes and greater discretionary spending, takes a central role in establishing the family's status in the community.

These assigned roles in the industrial orientation show less fluidity than in the agrarian perspective, and the proper performance of tasks carries more moral weight (Matthaei 1982:321). One part-time farmer expressed these expectations when asked if his wife's name was on the farm deeds. "The man should be the head of the family," he replied, and for him this should be reflected in having only his name on the deeds; the woman "should stay home and take care of the children." A full-time large scale farmer expressed his desire to "provide the living" as a matter of pride; "and if I couldn't, I hope folks would say I really *tried*." In the industrial model of marriage, women's earnings from jobs are more problematic because the successful breadwinner should provide sufficiently to keep his wife from "having to work off." It is recognized by both spouses that some women like to have a job because they want more stimulation than housework provides or want to buy "extra things" with a supplementary income. In these cases, the money she earns should be hers to spend entirely as she wishes and ideally is kept in a separate account as her discretionary fund. One affluent part-time farming woman with a full-time job said, "I have my money and half of his money; it's his responsibility to take care of the farm finances; my money is for extras."

The centrality of the husband's breadwinner role reflects a more hierarchical ordering of gender domains in the industrial model. Several older farm men assert that the husband ought to be "the leader, and the wife the follower." Said one wife, "I was always brought up with the idea of the man having more power." In other industrial model marriages there is more joint decision making, but the sense of joint partnership that typifies the agrarian model marriage is missing. Housewife and breadwinner spheres are not equally important, and final allocations of money are usually the husband's decision. As one husband put it, a wife's opinions are welcomed—"She can make *suggestions*"—but then he makes the final decision.

Women with a more industrial perspective express a range of attitudes toward the farm but are generally less emotionally attached. Some are hostile toward it, or at least reluctant to allow their families' lifestyles to be dependent on such an unreliable source of income. "Today, it's kind of embarrassing to admit you're a farmer," said one. Some enjoy a few aspects of the farm, but the strong personal satisfaction in the farm life expressed by many agrarian women is missing. Though her personal identity is not bound up with the farm, a woman may nevertheless say that farming is important to her: "It has to be important to me because my husband is out there." Knowing that her husband loves farming and has chosen it as a career, such a woman supports his decision, as might the wife of a plumber or a lawyer. Because these women recognize a special, compelling quality in the farm life and know their husbands "wouldn't be satisfied" with any other job, they try to be supportive, though they might personally have no interest in farming: "I don't love it, but I don't hate it. To be honest, I'd like to get out, but he wouldn't be satisfied." One wife of a part-time farmer is proud of what they have accomplished, but also says she hates the farm and would like to sell it to buy a retirement home.

For those women who aspire to the industrial model, farm work is degrading and entails a loss of femininity. "I always hated farm work," said one. Another woman watched from a window as cows got out of their pasture, but rather than try to shoo them back in and avoid any damage to them or to crops, she simply called her husband at work in town and told him of the problem. A woman with an agrarian perspective who works in town reported that the more industrial orientations of her coworkers make them "kind of look down on you" when she comes to work with dirty fingernails from farm activities. Many men share the conviction that women should not be involved in farm work. One large scale farm operator urged his wife to sell the farm if he should die first and to resist trying to operate it: "She's too *feminine*," he stressed. His statement reflects the greater value he places on her higher-status homemaker role than on farm continuity.

Companionship and Leisure

The desire for companionship, "family time," and shared recreation is another area in which these two marital models diverge. The more agrarian farm women cite family togetherness as one of the things they like about farming. Some parents and children drive around the farm together in the evening, looking at crops and checking on livestock. "It's very relaxing and makes you feel the family is together," reported one wife. Family time is found by some women at a hog sale or at daily family meals. These couples value the fact that farming lets a man stay close to home: "I like the way he's around all day—not off somewhere," say several women. Full-time homemakers especially appreciate farming's flexible hours.

For other women, who speak of loneliness because of their husbands' frequent absence, farming represents exactly the opposite. One middle-aged wife of a part-time farmer remembered how shocked she was early in her marriage to discover that farming meant her husband might be out until midnight and did not expect to share evenings with her. Recently, a young wife who did not grow up on a farm experienced a similar jolt; her husband told her she would "just have to adjust." She reports that she has become reconciled to his hours and has come to value seeing her husband during the day and having the opportunity to ride in the truck with him on occasion. The older woman says, "I enjoy seeing him enjoy farming."

Loss of companionship is a big complaint, especially among younger women. For a woman with a job, a farmer's late hours, especially on summer nights, means a couple has little shared time. She may need to go to bed early, while he stays up to irrigate. He may have more time to talk in the mornings, but she has to hurry off to work. Meals also have to be coordinated; she may want to eat quickly after work, but he comes in later. "Sometimes we eat at nine and sometimes at six— you just never know. I'm used to it, but it's aggravating sometimes."

For those women uninvolved with the farm, the lack of contact with their husbands violates their expectations about emotional closeness. Said one young wife with an industrial marital model whose husband operates a large partnership farm: "You have to play second place to the farm." Because of the daily pressures and the risks, "it takes a strong, strong man to be a farmer and a strong woman to put up with it." When her husband has to choose between the farm and his wife and children, she ends up feeling somewhat cheated: "What about *us*? It probably never crossed his mind that any of us might need him." For some couples, these different expectations remain a troublesome issue for years, and the women speak with bitterness and venom when asked about their attitudes toward farming. Other couples make their peace and come to "an understanding" about vacations, time for children, and other emotional issues.

Wives with a more industrial orientation often desire to leave the farm to vacation once or twice a year, camping or traveling. Vacations are considered necessary to an acceptable standard of living. Other leisure activities such as eating in restaurants or going to movies are also discussed. These attitudes toward recreation reflect values shared with many nonfarm Dodge Countians but can conflict with the farm's demands for careful livestock care and all-night irrigation at unpredictable intervals.

The Role of Husbands

This analysis so far has left out the husbands, but clearly marital ideologies are affected by the negotiations between spouses. Men often talk of the benefits of having a more active farm wife who helps out on the farm and supports its demands. One young farmer asserted his wife saved him more money by being at home and helping on the farm than she could earn in town. Other men forego these advantages in favor of an industrial model that upholds their status aspirations and sense of accomplishment. One large scale farmer reported that he and his wife agreed early on in their marriage that "my job is to make the living; her job is to make the living worthwhile."

Men's attitudes can constrain women's farm involvement. A husband who laughs at his wife when she attempts to learn to drive a tractor or who never speaks about farm issues to her can discourage an interest she may feel. One man never volunteers information to his wife and said, "She doesn't know how to question me." One woman who relishes her own active farm role criticized a male relative who farmed with his father and had less need of extra help for failing to include his wife in farm activities: "He should have made her a part of it." This is not an isolated example; women are often less involved with farm tasks on partnership farms. Several of these women explained that their husbands excluded them to simplify thorny family politics. Said one who wanted to be more involved: "You're second place, and you're not born into it, and you're not a part of it." However, usually when the men on partnership farms share an agrarian orientation, they make efforts to help wives learn unfamiliar tasks and expect shared farm work and decision making. On the other hand, some women on large partnership farms are peripheral to the farm and prefer it that way. ". . . And I'm not interested in getting into it," emphasized one older woman.

The Symmetrical Model

For the youngest group of farm women—those in Generation 3, in their twenties and early thirties—a variant of the agrarian marital model has emerged. I have called this a symmetrical orientation to marriage, based on work by Arlie Hochschild (1989) and William Everett and Sheila Everett (forthcoming). The symmetrical model is the most individualistic of the three, and its adherents expect that both men and women will seek personal satisfaction and a sense of achievement in work. Two individuals may choose to pool resources and operate a farm, but they do so to fulfill their own separate ends (Collier 1989:28). In this model, marital obligations and division of labor are more open to negotiation based on the preferences of the individuals involved.

The symmetrical orientation echoes the agrarian in many ways: both spouses are expected to be responsible for financial contributions to the family, though the wife may choose to be a full-time homemaker while children are young. The work of both men and women is considered important, though men may be able to earn more money, and decision making is meant to be shared. Domestic labor is regarded as the responsibility of both spouses, although, in fact, men's participation in household work is still rare. This division of labor is more likely to be seen as an unfortunate holdover from the past (Matthaei 1982) instead of as an ideal arrangement as in both the agrarian and industrial orientations. Women are less likely to take pride in their homemaking skills, though some are wistful that their hectic lives leave them little time for the cooking or mothering they remember from their own childhoods.

Couples with a symmetrical model, like agrarian couples, expect both spouses to share in supporting the family. "I'm not the type to sit at home and let the husband provide the living," one woman in her thirties said disdainfully. In some of these families, the husbands may say, "My wife makes the living." He recognizes that his efforts go to keeping the farm afloat, and though both spouses long for a less stressful farm economy, the wife's contribution to the household is not seen as diminishing his status. Many of these couples expect that two breadwinners are necessary, given the costs of living these days.

The symmetrical model of marriage also echoes the agrarian in that women embrace the farm and its activities with enthusiasm. This identification with the farm and enjoyment of it is seen, however, as a choice based on personal interests, not an automatic component of loyalty to the family. Individual preferences are the basis of the symmetrical marriage, as husbands and wives negotiate farm work, jobs, and child care, in an effort to allow each spouse personal satisfaction while keeping a farm and family afloat.

For some women, symmetrical ideals are an outgrowth of the agrarian cooperation of their parents. The model adds greater individualism and an expectation of off-farm work to women's roles. For others, a symmetrical orientation reflects a conscious rejection of the industrial traditional marriage they grew up with. Some men share a symmetrical perspective but have adopted it as "only fair." They reject their fathers' sole breadwinner model because it places women in an inferior position. Others see their mothers as always having contributed to the family and are comfortable with this modern symmetrical variant because they see it as a continuity with the gender roles of their natal families.

This more egalitarian marital model is found among Generation 3 women who have jobs they enjoy and a strong commitment to off-farm work. They value highly the opportunity to contribute to society outside of the home. Though levels of education vary, these women tend to have had more college education, by an average of two years. Some women in Generation 2 (in their mid-thirties and forties) share these same characteristics of education and jobs but do not expect to share breadwinning responsibilities with their husbands. Thus, the symmetrical model seems to be a reflection of the broader societal revolution in gender roles that has affected these younger women (Francesca Cancian 1987; Hochschild 1989). All made personal choices to support the farm life and to embrace its success, and in their marital roles, they are very similar to agrarian women. Because the numbers of symmetrical marriages are small, in the rest of this analysis, they will not be treated as a separate group but rather as a variant of the agrarian perspective. However, since the symmetrical marital model seems to be stronger in some other parts of the country, it might need to be separated from the agrarian perspective for some different kinds of analysis.

Emerging Marital Models in Dodge County History

The presence of the agrarian and industrial marital models in Dodge County today represents a historical process of economic, social, and ideological change. Declining agricultural and domestic labor demands, rising farm affluence, and the personal aspirations of individual women are all part of the interplay of these two perspectives. The "new" moral economy of the family connected to industrial society emerged to challenge the agrarian way of life much earlier in the Northeast of the United States. Mary Ryan (1981) has described this transition as a response to the expansion of capitalism in the early 1800s and the growth of an urban middle class. The increasing affluence of small town and urban families allowed them to adopt a more upper class marital model that had been in existence for centuries. Women shifted their identity from being "a profitable farm wife" (Barron 1990:16; Adams 1988:466) to being guardians of the family's status through domesticity, consumption, and community work.

Dodge Countians undoubtedly were aware of this industrial marital model at the end of the 1800s. From the North came contacts with national elites through the railroads, timber operations, naval stores industries, and commercial enterprises. Incoming migrants from the southern plantation belt were also familiar with many of these aspects of feminine gentility and domesticity (Fox-Genovese 1988). More affluent town families were better able to live out this new moral economy. Because some women on large agricultural estates still had central roles in farm and household production, the shift of women's attentions entirely to the sphere of consumption was more easily accomplished by families removed from agriculture. Women keenly recall that in the Depression era the industrial marital model was sufficiently widespread to be held up as a more prestigious and higher-status orientation. At a time when most farm women were active in agricultural labor and mired in the poverty of the era, however, few were able to aspire to such a lifestyle.

For Dodge County families on small farms prior to World War II, the agrarian ideology of partnership and shared labor continued to be both adaptive and necessary for survival (J. Jones 1985:106). Whether tenants or small owners, such farm families struggled with depleted soils and poor prices through shared efforts in the fields and homesteads. Men and women were dependent on each other for the production of food and its processing, as well as for its preparation. From making soap to sewing, women's production was essential. The financial pooling observed today among agrarian families reflects the realities of the Depression era when, as we saw in chapter 1, few families had the surplus to allow women a separate discretionary fund. Some writers emphasize a patriarchal family structure on small farms during this period (Sachs 1983), but the fact that the majority of Dodge County families owned no land and moved regularly and that men faced various political impediments in voting and in the exercise of their legal rights suggests that masculine power may have been correspondingly weakened. Although there were undoubtedly pressures toward patriarchy and strains over resource allocations to men's and women's domains, memories of a less hierarchical family distribution of power may accurately reflect greater interdependence of husbands and wives in agrarian families.

For more affluent farm families in the Depression era, resources were available to permit adoption of the higher-status industrial patterns. Hired hands, tenant families, and household help provided the labor to free wealthier farm women from agricultural work and from much of the drudgery of domestic work as well. Some women embraced the homemaker ideal as part of a desire to leave the hardships of rural conditions and a preference for the comforts of town lifestyles.

As farm life was transformed after World War II, women's roles in Dodge County underwent changes that had also occurred in the North, though considerably earlier (Adams 1988; Sachs 1983). Domestic work was revolutionized: cooking, laundry, cleaning, and sewing became much less arduous with the advent of paved roads, electricity, indoor plumbing, gas stoves, washing machines, and purchased clothing. Time spent performing tasks such as ironing was reduced by the introduction of synthetic fabrics, and vacuum cleaners replaced twig brooms. Mechanization of farm tasks and federal programs brought greater affluence to those families who stayed in farming and reduced the need for women's farm labor as well. More and more farm women aspired to achieve the industrial ideal of a homemaker lifestyle. As noted in chapter 2, the extension service and the mainstream national culture both emphasized this consumer role and deemphasized women's roles as "farmers" (Fink 1986b; Adams 1988). For some women, a changing relationship to technology and production fostered a different consciousness about farm life (Fink 1986a). As men became specialists in machinery and women who did not have such skills were no longer able to help out with farm tasks, female identification with the farm lessened. Women's own farm enterprises—the production of chickens, eggs, cream, and butter—declined as well. As women's productive skills were no longer needed, a man might marry a woman from a nonfarm background without jeopardizing the farm's success.

The changes in marital models can be seen through the generations of Dodge County women and intertwine with status aspirations, social class, and farm background as well. Since the generations identified in previous chapters are linked to the date of farm establishment, for table 6-2 I have coded women by generations based on chronological age, since values have more to do with peers and societal influences than the point at which husbands chose to start farming. Women in Generation 1 are in their fifties and sixties, Generation 2 women are in their mid-thirties and forties, and the youngest generation includes women from twenty to thirty-four. To code each woman in the study as having a more agrarian or more industrial marital model, I found that family financial responsibility, personal aspirations with regard to the farm, and emotional attachment to the farm life were the three most useful dimensions.[4]

The more senior women on the more typical middle-sized farms are much more

Table 6-2. Marital Models by Farm Type and Generation

	Percent Agrarian	Percent Industrial
Full-time farms		
Generations 1 and 2 (ages 35–70)		
Large scale (n = 16)	44	56
Medium scale (n = 19)	79	21
Generation 3 (ages 20–34)		
Large scale (n = 13)	69	31
Medium scale (n = 12)	33	67
Part-time farms		
Investors (n = 6)	33	67
Standard (n = 23)	52	48
All farm women (n = 89)	56	44

likely to support agrarian ideals (79% of Generations 1 and 2). The few in this cohort who hold more industrial marital models today were either active in jobs off the farm for much of their lives or their husbands had been nonfarmers or part-time farmers for a substantial portion of their marriages. The women over thirty-five from large farms are more evenly divided between the marital models (44% are agrarian). Some seek the more prestigious housewife role, but others from elite farm families are as committed to the farm and involved in its work as those on smaller farms. Women from more affluent farm backgrounds show the same diversity of marital models.[5]

Among Generation 3 women, farm scale also seems to play a role in determining marital model and is linked to status aspirations. As farms declined in number in Dodge County during the 1950s and 1960s, the industrial ideology became not only the middle class ideal in town but common in rural areas as well. The younger women on Dodge County farms today who emphasize their ignorance of farm tasks ("Don't ask *me* . . .") are claiming the higher-status domestic role. Many of the wealthier Generation 3 women, though new to the farm, have nevertheless embraced agrarian ideals and desire a connection to the operation.

Generation 3 women on medium scale farms are twice as likely to hold an industrial ideal, a fact that may reflect their more tenuous connection to status and affluence and an aspiration to the more traditionally elite gender roles. The desire to rely on the husband as the primary breadwinner may also relate to actual earning power, since their lower levels of education on average may reduce their access to higher-paying jobs. Unfortunately, the numbers of employed Generation 3 women are too small to test this relationship between marital model and earning power.

As table 6-2 shows, young women on large scale farms are not reluctant to embrace an agrarian ideal and therefore see no loss of status in this orientation. These farms are affluent enough—together with off-farm income in some cases— to provide a desired middle class standard of living. Some of these agrarian women are more highly educated jobholders, whose marital models follow the symmetrical model.

In sum, neither class background nor farm scale neatly correlates with marital model. For older women from more elite backgrounds, there is considerable diversity, with a slight majority tending toward an industrial perspective. For younger elite women, the pattern is reversed, and more privileged women are likely to embrace the farm. This flip-flop of generational patterns seems to reflect the changing affluence of the farm life as well as new opportunities for women in the work force and changing societal ideologies about gender roles.

Farm women are much less likely to be drawn from agricultural backgrounds today, and this trend is also connected to marital orientation. Of Generation 1 women, 83 percent are from farm families, but this figure falls to 59 percent of Generation 2 and to only 28 percent of Generation 3. This decline is perhaps connected to the fact that agrarian marital orientations fell from two-thirds of all Generation 1 women to a half of those in Generation 3.[6]

Black women participate in both the agrarian and industrial marital models with statements and contributions that fit within the same range as white women. Because the numbers of black women in the study are small, they cannot be described separately without presenting details that might identify individuals. More black women are older and from smaller farms and hence tend to be agrarian in their perspectives, but some women aspire to the higher-status industrial model and its homemaker role. Several of these women rejoiced that they had escaped from the rigors of agricultural field work, but many black women express strong positive feelings about farm life. Several downplayed their hard work on the farm today, noting how much easier their lives are now than they were in their youths. With regard to the symmetrical variant of the agrarian marital model, however, there were no cases among the black women in the study. Those who had enjoyed their jobs and who had been committed to their work were all older and articulated a more industrial perspective. All the African American women in the study either grew up on farms or remember their parents doing farm labor.

Models of Money Management

Management of family finances is an area in which the ideal roles posed by the two marital models can be seen in sharp contrast. John Bennett's research on Canadian farmers found that one of the central challenges to successful farm management is the balancing of demands from the farm and from the household (1982). The agrarian and industrial marital models in Dodge County lead to different expectations with regard to these husband-wife interactions.

Because the agrarian ideology assumes the goals of the household unit are shared, contributions of money, labor, or savings are all valued toward the family's success. Where there is income from the wife's job, the money is usually pooled toward a "shared pot." In the case of one couple that was entirely dependent on farm income, the wife (now a widow) reported that her husband saw her as integral to farm success and money management decisions. "He knew I contributed, and when there was something left over at the end of the year, he'd say: 'You've been needing a new stove—here, let's go look.' He always wanted me to be a part of it." A woman with a part-time job explained that she and her husband pool their incomes by dividing up expenses. Her money buys appliances, linens, and clothing; his money goes toward the car, the groceries, and the farm. She sees this division of labor as the same as if they both had off-farm jobs. "We're working together," she stressed several times, each paying for a part of the whole. "Maybe I'm old-fashioned, but I think marriage is fifty-fifty, and you both do what you can to make things run more smoothly."

Family finances are rarely discussed as an issue of tension in agrarian households. In some cases, income levels do not permit much latitude in consumption decisions, and in other cases, couples are older and priorities for expenditures have long since been worked out. Though accounts may emphasize the ideal of cooperation and downplay actual conflicts, they also reflect shared priorities. One older agrarian woman asserted that if the family puts a desire for a car ahead of the farm, it may end up bankrupt: "Farming has to come first or else you'll suffer." Several women with an agrarian marital model stressed that they shopped as a couple and "always worked closely with each other."

In the industrial marital model, the breadwinner role is expected to have more control over financial decisions. Said an older woman on a large, sophisticated farm, "If it involves very much money, it's his decision, because I'm not capable." Some couples with an industrial perspective emphasize that it is the husband's domain to make financial allocations but acknowledge considerable interaction prior to the final decision. One woman on a small part-time farm keeps the books and notifies her husband when a bill needs to be paid. She knows a calf will be sold to pay it and may even have an idea which calf should be sold. She informs her husband when they can afford to trade in a car or truck for a new one without exceeding these budgetary limits. Though they both agree the husband has the right to allocate money differently, she admits that he usually follows her suggestions.

Husbands who expect to be sole providers are often uncomfortable when their wives work off the farm because it makes them feel they are "falling down on the job." When wives choose to work off the farm out of personal preference, however, the husband's success as a breadwinner is not challenged. Her money is seen by both spouses as a discretionary fund to be used for "extras." In the difficult times of the 1980s, the use of this discretionary fund was more often seen by women as "for the family," not "personal extras." When asked, husbands often admit that their wives' income is spent on college costs, children's clothes, and other household expenses. A man may shore up his perception of his breadwinner role by expressing complete ignorance of his wife's expenditures: "I don't know *what* she does with her money, I really don't!" exclaimed one husband. Though most couples with an industrial model aspire to its financial individualism, only 12 percent of the families studied had financial situations sufficiently strong to enable wives to keep their income for their own personal spending.

Each view of the management of marital finances claims a certain moral righteousness. Women who hold to the higher-status industrial model protest that their money or their contribution "is not really needed." If it were, they would "help out." Agrarian women who expect to contribute to the family consider a wife with her own discretionary fund to be "selfish." Keeping separate accounts imposes an individualistic autonomy within the supposedly shared domain of the family. Several women with agrarian orientations reported that their coworkers in town ridiculed them or called them "stupid" because they contribute to household bills or to the farm. Those with an industrial perspective say, "It's like throwing money away. . . . You're liable to lose it." Women with a more agrarian orientation reply, "But it all comes back to me in the end!" A medium scale farm woman who reported that a friend had told her she was "crazy to put my money in the farm" argued, "I'd rather have the house paid off than have pretty things in it." The distance from the farm found among women with an industrial perspective is expressed by a woman who works as a clerk who claims that she is willing to "help out" during the farm crisis to buy groceries, pay some household bills, and buy most of the family's clothes, but she does not want her money to go into the farm because "my husband is a talented man and could do lots of other things and make a good living. He chooses to farm, so let him do it!"

This industrial perspective clearly inhibits a farm family from throwing all its resources into an effort to save the farm. Desires on the part of both husband and wife for higher status and more affluent consumption standards conflict with the necessity for a "tighter belt" when farm profits decrease. On the other hand, women who hold to the "shared pot" ethic sometimes were very uncomfortable when discussing other ways of handling family finances. Their tension can be seen as an awareness that the pervasive individualistic values of a market society threaten their lifetime orientations. The market-based practice of keeping separate funds not only devalues their family contributions, since most are unpaid or paid less than men, but also underlines a different definition of family "success." Their commitment to the farm and to the joint family enterprise can be criticized by the industrial perspective as "stupid," and their view of success becomes muddied by the question, "Whose farm is it?" Where domestic and farm domains are integrally linked and both valued, such questions do not arise. The agrarian family woman is understandably agitated when discussing such intrusive values, and her agitation betrays the extent to which she was already struggling with the increasing dominance of the industrial perspective.

Given these connections between marital models, frugality, and consumption patterns, it should come as no surprise that the cautious and ambitious management styles described in the previous chapter are commonly parallel to marital models. Though not all spouses see eye to eye or share values, it is reasonable to expect more harmony than dissonance, and the Dodge County data support this view. In eight out of ten cases, women with an agrarian marital model are married to a husband with a cautious, debt-averse farm management style. Women with an industrial model are married to ambitious farm managers in 68 percent of cases (significant at the .001 level; chi-square = 11.5). Therefore, money management in the family is often echoed in money management on the farm.

Jobs and Women's Farm Work

Though differences in financial management reflect the diversity of the two marital models in Dodge County, women's work on the farm and off shows a dramatic transformation across all types of farm families. Farm women are now more likely to have a job—full-time or part-time—than to be a full-time homemaker, and this

Table 6-3. Off-Farm Employment of Farm Women

	Percent with Off-Farm Jobs
Full-time farms (n = 65)	63
Part-time farms (n = 35)	57
Large scale full-time (n = 29)	66
Medium scale full-time (n = 36)	61
Agrarian role orientation (n = 49)	53
Industrial role orientation (n = 39)	64
Generation 1 (n = 29)	45
Generation 2 (n = 42)	68
Generation 3 (n = 27)	67
Total (n = 102)	61

change has brought much-needed cash into financially strapped families. It has also created tensions as farm families worry whether they are losing more than they are gaining by this choice. Though we saw in chapter 3 that opportunities for employment for women in Dodge County came more slowly than for men, farm women who were interviewed never complained that they wanted to find a job but were unable to do so. Low wages were a common complaint, but most women who want a job find one and stay with it for long periods.

The average farm woman in Dodge County makes $13,000 a year, a figure that combines the few part-time jobs with the majority of full-time jobs. Among older (Generation 1) women, incomes between $5,000 and $9,000 are common, in part because some work fewer than forty hours a week but also because their jobs in small businesses, factories, and child care are not high paying. In Generation 3, a larger proportion of teachers and civil service workers earn salaries as high as $25,000, though this level is not the norm.

Table 6-3 shows the percentage of women working off the farm during the study period, including those women laid off temporarily and those who worked all their lives but recently retired. Although older women are less likely than Generations 2 and 3 to have a job, a large percentage (45%) work off the farm. The link between age and employment is, however, statistically significant at the .01 level (chi-square = 8.82).

Though 61 percent of farm women have jobs, only 43 percent indicated they would prefer this type of work. When asked what their ideal daily work would be, nearly half said homemaking and 9 percent said they would rather do full-time farm work. The fact that four in ten would rather be employed reveals the extent to which rural industrialization and the availability of jobs for women outside the home have given many women an opportunity for work that they prefer to traditional homemaking activities. Another two out of ten farm women have taken jobs to help out the family and the farm, though they would rather stay at home.

African American women in Dodge County have had fewer opportunities during the crisis to help out the family through off-farm work. Historically, opportunities for jobs outside of domestic work have been rare, as we saw in chapter 2 (J. Jones 1985). As a result, the majority of black women in the study (79%) do not work outside the home, which reflects both the lack of lucrative opportunities available and the achievement that it represents to be able to avoid wage work. As noted in chapter 3, black families who are property owners are a privileged minority in Dodge County, and their ability to be self-employed is not easily sacrificed. Even in this group, however, the desire to provide additional benefits to children led some women to take work off the farm during the crisis.

Several men and women in Dodge County commented on the effects of jobs on women's status and self-concept. Jobs are almost always located in town, and therefore a woman usually has her own vehicle for transportation. A new wardrobe is common, and though women rarely discuss this aspect of jobs, they clearly enjoy the opportunity to dress with more sophistication. For women who work as cooks or in factories, clothing is less an issue than the discretionary spending made possible by a salary. Whether buying children a new pair of jeans or running shoes or providing the family with a new couch, employed women have opportunities to express an independent sense of style that many appreciate.

A woman's status and power within the family may also expand as she gains new skills, self-confidence, and new contacts with the public world "out there." Women who work as clerks or in banks or other businesses become familiar with financial dealings that used to be the province of farm men. Interaction with townsfolk and assimilation of their knowledge can make farm women more respected at home. Reported one woman from a moderately large farm, "When I got a job in town my children learned Mom isn't stupid after all." To the extent that parents and children have absorbed the contemporary devaluation of the homemaker role and adopted a market approach to the value of labor, jobs give women greater value.

Most often, men and women emphasize that women take jobs to help the family, saying, "It just takes two nowadays." A few women and men who hold a symmetrical marital model acknowledge that a wife may prefer off-farm work to homemaking and that she should pursue what is best for her as an individual. For the more agrarian families, the woman's income also provides a cushion that allows the farm to experience lower profits without concern for household expenses. For the industrial family, the additional income is seen with more ambivalence. Whether women see their jobs as temporary or permanent, appropriate or inappropriate, they interpret their efforts as contributions to their families' overall welfare and long-term success. Spouses acknowledge their desire for higher incomes to keep up with the rising costs of living, and the pressures of new lifestyles, as noted in chapter 5, are part of these financial calculations.

When the family's desire for greater affluence requires the wife to have a job, it creates a conflict with traditional notions of proper child care, and farm couples wonder—as do many other Americans—if more money is really what is best for the family. Many Dodge County women with jobs also have young children and have chosen to place them in daycare.[7] Several parents worried that their children became ill more often in such settings, but a more common concern is the way jobs restrict time with children. The larger issues of how children are socialized—how future generations will turn out—are a primary source of anxiety for farm families. Although one woman admitted that she feels some pressure to share financial responsibilities with her husband, she would rather "do without" than get a job and "face problems with my children" because she was not at home with them. "Lots of people use their work as a way not to deal with children on a day-to-day basis," accused a middle-aged homemaker.

Ambivalence about changes in child rearing, however, is not limited to families in which women take off-farm work. One full-time homemaker worried that her children had grown up less independent and less capable of making decisions themselves because of her own willingness "to do for them." When she was a teenager, she had done most of the family cooking because her mother had a job; she recently was shocked to realize that her daughters had finished high school and did not even know how to make biscuits. Her story reflects aspects of the industrial marital model combined with a middle class lifestyle in which the work load of domestic tasks (as well as farm tasks) has declined so that children are no longer needed to help. In the case of her children, the change in the household economy has limited their domestic skills and altered their relationship to the family.

In addition to increases in paid employment, women's lives in Dodge County have seen dramatic changes in work on the farm. Today, most women do very little regular farm labor, and some do not even help out on an occasional basis. This decreased involvement in farm labor is not limited to women with jobs, women who grew up in town, or women with an industrial marital model. Across the board, most farm women do not have a major role in agricultural production. When asked in general terms whether they participate in farm work, only a third of full-time and part-time farm women agreed that they "do farm work" (32 of 95 women). This level of farm involvement is greater for full-time farmers (40%) than for part-time farm families (22%), but it is notable that a majority say they are not involved in farm labor.

To test these self-perceptions, I adapted the 1980 National Farm Women's Survey (Rosenfeld 1985) to ask the women in the study whether they carried out a series of farm production tasks or farm helper tasks on a regular or occasional basis.[8] Of eight farm production tasks (such as field work with machinery, marketing farm production, and making farm purchases), 59 percent reported carrying out none of these tasks in the previous two to three years. Only 11 percent said they did three or more tasks (the mean was 0.9 tasks). Women with an agrarian orientation showed a slightly greater involvement with farm production (a mean of 1.1 tasks, not a statistically significant difference), but nearly half (49%) reported doing no such tasks. Women on full-time and part-time farms show only minor differences in farm work levels.

Dodge County women are more likely to be engaged in farm helper tasks, such as occasionally helping out with field labor, animal care, or truck driving at harvest. Of six such tasks, the average number performed is 2.5, and only 15 percent of women say they do none of these tasks. Women with an agrarian orientation average 2.7 tasks, and only 4 percent report that they do no farm helper tasks.

There is, of course, considerable variation because a few women love farm work and do a substantial amount. One highly active young mother on a medium-sized farm says, "I want to be part of the farm and you have to be out there in it." Occasionally, she does field work with machinery (weeding, mowing hay, or harvesting), regularly drives trucks at harvest, and often does field labor such as hoeing peanuts. In spite of these contributions, she does no government program management, makes no farm purchases, and is not involved with marketing or animal care. Most often, women who do only one or two farm production tasks help with hauling at harvest and care for animals.

An example of a woman who reported four helper tasks is a young woman who claims that she occasionally helps with harvest hauling, irregularly does minor work with the hogs, and does a little bookkeeping. Regularly, she drives to town for machinery and parts and does other farm errands, the most common helper task since even women with jobs can run errands while they are in town. Occasional animal care and harvest help are the next most frequently reported types of work.

Women's tasks on farms are affected by their husbands' preferences and the farm's labor needs. In addition, some women choose deliberately to avoid learning some tasks (bookkeeping was mentioned by two) to avoid the possibility of that work being added to their already heavy load. Others are content to do the bookkeeping because they have more education than their husbands or because they enjoy the task. It is interesting to note, however, that in spite of the popular conception that farm women keep the books, only 31 percent of Dodge County women on part-time and full-time farms say they do bookkeeping on a regular basis, and nearly half (48%) say they never do bookkeeping and accounts.

Domestic Work

In addition to work on and off the farm, Dodge County women have primary responsibility for household tasks, and the burden of a "double day" at a job and at home is exhausting for many. Virtually all Dodge County farm women do their own domestic work. Said one woman who does daily care of hogs as well as housework after a full day working off the farm, "I work eight hours there [at her job] and then come home and do eight hours here. I'm *tired*." Meals, cleaning, laundry, and child care make up the bulk of this domestic work. Many farm women spend a month or more doing heavy canning and freezing, storing a year's supply of vegetables and soups for future meals. Though the long hours of domestic work that were typical of the Depression era have been greatly lightened, the effort of cleaning up after a farmer, living where mud and dust make housework an endless battle, and providing the hearty meals that characterize the local diet is easily a full-time job. Most husbands contribute very little time to domestic tasks, even in situations where both spouses have off-farm work. There are perhaps half a dozen exceptions in the sample of over a hundred households interviewed. Wives who insist get some help with cleaning or laundry, though children are more likely to be pressed into service than husbands.

For full-time homemakers, both agrarian and industrial, the nurturing work of creating meals and running the household is often described as a source of satisfaction and accomplishment. "It's a good feeling to sit down to eat and know that everything on the table is provided by your own hands," said one part-time farm woman. A young but highly committed agrarian woman said: "When I make a breakfast of grits and biscuits and sausage and my family leaves the table full, I feel *proud*. I have a sense of pride serving my family, but that's gone from America. Women today take the kids to McDonald's instead. Or buy a cupcake from the grocery. Not that that's a bad cupcake, but you can't have the same pride," she concluded.

This woman, like several others, expresses her pleasure in caring for children, keeping a clean home, and providing daily meals but recognizes that these tasks are devalued in the media-generated world that increasingly penetrates rural America. For some women, this devaluation of the homemaker role presents a much-welcomed opportunity to get "out" and join the world of paid employment. But for others, it represents a painful contradiction to the values by which they have oriented their lives. Nurturing emotional bonds among family members, taking care of the elderly and the sick, and providing the elaborate meals that bring together the family three times a day are part of the fabric of what is valued about farm life.

Whose Farm Is It?

Whether the farm is seen as a joint family enterprise or the husband's career is reflected in the extent to which the wife considers herself—and is considered under the law—a co-owner of the farm estate. The marital conception of the farm as a joint estate is rarely reflected in the farm's deeds and debts. Only a third of farm owner couples include the wife's name on any deeds; about half of these are cases in which the land in question was inherited by the wife. Legal responsibility for farm debts is also carried exclusively by men for 75 percent of all married farmers. In most of the cases in which the wife is a co-debtor, her name is included because it appears on the farm title. In a few other cases, the wife's job helps to back up the loan.

Concerns about women's legal rights to farm property have surfaced particularly in the Midwest, where farm women's groups have protested that wives' contributions to the farm are sometimes discounted in divorce proceedings. Income and labor invested in the operation have at times been ignored in the division of property. Legal title in the husband's name alone and the customary role of the man as "the farmer" can make farm women's contributions invisible under the law (Fink 1986b:207).

I did not hear these concerns about legal titles or property rights expressed in
Dodge County. As summed up by one woman, "What's mine is his and what's his
is mine." In fact, Georgia law has traditionally recognized the wife's investment
in a farm held only in her husband's name and assures her inheritance of a share
upon her husband's death at least equal to the share her children receive. Women's
rights in the situation of divorce have not been so clear, but most farm women in
Dodge County that I talked to felt secure that the "family farm" was indeed a joint
estate from which both they and their children would benefit.

Dodge County men echo their wives in seeing the farm as part of the marital estate, whether or not it is legally registered as such: "What's mine is hers,
anyway." They also assert that they want to protect their wives from the financial
vulnerability of farming. As a man with a more industrial model explained, "The
farm was my risk and my endeavor."

There are relatively few cases of divorce among Dodge County farm couples,
but data from these cases do not support men's and women's assertions that the
farm is a jointly held estate. By 1989, there were thirteen cases of divorce among
the full-time and part-time farm families in the study, and in only one case did
the wife receive a share of the farm or its value as part of the settlement. In four
cases, the farm had been inherited from the husband's family, and he retained the
entire farm after the divorce. It might be argued that the wife's efforts in these
cases did not contribute to obtaining the farm and thus it was appropriate that she
not receive a share of the property. In four other cases, the couple purchased land
during the marriage, and again this land remained with the husband. In the final
four cases, no farmland was owned at the time of the divorce.

Women's property rights in divorce cases seem not to be an issue in Dodge
County for several reasons. First, divorce is still quite rare among farm couples.
(Prior to 1982, there were only three divorces among all the men and women on
full-time farms in the study.) In addition, some divorced women see farming as
the husband's career and are not interested in claiming a share of the estate. Some
seek a divorce to get away from the farm and want to put conflicts with the husband's family far behind. Finally, some women's lack of concern for the possible
loss of their rights to property seems to reflect a general disdain for farming and
a judgment that the property is not really worth all that much anyway. Especially
for women with a more industrial marital ideology, their attitudes toward legal
rights reflect their expectation of support by a husband rather than involvement in
an equal partnership in a family enterprise.

The farm crisis has brought these legal issues into sharp focus for families facing
hard times. In half a dozen cases, wives of farmers forced out of business have

been able to buy back the farms in their own names. The strategy to keep the wife's name off of deeds and debts was successful, since after bankruptcy or foreclosure, the wife's credit rating was not affected. She was able to arrange bank financing in her own name to save the home or the farm or to invest in a new business.

Such legal processes, however, sometimes violate the couple's industrial marital model. One such woman whose family finances are now entirely in her name protests that "he's really the breadwinner" and emphasizes that her husband does the primary work that supports the household. Women who have gotten loans to buy houses, buy back foreclosed farmland, or refinance farm debts feel a new, personal involvement with the farm and with the family's finances. Especially if they are unhappy with their husband's choice to farm, such a role may be unwelcome. For a few agrarian women, their new legal autonomy is a facade that must be adopted to help the family. "It doesn't mean anything," they assert, though it intrudes an individualistic legal structure into the heart of the family farm. It is ironic that a legal separation of husbands' and wives' interests on deeds and loans has enabled some women—whether or not they are pleased with the opportunity—to obtain a second chance to keep the farm in business.

Moral Economies and Women's Opposition to Farming

Considering this background of the changing moral economies of Dodge County farm families, the reasons why some women express anger and hostility toward the farm are clearer. A quarter of the women from full-time farms (and 37% from part-time farms) are negative about farming and opposed to their husbands' preference to farm. This means, of course, that a majority are generally positive about farming, and even if they are personally uninvolved or ambivalent about the farm, at least they encourage and support their husbands.

The negative assessments reveal the interaction of past status, present realities, and aspirations. Especially for women in Generations 2 and 3 who desire upward mobility in an industrial definition of success, the farm's fluctuating income and high risk pose a substantial threat not only to the family's social status but to the woman's own personal sense of accomplishment and obligation to the family. Some Dodge Countians refer to women's anxieties in this regard as a simple desire to accumulate possessions. Said one husband, "Farmers have always been poor, and [women] think they won't be able to have the things they want." Some women echo this assessment and emphasize the "selfishness" of negative attitudes toward farming: "They have to give up new clothes or their own money to spend on what they want."

The analysis of marital models presented in this chapter allows us to go beyond such a judgment of materialistic individualism to see several other dimensions to women's opposition to farming. First, it is the *family's* loss of income, and consequent loss of status, that energizes most women. A desire to give children what they want, what their peers have, is a part of this frustration. A new house or a new car marks the success of the family unit as well as contributing to the greater comfort of all. One woman from a large scale farm in deep financial trouble reported her attempt to encourage her husband to quit farming: "I have too much ambition. I want things—*nice* things—and I don't want to suffer for the farm. It's not worth it. I told him: When you're fifty, *if you live that long*, you'll look back and say 'Why did I put myself through this just for that piece of land out there?' "

Men who share their wives' frustration with farming's poor return sometimes emphasize that the farm is a long-term investment. They value the inheritance they will be able to pass on to their children and point to the family's accumulation of equity and future income. Wives sometimes reject this long-term view because they perceive that limiting household consumption in the middle of the life cycle, as children are reaching their expensive years of adolescence, affects courtship possibilities that might lead to the marriage of their children into families of desirable status and means. Children who are bitter about family poverty may also seek to marry early and perhaps less carefully. Even more important, strained finances may hurt a child's chances for college or technical training, a major loss in future earning power.

Thus, especially for the industrial orientation, a woman's greater ambivalence about farming reflects her primary role as mother and reproducer of the household. Getting her children started off well in life, especially seeing them educated and properly married, is a central component of a woman's success. The farm can hurt this process by making children look poorer than they "really" are. By the time the farm is paid off, the children have long since left home, and one of the main purposes of consumption—the enjoyment by family—has passed. Thus, women's commitment to the upward mobility of their children may place them squarely in opposition to the farm's need for frugality.

A second dimension of women's hostility to the farm is the struggle to balance the household budget that falls to the wife as the "consumer" specialist. One woman, answering first that "seeing God's wonders" was one of the things she liked about farming, used the same reason in explaining what she did not like about farming: "Seeing God's wonders, including fields burned off and a loss, and thinking about how can I put this bill off, and find enough to pay this one to get him off me—and put that bill off." As Lillian Rubin (1976) found among California couples, farm women often bear the painful brunt of creditors' calls and grapple with stretching the family's income to cover necessities.

A final aspect of women's hostility to the farm involves the increased pressures of the crisis that further threaten goals of family togetherness and shared activities. "Time for the family" and "vacations together" are among the first casualties in the battle with droughts and low profits. These industrial model goals for family time not only conflict with the long hours demanded by farming but represent a means to social status harder for farmers to achieve. The women whose views of marriage conform to the agrarian marital model join their husbands in bragging about how many years they have gone without a vacation because of farm demands. The heavy work load of balancing job, family, and household tasks affects women from all marital perspectives, but the shared commitment to the success of the farm that is part of the agrarian model makes these farm women more able to focus their blame, anger, and disappointment on bad weather and poor prices instead of on their husbands and their choice of farming as an occupation.

Conclusion

Just as chapter 5 concluded that there is no consensus on prudent farm management today, there is also no agreement on proper roles for husbands and wives on Dodge County farms. The changing regional economy has brought with it a changing moral economy of the family and new values with regard to individualistic choice and work autonomy, commitment to the farm enterprise, and personal aspirations. Women have withdrawn from productive activities on the farm, and 61 percent have turned to employment off the farm. These changes in work roles threaten certain cherished aspects of homemaking, child rearing, and farm life. Ideals about the management of family finances also show the impact of greater individualism and the decline of a commitment to a marital "shared pot." Such desires for autonomy bring new satisfactions to women and new opportunities for personal fulfillment but also challenge the coordination of farm and household, especially in a prolonged crisis period.

Some of women's increasing distance from the farm can be attributed to the southern context, where there has perhaps emerged a greater status emphasis on separating women from the farm, especially from farm labor. This emphasis reflects the greater rural stratification of this region, the deeper and more recent poverty of the sharecropper era, the more labor-intensive cotton and tobacco culture, and the disdain for manual labor that accompanied the institution of slavery (Daniel 1985; Kirby 1987).

In other ways, these changes within the farm family are not unique to the South. The work demands of a particular commodity system are always important in constraining ideal gender roles, and throughout America, rowcrop and livestock production creates less demand for women's labor than dairy production, vegetable or truck cropping, or tobacco farming (Daniel 1985; Sachs 1983; Simpson et al. 1988).[9] Also, as farming becomes more mechanized and women are less knowledgeable about the farm and its machines, they are less able to participate in the operation.

Some of the alternatives encoded in these marital models echo wider value conflicts within American society. Individualism and its place in career choice, money management, child rearing, and other aspects of homemaking are debated issues in cities and suburbs as well. Definitions of "a good husband" and "a good wife" reveal shifting aspirations and emphases throughout American society. The materialistic pressures of industrial society are troubling to couples in diverse walks of life, and a desire to preserve (or create) an alternative value system energizes many who are not bound up in the household economy of the family farm.

The Dodge County data suggest that these marital models influence ways of defining success, which in turn affect how money is spent and how families respond to hard times. One young man on a struggling but ultimately successful large scale farm testified that his wife's "moral support over the years has been more important than anything else in keeping me going." His wife agrees with other women who embrace an agrarian ideology and who say farming is the best life, "not because it can offer you luxuries, but because it gives you some of the best life has to offer." Reflecting an alternative, less materialist definition of success, these women share a vision of marriage and its linkage to a joint family enterprise, run in a less ambitious, less competitive farming style. For other women who lean toward the homemaker role of the industrial marital model, the farm may provide the affluence necessary to meet their status goals, but during a recession, their sense of personal success is more at risk.

SEVEN

Boom, Bust, and Insolvency:

The Farm Crisis and Its Impact

on Farm Families

The early 1970s were boom years in the farm economy, but conditions then deteriorated in the second half of the decade. Droughts hammered the Coastal Plain of Georgia and farm incomes plummeted. Dodge County farmers responded with a series of strategies to cut back failing enterprises, earn more money, and safeguard the farm. For some, management styles began to shift as well. The institutions surrounding farmers, particularly the banks, other lenders, and federal agricultural programs, responded in a series of efforts to help farmers survive. Some of this aid was ultimately harmful, as debt levels rose, and some operators were forced out of business. This chapter recounts the history of the farm crisis as seen from the perspective of Dodge County farmers and describes as well the emotional cost to farm families.

In the history of the boom and bust years of the 1970s and 1980s, we can see the consequences of trends described in previous chapters. Capital intensification raised the costs of annual operation and made farmers more vulnerable in an economic downturn. The increasing bureaucratization of farming and the intrusion of lenders and farm experts played a role in limiting farmers' responses to the crisis and also in making them feel less responsible for their decisions when things turned out badly. In the accounts of Dodge County families in stress during the crisis, we can see the different agrarian and industrial meanings of success, in farm management, in household consumption, and in marital roles. The hardships of the bust years forced Dodge County families to reassess their goals as well as their strategies to reach those goals. Throughout this chapter, we will see the power of national and international markets as they shifted the ground on which farmers tried to stand. The integration of the Dodge County economy with these markets has brought new affluence to farmers, but in the 1980s it seemed that it might take this prosperity away.

The boom years of U.S. agriculture began in 1972 with the so-called "Russian wheat deal" in which the Soviet Union purchased eighteen million tons of cereals from the United States (Schertz 1979:48). One-fifth of the total U.S. wheat supply was sold, and prices more than doubled. Other countries increased purchases of U.S. agricultural commodities as well, both in compensation for poor weather conditions and in response to the declining value of the dollar. "Many farmers received incomes never imagined before" (ibid.), and Dodge County participated in this boom. One young man who farmed a hundred acres for the first time in 1973 cleared a full $25,000 profit. "It set us on fire," he reported. Nationwide, farm incomes rose an unprecedented 39 percent in one year (Brooks, Stucker, and Bailey 1986:392), and these trends attracted an expanded cohort of new operators, as discussed in chapter 2.

Booming farm profits fueled the ambitious management style throughout the United States, and expansion of farm acreage and investments in facilities and equipment resulted (Friedburger 1988). Tax regulations also encouraged farmers to reduce taxable income through these investments. In Dodge County, as throughout the country, real estate prices rose and rents increased. Inflation became a national concern and pushed farmers to invest sooner, rather than later, to avoid paying higher prices. Inflation joined with the boom in prices to make farmers much wealthier, at least on paper. Farm assets tripled in the 1970s from their values a decade before (Schertz 1979:33). Investment in equipment and assets thus became a hedge against inflation, and tax laws rewarded such expansion.

Rising farm real estate values were advantageous for established farm owners but made entry for young farmers more difficult. Although many farmers recounted that in past decades they paid for land primarily from savings, soaring land prices made savings inadequate as a way to finance expansion. Lending institutions became heavily involved in loans for expanding farm scale and other investments during the boom years. Farm debt soared. By 1978, national farm debt reached $120 billion, ten times the pre-inflation level of 1950 (Schertz 1979:56).

By the early 1980s, forces driving the agricultural boom had reversed direction (Murdock and Leistritz 1988:14). Exports fell due to a combination of factors: President Carter's grain embargo to the Soviet Union, worldwide recession, the rising value of the dollar, increased domestic agricultural production in many countries, and foreign competition for U.S. farm commodities. Federal farm policy also played a role; the 1981 Farm Bill set prices above market levels and

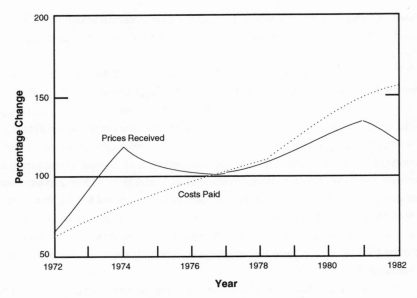

Figure 7-1. Prices Received and Costs Paid by American
Farmers, 1972–1982 (Percentage of 1977)

Source: USDA 1983:11.

encouraged overproduction and international competition. As exports fell, so did crop prices. Costs of production continued to rise, however, and net farm incomes jolted downward. As figure 7-1 shows, costs paid by farmers rose faster than prices received. Land values began to drop, threatening the level of assets bankers held as collateral on loans. Further credit was cut off to many producers, and nationwide the percentage of farms going out of business nearly tripled from 1982 to 1986 (ibid.:17).

Booms in U.S. agriculture had occurred in the 1910s and 1940s as well as the 1970s. In both earlier periods, national and international forces boosted farm incomes, leading to rising land values and investments in other farm resources. These "relatively short periods of favorable returns appear to create expectations that these returns will be permanent" (Murdock and Leistritz 1988:21). Then conditions change, land values deflate, and "an extensive period of depressed farm earnings generally follows" (ibid.). In the 1980s bust, however, farmers were more vulnerable because farms were larger, more dependent on purchased inputs, and more indebted. In other words, it was much more difficult to cut costs successfully, substitute family labor, and retrench in the ways that had been possible in previous economic downturns.

The Boom in Dodge County

The primary impact of the boom on farmers in Dodge County was to encourage a more ambitious farming style. National newsletters and advice from commentators on farm exports and futures markets all reinforced a new enthusiasm for expansion and speculation. Some large scale farmers attempted to play with "the big boys," aware that their rapidly increased net worth made them "rich" and trying to be "smart" with that wealth. Some explored futures markets, insurance company lenders, and other new financial strategies. One young farmer attended the University of Georgia and reported that the message he received was, "You're not going to be a dirt farmer any more—it can be a glamorous life." This man took a number of risks with a substantial inheritance (and ultimately lost the farm).

Medium scale, cautious farmers were also caught up in the pressure toward a more risky management style. In one case, a father and son partnership on a modest-sized farm was steadily profitable into the late 1970s. An opportunity to buy a nearby 200-acre farm became available, and the risk seemed minimal. The increased acreage required larger equipment, which they purchased secondhand. The boom was soon followed by the bust; several fair years and modest progress on these loans were succeeded by a severe drought year and a tremendous loss. Low-profit years followed, and it soon became clear that bankruptcy or voluntary liquidation of the farm and a career shift to steady off-farm work was the only option. Some cautious farmers remember the boom period with pain. It was a time when experts promoted behavior that was inconsistent with their preference to avoid debt and expand only carefully. One older farmer admitted he stopped going to extension service meetings at that time: "They tell you to grab out there and get it." As the boom encouraged farmers to expand, beginning farmers and poorer farmers were at a disadvantage. The best-quality land sometimes rented for more than the highly leveraged farmer could afford to pay. One second career farmer complained that "the upper class farmers can force out middle-type farmers like me" by outcompeting them for the best land rentals.

The Bust: Drought and the Cost-Price Squeeze

The boom of the mid-1970s was followed in Dodge County by a slow collapse. The bust had two components: successive years of drought and shifts in the balance between costs farmers paid and prices they received, known as the "cost-price squeeze." The droughts began in 1977, as midsummer rains ceased and crops "went down like a wilted turnip." Rustling brown leaves and stunted plants brought skimpy harvests. The 1978 crop year was also dry, and high heat battered spirits as well as crops. The drought patterns were not uniform over the county— some farmers received good rains or adequate showers. The third year, 1979, was somewhat better and, encouraged, many farmers rented extra land "doubling up to catch up."

Then came 1980 and a more devastating drought than either 1977 or 1978. Temperatures in the hundreds were unabated. In other regions of the South, whole chicken houses were lost to the heat, and even city folks panted in the relentlessness of the summer weather. One agricultural expert said it would take two good years to begin to make up for the 1980 losses alone. One cautious large scale farmer recalled, "I lost $100,000 in 1980." In Georgia overall, farm income sank to Depression-era levels. Instead of recovery, however, intermittent rains continued to be the pattern in 1981. Said one ambitious large scale farmer, "I have always bored with a big auger, with faith in my abilities—and have been able to bring it off—but the elements—I can't handle that."

National Weather Service records show that the droughts experienced in Georgia for 1977–81 conform to a thirty-year cycle of dry spells. Low rainfall in 1952 and 1953 were particularly remembered by older farmers. Some of these 1950s dry spells apparently fell at less critical times for crops than the dry years in the 1970s, and thus farmers did not anticipate such a severe or extended drought. In the mid-1980s, it became clear that the jet stream had shifted. An El Niño in the Pacific set off other atmospheric changes.[1] Some commentators worried that deforestation from pulpwood harvests had changed the movement of clouds; others felt the replacement of hardwood forests with pine stands changed evapotranspiration processes and water cycles.

This study began in 1982, a year of quiet, steady rains throughout the summer. It was a superb growing season, and some farmers reported making their highest yields ever. As with the drought years, however, there was continued variability; some farmers reported mediocre harvests, and a few had insurance-certified disaster losses due to low rainfall toward the end of the summer. Differential timing of crops partly accounts for this variability, but rainfall patterns in general were inconsistent across the county for most of the decade.

Harvest time in 1982 brought little joy, however, because profits were low. Costs had continued to rise and grain prices were poor. Farmers with pressing debts were forced to sell immediately and found themselves dismayed at the scant reward for their efforts. The reality of the two-part disaster began to be apparent. Though none of the years between 1982 and 1987 brought as bad a drought as 1980, many farmers experienced dry conditions year after year. By 1989, some had given up expecting the old pattern to return and concluded that the weather had changed: "We just can't get the season," complained older farmers without irrigation. Even lucky farmers who received adequate rains were hurt by the poor economic conditions.

The cost-price squeeze began with the Arab oil embargo of 1972, which set off inflationary pressures throughout the U.S. economy. In 1979, another petroleum price hike fueled inflation, and Dodge County farmers felt these jolts throughout a range of input costs. Machinery prices went up sharply. One farmer reported buying a particular tractor in 1971 for $5,926; in 1978, the same tractor cost $19,000. One man's fertilizer bill went from $80 a ton in 1972 to $230 a ton ten years later. Diesel jumped from 22 cents a gallon to $1.05 in the same period. Chemicals rose as well, and even seed costs went up, in one case tripling. It was not uncommon for a farmer's costs to double in a five-year period.

Rising loan interest rates also caused concern, as farmers faced double digit rates. Said one farmer, "I'd be happy with a 9 percent profit each year; I'd accept that as a fair return to my work and investment. But no one can make 9 percent profit on top of 15 percent interest. The interest eats up all my profit." By 1983, the Federal Land Bank's floating interest charges were 18 percent—a devastating blow to many farm balance sheets. Rates between 12 percent and 16 percent were common in this period.

Meanwhile, crop prices either fell steadily from their highs in the mid-1970s or remained steady. With constant or falling income, rising costs made some farmers panicky. Others were angry, blaming the government and the unions for rising costs. Many were depressed. Said one: "Farming is just *disgusting* right now." Discouragement reflected both the reality of the poor weather and high costs but also the loss of dreams. Farmers who expected to do very well were being forced to face the erosion of those hopes, not to mention the very real possibility that they might go out of business.

The crisis was seen by many older farmers as worse than the Depression.

Depression losses were more widely shared, they felt, and the annual costs of production were much lower. "Things are not as certain now as in the Hoover Days. . . . You wouldn't have anything then, but now it's variable. You can lose so darned much so fast." Financial stress came faster to some Dodge County farmers than others. A few lost on crops but were lucky with livestock. Some established farmers depleted their nest eggs and were forced to borrow operating money for the first time. This new vulnerability to debt raised tensions as well.

By 1983, Dodge County saw a range of businesses hurt by the drought. Though farmers' low yields were felt immediately, inadequate rain hurt timber growth as well, but with delayed effect. Pulpwood companies that rent land for timber production began to plan for smaller timber harvests, though the vulnerable younger trees might not be harvested for five years or more. Local stores, especially the crossroads country stores, saw their businesses decline as droughts closed up farmers' wallets. Farm supply stores were especially vulnerable to delays in repayment as well as to bankruptcies. In Dodge County or nearby, several farm suppliers, an equipment dealer, and a grain dealer went out of business. All through the Coastal Plain, the farm crisis brought an economic downturn to small towns and rural communities.

Land prices fell steadily after 1983; from a high of $800 an acre, the best land in the county dropped to nearly $500. Average land values settled in the $300 range, and farmers whose loans were based on a net worth of overvalued land faced difficulties with lenders. Equipment values dropped as well. By 1983, farmers expected to receive less than half of the former value of equipment if they tried to sell. The used equipment market was glutted, and the farmers who wanted to buy secondhand machinery were often unable to afford any extra expenses. The declining salvage value of farm equipment further lowered farmers' net worth.

These conditions in the early 1980s greatly hampered the efforts of a number of operators who began to think of voluntarily cutting back or getting out of farming entirely. One older farmer tried to rent out one field to generate some steady income but reported, "I couldn't find a sucker who'd take it." Retrenchment became a successful option for a few, depending on the financial condition of neighbors who could take on extra acreage, but many turned first to other strategies to survive the crisis.

Strategies in Response to the Crisis

The first five years of the crisis were a period of experimentation and adjustment; changes in crop and livestock mix, farm acreage, and amount of off-farm work were the most common strategies reported. Irrigation was a major innovation, but in 1982 it was still limited to mainly the large scale farmers. Many of the cautious farmers, large and medium, were not persuaded that the drought would last long enough to make the investment in irrigation worthwhile.

About half the full-time farmers and 20–30 percent of part-time and retired farmers reported changes in crop and livestock mix between 1978 and 1982. When drought losses reduced feed supplies, some farmers sold livestock. Others, especially a few encouraged by the Farmers Home Administration, expanded their hog facilities to generate cash. Planting a quick crop of watermelons was another way to increase earnings without disturbing the overall crop mix, and a number of farmers with access to the right kind of soil added a few acres of watermelons. One or two in the county tried to produce vegetables of different kinds.

Most of these strategies had negative consequences. Cutbacks in livestock, especially hogs, lowered income although the decision may have been prudent to avoid even greater losses. Low hog prices hurt virtually all of the farmers who tried to expand hog production; this strategy had been attempted throughout the Southeast, and supplies were glutted. The market for watermelons was also flooded in those early years, and some farmers chose to let their melons rot in the fields because prices did not cover the cost of harvest and transportation. Vegetables were very vulnerable to late frosts and early dry spells, and one farmer who managed to get a good crop faced serious marketing difficulties.

Shifting crop acreage among the standard rowcrops to take advantage of the highest prices was a more successful strategy, at least in the short run. Many farmers, for example, responded to good soybean prices with an increase in soybean plantings. Soon prices dropped as national supplies rose, and infestations of new diseases and insects lowered yields. More affluent farmers tried to expand their acreage of high-value crops like peanuts, tobacco, and cotton by buying allotments or building up a cotton base. Some farmers continued to make money steadily throughout the crisis as a result of efficient hog production, good government program access, or a carefully balanced mix of rowcrops and livestock with low production costs.

An important strategy to recoup drought losses in the early years was to rent additional acreage. About a third of full-time farmers tried such expansion, renting land from retiring farmers and from newly harvested Soil Bank timberland. Slightly more farmers (43%) chose the opposite strategy of cutting back acreage by giving up some rentals. They cited the costs of hired hands and the increased risks of loss as their reasons.

In the second half of the crisis decade, Dodge County farms continued to show a rough balance between those who tried to cope by expanding and those who cut back, and irrigation was sometimes related to such decisions. Retrenchment was the pattern reported on most medium scale farms, as only the best land was kept in production. Some younger families benefited from purchases of new acreage and inheritance, expanding as part of the normal life course. Irrigation facilities were added all over the county, and large scale farms were more likely to have all major crops covered by this form of crop "insurance." Several younger medium scale farmers began to recognize the necessity for irrigation as well, but in general the older medium scale farmers assessed the investment as too costly for their farm profit levels. Some also felt the extra work of irrigation was unacceptable.

The Conservation Reserve Program was important in encouraging farm scale reductions in the later 1980s. The program allowed Dodge County farmers with "highly erodible land," as certified by the Soil Conservation Service, to put farmland into trees (usually pulpwood) or grass, in return for a sizable annual payment from the government. This program took thousands of acres in the county out of farm production, giving an assured income to the owners. Where a large farmer had the land to spare, this program was highly beneficial, and it helped retired farmers and widows as well. On the other hand, some farmers lost highly desired rental land. The program was successful in its goal to lower overall crop production, thereby reducing national surpluses. More than one large scale farmer boasted, however, that he could give up a percentage of his cropland and still keep production constant by working the remaining land more intensively. The conservation program also reduced the secondary benefits of farmed land throughout the county, such as the purchase of diesel, tractor parts, and crop dusting services. It therefore had a dampening effect on the local farm economy. For individual families who received its payments, the Conservation Reserve Program allowed some debt repayment, another of the original goals of the program. The paper companies and timber companies also benefited greatly from the vast new acreages of softwoods planted, which will provide enhanced pulpwood stocks in twenty years. The fact that they can count on buying this timber when the trees are ready to be harvested saves them the rental on land for the next two decades, and more than makes up for the drought losses they suffered.

Cutting costs was a response to the drought reported by many farmers. Many used chemicals or diesel more sparingly. Some cut back fertilizer or lime, knowing they were "drawing down the bank account" of the soil's fertility but hoping good times would return before the consequences caught up with them. By such practices as saving their own seed or experimenting with more careful irrigation, farmers tried a range of ways to reduce cash outlays. Farms also reported cutting back household expenses. One woman froze more homegrown vegetables; others no longer ate out at restaurants or tried to lower electric bills. One frugal young couple faced the financial stresses of the drought years with physical stresses as well. They had no air conditioning and reported, "It got *hot*! Sometimes it would be 103 degrees in the kitchen."

Adding off-farm income was another major strategy. About one-quarter of farm households took additional work off the farm in the first five years of the crisis; another quarter added off-farm income in the second half of the crisis. For most, increased income came about through the wife's obtaining a new job. In a few cases, the husband took a part-time job as a school bus driver or timber worker. In eight cases, farm debts became so critical that both the husband and wife sought full-time off-farm work, and they cut the farm operation back sharply to a level they could handle evenings and weekends. New jobs increased the labor demands on women's time. Pressures to complete household chores and occasionally help out on the farm were reported as overwhelming by some women. "I don't know how the wives can stand it," said one man who recognized the heavy work load that home, children, farm, and off-farm job placed on his wife. The worry from the crisis was also a part of that load. "I thought I was going to crack up," reported one woman.

As the crisis years were drawing to an end, over half the farms in Dodge County reported a decline in their use of hired labor. The number of very large farms that hired three or more workers fell. Farmers now who use hired labor are more commonly younger operators who seek one helper to manage 250–400 acres of rowcrops. There is also a small group of younger large scale farmers in good financial shape who have expanded their use of hired hands.[2]

Rethinking the Ambitious Management Style

By the late 1980s, adaptations to the farm bust in Dodge County showed movement away from an ambitious farming style. Overall, more families cut back acreage, cut costs, and reduced the use of hired hands. Farm expansion via credit was seen as too risky, and most farms held constant in size or let some rentals lapse. Poorer lands were taken out of crop production and put into trees or pasture. A small group of operators found their profits sufficient to expand and to use more hired help, but even within this fortunate group, credit was used more cautiously and investments were made more commonly from savings.

As economic conditions no longer sustained the ebullient hopes of the boom years, farmers' assessments of "a good farmer" showed some changes over the eight years of this study. The large scale farmer who recounted that he began farming with the dream of retiring as a millionaire found himself unsure his farm would survive. He reassessed his judgment of his cautious father: "He was a *successful* farmer." This newfound respect for his father's farming style represents a partial rejection of the upward mobility that ambitious farming was supposed to bring. As this man's life has unfolded, the attractions of social status have not been worth the work and worry his large farm has brought. As with several families who say they "lived beyond their means," he is not particularly pleased with the ways his children have used the affluence he provided them. A level of disillusionment with their choices is part of his reassessment of his own dreams.

Other more cautious farmers express the greater weight the crisis has brought to their chosen occupation, but they are more likely to end on a positive note about the value of the farm life. One older medium scale farmer commented that it is "disheartening" to think of men who took off-farm jobs back in the 1950s and now have "pretty good retirement and don't have to work none." Meanwhile, he continues to work hard and is financially "in the hole." But, he concludes, "I could have done the same, and I believe, looking back, I wouldn't have." "It's a heap of satisfaction," he said twice. A black farmer expressed his disapproval of what he perceives as a general devaluation of farming and an emphasis on material accumulation. His white neighbor agreed: "We care too much about money and material things now," he said. "It used to be, a man who didn't have much but who worked hard had community respect, but no longer." Another medium scale farmer mused that he "might have been better off" had he accepted a job that he was offered as a young man, but he would not have been as satisfied. By "better off," he refers to financial considerations and especially his home and furnishings. He and his wife live in a small, white frame house, have few household appliances, and have never taken a vacation. But this farmer is unambivalent about his joy in farming—"I just love it," he said.

Among the most disillusioned are the highly educated beginning large scale farmers. They feel keenly the status losses of their choice to farm, even when their financial situation is strong. Farming was to be the means to an affluent life for this ambitious group, and those dreams are fading. Several talked about resenting the time demands of farming and the relentlessness of worry. They want to be able to take weekends off, schedule vacations, and keep to these schedules. Seeing the lifestyle their nonfarm friends enjoy has taken the fun out of farming for some. "It's too low a return on equity," said one, "and too much work for too little pay." Even when the farm accounts are in the black, financial disappointments permeate their assessments of farming, and noneconomic rewards do not outweigh this dissatisfaction. This sense of failure—in the midst of success by the agrarian definition—reflects their unfulfilled dreams of a middle or upper middle class life. Farming has to provide "at least the average standard of living of the other children in school." Inability to live as well as other college graduates and some professionals in town is a source of frustration. In the social ranking of Dodge County, they had expected farming to support their dreams but are now forced to face the possibility that it cannot.

Most cautious farmers accept that farming cannot guarantee a high standard of living. One woman attributed her farm's success to knowing how "to stretch the check." She feels some young couples have a hard time holding back from spending large crop checks, especially when "peer pressure" urges them to indulge in things like a four-wheel drive vehicle. In many parts of the county, "young people are just living too high for farming and that's why they can't make it," she said.

In the aftermath of the crisis, younger farmers who had embraced an ambitious management style developed a new respect for the older, more cautious ways. One large scale farmer who had been confident his superior education would lend him a competitive advantage said, "We were going to tear the world up . . . but we found those old farmers knew more than we thought." Several farmers emphasized a new preference for smaller scale: "When I started out, lenders, the extension service, any magazine or journal you could read all said bigger is better." Now, this young operator argues that the larger-sized farm, worked with hired hands, is not more competitive and seeks to scale back his own operation to what he can work by himself. Not all young farmers have abandoned their ambitious goals, however. One still wants to "farm and be big at it . . . be a success . . . clear a million dollars. But I can't go at it big at the beginning; I'm having to work my way up."

Institutional Responses: Lenders and Federal Disaster Aid

The responses of lenders in Dodge County helped some farmers and hurt others, and the same can be said for the effects of federal disaster aid. The emotional tension created by the crisis was often directed toward these institutions that surround, support, and constrain U.S. agriculture. In 1985, a new Farm Bill directed billions of dollars into the farm sector and was critical in reversing the downward spiral of the cost-price squeeze. By that point, however, it was too late for many of the farms that were to be forced out of business by the crisis. Since very few farmers voluntarily chose to discontinue farming, the banks, Farm Credit System, and the Farmers Home Administration were usually the agents that cut off credit and forced farmers into a reckoning with their debts.

Of the farm lenders used by most farmers in Dodge County, the local banks were the least threatened by the crisis. In general, the better off and more cautious farmers used banks for their loans, and few of these farmers experienced a decline in net worth so severe as to threaten their creditworthiness. Local banks' ceiling on indebtedness at one-half of net worth also protected them, even when asset values fell sharply. Some farmers were cut off from further loans until debt levels were reduced, but banks rarely tried to foreclose, preferring to renew unpaid loans and to assume eventual repayment. In most cases, this confidence was justified. In fact, even in some cases of bankruptcy in which a farmer's bank loan was implicated, the operator informed the bank privately that the debt would eventually be repaid, and this promise was made good. Most farmers felt they had been treated fairly by the local banks and wanted to repay those debts. Of course, they also wanted to assure future credit. By the end of this study, some farmers forced out of farming by other lenders had indeed been successful in obtaining new credit with local banks.

The two New Deal lending agencies that operated as credit cooperatives—the Federal Land Bank and the Production Credit Association—were both active in farm lending prior to the crisis. As repayments faltered and the cooperatives faced a credit crisis of their own, offices and personnel were cut back. Dodge County lost branches of both organizations, and farmers had to travel to the next county to arrange credit and payments. This inconvenience, together with more stringent lending rules, pushed many farmers to abandon the Production Credit Association for annual operating money, turning instead to local banks or the Farmers Home Administration. In any case, only the operators in strong financial condition remained with the Production Credit Association. The Federal Land Bank continued to be the lender of choice for long-term land purchases, but for much of the 1982–87 period, new land purchases by farmers were rare.

The Farmers Home Administration (FmHA), supported by federal funds, was also created by the New Deal, but its mandate was to provide supervised credit to new and high-risk farmers. As such, it was designed to be the lender of last resort to provide credit to farmers with insufficient assets for bank loans. Its interest rates varied according to different programs but often were below local rates. As discussed in chapter 2, the boom years saw an expanded cohort of beginning farmers in Dodge County, and many of them were financed by the Farmers Home Administration. As early drought losses hindered repayments, some operators argued for higher assessments of land and equipment values, and with these higher calculations of assets, loans were allowed to increase. Supervision of borrowers became increasingly perfunctory as staff was not expanded in keeping with the work load. Personnel turnover also hurt the maintenance of farmers' records. In some years, Congress and the Washington FmHA bureaucracy provided new loan authorizations too late in the spring to be of use in farmers' planning for spring plantings. Working with FmHA became increasingly frustrating for many operators.

Farmers Home Administration lending grew more complex in the drought years. After 1977, a disaster program provided payments at 3 percent interest to eligible farmers. After 1978, a 5 percent program allowed many farmers to consolidate their loans and pay off more expensive creditors. Other special programs were targeted at particular groups of farmers. When Congress became dissatisfied with the pace at which FmHA disbursed drought relief funding, another relief program was administered through the Small Business Administration (SBA). Though the Small Business Administration had no experience in agricultural lending, it was able to make available substantial amounts of money to debt-strapped farmers (and to other eligible landowners who managed to fill out the complex forms). It was widely rumored that these loans would not have to be repaid. (Interestingly, the 1929 report of the Dodge County Agricultural Extension agent warns of similar rumors with regard to "distress money" provided by the Farmers Seed Loan Office. A letter from that office circulated to farmers in 1929 said, "It has been reported in some sections of the seed loan area that the United States Government does not seriously contemplate the collection of these loans this fall. Such reports should be corrected at once.") A range of farmers borrowed SBA money, and as we shall see in chapter 8, only a few did not come to regret it.

Pressure was placed by Congress on the Farmers Home Administration to make disaster help more available to suffering farmers. Members of Congress criticized the agency for unspent funds in congressional hearings and threatened to reduce the FmHA budget. Local FmHA personnel worked with interested farmers to create farm plans that would justify renewed loans. It was in this context that several farmers were forced to add hog operations or plant watermelons to justify new loans. Several newcomer farmers were shocked by their drought losses in the early years and wanted to cut back. Farmers Home Administration personnel were more optimistic about a turnaround in the economy and urged them to keep on. "You can't quit now!" one man reported being told. Others were unable to show repayment of FmHA loans and therefore were prevented from scaling back on farm acreage.

In the early drought years, the FmHA's generosity was greatly appreciated. Young farmers and second career farmers trusted the agency's calculations of their ability to repay and cast off the cautious warnings of parents and neighbors. One young farmer was doing well paying off a medium-sized farm and equipment when the early drought years caught him without irrigation. Hearing of the FmHA disaster loan program, he went in with documentation of a $17,000 loss. Farmers Home Administration personnel told him he was eligible for $67,000, based on his farm situation, and in light of the low interest, the young man accepted the loan. "You can't lose," he told his father. The next four years were all bad crop years, interest and principal mounted, and by the late 1980s, the farmer was out of business. In a similar case in which FmHA urged a beginning farmer to take more money than he originally wanted, the farmer is bitter now. "Of course I blame FHA [FmHA], and no one was twisting my arm to make me take it. But I look at it like putting out sugar and then sugar attracts flies. They held out a handful of sugar to me." [3]

The large checks some young farmers received were "mind blowing." "I just didn't know how to manage it," said one who received $40,000 one spring. "You're rich—momentarily." "Lots of people think they can't ever spend that big a check," agreed his wife. "FHA should have told me not to buy new equipment," complained this farmer, who pointed to the more careful supervision and regular farm visits by FmHA personnel in his father's day. In this case, the farmer felt that eventually he could have paid the debt, but the agency cut off further credit in 1985 and forced him out of business.

As the crisis wore on and debts mounted, the Farmers Home Administration became more cautious in its advice. Some farmers wanted to expand rentals or plant risky crops but were denied additional funding for these plans. Much of this supervision was unwelcome and provided a target for farmers' resentment.

A farmer who watched a neighbor come out well in a risky venture while he had been denied the same opportunity by the FmHA and again could not pay his bills felt some of the blame for his loan delinquency fell on the FmHA's shoulders. Some argued that the agency's intrusion into their managerial judgments left them with less responsibility to repay their loans.

Several farmers reported applying for disaster loans through FmHA or SBA and then getting cold feet: "We saw we were in too deep." However, the agencies made refusing the money very difficult—"We had to *fight* to make them take back the check," said one couple.

One frustration to families sinking under a debt burden was that if they had one loan to the Farmers Home Administration at 3 percent and another at 16.5 percent and they brought in a check to make a payment, the money would be applied to the 3 percent loan, leaving the other to amass interest. FmHA rules required that payments be applied to the least secured loan, which was often the disaster loan made at subsidized interest. Earlier loans, at higher interest rates, were already secured by land or equipment. This logic was of little solace to the struggling farmer.

It is unfortunate that confidentiality regulations keep this account of farm lenders necessarily one-sided. Lenders cannot talk about their problems with farmers and are much more reticent than farmers about discussing the crisis. From farmers' accounts, though, it is clear that lenders commonly experienced verbal abuse. Threats of physical harm to loan personnel were also recounted by farmers themselves and by third parties. Lenders were frustrated by changing regulations, understaffing, and the hopelessness engendered by the persistent droughts. Several were certainly angered by the recalcitrant, defensive, and hostile behavior of some farmers. Not all cases, however, were marked by rancor between debtor and creditor. One operator forced out of business characterized his experiences with FmHA personnel as "not unpleasant—I'd compliment them."

Bankruptcy, Foreclosure, and Settlements

The Farmers Home Administration was involved in lawsuits for much of the early 1980s, and action on delinquent cases was erratic. Lawyers battled over whether the agency should be allowed to foreclose on farms in arrears or whether its congressional mandate required it to give delinquent farmers a three-year grace period. Critics of FmHA in the Midwest charged that foreclosed farms were being sold to the highest bidders, thereby displacing family farmers in favor of corporate

and nonfarm investors. Low-resource and minority farmers claimed unfair treatment as well. When these issues moved toward legal resolution and new guidelines
for settlement of delinquent loans finally appeared in 1989, farmers in Dodge
County were presented with a series of relatively favorable options. Cases that
were settled before 1989 tended to be somewhat harsher in their demands on farm
families.

The Family Farmer Bankruptcy Act became law in November 1986 and created
a new Chapter 12 in the legal code to help farmers weather the crisis and keep
their farms. The law allowed farmers to reduce their level of indebtedness to the
new reappraised value of the collateral held by the lender. The remainder of debt
not covered by collateral was required to be written off by lenders (though the
farmer must try to pay for three years). Farmers were expected to repay all of the
debt amount covered by the revised asset value. By 1988, this new law affected
all types of lenders, and they increasingly turned "to privately negotiated reorga-
nizations to avoid the administrative costs of a formal bankruptcy proceeding"
(Innes, Keller, and Carman 1989:29). Such negotiated settlements reduced legal
fees, court costs, and delays while ending in much the same result as a formal
Chapter 12 bankruptcy.

In Dodge County, delinquent FmHA borrowers were the main group to participate in such voluntary settlements, and by 1989 most of those in the study with
serious financial problems either had gone through such a negotiation or were
contemplating one. In such settlements, the farmer's land and equipment were ap-
praised and the total asset value was applied to the outstanding loan. Depending on
the farmer's other debts and income sources, the remaining debt after the farmer
made some sort of payment on the balance was usually "written off." In one case,
the farmer offered to pay 1 percent, then 5 percent, but the agency finally accepted
an offer of 10 percent. Others made more substantial settlements. The money for
these payments was obtained from family members, saved from off-farm salaries,
or earned from the sale of some other asset. FmHA required farmers to sign an
agreement that allows the agency to act at some later date to recoup canceled
debts from farm income. In a bankruptcy proceeding, such continuing liability is
eliminated.

By 1987, FmHA procedures began to allow "buy-backs" of assets by beleaguered farm families. Lenders learned from bitter experience that public auctions
of land and equipment gave poor returns on the value of assets. If a farm family
was allowed to place a bid in the amount of the lender's assessed value of land or
equipment, it saved the lender time, fees, and paperwork to accept such a bid. It

also concealed from public outcry the extent of farm loss, an issue more salient in Georgia after armed farm activists defended a black farmer from foreclosure in a nearby county. Buy-backs were welcomed by farm families because they avoided the public humiliation of land and equipment auction. Though usually only a portion of the original farm was saved, if important equipment was retained as well, the farmer was able to go back into business, often after some delay. The original farm operator was usually ineligible to buy back the farm because FmHA would then be able to sue for the outstanding balance of the loan. As noted in the last chapter, the wife was sometimes able to obtain a loan for this purpose because her name was not tied up with the farm debts. In other instances, a father or brother bought back the farm and allowed the original owner to continue the operation.

In cases where foreclosure or bankruptcy was the outcome of the crisis, land was customarily auctioned on the county courthouse steps on the first Tuesday of the month. The time of the auction was not announced, and bidders were seen waiting sometimes half a day. In the sales that I witnessed or heard described, only a small group of family members, lawyers, and bidders assembled, and if someone in the family bid the assessed value of the land, competitive bidders kept silent. In no case was a Dodge County family outbid for farmland in such an auction. Most commonly, no one bid the assessed value of the land, and the lender took possession of it. The county newspaper listed an average of two to five foreclosure notices a month during much of the crisis, but almost all of those involved were nonfarmers who had defaulted on loans for cars or houses. In the rare case of a farm foreclosure announcement, it most often was settled without a sale. Many advertised land auctions were the result of duels between lenders and recalcitrant, embittered farmers. Once land was publicly listed for auction, the family moved to make a payment or arrange a settlement, and the foreclosure process was aborted. Some land auctions that did occur were part of complex legal maneuvers to limit the family's liability for debts. More and more, as the crisis years ground on, lenders directly sought out investors, bankers, large landowners, and other possible buyers to move their inventory of land.

By the end of the 1980s, the pace of negotiated settlements with the Farmers Home Administration had accelerated in Dodge County amid widespread criticism of the policy. These arrangements left many solvent operators "hot under the collar." Most critics of FmHA write-offs did not understand the new regulations of the 1986 Family Farmer Bankruptcy Act and the way write-off procedures reflected this legal change. Older farmers in particular resented that FmHA supported beginning farmers who, in their opinion, should not have been supported:

"Just bought them a bag of groceries." These young farmers raised rents for other farmers, made serious mistakes, and went out of business. The established farmer complained, "I had to pay *my* debts while these young men got theirs written off and kept their farms, houses, everything!"

Even some farmers taking advantage of debt settlements are ambivalent. Said one, "This doesn't really square with my own philosophy," but the opportunity to help his family by eliminating burdensome debts outweighed his scruples. An older farmer asserted he never took on a debt he did not intend to pay, but after negotiating a write-off, he felt not only all his hard work but also his reputation had gone down the drain. Some operators justify the settlements by claiming that the canceled debts are mostly interest and thus represent only a paper loss to FmHA. Another farmer expressed resentment of criticism over his write-off because, he argued, the money he borrowed went to pay off suppliers and other creditors; *they* were the ones to benefit from the loan, not he. Other operators remained so angry with the Farmers Home Administration for past difficulties that they refused to negotiate or even respond to letters. In 1989, one delinquent borrower tried to read the hefty package of forms that explained to him his rights but gave up in disgust, throwing it in the trash.

The delinquent loan settlements offered by the Farmers Home Administration had several other effects in addition to reducing the costs of bankruptcy proceedings. They were designed to avoid the flooding of the real estate market, which would further destabilize the farm economy. Highly visible farm auctions and lowered confidence in farmers' credit had the potential to hurt financially sound farmers as well as those in trouble. Some lenders even expressed concern that since the collapse of the farm economy had contributed to the nationwide Depression of the 1930s, the same sequence could happen again. The Farmers Home Administration felt that making settlements was realistically the only way to recoup money from the deflated farm economy. Another goal was to cut the losses in relatively hopeless cases to stop the endless spiral of red ink.

In assessing the impact of the agency in the crisis, it is important to keep in mind that several successful younger farmers were put in business by FmHA and were able to repay their loans. Part of the high delinquency rate was due to the larger cohort of young and second career farmers. In effect, the increased financing for these new operators created, albeit briefly, a more open door to the occupation of farming. No other lender is available to support deserving low-resource and high-risk beginning farmers. Although the policies adopted by the agency have been controversial, they have also had benefits for many in the county, especially those whose heavy debts are now nonexistent. For the more cautious families who sacrificed a great deal to pay off their debts, the write-offs make them question the wisdom of their principles.

Fraud and Dishonesty

As the farm crisis ground on, and contradictory government programs succeeded each other, fraud and dishonesty in handling the crisis became a frequent topic of conversation. Said one farmer, "Farmers used to have as much honor as anyone. A farmer would never try to beat anyone out of money or steal—but that's not true now." Said one part-time farmer, "Thanks to my job, I've never had to stoop to that, but I won't say that I wouldn't do it." An overextended large scale farmer admitted that in the past he would never have considered falsifying a document or fudging on a federal program, but now he is not so sure. He has struggled with the enormous pressures of high debts for so many years, and his exhaustion is a part of his changing sense of what is right. Watching others "get away with it" also makes it easier for him to consider fraud. One woman asserted, "Everyone knows if you're going to farm, you have to do dishonest things." Many farmers complain that commodity programs, disaster help, and other agricultural assistance are set up arbitrarily. "There's no fairness in it," complain all types of farmers. Cheating on these programs is held to be rampant. Even a federal criminal investigator expressed this sentiment. For decades, farmers were never the target of his work, he reported, but their world has changed and their behavior with it.[4]

Resentment over crop insurance fraud is most frequently expressed by honest farmers. Some operators are accused of planting crops with minimal seed and fertilizer, without irrigation, gambling that the year will be dry and that they will be compensated for the low yields by an insurance company. For a farmer whose past yields have been recorded at substantial levels (and who is therefore eligible for a substantial insurance payment), it is hard to prove that a low return is caused by inadequate inputs rather than drought. More conscientious farmers watch their highly indebted neighbors continue farming because of cash infusions from insurance payments that hold off debt pressures, while they themselves are forced out of business. Such inequity is demoralizing and creates an atmosphere of degenerating confidence.

Farming provides many opportunities to conceal earnings or dishonest dealings. Lenders struggle to identify whose crops are in a field, and neighbors are often purposely unhelpful. One farmer went bankrupt and supposedly quit farming. His frustrated lenders were suspicious because the fields he had rented continued to show planted crops. In reality, the rented land had reverted to the original owner, who had leased the land to another farmer, but such transactions are not recorded publicly or even discussed. Driving past the field, the lender might easily assume the bankrupt farmer fraudulently continued to produce. One part-time farmer reported borrowing from a local bank with no intention to repay the loan. He manipulated every program because "when you're sliding down the wall, you grab at every bump that comes along."

It is difficult to substantiate these claims of widespread dishonesty. A few highly visible cases set a tone, particularly in certain sections of the county. Some farmers discuss dealings with local agricultural businesses as a constant battle to avoid being cheated. One farmer recounted his own experiences of being short-weighted by a grain dealer, cheated on fertilizer content, and victimized by being sold old seed as new.

At the same time, it is clear that farmers accuse each other readily of various farming strategies, financial decline, or fraud with minimal and often no evidence. A lively gossip network spreads these rumors, and occasionally I was able to find evidence to prove them false. Therefore, it is hard to know for sure the extent of fraud or dishonesty. What *is* certifiable is the atmosphere that generated such accusations. Again, the rumors were more pervasive in some communities than in others, and where they were spread, farmers saw the fraud as a trend caused by the crisis.

Dishonesty is less commonly discussed by the cautious medium scale farmer; when it is, there is an anger and a distance in the farmer's tone. Fraud seems to be more often seen among the highly indebted, ambitious farmers, for whom an affluent farming style and lifestyle are part of claims to a high (or higher) social position. One Dodge County official familiar with fraud in various forms judged that most cases were to be found among the larger farmers: "People are just not willing to lose what standard of living they've been able to amass over the years," he said. Though this link between fraud, farming style, consumption, and social status cannot be proven, there is a logic to the idea that "clever" dealings with regulations are more palatable to the highly indebted ambitious farmers.

Emotional Impact of the Crisis

For farmers facing farm loss, bankruptcy, or foreclosure, the drought years obviously have been traumatic, but for farmers in good financial shape, stresses have been severe as well. In 1987, almost a decade after the first drought years, many of the most prosperous farmers were exhausted and discouraged. "I'm not as interested in farming anymore. I have no desire to farm," said several younger men. "Being a farmer today is just like being a mule used to be—you work and work all day with that carrot dangling right out in front of you, but you never get it," said a middle-aged farmer. Some older men long to retire, rent out their land, or plant it in pine trees. One black farmer lamented the general decline in the centrality of farming to the community: "When I was in school, farming was considered the backbone and children were let out of school to help their parents. Farming used to have a bright, shiny side, but now it has a dark, gloomy side."

Financial stresses hurt families of all types, not just those heavily in debt. Said one medium scale farm couple: "We feel it [the bad times] as hard as a thousand-acre farm—it's hurt us as much as a big debt." Another said, "I've learned to depend on the Lord and He's provided. Just when we couldn't pay the telephone bill, money would come in from the Goldkist dividend. . . . It's been rough to make ends meet, but we've been able to." One farmer in good shape says, "It weighs on you. . . . Maybe this year will be the one."

Many farmers complain bitterly of the personal cost of the drought. One older man claimed, "I made a good living on the farm—from 1973 on back." In good years, he bought a car or farm equipment and was proud that he could paint his house or make some home improvement every year. Then the cost-price squeeze wiped out his profits. Frustrated, he exclaimed, "I've had enough of working for nothing, feeding people which don't appreciate it." His run-down house lowers his self-esteem as a husband. In anger, he blames the government: "Nixon messed it all up." A part-time farmer from a more affluent family expected his farm to augment his household income. As debts have piled up, he feels depressed by the loss of his desired lifestyle: "I expected to be higher on the hog by now. Farmers all over have lost ground; you can see it in their not *having*. Not being able to trade cars, for instance."

Family ties are affected as well. Children must be extra careful about expenses and may have to do additional farm work. "I hate to see them toting irrigation pipe," said one mother. But overall, in this case, she felt her family's quality of life had improved because "we have accepted the situation and worked together."

"I haven't been able to do for my family like I want," said one black farmer. He used to be able to give them "loving things" but is no longer able to. In a different case, the husband reported that his wife was suspicious that he was seeing another woman because their household budget had declined so precipitously.

The stress of the prolonged crisis is blamed by many families for increased health problems. Carrying irrigation pipes was said to cause back problems, hernias, and strains. Ulcers, depression, and new allergies were reported in several families. The first five years seemed to unite families as they faced the onslaught of the crisis together. But as the next five years dragged on, the broiling summer temperatures and the silent pain of dying crops took their toll. By 1989, the number of divorced and separated full-time farmers had doubled from 1982, though still far below nonfarm levels.

The process of financial decline can be excruciating and embarrassing. Sleepless nights and worries about bills and repayment of farm loans were reported in many families. As finances deteriorate, women are most often responsible for juggling creditors' demands. On one nearly bankrupt farm, the wife claimed that many husbands do not know the truth about the family's finances because their wives keep it from them. "He never sees the personal [household] bills" and therefore does not know that the children do not have shoes or clothes or how far behind the payments have become. Negotiations with local stores, utilities companies, and other creditors are tough: "It's a pain I can't describe," said one woman. "When you go in to explain to people that you can't pay your bills and you can see in their eyes that they're thinking: 'What kind of tale is that?' But it's the honest truth. And you're trying as hard as you can and it just isn't there."

Not everyone is conscientious about scrimping on personal expenses. Some families are unwilling to change aspects of their lifestyle to save a small amount to put on a large farm debt. Especially for some large scale operators, there is little incentive to work extra hours and cut corners to clear $50,000 on a harvest when it will hardly make a dent in a debt of $500,000 or more. Families who have only equipment as collateral sometimes feel less vulnerable, and, especially if they blame the Farmers Home Administration for their troubles, they are not inclined to scrimp in order to make progress toward repayment. One farmer who went bankrupt in 1982 remarked that some people feel if they are going to go bankrupt owing $100,000, they might as well go bankrupt owing $500,000.

At the same time, there are some farmers who have made money steadily through the crisis. Though a minority, they are typical of the farmer who asserts, "Now, farming has been *good* to me." Droughts have hurt these operations, as has

the cost-price squeeze, but for various reasons—large peanut allotments, irrigation to assure high yields, good hog production, diversification, and low costs—
they have come out ahead, year after year. These farm families are generally quiet
around the county. They avoid talking about their success and their luck. Out
of respect for the pain of their neighbors, and out of a desire not to be seen as
bragging or criticizing the unsuccessful, they keep their financial situation to themselves. Their behavior is also in part political. Government efforts to aid farmers
through the crisis help them too, and their softening of the public perception of
the crisis as an unmitigated disaster might lead to the discontinuation of such programs. Because the conditions that control farming are national and international
in scope and the perceived dimensions of the crisis are often more important than
the reality, political self-interest joins with Christian compassion, some degree of
modesty, and a desire for privacy to conceal these less-troubled cases.

The 1985 Farm Bill and the
Beginning of the End of the Crisis

The Food Security Act of 1985 began a slow turnaround for Dodge County
farmers. Farmers who participated in a series of grain and other crop programs saw
increased earnings. Around the nation, federal payments to farmers skyrocketed
in 1987, and 1988 "nearly matched the previous year's level" (USDA 1989).

In Dodge County, large scale farms received a mean of $28,000 in payments
from set-aside and disaster programs in 1986. Medium-sized farms received an
average of $3,700. This disparity allowed several of the larger farms to pull out
from under their debts and to see some light at the end of the tunnel by the close
of the decade. Medium scale farmers took an understandably more pessimistic
view of the crisis. Continued drought, little relief from high input costs, and only
small increases in product prices left them as discouraged as some of the most
indebted. In some cases, however, heavy reliance on the peanut program allowed
even medium scale operators to make progress on their debts. The 1989 growing
season was a wet one, and between the Farm Bill and the restoration of rain, a
slow consensus emerged that perhaps the worst of the crisis was over.

EIGHT

The Determinants of Farm Survival

As the crisis years were drawing to a close, a third of full-time farmers were out of business, and still more were gasping under heavy debt loads. Yet another third had withstood the losses from droughts and poor prices, and some had even made money. Who are the farmers who made it, and how are they different from the ones who went under? What were the keys to farm survival in the 1980s?

Conventional wisdom in Dodge County points to several determinants of farm survival. Skill is one common explanation; smart investments, shrewd deals, long hours, and hard work are also considered important. Other factors are sophisticated equipment and technology use. Recognizing the severe economic pressures of the bust years, several large scale farmers said, "If only two farmers survive in Georgia, I want to be one of them." More conservative farmers point to this entrepreneurial expansion and willingness to borrow as the road to disaster. One older operator said, "Young farmers today don't know the value of a dollar. They borrow too much, get too deeply into debt, and can't get out." His wife agreed: "Young farmers blame *farming* when the problem is they borrowed a lot of money and got into trouble. Debts always worry me."

The desire for a higher standard of living, or "living too high off the hog," is also seen as the cause of some farmers' demise. Some medium scale farmers complain that their problems are due to unfair competition with large farms because of special benefits from federal programs. Beyond the conventional wisdom of farmers themselves, researchers have pointed to expansion at the wrong time as a determinant of farm vulnerability. Other important resources that affect survival are soil quality and family help in access to land or equipment.

This chapter presents the results of statistical analysis that tested all of these assumptions about what determines farm survival. The analysis emphasizes full-time farms since they are of greatest interest, but part-time farms and retirement farms are also shown later in the chapter to be affected by many of the same dynamics. I have taken the farm enterprise as my unit of analysis, not the farm operators, but chapter 9 focuses on the consequences of farm loss for the individuals and the families caught up in the crisis.

All through the Dodge County story, we have seen that farm scale (large and medium) and age (generational cohort) have an effect on many aspects of farm life, and the patterns of farm survival must also be understood in those contexts. Table 8-1 presents two measures of the impact of the crisis on Dodge County farms. Cases forced into bankruptcy, foreclosure, or "voluntary" liquidation to settle delinquent debts are shown as "out of farming."[1] The second measure, "poor financial condition," includes all cases forced out of farming as well as those with high debt-to-asset ratios who are vulnerable to future farm loss. In many ways, debt-to-asset ratio is a better measure of the impact of the crisis because some highly indebted large scale—and a few medium scale—farms have been able to postpone foreclosure and hold off their creditors by their skillful loan manipulations and by the sheer magnitude of their debts. In some cases, both they and their creditors know that they are postponing the inevitable. Since data on farms out of business in 1989, therefore, would underrepresent large scale farms and over-represent medium scale operations, which were forced out more quickly, I have chosen to use debt-to-asset ratio as a better indicator of future farm survival.[2]

Debt-to-asset ratio is widely used as an accurate measure of vulnerability in the crisis (Leistritz and Ekstrom 1988a; Smale, Saupe, and Salant 1986; Jolly et al. 1985).[3] A low debt-to-asset ratio is a good insulator against farm loss because farms free of debt can only be forced out of business through nonpayment of taxes, and these costs were sufficiently low in Dodge County to pose little threat in the 1980s. Debt-to-asset ratios take the farm's income-generating potential into account in balancing the overall level of indebtedness. Lenders also evaluate debt levels in the context of the farm's assets, and the lenders' judgments are critical in determining which farmers are allowed to continue in operation.

Farms in Dodge County with debt-to-asset ratios over 75 percent all experienced severe financial stress, and most were out of business by 1989. Farms with low debt-to-asset ratios—under 30 percent—have not faced financial pressures that threaten farm survival. Only 10 farms out of a total of 58 full-time cases fall between these two levels. One farm with a debt-to-asset ratio of 49 percent began voluntary liquidation proceedings as this study ended, and the two farms above

Table 8-1. Farms in Crisis by Scale and Generation

	Number	Out of Farming	Poor Financial Condition
Large scale			
Generations 1 and 2	13	5 (38%)	7 (54%)
Generation 3	8	1 (13%)	4 (50%)
Medium scale			
Generations 1 and 2	20	2 (10%)	5 (25%)
Generation 3	17	11 (65%)	13 (76%)
Total	58	19 33%*	29 50%**

*Chi-square = 14.26, d.f. = 3, p < .01, lambda = .26.
**Chi-square = 9.85, d.f. = 3, p = .02, lambda = .34.

this debt level were considered high risk by their lenders and described themselves as under serious debt burdens. The cases below the 49 percent level experienced losses from the drought years, but none was in danger of losing the farm. Thus, I have divided the full-time farmers by debt-to-asset ratio into "good" and "poor" financial situation groups at the 49 percent level, a mark that, in fact, puts half the sample in each group.

Farm assets were calculated by combining the value of land, farm equipment (including trucks), irrigation systems, livestock, livestock facilities, and other investments such as grain bins, ponds, and barns. The value of equipment and other investments was obtained with the help of a local professional appraiser, assuming an average sale price and fair equipment condition. Land values were calculated with the help of data on recent sales, discussions with lenders, and an evaluation of each farm's characteristics (see appendix 1). Debt levels and asset values for this analysis were obtained primarily through interviews in 1987 but were updated in 1989. The data from the original 1982 survey that began the study were used to fill any gaps and to reconstruct changes in farm management style.[4]

Table 8-1 shows that large scale farmers have for the most part remained in business, but half of them are in poor financial shape. Though the numbers are small, they support the conclusion in chapter 4 that large scale does not protect a farm in the current crisis. In Dodge County, as in other areas of the country, expensive and sophisticated farms have been shown to be highly vulnerable in an economic slump. The older and younger generations of medium scale farms show a different pattern. The established farms of Generations 1 and 2 are mostly in good shape.

Only a quarter have high debt loads. The Generation 3 medium scale farmers have been extremely vulnerable, and three-fourths face critical debt loads.

Farm Expansion and Disaster Loans

What has brought about these different levels of vulnerability? Multivariate and univariate analyses based on data from interviews with Dodge County families point strongly to two particular actions that greatly raised debt levels: farm expansion and acceptance of special low-interest disaster loans (see appendix 2 for details about these analyses). Farm expansion in the 1970s was found by studies in Wisconsin (Salant and Saupe 1986), Texas and North Dakota (Murdock and Leistritz 1988), Minnesota (Rosenblatt 1990), and Iowa (Friedburger 1988) to be a critical determinant of 1980s farm viability. Expansion means a significant investment in facilities, land, or equipment that increases the scale of farm production. Of the 58 farms in the sample, 38 expanded in the 1970s. Some went into debt to do so, while others expanded by using savings. The data show, however, that such a decision was risky:

	1970s expansion	no expansion
good financial situation	13	16
(n = 29)		
poor financial situation	25	4
(n = 29)		

(chi-square = 9.23; p < .01; lambda = .41)

Expansion in the 1970s shows a highly significant correlation with poor financial situation at the end of the 1980s. Of 20 cases which did not expand, four-fifths are in good shape. Conversely, of the 38 that expanded, two-thirds are in poor shape. The figures show that 25 out of 29 farmers in poor shape expanded in the years just prior to the crisis. The lambda measure suggests that 41 percent of the overall variance in poor financial condition can be accounted for by this one decision (or series of decisions).

Farmers expanded their operations in the 1970s for several reasons. For some operations, it was a necessary part of beginning a farm or accommodating a son. Thus, it would have occurred despite the boom years and may have been seen as a rare event in the life cycle. Other cases involve a long-awaited opportunity to buy or rent land from a neighbor or family member. More commonly, however, 1970s expansion resulted from the high spirits of that inflationary period and was part of an ambitious farming style that sought larger scale and higher income.

The other important variable in raising debt levels revealed in the statistical analyses is the acceptance of a disaster loan. As we saw in chapter 7, disaster programs of the Farmers Home Administration and the Small Business Administration offered loans at very low interest. Many farmers in good financial situations considered taking these loans in order to obtain cheap credit for various purposes, although more conservative farmers tended to reject disaster loans as too dangerous:

	disaster loan acceptors	nonacceptors
good financial situation	6	23
poor financial situation	23	6

(chi-square = 17.66; $p < .01$; lambda = .59)

The figures above show a strong relationship between those who accepted financial assistance in the early years of the crisis and those who were out of business or in financial trouble by the late 1980s. On the surface, it may seem that accepting a disaster loan has no relationship to the causes of farm survival since farms already having difficulties would be the ones to seek this help. In fact, discussions with a number of farmers who accepted disaster loans revealed that their farms had been in quite good shape and might have survived without the additional burden of these "cheap money" loans. It is striking to see that of all the 29 disaster loan acceptors—from solvent and marginal farms alike—only 6 were able to take advantage of these programs without placing themselves in jeopardy. Of the 29 more cautious farmers who avoided these debts, nearly 80 percent remain in good financial shape. For statistical purposes, however, the measure is somewhat circular because debts are used as part of the dependent variable.

By combining these two indicators of farm operation, I created a new measure that reflects a particular orientation to farm management and debt that placed the farm at risk in the 1980s. Forty percent of the full-time farms in the study expanded as well as accepted a disaster loan, and nearly all are in poor financial shape:

	1970s expansion and disaster loan acceptance	remainder
good financial situation	2	27
poor financial situation	21	8

(chi-square = 23.3; $p < .01$; lambda = .66)

Only 2 cases remain in good financial shape out of 23 who expanded the farm and accepted disaster loans. Logistic regression reveals that the odds of a high debt-to-asset ratio are increased 35 times by these two actions.

These findings reveal a surprising fact—that few farmers are in trouble solely because of the drought or declining profits from the economic slump. Though a great many farms were hurt by low earnings, and in some cases catastrophic drought losses, if they were in the more fortunate group that did not expand in the 1970s, they were rarely made vulnerable to farm loss. In the figures given previously, we can see that only four farms that did not expand in the boom years ended up in poor financial condition. Each of these four represents a true drought loss case. All of these operators were approaching or over sixty, two faced debilitating illnesses, and one had a difficult death in the family. One is now out of business, and the other three face debts that are sufficiently large that it is unclear whether they will be able to pay them off. These cases suggest, then, that physically vigorous farmers, even without irrigation, have generally not been driven out of business by the drought years or the larger economic crisis. The key to survival seems to be farm management choices that avoid accepting risky debts and that permit the operation to absorb losses without going over the farm's financial limits.

Ambitious Management Style

The complex orientation of the ambitious management style to the farm, personal success, and family status and lifestyle is clearly connected to financial vulnerability in the current crisis. Based on my subjective codings of management style presented in chapter 5, the data show a strong relationship between the ambitious management style and high debt-to-asset ratio:

	ambitious management style	cautious management style
good financial situation	1	28
poor financial situation	22	7

(chi-square = 28.82; p < .01; lambda = .72)

Ambitious farm managers are also more likely to be out of business. Of the 23 operators coded in this way, 15 were already bankrupt, foreclosed, or engaged in liquidation in 1989.

Although the ambitious style was considered more progressive, up-to-date, and even admirable in the years after World War II and on into the boom, it has been shown to be highly risky in a downturn. This finding is true not only in Georgia but also in Iowa: "Ironically, many of those most at risk display personal and farm-firm characteristics that formerly were felt to ensure survival in a competitive and rapidly changing industry. . . . Those most susceptible to displacement seem to be persons who heeded the call during the 1970s to plant 'fence row to fence row,' treated farming as a business, were quick to adopt new technologies, and sought economies of scale. . . . In comparison, farmers most likely to weather the current crisis are those who, because of limited financial resources, poor credit standing, or conservative orientations, forfeited opportunities during the 1970s to expand their operations" (Bultena, Lasley, and Geller 1986:445–47). Steve Murdock and others found similar patterns in the Great Plains, where "producers under the most severe financial stress are often users of sophisticated financial management techniques who avail themselves of information from technical sources" (1986:425).

The more detailed information from the Dodge County study can help to shed light both on the ways management style is implicated in farm survival and on the reasons that certain exceptions exist. To understand the seven cautious managers who are in poor shape and the one ambitious manager in good shape, we must turn to a more textured analysis of farms within their more homogeneous groupings by scale and generation. In this context, we can also explore the role of farming skills and favorable resources (good soil and good allotments), the other two variables found to be important by the statistical analyses.

Before looking at the large scale and medium scale farms separately, however, it is useful to consider three aspects of management style for the entire sample, to see how they relate to financial situation: the use of hired labor, the level of consumption, and family goals as reflected by the agrarian and industrial marital models. The use of hired labor and a higher than average level of household consumption were identified in chapter 5 as components of an ambitious style; both are more amenable to quantitative analysis than the subjective dimensions of work ethic, concern with status, and desire for large scale that were also discussed as elements of the ambitious style. The data show that the use of hired labor correlates with high debts at a statistically significant level, but there is considerable variation:

	high use of hired labor	low use of hired labor
good financial situation	7	22

poor financial situation   14   15
(chi-square = 2.69; p = .10; lambda = .24)

In computing these figures, for large scale farms, the use of one full-time worker or more for every full-time operator was coded "high use." For medium scale farms, the use of one-half a full-time worker or more was coded "high use." The patterns shown support the idea that greater use of hired labor is more common on farms that are at risk financially. Looking at individual cases, it is clear that the large scale farms that use less labor—often because they are family partnerships— are more likely to have a cautious attitude toward debts, as well as the care of crops and livestock that leads to high earnings. The medium scale farms that tried to use hired labor also tend to be more vulnerable. These figures suggest that the use of hired labor may be a risky strategy, supporting the idea that there are diseconomies in large scale (Reinhardt and Barlett 1989). Medium scale farms generally avoid these disadvantages, and family partnerships can do the same while permitting a larger operation.

Another component of the ambitious operation is lifestyle, and as we have seen, consumption standards are an important marker of success for many Dodge County farmers. On the other hand, some Dodge County residents say farmers in trouble "brought it all on themselves" with an overly affluent lifestyle. Such a conclusion rankles among many farmers but is clearly true in some individual cases. One operator who went bankrupt jokingly admitted the role of high consumption standards in his own farm's demise: "You can only make it in farming today by having one dim bulb, no indoor plumbing, no phone, no car—like the old days." To test this relationship between affluence and farm viability, I used the data on houses, cars, and household appliances discussed in chapter 5. For a total of 68 households on the 58 farms in this study, I compared family consumption levels with the norm for the other families of the same generation and scale of farm. Those whose lifestyle was more affluent than that of their peers in at least two of the three dimensions of houses, cars, and appliances were coded as "high consumption."[5]

	high consumption	low or average consumption
good financial situation	9	27
poor financial situation	16	16

(chi-square = 3.54; p = .06; lambda = .22)

The data show that a lifestyle more affluent than that of one's peers is often linked with high debts; the odds of a farmer with a higher level of consumption being in the "poor" group are increased almost three times. On the other hand, consuming at an average or a modest level is more often characteristic of families who have gotten through the crisis in better shape.

A final aspect of the ambitious or cautious management style involves family goals and aspirations with regard to the farm. In chapter 6, we saw that the agrarian and industrial marital models reflected very different commitments on the part of women to the farm life and to the sacrifices necessary in the crisis. The data show that women's marital model seems to play a role in farm survival as well:

	industrial marital model	agrarian marital model
good financial situation	6	18
poor financial situation	13	11

(chi-square = 3.14; p = .07; lambda = .29)

In farms that are in good financial shape, it is much more likely that the woman has an agrarian marital model. Farms in poor shape show a split in women's marital models. Though women's ideals about marriage are certainly not determinative of farm survival, they support the cautious management style that lowers the risk of farm loss.[6]

Large Scale Farms: Cautious Managers and Silver Spoon Farmers

By looking at the large and medium scale groups separately, we can explore the role of other variables that may account for different patterns of farm survival. Table 8-2 shows the connection between management style and financial condition. For both older and younger operators, the ambitious style is highly risky. The one ambitious farmer in good shape is a Generation 1 operator who did not expand in the 1970s. He had already amassed the size of farm he desired, his living standards were high, and he had no son to bring into the operation and thus avoided risky new investments. All the other ambitious operators expanded in the years before the crisis, and most took on disaster loans as well.

The cautious large scale operators faced the downturn from a less-leveraged position and worked to boost profits and cut costs. They differ from the ambitious farmers in preferring to do their own work, therefore using less hired labor. They do not show lower levels of household consumption, however; their operations

Table 8-2. Financial Situation of Large Scale Farms
by Management Style and Generation

	Number	Poor Financial Condition
Generations 1 and 2		
Ambitious	8	7
Cautious	5	0
Generation 3		
Ambitious	3	3
Cautious	5	1
Total	21	11 (52%)

support a substantial degree of comfort. A few took disaster loans and some expanded successfully, but their cautious management style allowed them to handle a degree of risk.

Beyond these concerns of management style are two other issues revealed by statistical analysis to be important: resources and skills. We saw in chapter 4 that medium scale farms generally ranked below large scale farms in both dimensions but were not thereby prevented from continuing in operation successfully. Here, we can look within the large scale group to see if certain advantages in resources or skills play a critical role. A range of variables that might be expected to be significant did not show any correlation with the financial situations of large scale farmers, including access to family land or equipment, higher education, family background, wives' labor contributions, off-farm income, years of experience, and overall production skill (see appendix 2, table A-1). The two resource variables that show high lambda values are good quality soil and federal program rights. Of eleven cases with resource deficits in one or the other area, nine are in poor financial shape.

Lower crop production skills also correlate with higher debts. Though most large scale farms have good skills by the codings described in chapter 4 and in appendix 1, of the 5 cases (out of 21) with poor skills in crop production, all are in poor financial shape. The magnitude of these skill and resource disadvantages can be seen in a few figures. The median product sales per acre of the established large scale farmers (Generations 1 and 2) is $313 for those in good shape and $116 for those in poor shape. The debt levels between these two groups are also striking:

$126 per acre for the group in good financial condition and $486 for the group in poor condition.

The cases with resource deficits and poorer skills are found in both age groups, and all but one are ambitious in style. Thus, these operators seem either to have expanded beyond their access to high-quality cropland or to have insufficient yields and federal program benefits to keep up with the debts they contracted. Several large scale farmers had adequate resources to sustain a large operation and an affluent standard of living, had they not chosen to expand at the time they did (or to the extent they did). Some of these established operators were particularly fortunate in their access to large family estates, abundant capital, and good machinery, yet they went out of business. Extraordinary advantages were occasionally squandered by optimistic operators who were sure the economy would turn around. They tended to respond to the crisis with the same levels of expenditures they had grown accustomed to during the boom years; several bought expensive irrigation systems or took advantage of opportunities to buy land. In contrast, many cautious farmers thought about expensive irrigation systems or expansion but postponed such expenses until their financial situations were more secure.

A commitment to the ambitious definition of personal success framed the choices of a number of these large scale operators and their families. Several were unwilling to cut back their standard of living in the face of declining incomes. One such farmer said that meeting his parental obligations was more important to him than saving the farm. "I want my children to have the things that others do in school. Not to the point of throwing money away, but I don't want my kids looked down on." His kids do not go without anything they need, he said, and they get most of what they *want*. "I wouldn't want to stay in farming if I can't provide that." In this case, farm debts remained unpaid while lifestyle was maintained, even to the point of bankruptcy. This operator then turned to off-farm work to support his desired lifestyle and his sense of success as a husband and father. Women's aspirations also affect these management decisions; in all but one of the six large scale farms that have gone out of business, the couples share an industrial marital model that places family lifestyle ahead of the farm.

The determinants of survival for Generation 3 large scale farmers reflect a mixture of the forces that lead to both a more closed and a more open farming occupation. What distinguishes the four in good shape from the four in poor shape is, first, the magnitude of their debts: a median of $24 an acre, as opposed to $432 an acre, respectively. Second, and related to these debt levels, is the amount of family help they have received, especially in access to land and fully developed, prosperous farms. These young operators have extraordinary advantages and can be labeled "silver spoon" farmers, using John Bennett's (1982) label for similar Saskatchewan farmers. Both high start-up costs and any disadvantages of inexperience have been avoided for such farmers. They reflect the latest phase of the pattern observed in chapter 2 whereby Generation 2 farmers received considerably more family help than those in Generation 1.

If the silver spoon farmers were all in good shape and the self-made young farmers were all out of business, it could be argued that family privileges are essential to getting through the crisis. Fortunately for those who would like to see farm survival more dependent on personal efforts than class background, there are four Generation 3 operators who are extremely hardworking and productive and whose skills and sales are among the highest in the county. These "whiz kid" farmers were supported by the Farmers Home Administration, most have been able to establish family farms without parental assistance, and they have worked rapidly up to a large scale. Two are in excellent financial shape, and although the other two have high debts, they can confidently be expected to survive. The whiz kids are highly visible in the county and are part of the reason why many Dodge Countians believe skill determines survival.

Thus, the successful large scale farmers either avoided debt in the first place or responded rapidly to changing economic conditions and scaled back their expenses. Their operations were built with an awareness that retrenchment or caution might become necessary. Such a shift in style did not threaten them; their self-image and satisfaction in farming were based less on scale and status than on skill and survival. For some younger large scale farmers with access to family resources, good soil and allotments permit them to begin operation even in the midst of the crisis. A few cases without the advantages of these silver spoon farmers have become successful with superior skills. Ambitious farmers without strong skills and good resources face (or have faced) farm loss.

Medium Scale Farms: Cautious
Managers and Second Career Farmers

In the beginning of this chapter, we saw that the older medium scale farmers have come through the crisis with the least loss, while the Generation 3 group faces high levels of debt. Of Generations 1 and 2, only 10 percent were out of business as the study ended, but two-thirds of the younger group were forced out. Why do

Table 8-3. Financial Situation of Medium Scale Farms
by Management Style and Generation

	Number	Poor Financial Condition
Generations 1 and 2		
Ambitious	1	1
Cautious	19	4
Generation 3		
Ambitious	11	11
Cautious	6	2
Total	37	18 (49%)

age and experience seem to make more difference in the success rates of these farmers? Why have the young medium scale operators been so vulnerable?

Among the established Generation 1 and 2 farmers, we have seen in chapter 5 that a cautious management style is typical, and table 8-3 shows that most are in good financial shape. "I haven't lost any money," said one, "which means I'm doing real well." The case of another older couple provides an illustration of medium scale survival strategies. They not only weathered the crisis years but toward the end of the decade bought land and are in a position to do so again, should a good opportunity arise. They live modestly in a cinder block house and have passed the stage of high expenses with their children. Drought losses hurt their yields, but they used government program payments and savings to buy an inexpensive irrigation system, which made them less vulnerable in dry years. They fix their own equipment, cut corners with such purchases as a secondhand tractor with no cab, and avoid expensive vehicles like four-wheel drive trucks. Their frugality on the farm is augmented by a small income from the wife's part-time job. Though their decision to risk buying irrigation might seem to be an important factor in their success, many conservative medium scale farms have survived without irrigation.

Among the older medium scale farmers, a few experimented briefly with more ambitious expansion. In one case, a man who owned 250 acres rented 450 more, bought extra equipment, and hired a full-time worker to try to increase profits. Instead, he suffered a considerable loss and rapidly retreated to a size he could work himself. One of the cautious farmers in financial difficulties was still trying to retrench when the study ended. The one ambitious farmer in this group, who contracted the highest per-acre debt level in the county, confessed, "We lived beyond our means."

The remaining four older cautious farm families in trouble are the cases discussed above in which the additional stresses of the drought combined with advancing age or illness to result in serious income losses. Said one woman, "Until this disaster period, we never knew what a debt was—we never thought about trying to get ahead much." This couple was frugal in their lifestyle, but low yields made them unable to pay back their operating loans, and they struggled to make a good enough crop to keep up with interest costs.

Among the established medium scale farms, the variables of lower skill, smaller allotments, and poorer soil seem to play no contributing role in leading to financial distress, as occurs among the large scale farms. Overall, this group is modest in its production, with a median of $86 in sales per acre, but modest also in debts, at $39 an acre. The cautious farmer's aversion to debt and acceptance of a lower standard of consumption—on the farm and in the home—have been the keys to survival.

Turning now to the group with the highest attrition rate, of the seventeen Generation 3 medium scale farms, only four (24%) have good debt-to-asset ratings. This group was susceptible to the drama of the boom years that promised high incomes in return for expansion and borrowing. Most went heavily into debt to start their farms but had insufficient experience or equity to survive immediate drought losses. As we saw in chapter 7, farming journals, experts, and bankers alike pushed them toward a growth ethic. A highly leveraged farm was seen as progressive and dynamic; it symbolized an ability to manipulate credit, machinery, and hands in a more sophisticated way. Some had considerable help from families, with access to land and equipment, but their ambitious goals and acceptance of disaster loans in the early crisis years made recovery very difficult. A few overinvested in machinery, and one even admitted that he could have tended twice as much land with the equipment he had. Others attempted risky ventures in livestock or other facilities but had no cushion to withstand a major loss. Many of these ambitious younger farmers were supported or encouraged by wives with an industrial orientation, some of whom had not grown up on farms and had no basis from which to counsel caution. The drought years placed an unrelenting pressure on these young farmers, many of whom had no irrigation.

A major factor affecting the survival of this group is that ten of them are second career farmers who gave up full-time jobs in some other line of work to return to farming in their middle-adult years. Only one is in good financial shape, and most are now out of business. Some had parents who farmed, while others had been associated with their grandparents' farms. Second career farmers face a host of disadvantages, as one case illustrates. This man loved his father's occupation and always wanted to farm, but after high school he chose the more secure income of an off-farm job. Frustration with his job combined with accessible agricultural loan money encouraged him to switch occupations, just as the good years in farming ended. He borrowed heavily to buy equipment, rent land, and pay for fertilizer, seed, gas, and living expenses. He had no familiarity with the land he rented, no family financial support or backup skills, and no equity in the farm. The land available to rent was not of the best quality. In addition, his family had approached an expensive phase of child rearing. Though his wife tried to be supportive, she had not married a farmer, was not from a farming background, and had little patience with the mounting debts. Her job kept this farm in business through a number of years, but eventually their high debts became impossible to pay, and they gave up.

When we remove the second career cases from this cohort, its survival rate becomes much more similar to the large scale farmers; 57 percent (four out of seven cases) are in poor financial shape. Not all of these young farmers with high debts will go under; some are unusually skillful—similar to the situation we saw with the younger large scale farms—and will probably be able to repay their loans. Though debt levels as high as theirs for both large and medium farms are cause for concern, the data show that younger operators have been able to enter farming successfully in the crisis years. The higher rate of loss overall for the younger medium scale group reflects the sharp rise in second career operators that boosted the cohort size; the "boom" in new farmers, we can see now, was to be short-lived.

What distinguishes the more fortunate cases of the four young medium scale farmers who have managed to begin farming without high debts? All have received substantial help from their families, through land inheritance or rental. This help is modest in scale compared to some of the silver spoon farmers, but combined with a cautious management style and a thrifty lifestyle, it helped to contribute to a sound financial condition. Although clearly not silver spoon farmers, these more fortunate medium scale operators might be labeled "stainless steel spoon" farmers. They reflect the same process we saw among the larger operations in which substantial family support facilitates successful entry into farming at an extremely difficult historical moment.

Besides the cheaper access to land of the more fortunate group, land quality tends to be somewhat better and they are generally more highly skilled. This financially secure young group has a median of $292 in sales per acre, over double the level of the rest of their cohort. Their debts are much lower as well. This group managed to make substantial fixed investments on their farms, not through loans, but through savings. Lower consumption standards, however, do not distinguish this small group from the others; most younger medium scale farmers live similar lifestyles regardless of levels of financial success.

Different expectations about work also distinguish some younger farmers. Farming with machinery and chemicals is seen as much less strenuous than farming in previous decades, and some young operators did not expect to have to work as hard as farming today demands. Staying up nights with farrowing sows, working most Saturdays, deferring vacations, and putting in long hours from early mornings to late summer nights came as a surprise to some young farmers, especially those whose parents were not farmers. Though the majority put intense work effort into trying to make it, a few fit the stereotype expressed by some older farmers who say that "these young farmers don't know how to work."

In sum, the cautious management style served medium scale farmers well, and most who resisted the pressures of a more entrepreneurial management style have continued to farm successfully through this period. The crisis years betrayed the hopes of many second career farmers that an independent life on the farm might provide them the work environment they loved while also sustaining a satisfactory livelihood. The high costs of becoming established as a new farmer—a trend that has continued since the technological revolutions of the 1950s and 1960s—makes entry difficult. Especially with droughts and low profits, young farmers with family support have a clear advantage. As we saw with the large scale operators, the benefits of these advantages can be diminished by taking chances with expansion, high debts, or dreams of affluence. All medium scale farm families value higher income and desire a comfortable lifestyle, but they do not compare their situation to large scale farmers. Many, like the McClintocks in chapter 4, are proud of owning a farm and having a nice brick home and an appropriate array of appliances and vehicles. Though their aspirations for the farm are more modest—and less risky—than the goals of many ambitious farmers, their standard of living represents evidence of having "made it" just the same.

Part-Time and Retirement Farms

When this analysis of the determinants of farm survival is extended to the part-time and retirement farms, the data reveal many of the same vulnerabilities as found among the full-time farms. Of twenty-five farmers in the retirement group, only two faced financial difficulties. Both experienced severe health problems that inhibited their debt repayment. One bought land just before the crisis began, and the other accepted a disaster loan. Both were small in scale, having cut back from larger acreages, and both had been generally cautious in style, until accepting these recent debts.

Of forty part-time farmers in the 1982 random sample, only nine faced high debts. Most of these farms in trouble were clearly cases in which a more cautious management orientation had been betrayed in either the excitement of the boom years or the pressures of the bust. Some were newcomers to farming and lacked the skills to survive the drought years. Many were seduced by the disaster loan programs. Of these nine with high debts, four were forced out of business, and three were still struggling with lenders and negotiations as the study ended. The remaining two had been able to salvage the farm with family help.

The vast majority of part-time and retirement farms, however, weathered the crisis without major financial stress: 90 percent of the retirement farms and 78 percent of the part-time farms. Many were frustrated by the decline in earnings, and some were bitter about losses, but most had managed their operations in a way that safeguarded them through the bad years. One part-time farming couple agreed that they lost money on their farm but are comfortable with their decision to take this risk. Said the husband: "I have no regrets—I love farming."

Part-time and retired farmers, like many medium scale farmers, were unaffected by poor resources and skills. Very few invested in irrigation, peanut allotments were very low, and many suffered the disadvantages of poor soil as well. By the skill measures, most were less-skilled operators, and farm product sales per acre, with a few exceptions, were not high. Through a cautious management style, these small scale operators avoided debts and kept losses under control. The loss of extra income was painful to some families, but others, especially the elderly, did not expect farming activities to continue indefinitely and were able to live on Social Security or other income. Their experience in the crisis confirms the general patterns seen for the medium scale farm operations.

Conclusion

This analysis of the determinants of farm survival has revealed a number of surprises. One conclusion is that drought losses alone did not produce a high-risk situation; most Dodge County families were able to cut corners, reduce living standards, or take on sufficient off-farm work to supplement poor farm earnings without jeopardizing the farm with debts. As I looked at the scorched fields and heard the reports of drought losses, I did not expect that, in the end, most families would be less injured by these hardships than by certain choices they might make. Another surprise is that the purchase of irrigation did not turn out to be a good predictor of survival. Although irrigation facilities certainly increased yields on many farms, the high costs of purchasing and operating the systems were a heavy burden in other cases. Irrigation turns out to be both a way to reduce environmental risk and a risk factor itself.The study also revealed that high levels of off-farm income did not correlate with farm survival. Though some families were able to hold on longer than others because of this subsidy to the household budget, few were able to earn sufficient amounts off the farm to put a dent in heavy farm debts.

Skill was also not consistently related to farm survival, though it was more important for the large scale than the medium scale farm operators. In general the refrain of the agricultural experts in the 1970s, "You have to be efficient to survive," pushed farmers toward larger scale and ignored the option of the medium scale farming path. Lower yields, sales, and overall skill have been shown to present no major problem for established farmers whose goals and consumption standards remain modest.

Large farm scale, technological sophistication, and good investments in facilities were found to confer no distinct advantage in the crisis. Nor can it be concluded that "small is beautiful"; the medium scale farms in Generation 3 were found to be very vulnerable to high debts. Only among the small, part-time farms does limited scale correlate with survival—in this case, because the farm is not the primary occupation of the farmer.

Over the recent history of Dodge County, we have observed the increasing concentration of farm resources and the role of federal program subsidies in supporting large farm scale. I expected that unequal access to such privileges would create benefits for some farmers in this crisis period. In this domain as well, the medium scale farming path shows that many operations can overcome resource disadvantages. Though high earnings from peanut, cotton, tobacco, and other government programs are clearly important in particular cases, they are not predictors of success. Other resources, such as cheap family land, loans of equipment, superior soil, and labor contributions from wives and children, were also shown to be benefits to individual farmers but were not correlated with survival. A higher level of education is another privilege that increases earnings outside the farm sector but did not relate to the financial status of farmers in the crisis. Although there are definitely some skills learned in college that bring benefits to farm operators, many management traditions that enhance survival are not taught in school. It seems, therefore, that opportunities to enter farming for less-advantaged families remain open in spite of the impact of the crisis.

The management orientations linked to survival are encapsulated in the cautious/ambitious dichotomy, which defines a farmer's goals and attitudes toward farm scale, manual labor, debt, and social status. The large scale farms that followed the ambitious style into the crisis years mostly ended with suffocating debt loads. Only a few, with very high skills and extraordinary resources, were able to pull out from under the burden. Cautious, debt-averse operators, whether medium or large in scale, found themselves better able to withstand the crisis. Some were even able to make money during these years. Their commitment to careful crop and livestock management, lower use of hired labor, and satisfaction with the work ethic paid off. The abandonment of the cautious management style brought high risks, and those who accepted disaster loans, undertook land or facilities expansion, or borrowed heavily to start farming found themselves in treacherous financial straits.

Farm survival can also be jeopardized by the high consumption standards characteristic of the industrial marital model of personal success. More accurately, the desire for affluence that is often part of an ambitious management style may not permit the retrenchment or frugality necessary to stay in farming. Farm operators who took up farming as a second career were found to be particularly vulnerable in this regard. The data on marital models suggests that women who are more concerned with the farm's success and more personally committed to the farm life and who expect to share responsibility for the family's financial well-being can contribute to farm survival by supporting a cautious management style. Such women are more likely to accept greater lifestyle stringency and are less likely to label the crisis situation a failure on the part of their husbands, thus eliminating some of the financial pressure on the farm. For the medium scale farmers, this contribution of farm women is particularly important.

We have seen that life cycle considerations have affected the financial situations of farms at several points in the Dodge County story, with expenses involved in farm start-up and the high costs of raising children during the middle years. But in each of these life cycle moments, management style or the amount of family help takes precedence in farm survival. The young large scale operators I have called silver spoon farmers avoided the high debts forced on many second career farmers. As for the expensive middle years, the Generation 2 farmers who are medium scale are all cautious in style and most are in good financial condition, whereas the Generation 2 farmers who are large scale are mostly ambitious and in poor financial condition.

The conflicting visions of farm success presented by the cautious and ambitious management styles—which are linked with the two marital models—reflect the larger cultural divergence between an agrarian and an industrial way of life. Concerns with long-term planning, money management, and commitment to a multigenerational agricultural business clash with the emphasis on short-term gains, expansion, and risk-taking entrepreneurship that are highly valued in a capitalist system. In a short period of time, the tables were turned on the ambitious farmers in Dodge County, and they watched their management strategies drag them deeper into debt. Just as in the Depression years, the cautious operators were better able to hold on through year after grueling year. Their style of farming represents an alternative path, and as the overall number of farms throughout the country continues to fall, their numbers decline as well. The large and medium scale cohorts of younger farmers in Dodge County provide evidence, however, that the cautious style has been successfully transmitted to a new generation, even in the face of adverse economic conditions.

It remains to be seen whether the final outcome of the crisis will be a shifting, once again, of management style prestige away from the more ambitious ethic. If farm incomes in the 1990s surge, the loss of one-third of Dodge County farms may come to be seen as a temporary setback, and the goals and farming styles that motivated the ambitious farmers may once again come into vogue. If farming conditions remain bleak, the modest lifestyle and work ethic of the cautious farm family may come to be recognized as the only sure means of survival for the family farm in the United States.

NINE

The Aftermath of the Crisis:

Structural Change, Sustainability,

and the Meaning of Farm Loss

"I enjoyed farming 'til it got to where it beat you," said one older woman. "Farming is a gamble and I lost," admitted a younger farmer. The mother of a young farmer who was foreclosed said, "It was the worst experience in our lifetime." Though similar in their pain, each family's story is unique, as these Dodge County men and women endured mounting hardships, stress piled upon stress, and ended by going out of business. The loss of farming as an occupation, an investment, and a way of life means different things to different families. For some, farming brought dreams of success based on an agrarian ideal. For others, it represented a chance to "get rich" or achieve status based on a more industrial ideal. The loss of such dreams is a pain felt so deeply it will "never go away." Compared to families in more isolated farming areas, such as North Dakota (Leistritz et al. 1987), Dodge County families have not faced as much hardship in loss of homes and the need to relocate. Nevertheless, the impact on families and communities has been substantial, and the second part of this chapter will explore the distinct dimensions of the process of leaving farming. Through the stories of men, women, and children, this chapter will also take stock of the meaning and emotional impact of farm loss for those involved.

Another aim of this project has been to determine the impact of the crisis on rural communities; I have in particular been concerned to assess changes in the structure of agriculture. As explored in the Introduction, postwar trends in U.S. agriculture led to predictions that the crisis would favor the elite farms, push medium scale farms out of business, and lead to a structure of agriculture made up of fewer and larger farms. Such a trend could be expected to have adverse consequences for Dodge County's communities and the broader social welfare. This chapter will explore the extent to which land and capital have become more concentrated in Dodge County and will assess the implications of irrigation as the latest phase in the technology treadmill. In addition to evaluating the ability of Dodge County farms to survive economically, there remains the issue of ecological sustainability. The drought and farming practices have brought a number of environmental changes, raising several questions about future farm viability.

Concentration of Resources

Have resources become more concentrated as a result of the crisis in Dodge County? To answer this question, I compared changes in total farm acreage and total farm sales for the large and medium scale farms. As in the last chapter, it is useful to divide each scale group into established and beginning farms. Levels of capital investment per farm and returns to land and capital investments show some surprising patterns among the four groups.

If the crisis accelerated trends toward larger farms, we would expect to see the large scale groups of operations growing in average size and in their proportion of the total farmland in the county. The established large scale farms might particularly be expected to take advantage of land for sale since their own original land purchases and equipment investments should have been paid off in the good years. Table 9-1 shows, instead, that established Generation 1 and 2 large farms have held constant in their land share, at 48 percent.[1] Their mean farm acreage has also been quite stable. The data reveal the concentration in landholdings represented by the large farms—although they are less than a fifth of all farms and a quarter of all operators, they control nearly half the acreage. But this concentration did not increase over the crisis years. Some operations were able to expand in this period, but their gains were balanced by those forced out of farming. Established medium scale farms show a similar stability in size; their proportion of county land has remained essentially unchanged, and their average acreage declined only about 40 acres. Their smaller farm size in 1986 reflects not so much a loss of farm units but a retrenchment in farm size, as extra rented acres were given up and farm operations were streamlined in the drought years.

Younger large scale farmers show the greatest gain in land share, from 21 percent of total farm acreage in 1981 to 28 percent in 1986. The role of partnerships

Table 9-1. Land and Sales Distribution by Farm Group

Farm Group (Number of Operators)	Percent of Farms (Percent of Operators)	1981 Percent of Total Land	1986 Percent of Total Land	1982 Percent of Total Sales	1986 Percent of Total Sales
Established large scale (n = 19)	18 (24)	48	48	41	49
Beginning large scale (n = 16)	16 (20)	21	28	26	29
Established medium scale (n = 22)	39 (28)	17	15	14	11
Beginning medium scale (n = 23)	28 (29)	14	9	19	11

is visible in this group: although these younger farmers make up only 16 percent of farm units in the county, they comprise 20 percent of operators. They began the crisis period with an appropriate share of land and expanded to a somewhat larger proportion. This gain came at the expense of the many medium scale Generation 3 farmers forced out of business, whose share dropped from 14 percent to 9 percent of the total. These figures show that the younger, more elite farmers as a group have been able to follow a normal life cycle pattern of expansion. They are the main group to take the high risk of buying new farmland.

The figures conceal the fact that the successful medium scale Generation 3 farmers also bought land, because their gain is canceled out by the loss of land from those forced out of farming. To assess the long-term trends in land ownership and farm size, it is necessary to take account of the expanded Generation 3 cohort that includes the influx of second career farmers attracted by the boom years. If we exclude the highly vulnerable second career operators from the beginning medium scale group, its share of land in the county shows only a small drop, from 7 percent to 6 percent. This cohort thus has only a small amount of the total land in farms, but it has been able to hold its own in the heat of the farm crisis, in spite of losing a number of its members. On the other hand, this less-privileged group has not been able to expand average farm size. As other trends discussed below suggest, medium scale farms may be following a somewhat slower pace of enterprise development.

Unlike the acreage measures, the share of total farm sales in the county shows a somewhat clearer pattern of increasing concentration of earnings among the large farms. Established large farms in 1986 sold almost half of the county's agricultural products, and the newer large farms account for another 29 percent. This leaves only 22 percent of sales for all the medium scale farmers, a decline from 33 percent in 1982. The figures illustrate that larger farms have benefited from more secure yields because of irrigation and from larger payments from various federal programs. Their higher sales provide a more comfortable income, but it is not clear that the medium scale farms suffer a disadvantage in continuing to farm, once established. Their share of sales declined more markedly for the Generation 3 cohort, from 19 to 11 percent, but this proportion reflects the problem of the expanded cohort size. When the second career farmers are excluded, the beginning medium scale operators shifted from 12 to 8 percent of the county's sales, a more modest decline. These data suggest that there has been some movement in the overall structure of sales, but it has not been large.

Further concentration in capital investments on the farm is another possible outcome of the crisis years. The younger large scale farmers showed a high rate of farm investment in 1986. Average value of machinery, farm buildings, ponds, and irrigation systems equaled $216,136 per farm; for the established large scale group, the figure was $269,437. Medium-sized farms averaged $31,000–34,000, one-eighth the level of capital investment found among large scale farms. It is unfortunate that I do not have data from 1982 to track shifting patterns in this level of investment from earlier in the crisis, because there is considerable variation from farm to farm. Some medium scale farms have added irrigation but, of course, larger farms have done so as well, and it is unclear if their relative proportions of total county farm investments have changed. Since many of the heaviest expanders went out of business, it is hard to determine whether capital became more or less concentrated over the crisis years.

A final issue with regard to resource concentration is the relative efficiency of resource use, and I examined returns to land and capital for the four farm groups. The survival of medium scale farms in Dodge County is not due entirely to the more modest aspirations and lifestyle of operators; as a group, they are highly efficient with the land and capital they use. Table 9-2 shows that the beginning medium scale farms earn the highest sales per acre at $228 and $205 in the two time periods, substantially above either the large scale established or beginning group. (When the second career farms are excluded, their earnings rise even higher to $317 in 1981 and $243 in 1986.) The established Generation 1 and 2 medium scale group shows lower sales per acre, conforming to the skill patterns discussed in chapter 4. The medium scale groups are, not surprisingly, lower in their capital

Table 9-2. Comparison of Sales and Fixed Investments
per Acre by Farm Group

| | Mean Sales per Acre | | Mean Equipment and Facilities Value per Acre |
	1981	1986	1986
Established large scale	$147	$187	$173
Beginning large scale	210	193	287
Established medium scale	138	134	126
Beginning medium scale	228	205	118

investments in facilities and equipment; these operators are cautious in their farm investments and seem to limit their purchases to those with higher than average payoffs.

Although the estimations of equipment value used here are valid only within a 10 percent margin and are affected by the fact that younger farmers generally have newer equipment, these figures suggest that younger medium scale farmers are highly competitive in the efficiency of their use of capital. The advantages that more elite farmers enjoy in economies of scale and in government program payments do not result in more efficient earnings per dollar invested.

In sum, the figures suggest that in spite of the drought and the economic slump, the medium scale path remains viable. The large scale farms have increased their overall share of sales in the county, but the data on control of acreage shows little support for the idea of a long-term displacement of medium scale farms. Even the Generation 3 medium scale group has been shown to have held on to its share of land, when the expanded boom years cohort is taken into account. The advantages enjoyed by large scale farms in government payments are seen clearly in the overall sales figures, but the medium scale farms continue to earn well on their modest acreage.

Cannibalism and the Farm Crisis

Many researchers expected that the farm crisis would bring an opportunity for large scale farms to expand and would speed up the process of cannibalization by which the weaker, usually smaller farms would lose out in competition with larger, more innovative farms (Pfeffer and Gilbert 1989). This expectation derives in part from the growing size of large farms all over the United States in the post–World War II era and from the trends inherent in the technology treadmill. Willard Cochrane's (1979) concept of the technology treadmill claims that farm mechanization and other forms of technological advancement have created in U.S. agriculture a consistent pressure toward farm expansion. This theory argues that the "early-bird" adopter of an innovation reaps a gain, usually through increased yields. As more and more farmers use the new technology, the increased supply of farm products drives prices down. The later innovator is at a disadvantage because he or she must make the same investment to keep profits from falling but does not experience the same reward in the form of higher income. "Farm technological advance in a free market situation forces the participants to run on a treadmill." The "strong and aggressive farmers" are then in a privileged position to buy up the "laggard" innovators, who are "weak and inefficient . . . [resulting] in widespread cannibalism in American agriculture" (ibid.:389–90).

The droughts combined with the cost-price squeeze in Dodge County have turned these predictions on their head. The large scale "early bird" farmers were shown in chapter 8 to be much more likely to be forced out of business or endure an agonizing decade of struggle with creditors. The "laggard" medium scale farmers whose size and cautious management style made them resistant to the latest technological advances were able to survive the crisis with less danger. Some of the large scale farmers were successful in paying off innovations early on— irrigation, expanded hog facilities, or heavy machinery—but in the end, these investments did not always help much in surviving the crisis. Some technological innovations did not bring the expected benefits, often because maintenance and annual operating costs were high.

There is also little evidence that the crisis allowed large farms to expand greatly through purchasing land at the expense of farmers forced out of business. The full-time farmers in the study were asked to list all land purchases in the history of their farms, yielding data on 108 land transactions from the 1940s to the 1980s (most, however, were in the 1960s and 1970s). For each case, the relationship of the buyer and the seller was specified, and most farms were found to be purchased from retired farmers, their heirs, or close relatives who chose to sell for reasons unrelated to farm financial stress. Only 16 percent of the land ever purchased by the farmers in the study came from farms forced out of business. (This coding includes kin and neighbors forced out of business.) Thus, acquisition of land through farm failure has been relatively rare in Dodge County.

The crisis years increased the percentage of land bought from displaced farmers, but mainly because so little land changed hands. Between 1977 and 1986, only 2,790 acres were bought or inherited in the county, the equivalent of only one or two large farms. Of this acreage, 45 percent came from farms forced out of business, and half of that was one large transaction. Removing that one sale from the county total of acreage bought during the crisis years brings the percentage of land gained through others' misfortune to 21 percent, only slightly higher than the proportion over the whole forty years (16%). Relatively few farms expanded in this period, due to the adverse financial situation, and there is no support for the expectation of widespread cannibalism of medium-sized farms by large farms. In many cases, land lost by farmers reverted to or was bought by relatives or by investors who put the land into timber.

Irrigation and the Technology Treadmill

Irrigation is the latest of the major technological changes in agriculture, as outlined in chapter 2. It ratchets upward the annual costs of production and presents dilemmas to farmers because it reduces environmentally caused risk while increasing financial risk. Early adopters of irrigation in the 1970s were mostly large scale farmers who made the investment to protect and boost peanut and tobacco yields. Some found irrigated cotton, corn, and soybeans were profitable as well. Once the drought years hit with force, those who had irrigation benefited greatly, though they also complained of the increased costs of production. Economic research at the University of Georgia suggests that irrigation is often too expensive to permit farms to break even, given current crop prices. It does, however, lower the risk of complete crop failure.

Irrigation represents a form of labor intensification as well as capital intensification; farmers must spend more hours when they have an irrigation system running and must manage its operation carefully. Many farmers complain of the heavy physical and psychological burden. But in view of the fact that a number of Dodge Countians believe that the local climate is becoming permanently drier, they have opted to invest in irrigation.

If rainfall conditions were to return to the norm prior to 1975, it is not clear that irrigation would remain essential to Coastal Plain agriculture. It does give crops more ideal growing conditions, but farmers report that disease and insect damage from the moisture are increasing as well. Costs can also be quite high when the expensive equipment begins to need substantial repair. Irrigation thus presents some clear economic trade-offs as well as some unknown ecological challenges.

Nevertheless, irrigation's role in preventing major losses is increasingly recognized by even the medium scale farmers. A number of the successful younger medium scale farmers have decided to buy irrigation systems in light of these benefits. Given that irrigation is not feasible for all parts of the United States and that commodity prices are determined by national supplies including production from nonirrigated areas, it seems that this particular technological innovation has not come to later Dodge County adopters with any noticeable disadvantage. Some medium scale farmers benefited from the opportunity to buy secondhand irrigation systems from "early birds" who have now been forced out of business. Unlike the early adopters who often chose expensive systems and took on large debts, the later medium scale adopters tend to pay off their equipment costs quickly and finance them in part through savings. Younger farmers seem to find this major investment more feasible, given the years ahead in which they can reap its benefits. One Generation 3 farmer said that irrigation is changing the whole way farming is carried out in the county. Those operators who are unwilling to risk the high start-up costs of irrigation have turned to hog production or growing vegetables. So far, evidence suggests these are viable alternatives to rowcrops. The continued survival of the nonirrigated medium scale rowcrop farms also shows that established farmers are not forced onto the treadmill in this instance.

To support the investment in irrigation, some farmers have increased their farm size. Large pieces of equipment such as cotton pickers and grain combines also require a larger farm to justify the high cost. Several of the highly successful Generation 2 and 3 medium scale farms are expanding cautiously and adding to their equipment inventory with some of these items. This pattern suggests that an enterprise life cycle of expansion may be occurring more slowly among the medium scale farms.

In addition to making irrigation and equipment purchases from savings, another strategy that supports safe expansion is family partnership. We have seen that a substantial number of large scale farms have been partnerships for generations, and it is clear that some of the financially stable younger medium scale farms have benefited as well from the pooled resources and close cooperation of several households.[2] Both frugality and partnership provide ways for medium scale farmers to respond successfully to the pressures of the drought and the crisis that strengthen rather than erode their desired farming style.

Ecological Impact of the Boom and Bust

An issue related to the economic sustainability of farms is the ecological impact of the drought and the crisis on Dodge County and the implications for the future of agriculture in the region. The disastrous droughts over the decade raised several questions about long-term environmental change, especially in creek levels, fish populations, and aquifers. Many families report that the creeks in the county never used to dry up but that during the long dry spells of the 1980s, many did run dry. One farmer remembers that the creek running through his property used to be a powerful brook, full of fish and cool enough to chill drinks for the family as they worked in the hot summer fields, but that during the mid-1980s he could ride a bicycle up the creek bed. Fish have disappeared from many parts of the county, and some farmers have built and stocked ponds to replace this lost food source. Evidence exists that in many parts of the county, the drought has caused the water table to drop, which may be the reason the creeks have dried up. The rapid increase in irrigation has also affected water table levels. Farmers pumping water from ponds or wells have altered local hydrology and in some cases have even emptied their neighbors' drinking wells. The impact of irrigation seems to be quite localized, but it is possible that a hundred or more systems pumping water during dry months have affected the whole region.

Some people attribute the loss of fish in the creeks to the simple lack of water, but others feel agricultural chemicals play an important role. Runoff of pesticides, fertilizers, and herbicides undoubtedly affects the flora and fauna of nearby streams. Aerial spraying, especially of powerful chemicals used in cotton production, also distributes poisons broadly. Questions have been raised about the effects on wildlife populations as well as humans.

A final reason for dry creek beds is erosion and changing soil tilth. Dodge County soils are highly variable, but most are susceptible to rapid erosion. One farmer took me behind his house to the edge of his lawn and pointed out a drop-off of nearly a foot from the grass to the plowed field. When he began cultivation of that land over twenty years earlier, he said, the two surfaces had been level. Such a dramatic measure of soil loss is rarely seen, but after every rain, road edges all over the county are filled with silt. Such erosion creates boggy, swampy lowlands in place of the woodsy creeksides encountered by early settlers, and water-borne sediment may affect fish as well. New agricultural techniques have also had an adverse effect on soil organic matter levels. When manures and crop residues are no longer incorporated to refertilize some fields, the loss of tilth increases both erosion and the runoff of fertilizers and chemicals.

Some commentators worry that increased irrigation is depleting underground aquifers. In fact, aquifer levels did drop sharply at the peak of the drought. But water levels returned to normal in the later half of the 1980s, though irrigation continued to expand, suggesting that the two may not be closely related. Chemical contamination of underground water is a different matter, and early research has raised warnings about the long-term impact of farm chemicals on drinking water.

Weather researchers do not agree on the causes of the prolonged drought, but it is clear that such a persistent change in rainfall patterns is unprecedented. The cultivation of timberland for pulpwood production may be related to such weather shifts. Replacing natural stands of diverse hardwoods with monocot conifers creates a new microclimate. As many farmers have "cleaned up" mixed woodlands to plant pines and as county timber acreage has increased from the Conservation Reserve Program as well, evapotranspiration rates and soil moisture levels are both affected. County statistics reveal no significant levels of deforestation because the huge tracts of Soil Bank timber that were cut in the 1970s and 1980s were mostly replanted to pines. But new pine seedlings are a very different ground cover from a mature pine stand, and it is possible that the radiated heat from these clear-cut areas affects rainfall patterns.

Farming practices changed in ways that both harmed and helped the environment between 1972 and 1987. Maintenance of Depression-era soil erosion terraces became more difficult in the boom years, because growing farm sizes required larger equipment. Many farmers found their equipment too wide for the smaller terraces and plowed over them. Some farmers have built new terraces, but this process is slow and does not always stop erosion. Other operators have been reluctant to invest in the effort involved in building larger terraces and grass waterways. Though a handful have tried no-till planting methods, it is common in the county to leave no plant cover on the fields after harvest.

Many farms have had to intensify production, and some of these practices have increased ecological degradation. Double-cropping of fields reduces erosion but also depletes nutrients and, depending on the methods used, can add to soil compaction, buildup of chemical residues, and loss of organic matter. Intensive hog production dumps concentrated wastes in small areas, changing soil pH, contaminating local water with organic debris, and breeding swarms of flies and other insects. Farmers with large hog operations on the ground have to be careful not to allow disease concentration, or they may run out of "clean" land.

The demands of the crisis forced some farmers to abandon desirable crop rotations. Newcomer farmers, with less-than-ideal rented plots, often felt especially compelled to push for maximum earnings even at the risk of soil depletion or weed infestation. Although they were a minority, some farmers of all ages reported cutting back their applications of fertilizer and lime.

On the other hand, federal programs helped to pay for soil erosion improvements, and a number of farmers instituted these changes, even in the worst years. The use of agricultural chemicals, as noted in chapter 7, was reduced for financial reasons; several farmers reported that their need to cut costs led to substantially lower usage. Several other changes in production techniques, such as more careful weedings and the use of shredded crop residues as mulch, are ecologically beneficial as well.

Though this study did not include a medical component, there was considerable anecdotal evidence of chemical stress on farmers, particularly in pesticide poisonings, allergies, and cancers. Early research has raised warnings about the long-term impact of farm chemicals on drinking water. Several farmers had to give up production of certain crops because of debilitating reactions from chemical contact. Even neighbors are affected. One nonfarming woman with allergies was misted through her car window by irrigation water containing chemicals. Her face puffed up so that she could hardly see, and she was forced to stay in the house until her neighbor's irrigation was completed. Reports of dangers from chemical use scare some farmers, but protective clothing and masks can be highly uncomfortable during a Georgia summer and are rarely seen.

Questions remain about the long-term ecological viability of agriculture as it is now practiced in the county, but there is no evidence that environmental problems will demand rapid changes. More likely, there will emerge unforeseen costs and difficulties that will slowly push farmers in new directions. Although water contamination, pesticide use, and soil erosion may be time bombs, it is difficult for farmers to adjust their practices when feedback may take twenty years, and data, in any case, are confusing. For most families, the ecological and medical dangers of current farming methods are a distant rumble of thunder amid the more pressing threats of drought and financial crisis.

Dimensions of Farm Loss

Within this context of the economic and ecological sustainability of farming in Dodge County, we can turn now to the human experience of the families who lost their farms in the crisis. Though wrenching loss may be only one episode in their lives, it is a privileged moment for us as outsiders, because it reveals not only the workings of farm families and communities, but also the interactions of our deepest values and dreams. As fellow citizens, we are concerned about the long-term health of our creeks and agricultural lands, but we also care about the families who have suffered the most in the crisis. In this section, statistics will be based on families and farm *operators*, not on *farms* as in preceding chapters, in order to take account of the different experiences of individuals on partnership farms.

Farm loss involves several painful dimensions, but not all are experienced by every farm family who is forced out of business:

- loss of a desired occupation;
- loss of farm property;
- loss of a home; and
- loss of income and the uncertainty of finding a new job.

It is often assumed that foreclosure or bankruptcy automatically includes all four dimensions, and poignant movies about families losing their farms reinforced this idea in the popular mind during the 1980s. In fact, such devastating and multifaceted losses are true for only a minority in Dodge County.

One of the most difficult aspects of the crisis, for those going through it as well as for those trying to measure it, was the long delay at every stage. In 1982, farm experts predicted that 20 to 50 percent of farms would be lost in the county, but even by 1984, few were out of business. When cut off by the main farm creditors, some farmers obtained seed, fertilizer, and diesel on credit directly from suppliers. Funds from family and from sales of crops and livestock kept these farms going, though often at a smaller scale. When farm families gave up, understaffed lenders moved slowly to foreclose, and a partial payment on an overdue loan sometimes forestalled legal action. In the case of those who accepted the necessity of a voluntary liquidation, negotiations over depreciated assets also dragged on for years. In one such negotiation, even though the farmer cooperated completely, it was four years before all aspects of farmland, equipment, and home were settled. Another family ceased operation in 1982, but their land was not sold until 1986. Many insolvent farmers attempted to string the process out to the bitter end, hoping for some miracle that would save the farm. The emotional toll of these long years of suspense was enormous.

Looking first at the ability to continue as a farmer—the desired occupation of the 77 full-time operators in the study—25 farmers or 33 percent were forced to give up farming, as shown in table 9-3.[3] Four of these could be considered to

Table 9-3. Dimensions of Loss for Full-Time
and Part-Time Operators

	Lost Farming Occupation	Lost Land*	Lost Home	Unemployed after 6 Months
Full-time farmers (n = 77)	25	11	2	0
Part-time farmers (n = 41)	8	3	0	1
Total (n = 118)	33	14	2	1
Percent of total	28	12	2	1

Note: Excludes deceased operators and those who retired for medical reasons.
*Includes cases in which all or part of the land was sold or conveyed to a lender. Not included are the 11 cases in which the farm was subsequently bought back.

have left farming voluntarily in order to safeguard the family farm before debts mounted too high; the rest left involuntarily. Of the 41 part-time farmers, 5 (12%) were forced out of farming and another 7 (17%) quit voluntarily. Four of the part-time farmers who chose to leave farming voluntarily experienced job transfers or changes in work schedules that forced them to abandon farming; they said the decision was unrelated to agricultural returns and that they would have made the same decision even if times were good. Excluding these job-related voluntary exits from the total, 33 (28%) operators out of 118 full-time and part-time farmers in the study were forced out of business.

Most families stress that giving up farming is much harder than simply losing a job, though they know job loss is itself very difficult. "It's really hard when it's something you really want to do and you can't." "The fact is, you can't do something you want to do—the door has been shut and you have no choice. Nothing bothers Americans more than to tell them they have no choice. If you have pride in your work, you . . . keep asking yourself, where did I go wrong?" Describing the experience of being forced out of farming, one man calmly reflected that he had been his own boss for roughly a decade. Then came the worst drought year,and "the first half was enjoyable and the second half was a nightmare that'll never go away." One part-time farming couple forced out of business felt the experience was easier for them than for full-time operators. "At least we have a living," they said, referring to their jobs. Losing the occupation of farming can also be difficult because it tends to close the door to children who might wish to follow in their parents' footsteps. By making transmission of the farm lifestyle more difficult, farm loss also devalues the inheritance of land or skills that parents hoped to be able to pass on to their children.

Though nearly a third of all operators were forced to seek other work, most did not lose land (see table 9-3). Of the 25 full-time farmers forced into other jobs, only 10 (40%) lost some or all of their property. Two of the 8 part-time farmers who were forced to give up farming also lost their land. In 2 other cases, farmers in financial distress were forced to sell some land to stay in business (1 full-time and 1 part-time). A total, then, of only 11 (14%) full-time farmers lost property from the crisis as of 1989. This figure is low because a significant number of farmers were able to buy back their farms after they faced foreclosure, bankruptcy, or settlement with a lender. Ten full-time farmers and 1 part-time farmer were able to avoid any loss of property for the time being by buying back land. Some planned to make their farm payments with new jobs off the farm; others returned to full-time farming. Several families who tried to buy back their farms have experienced foreclosure since the study ended, and it is not clear if buy-backs will be successful in avoiding property loss in the long run. A third of the full-time farmers and a quarter of the part-time farmers that were forced out of business lost no land because they owned none (8 full-time farmers and 2 part-time farmers). The land they had rented reverted to the owners and was usually rented out again to other operators or was planted to trees.

The surprisingly low rate of farm loss—less than half of cases forced into new occupations—is due to three factors. First, it is related to the ability of families without property to enter farming by renting land and borrowing money to buy equipment. Such a pattern goes back to the earliest days of European settlement in Dodge County and the option of tenant farming and sharecropping; more recently, landless families were supported by agricultural lenders. Second, some operators who were landowners were careful to keep their property apart from farm loan collateral. Usually this land contained the house plot, and they were anxious to keep their homes secure. Lenders could try to recoup their losses, but the family could not be dispossessed. The third reason for the low rate of farm loss is the more lenient terms of loan settlement adopted by the Farmers Home Administration and the cooperation of local banks in financing buy-backs. These agencies made it possible in several cases for a farmer to write off crushing debt levels and return to farming.

Though a complete loss of property was not the typical experience in Dodge County, it should not obscure the anguish of those who did lose their farms. As one daughter said, "It's so unfair that you work all your life for something, and then someone comes and takes it from you." The public announcement of a foreclosure or sale often took families by surprise, making the jolt of public revelation more difficult. There were often long delays between the time a farmer was notified by letter that the case had been "accelerated to foreclosure" and the time any action occurred. One farmer was notified in the spring that his equipment would soon be repossessed. By the time I interviewed him in midsummer, he still had the equipment, he had planted crops with it, and he hoped repossession would be deferred until he completed his late-summer harvest.

When an equipment auction took place, the family had to endure the crowds of bidders and the loss of treasured machines, often the object of years of careful maintenance and repair. Said one beginning farmer, "It was an old, nasty, rainy day when we auctioned everything off . . . but that's all dead and gone. It happened, and there's no way to wipe it out. I've been upset and it didn't feel good, but it would have been a lot worse if we had lost property." One teenager recounted the day of his family's auction in a distant, faraway voice: "It just didn't seem real. That was *our* stuff. . . . It hurt." He remembered getting up that morning and thinking that it did not seem possible that by the end of the day, all their equipment would be gone to others. The father of a friend bought one tractor, but the young man said emphatically that he would never ask to borrow it or even to ride it: "Never! That part of life is *gone*."

The third dimension of the crisis—loss of a home—has been quite rare in Dodge County. When the research team first arrived in 1982, the county was reeling from a highly publicized foreclosure in which farmers lost not only their land and equipment but their homes as well. One other farmer experienced this trauma shortly after. But eviction from homes ceased after those early years, and farmers whose houses were part of their collateral were usually able to buy them back from the lender. The well-publicized cases in which homes were lost motivated many delinquent borrowers to regain control of house plots, pursue negotiations, or seek bankruptcy protection. The long delays in settlement were particularly traumatic when families did not know if they would be able to stay in the homes that—in most cases—they had designed and built.

The fourth aspect of being forced out of business is a sudden loss of income, which is assumed to be accompanied by a prolonged search for alternative work. This experience was not typical in Dodge County. For the 25 full-time farmers who left farming, looking for work was sometimes difficult and disappointing, but most found jobs quickly. Roughly half found skilled blue collar or technical jobs, a third found white collar positions or became small business owners, and 2 found employment as farm hands or mechanics for other farmers. Only 1 remained unemployed in 1989, and this farmer had experienced periodic unemployment prior to trying farming in the 1970s. In describing their job situations, the majority said they were pleased with their work or were at least sufficiently satisfied to continue at the job without searching for something better. Only 3 were so dissatisfied that they hoped to find a different line of work in the near future. Jobs were found in Dodge County or nearby counties, though some families complained about long commutes of over an hour each way. Loss of farm occupation, then, in Dodge County was usually not linked to painful family relocation.

For most families leaving farming, incomes improved sharply. The drought years were lean ones for family budgets, and most struggled to pay bills. Families averaged only $8,500 in off-farm income, and farm incomes were erratic or negative. Today, the families that have weathered the transition to new occupations average $25,300 from husbands' and wives' salaries. Of the families forced out of farming, about half conclude they are financially better off now. One couple exulted in their new affluence from the steady salary: "I could buy a Lincoln Town Car!" said the husband. The relief from creditors' pressure was another major benefit. "No one can *call* you," sighed one woman after their farm's bankruptcy was filed.

About a third of those forced out of business feel they are worse off now. After a valiant battle to cut costs and change crops, one older farmer expressed the grief felt by many: "There went my life's work, handed over to 'em." Even for those whose bitterness and pain linger on, there is freedom from the debt burdens and the suspense: "At least I can sleep." "I haven't a penny now, but I'm free and clear."

Emotional Consequences and Community Reactions to Farm Loss

Many marriages were greatly strained by the crisis, particularly as it became clear that the farm could not survive. The wife in one relatively affluent family described her feelings: "Depression sets in and invades . . . the family and the household. . . . You try to push it away, but you can only do that for so long, then you have to face it. . . . The hard part is, this slump will *last*." In this case, her husband was honest with the children about the situation, and it hurt her to see "the slump in their faces and their manner. It limits what we can do as a family. And it interferes with our self-esteem, especially in the kids. [It has been] a trend to setback, every year. Now it's so overwhelming. You just can't bow out gracefully, and there's no hope to the future."

Men tend to be less eloquent in their descriptions, hiding much of their emotion. "I'm hurting," admitted one, nodding his head. "The pain is more than I want to think about," said another. Several men cried as we talked about the experience of farm loss, and they seemed grateful for an opportunity to share "the mental anguish." Men were more anxious not to dwell on the emotional costs of the crisis: "You know we don't go on like this all the time—you have to put it out of your mind at times."

Women struggle to keep their own spirits up at the same time as they feel responsible for helping their husbands. "The biggest disappointment for me was for him. He would come home so discouraged and I wouldn't know how to lift him up or what to say—you don't know what to say, how to help. He didn't see any way out." One husband began to drink more heavily. His wife explained, "He's very defeated. He's at an age where if your dreams haven't materialized, they probably aren't going to. And it's hard because a wife can't do anything about it. It's been hell, these last two years." Several wives complained that their husbands did not realize the family needed attention too. The hard times have made marriage "a roller coaster" for some couples—very close one minute but "at each other's throats" the next. "Farming can either pull you together or tear you apart," said one farm woman.

Many couples reported that the crisis had opened up new communication between them, new depths of trust, and a new level of commitment. "I think he feels closer to me now," said one woman. "I feel closer to him now. He didn't used to talk much, but now he's more open." Many felt if the marriage had not been sound, the drought years would surely have driven them apart. In a few cases, couples have little interaction about the farm, and the husband's anguish is concealed from his wife. One full-time operator told me he felt like a failure, but his wife asserted that the hard times do not affect their marriage because he never talks about them. When asked if the crisis was hard on her husband, she replied, "I guess so, but I don't really know—we don't talk about the farm. I have nothing to do with it." More common are the women who report the short tempers and ill humor of stressed husbands: "The last five years have been living hell. You never strike a time when things are going just good." Children can be especially vulnerable during the crisis. Strapped families sometimes arranged for children to obtain the "free or reduced cost" lunch ticket at school, but in one family, the children pleaded to go without lunch rather than endure the humiliation in the lunch line. Unable to buy snacks at the snack bar, one teenager reported being taunted by his peers: "You grow food, but you can't buy it."

Most extended families are very supportive. One mother whose son endangered the family farm by taking on high debts urged him to consider bankruptcy or foreclosure—whatever was best for him. In the end, he saved the farm. But in another case, older parents blamed their farming children, considering them lazy or inefficient. "That [family disapproval] was a pressure on us—that's why it's been so hard," said one wife. Admitted a middle-aged man, "The worst part is the *family*. Getting out of farming affects so many people: your wife, your children, your parents." [4]

Reactions of neighbors and the community can make the experience of farm loss more bearable or more difficult. "Some people look at you like there's something wrong with you," reported one woman. In contrast, a young man from the other side of the county reported that neighbors had been supportive: "People hated to see it—people been real nice." In this case, the neighbors who bought his equipment offered to let him borrow it any time. Also, a neighbor facing a similar situation came to talk about strategies. Life with his family and friends at church continued the same. Another older couple reported that people came to the house to offer help and "to tell us they loved us." In this case, one church friend offered his whole life savings of $5,000, if they needed it. One overextended operator reported that most neighbors were "very sympathetic, very understanding. Of course, every so often you have a horse's ass." Facing these tensions, a few farmers withdraw from social interactions. They avoid going into town to escape seeing friends they cannot pay. This sense of betrayal of trust and loss of friendships haunts some farmers more than others.

One of the hardest aspects of farm loss is facing the sense of personal failure. Especially in the early 1980s, few farmers would admit any responsibility for their financial difficulties. They blamed the government, foreign aid programs, ignorant consumers, and labor unions. Interviews in 1987 and 1989 found farmers more thoughtful and less defensive. They were more able to admit errors such as expanding at a certain time, risking a disaster loan, or living "beyond our means." Others, in actuality, had no errors to admit. They had made sound, careful judgments but entered farming at the wrong time, with too little equity. They struggle with the guilt and a sense of the unfairness of their humiliation. A well-off farmer acknowledged that he would feel the same if forced out of business: "It would be a personal failure. I'd have a hard time telling myself it was just a business cycle." Said a young operator who went bankrupt: "I learned a lot from my mistakes. I miss the challenge of being in business for myself. I hope to get back in . . . if I can get up enough nerve—I'd be scared to try again after messing it up this last time."

The Meaning of Farm Loss

The meaning of farm loss varies with the social class background and aspirations of different farm families. Many of the medium scale farmers who took big risks pursued a dream of greater affluence through farming. These dreams were particularly important for the second career farmers. According to one such farmer who was about to be forced out of business after six years of struggling with debts: "I thought if you keep working, maybe you'll have a bit more. That's just dreaming, I guess. I could quit farming and be like other men who work their forty hours, then go fishing and are able to save a little money. But I want a little more too— and that costs."

For this man and others like him, farming represents a dream of upward mobility through entrepreneurship, hard work, and skill. Though the farm may have been a continual loss, they hang on, struggling with creditors. For them, getting off the tractor means giving up the dream. One wife commented on her husband's willingness to work so hard for such a low return after five years of interminable agony: "It's beyond my comprehension. He makes less than a dollar an hour and not once since he started farming has he been able to pay all his bills." In some cases, women cannot see the dream that motivates the prolonged agony of defeat. In this particular case, the wife understood, and had even shared, his dream but had given it up sooner. Her own commitment to the family's lifestyle and her children's peace of mind outweighed her husband's aspirations for "more" through farming.

For the medium scale farmer with dreams of greater affluence, the farm also represents an independent work life, a step up from punching a clock or driving a delivery route. When asked what was the worst part of getting out of farming, one older farmer replied, "I said I would never go back to that factory again!" Agreed another: "Going to work for someone else. It was springtime and not planting. Other folks are harvesting, and you're not. The enjoyable part, though, is the paycheck every week."

The pain of giving up a desired occupation also depends on the work that replaces it. For those who move on to comfortable salaries and white collar work, the sacrifice is obviously smaller. The spiritual dimension of work is lost, but many other rewards—insurance, pensions, vacations—are said to make up for the loss. The dulled eyes of some of the blue collar workers seem to reflect a deeper pain and a harder struggle to accept the new life. Said one with a shrug, "It's a job." These are the men and women who exult in their increased buying power and emphasize the industrial ideology that defines them as "better off now." To the extent that they can reject the agrarian values, they downplay their sense of failure and place themselves in the national mainstream of wage workers. They struggle to emphasize the positive aspects of the farm loss and admit, "That life is over." Said a medium scale farmer who quit after several bad years, "I couldn't make nothing on the farm, so why do it?"

Entwined with the agrarian love of the farming occupation is the desire to accumulate property. Part of the "mental anguish" of farm loss is the turmoil of the warring ideologies, one that values property and one that devalues it. Some farm operators in other parts of the country forego present income for future wealth and are comfortable being "cash poor but land rich." But in Dodge County, lower land values and the legacy of "Hoover Days" poverty undermine the notion that land ownership means wealth. The second career farmer above who claimed to want "a bit more" by trying to farm is referring primarily to income and lifestyle, from an industrial perspective, but he is also alluding to the agrarian status of owning land. One financially strapped farmer acknowledged that by staying on in business he was continuing to accumulate value in property, but he was not sure it was worth the physical and psychic costs: "I might not live to enjoy it," he said. A woman from a wealthy large scale farm family also reported ambivalent attitudes toward property: "Father said land wasn't worth a damn, but you can always borrow on it." Another woman pushed her husband to sell the farm in order to avoid leaving their children massive debts. Though these attitudes reflect a lack of loyalty either to farming or to particular pieces of land, there are, of course, some Dodge County farmers who talk with pride of the number of generations their families have been on their farms.

It is significant in this regard that most Dodge County farm families in financial crisis rarely mention the loss of property. In their evaluations of being "better off" out of farming, they seem to ignore the issue of capital gains and potential net worth; current income and an easier daily life come first. They rejoice in their higher postfarm incomes because they "don't have to pinch the penny so hard," explained one woman. It seems that most of these cases do feel the loss of their property and recognize they are no longer "accumulating" in the sense of long-term wealth, but they emphasize other conceptions of "having something" to downplay that loss. What the husband can provide, not what the family owns, becomes the focus of attention and the definition of success. Feeling these conflicting moral economies, families forced out of business struggle to devalue the farm as "an asset" and to redefine it as a luxury that comes second to living standards.

In a few cases, families who have faced years of struggle come to see the farm as a symbol of salvaging something from the wreckage of the crisis. One woman recognized this symbolic value not only for her husband but also for her children, and she agreed to take out the loan that would allow the family to buy back the farm. She admitted, "This land means absolutely nothing to me, but I cannot bear the thought that my husband and his brothers grew up on this land and our children grew up on it, and somebody else is going to come in and take it." For this family, their decision to hold on to the farm was a way to offset the humiliation, the financial stress, and the husband's loss of a meaningful occupation. They were willing to give up their personal incomes from off-farm jobs in future years to pay for the land all over again to keep the homeplace in the family. By making such a decision, they returned to agrarian roots, rejecting the industrial emphasis on lifestyle and devaluation of property ownership. When this same woman learned that some Dodge County farmers are content with the idea that when they are gone, their children will sell the farm, she pulled back her head in shock and said slowly, "That would be *really* hard to face." Her sacrifices to save the family's symbolic unity and self-respect require an agrarian foundation, and she found it hard to believe that other farmers did not share such traditions.

For the large scale farmers forced out of business, the personal meaning of the crisis has a different emphasis. The majority hope to continue as part-time operators after they buy back at least part of their land and equipment. Only time will tell if profits will be high enough to cover their payments and allow the farm to continue. After the buy-back is settled, the family trauma begins to heal. A sense of failure, embarrassment, and worry continue, but neither the desired occupation nor property ownership have to be given up entirely. Many of these large scale farmers have reassessed their ambitious management style. More careful in their use of hired hands, they have relinquished the dream of the gentleman farmer. The hope of enjoying a kind of planter lifestyle has been replaced by a quiet reorientation to a less flamboyant consumption level and daily work life.

The large scale farmers who have given up the occupation of farming have turned to white collar occupations and hope to create a new life without losing their place in Dodge County society. The newness of their replacement occupations and the uncertainty that these new businesses or jobs will support their status aspirations make it hard to assess the overall impact of the crisis. If they do become able to live as well as they hope, these families may also turn to an industrial ethic to justify their transition out of farming. As this research ended, however, many were still defensive and blamed their farm's demise on forces outside their control.

In sum, the crisis has strengthened the industrial ideal among many of the families forced out of business. Their commitment to a steady income and a high level of consumption aligns them with the nonfarm families of the county. Their devaluation of property ownership is on one hand a form of defense, a justification for the outcome of their attempt at farming. On the other hand, it is a recognition that farming does not provide a secure haven from the industrial world. Unlike in the "Hoover Days," a farm owner cannot retreat from the market and live off the land. Electricity, cars, medical care, and other changes discussed in chapter 2 bind up the farm family with the cash economy. Specialization has also removed the chickens, eggs, milk, and other farm sidelines that allowed a family in the Depression era to "eat at home" and avoid purchases of food. Farm families' reliance on grocery stores and a desire for the comforts of purchased appliances and clothes combine to reduce the importance of property ownership in the 1980s. Farm production itself has also become vulnerable to the market, as crops require fertilizers, chemicals, and expensive processing in order to be brought to the market for sale. These celebrated changes in the technology of farming and the affluence of farm life erode the meaning of farm ownership. Dodge County farmers who were struggling to establish a farm or accumulate resources recognize the power of the forces arrayed against a landowner. When forced out of business, some hold to the agrarian dream and admit their personal failure in achieving it. Others turn away from that dream and find new goals, reaffirming with the rest of the nation the centrality of income, consumption, and lifestyle as the measure of success and self-worth.

CONCLUSION

The story of the farmers of Dodge County—and their journey from frontier settlers to sharecroppers to commercial family farmers—has been the backdrop for the events of the 1980s farm crisis and the interpretation of its meaning. To assess the consequences of farm loss in this latest agricultural "shakeout," we have had to trace both the history of the locality and its connections to larger trends in U.S. society. The industrialization of the U.S. economy has meant industrialization of other aspects of the culture as well, and this analysis has looked at the resulting multiplicity in farm management styles, marital expectations, and personal goals. The crisis years checked the confident movement toward the industrial alternative and magnified the dissenting voices. The consequences of those years for different types of farms included a number of surprises, and many of the same trends have been found in other farming regions as well. As we look ahead to the future of family farms, and to the future direction of change in the broader American culture, the multiplicity, the dissent, and the surprises all have contributions to make.

The intersection of an agrarian and an industrial economy is found not only in Dodge County but in many parts of the United States. Wiregrass agrarian society showed a number of similarities with farm communities in the Northeast and Midwest, unlike the typical southern plantation areas. Early Dodge County settlers disdained luxury and idleness and valued a more egalitarian social order. The penetration of railroads, investors, and immigrants brought new entrepreneurial traditions to the wiregrass region, as in other regions of the country as well. Although Dodge County was marked by some uniquely southern traditions, such as the customs of a multiracial society, it provides a microcosm in which to see the tensions between the agrarian and industrial ways of life.

With the New Deal, southern farms came to look essentially like midwestern family farms, and the agrarian and industrial values were encoded in management styles of farm operation. Technological and biological revolutions in agriculture saw yields and incomes rise while farms became increasingly linked to industrial inputs and global markets. A degree of stratification continued, however, as some farms were extraordinarily privileged by large land areas, favorable federal program allotments, and better soils. New occupations absorbed many farm children, who gladly escaped into better-paying off-farm jobs. With greater status fluidity and upward mobility came an emphasis on consumption levels and lifestyle. Materialism, once an adaptive value that rewarded hard work, discipline, and achievement, lost its link with morality and came to be an end in itself (McNall and McNall 1983:81). In this aspect, the culture of Dodge County moved into the American mainstream.

The growing concern with income and consumption, though not new to farmers, did represent a shift in the dominant emphasis and supported the expansion and investments of the boom years of the 1970s. Encouraged by lenders and farm experts, many families borrowed, bought land and equipment, and enjoyed a new affluence while an unusual configuration of weather patterns, international trade, and monetary policies brought huge profits to the farm sector. A bumper crop of young people were drawn to farming, and their ranks were swelled by second career farmers who abandoned other lines of work in pursuit of their own dreams of success on the farm. The entrepreneurial spirit of the era of King Timber lived on as indebted expansion came to be seen as a necessary concomitant of fertilizers, combines, and new technology. Some older farmers—and some younger ones as well—upheld a cautious management style and maintained their resistance to the more ambitious approach. But many farmers, even some from cautious backgrounds, were caught up in the enthusiasm of the bonanza years.

The favorable economic conditions for agriculture were short-lived, and in the late 1970s, Dodge County farmers were devastated by year after year of drought. The cost-price squeeze on farmers nationwide and declining asset values combined with harvest failures in the Southeast to result in loan delinquencies, bankruptcy, and foreclosure. The adverse economic situation often led to a reassessment of family goals and of the ambitious ethic. The more cautious approach again gained ground, and some large farm operators even cut back their acreage and their dreams.

Just as the farm experienced new imperatives and clashes with older values, the family faced changing conditions of life and new alternatives. The interdependence of men and women in the "Hoover Days" and their gendered worlds of work on the farm became greatly simplified. Demands for field labor and animal care declined along with the heavy burdens of domestic work without running water and electricity. Many Dodge County farm women today do little work on the farm, and children often are spared regular farm tasks as well. The 1980s saw dozens of farm women taking new jobs in order to "help out." The losses of the crisis and the general decline in buying power of American families since the 1970s led most couples to attribute this decision "to necessity." For some, however, jobs also represent a preference that brings greater work satisfaction than homemaking. These two dimensions—a desire to contribute economically to the family and a desire for individual fulfillment—reflect distinct threads in women's new roles. As farm women struggle with the implications of these pressures toward individualism and new definitions of mothering that involve daycare for children, their expectations about men's work, financial support, and the control of money are also in flux.

As with the transformation of farming, changes in the moral economy of the family bring doubts and reservations. Primary among these are concerns about the ways in which the loss of daily child care may weaken the mother-child bond and fears that purchased daycare may harm the socialization of children. Jobs and higher income are sought for success, "for the family," but the resulting acceleration in life pace, more frequent divorce, and changed parental roles bring worries that efforts to serve the family are at the same moment irrevocably changing it. In Dodge County today, heterogeneous models of gender expectations wrestle inchoately with diverse definitions of personal success and moral virtue, producing dilemmas that underlie some of the deepest pain felt in farm families as the crisis has unfolded.

Transmission of Agrarian Values in a
World of Industrial Work and Knowledge

These conflicting aspirations for farm continuity and family income in Dodge County connect with deeper issues of work, knowledge, and prestige in American life. In ever more complex ways, the market economy now surrounds the farm family, although these articulations with the wider economy and polity are experienced as voluntary choices by the individuals themselves. When one farm woman with an agrarian orientation stressed, "We work together," she reflected a commitment to a joint enterprise with coordinated family labor that is increasingly less shared by the wider industrial society. The farmer's knowledge is also devalued, as the lifelong accumulation of experience with crops, animals, land, and weather is dismissed by some experts in favor of a computer program touted to make "sound economic decisions."

The power of science to alter plants, animals, and ecosystems challenges inherited traditions of the farmer's "craft" (Mooney 1988). American culture has also experienced a growing contempt for manual labor, an attitude once limited to elites. Farmers know that some are disdainful of the dirt and hard work of farming, and they experience a status ambiguity from their simultaneous roles as business owners and laborers.

The farmer's world combines the physical experiences of working with the human body and the natural biological processes of growth and seasons. "The kinesthetic sense infuses all the work. Married to the knowledge of materials, it produces a working knowledge that stands in sharp contrast to the working knowledge produced by formal education" (Harper 1987:131). The craft of the farmer depends on a certain attitude toward time as well, "stated most modestly as patience, most dramatically as a kind of contemplative attitude that sees all steps to an end as equal" (ibid.:148). Such an orientation to work seeks "realization and expression in an unfolding activity" (Thorstein Veblen, quoted in ibid.).

The transmission of these values to farm children becomes more difficult as farms decline in numbers. Many jobs off the farm today require a different sense of time, work, and knowledge. Though they do not provide the satisfactions of farming, they do offer steady incomes, benefits, and a more comfortable lifestyle. Pressures from the examples of neighbors and kin who work off the farm join with the technological developments in land grant schools and agribusinesses to challenge the ability of farm families to transmit alternative values. There is virtually nothing in the educational system which reinforces a distinct calculus, a resistance to the industrial ethic. Some farm children understandably avoid as much schooling as possible. Jobs in town, for women and children, also promote a different series of values. The decline in the amount of hand labor needed on many farms has removed women and children from much of the joint farm effort, distancing them from the skills, satisfactions, and identification with the farm as well as from the drudgery. From within and without, the family farm faces new pressures and new demands.

The mechanisms by which the wider American culture is reinforced are to a large extent cut off from agrarian values. Politicians, teachers, and preachers tend to be drawn from nonfarm groups or tend to adopt industrial values through their training. Exponents of the agrarian ideology like Wendell Berry are rarely read by

238   **American Dreams, Rural Realities**

farmers, possibly because the historically poor education provided in this region contributes to a general lack of interest in books. (The long hours of farming are also a major factor.) The agricultural journals farmers do read tend to promote a more entrepreneurial, capitalist spirit and provide few alternatives for the farmer who wants to resist these philosophies. Greater social stratification in the history of the rural South and a lack of a vital democratic tradition of dissent reinforce the silence of less powerful groups.

In Dodge County, a shared tradition of agrarian ethnocentrism that can stand against the industrial values of a consumer society is missing. Ethnic enclaves that might support such a tradition are not present, due to the mixture of groups and ideologies throughout the history of the county. Few in Dodge County can articulate their opposition to the profit-maximizing approach to the farm as a business, and they tend to fall back on generalizations about the farming "way of life." Compared to the way of life based on the entrepreneurial vision, this agrarian ethic means a lower standard of living and less opportunity to accumulate capital as a business. It seeks security through avoidance of debt. More positive qualities of daily life also exist: the satisfaction, autonomy, and achievement of performing meaningful work that is connected to the life of the spirit and nature. The realms of child rearing and adult work are blurred on the farm, as children combine play and work in their contribution to the family enterprise. Daily sustenance involves the product of this work, and families enjoy eating the food they have produced. Life is less mediated by the market and is more attuned to the organic rhythms of plants and animals. The world of farm and household is also connected to a community of like-minded people, in a "unity of work, play, and community interaction" (Mooney 1988:67).

Much of this agrarian way of life was eroded, along with Dodge County topsoils, in the timber boom years and the cotton tenancy that followed. Tenant mobility and migration undermined attachment to the land, and poverty and exploitation removed many of the satisfactions of the farm life. Job alternatives and the low status of farmers played their part in the devaluation of whatever agrarian ethic survived the Depression. Today, there remains among farmers a respect for skill and a sense of craft in the manipulation of seed varieties, chemicals, and machinery. Well-tended fields, hard work, and performing tasks "in a timely manner" evoke praise. But when each farm's equipment and chemical use are different and when a young farmer thinks an older one is "*stupid*" to work so hard, a common tradition of agrarian values is more difficult to sustain.

Some would argue that the willingness of most Dodge County families to embrace "success" through income and lifestyle represents an abandonment of property and a false belief that a "good job" means upward mobility. This acceptance of a life of wage labor and subordination to bosses can be seen as a testimony to the success of powerful classes in manipulating ideology to serve their own interests. For the Dodge County farmer, however, the choice is not between abstract "security" in landownership and "insecurity" in selling one's labor. The choice is the opposite—between security in wage labor and insecurity on the farm. Although from the long-term perspective of the next century or two—after the oil runs out, after a third world war, or after another Great Depression—it may be that access to land will ensure survival. The willingness of farm children today to give up a farm may come to be seen as incredibly shortsighted. But from the point of view of the Dodge County farmer, these are the ravings of intellectuals. The reality of a "good life" for one's children does not include a concern for such broad questions of security. When an industrial economy has provided this relatively fortunate class of rural Georgians with steady jobs and rising incomes for roughly fifty years, it is hard to credit the perception that property ownership yields more security than wage labor. Especially in the last decade, independent farm production has become increasingly precarious. Unless farm families are willing to give up their cash needs—for cars, electricity, and other modern conveniences—then farming provides security only to the extent that agricultural markets provide security, which must, from the evidence of many past decades, be severely questioned.

Lessons from the Farm Crisis

This account of the 1980s farm crisis has suggested a number of surprising consequences for the structure of agriculture and the survival of different types of farms.

Bigger farms were not necessarily better off. The first lesson is that bigger is not better. As the dust began to settle over a decade of droughts and economic disaster, half the full-time farmers in the county were in poor financial shape, and a third had been forced out of business. But despite predictions that the larger, more capital-intensive farms would have an advantage in survival, the overall vulnerability of this group was the same as for the medium scale farms. These groups represent two quite different farming paths, both of which provide satisfaction to their operators. Medium scale farms are usually operated by one farmer, and large farms are either multifamily partnerships or require hired hands. These two sizes of farms generally support two different lifestyles as measured by homes, appliances, and cars.

Farm survival depended greatly on management style, but it varied by the age of the operation. The newcomer farmers faced particularly large burdens in becoming established at a low-profit time. All but the youngest cohort of medium scale farms tended to be cautious in management style, and this orientation to debt and expansion preserved them from foreclosure and bankruptcy in the difficult years. More ambitious farmers—about half of the large scale group—were unable to withstand the double burden of lower yields and higher costs.

Debts were worse than the drought. Stunted and crisped crops were the most visible effect of the drought years, but the farmers who, in the end, were driven out of business were not those with the worst drought losses but those who had expanded at the wrong time, especially through purchases of expensive land and equipment. Expansion would not have presented a problem with the good profits of a decade earlier, but in the crisis years, debts simply could not be paid. Accepting low-interest disaster loans also turned out to be a mistake for most operators. For the ambitious large scale farmers, favorable allotments and good soil quality conferred an advantage. Those with superior farming skills were also more likely to survive. These issues of skill and resources were not as vital in determining the survival of medium scale farmers, especially those who continued to embrace a cautious management style. Advancing age and ill health were the only serious threats to continued farm operation for this group, though many suffered hardships from the strain on family incomes.

Among medium scale farmers, farm loss followed attempts to abandon the cautious management style and rent more land, expand equipment, and use hired hands. Higher levels of family consumption accompanied this process for a few. But for the most part, medium scale farmers failed because of timing. Many were second career farmers who took up agriculture with little equity and no intergenerational support. Those who inherited a farm or received significant family help in land or equipment had a much better chance for survival. The younger medium scale farmers forced out of business face the loss not only of their preferred occupation but also of their dreams of independent business ownership and the opportunity to "make money."

The efforts of institutions that extended new loans to help farmers get through the crisis were generally not successful. For the most part, these disaster aid programs made things worse for floundering farms. Had the crisis been short-lived, this aid might have been more advantageous, but in the end it only prolonged the day of reckoning for farmers in trouble. Dodge County is fortunate in that banks and other lenders did not adopt the policies seen in some parts of the Midwest, where falling asset values forced farmers to sell assets or provide new collateral to cover the parent loan. Most Dodge County bankers allowed farmers to roll loans over each year and later in the crisis provided capital for a few families to buy back their farms. Lawsuits that delayed the settlement of Farmers Home Administration (FmHA) cases were also critical in giving some large scale young farmers time to benefit from the 1985 Farm Bill. The experiences of Dodge County farmers with lenders have been at times excruciatingly painful, but in comparison to farmers' experiences in some other parts of the country, they were more favorable. Most fortunate, of course, were those who resisted crisis debts or who had the resources to begin farming without borrowing. It is a bitter irony that the same young farmers who are so resented by established operators for having been "bought a bag of groceries" by FmHA may well be the last remnants of the democratic homesteader tradition in which farming is an occupation open to all.

Farming is an increasingly closed career. Another lesson from the farm crisis is the importance of family help in transmission of the farm to a new generation. The most successful farmers in Generation 3, both large and medium scale, all benefited from family land and other aid. It is very difficult for farm profits in such hard times to support a family and pay for land and equipment in full, even with falling land values. Young men who worked into their fathers' operations or whose fathers made an effort to secure the resources to facilitate the son's entry were more likely to be successful. Georgia is now catching up to Iowa and other areas of the Midwest where "by the seventies, it was virtually impossible to begin farming without significant assistance from family members already involved in agriculture" (Friedburger 1988:73; Council for Agricultural Science and Technology 1988).

The willingness of some medium scale farmers to provide for transmission of their farms demonstrates that these less elite farms are able to reproduce themselves. Multihousehold partnerships are one way to spread out equipment and land costs, and there are substantial advantages in coordinating labor (and reducing hired labor) as well. Though a number of partnerships were forced out of business in the 1980s, they were vulnerable from their ambitious style and risky investments; partnerships following a more cautious ethic have allowed a number of younger men to enter farming successfully at this difficult time. Family cooperation has permitted some medium scale farmers to add irrigation and other expensive investments, with the expectation that children will benefit.

The very low recruitment of young men to farming in the later 1980s has raised concerns about the future supply of farm operators. The Dodge County data suggest such worries are premature. Young people have been able to begin operation, especially when joining their parents or siblings, and if conditions improve, more have said they will enter. A number of older medium scale farm operators have discouraged their children from attempting to start farms at such a disadvantageous time, but many of these young men are enthusiastic and may well take up the farm life when their fathers retire. Though the loss of so many second career farmers who entered after the boom years of the 1970s is a tragedy for the men and women involved, their willingness to give up other work to return to the farm reveals that the country is unlikely in the near future to face a shortage of farm operators. Most of these second career farmers suffered from poor soil, inexperience, and high debts, but some were highly skillful, and if they had been able to take over a family farm, they would have had a good chance to survive.

Farmers reassessed the ambitious management style. Another consequence of the crisis is that many farms have cut back in scale; roughly half of large scale farmers have either let go of some of their hired help or say they would like to. The technological sophistication of the farm now puts a premium on skill and attention to detail, and a number of farmers have shifted their goals toward a more cautious management style. Farmers in the 1980s sought ways to cut costs, use smaller and cheaper machinery, do their own repairs, and reduce chemical use. Some farmers, especially younger operators, have concluded that farming cannot support the affluent lifestyle or capital accumulation of their dreams. This reassessment has led to a greater respect for family frugality for some and the desire to get out of farming for others.

The years of this study also saw an increasing number of farmers expressing a sense of scientific limits and a disillusionment with technology. Since the 1950s, they had experienced ever-increasing yields and productivity breakthroughs, but these were perceived to have reached a plateau. "We've gone about as far as we can go in that direction," was a phrase repeated by a range of farmers. Several noted that award-winning "Farmers of the Year" had gone out of business around the South, further reinforcing doubts about the wisdom of the high technology path. The future competitiveness of U.S. agriculture is seen with greater uncertainty. Though ecological concerns about food quality, soil erosion, and water contamination had been considered minor compared to economic pressures, consumer fears and reports of the dangers of chemical contamination to farmers brought new doubts about the "progress" on which Dodge County prosperity had been based. It remains to be seen if the predicted revolution in biotechnology will restore confidence and generate a new round of productivity increases. It seems likely that growth in environmental concerns and the organic agriculture movement will present new challenges, especially given the warm, humid climate faced by southern farmers.

The crisis brought no trend toward large scale industrial-type farms. In the 1980s, the use of hired hands on Dodge County farms declined, and more farmers plan to move in that direction in the future. Evidence suggests that the use of hired hands made operations more vulnerable, which supports the findings of researchers who stress the competitiveness of the family labor farm in attending to the complex biological processes of agriculture (Reinhardt and Barlett 1989). The use of hired labor provides a higher income to the large scale farm owner, but to some extent, it is also an increase in risk.

Although this study focuses on families who own and operate farms, a brief study of farm workers confirmed that expansion of large farms and the use of hired labor would increase the levels of poverty associated with agriculture. Many farm workers prefer working outdoors and find farming more meaningful than other job alternatives, but their incomes are low and their work hours long. An expansion of the wage labor sector of Dodge County agriculture would not contribute to the overall social welfare of the county. Proportionately more farms in the county today use full-time hired hands than was true fifty years ago, when agriculture was dominated by tenancy. But there is no trend toward the further separation of management and labor into a more industrial-type farm organization, despite the fact that several aspects of Dodge County's history make such a trend plausible. Government programs, especially in peanuts and cotton, have encouraged capital intensification by supporting high returns per acre. The region has both an available pool of laborers who have farming skills and a tradition of organizing production on large acreages through hired help. There is also a history of respect for the owners of large estates, and though this ethos has been considerably modified as family farms have become dominant in the Southeast over the last thirty years, it would provide cultural support for a movement toward "factories in the field." The Office of Technology Assessment (1986:28) reports that the Coastal Plain has the potential to parallel California, Arizona, Florida, and Hawaii in the dominance of large scale capitalist farms.

Nevertheless, conditions in rowcropping are clearly not right for such an industrial organization of production to emerge. The lessons of the boom and bust support the paradox that if farmers receive the kind of prices and profits they feel they deserve, the attractiveness of agriculture to investors would increase and the family farm would be doomed. It is precisely the struggle between low returns and high risks that guarantees the future survival of owner-operated agricultural units.

Part-time and retirement farms remain important. Part-time and retirement farming operations continued to be a significant element in the county agricultural structure through the crisis, though declines in income hit the older farmers particularly hard. Part-time and retirement farmers do not expect to subsist off the farm and its earnings, and thus they were somewhat more protected in the downturn. Off-farm jobs covered losses for part-time farmers and pensions or social security for the elderly, but both groups tended to cut back their operations sharply, especially as the droughts continued.

Since part-time farmers comprise 37 percent of farm units in Dodge County, they make an important contribution in supporting local farm suppliers and equipment dealers. Part-time farm families have responded to pressures for secure and higher incomes by relying on off-farm jobs and are generally quite comfortable; in 1982, the combined pay of the average part-time farm family was over $33,000. Although they retain some of the commitment to the farm life of their small farm parents and appreciate many of the noneconomic benefits of farming, most have undertaken to farm primarily to earn extra income. The low prices and droughts of the last decade have made this more difficult but so far have not undermined the attractiveness of the part-time farming life.

Questions arise about the survival of black farms. African American farmers have not been uniquely affected by the crisis, but the trends toward decreased land and farm ownership by blacks in the South have not abated over the last decade. Very few young African Americans are attracted to the farm life, and like their white counterparts, many black parents encourage their children to seek a better life off the farm. Within the black community, farmers are relatively wealthy property owners, and their children's aspirations are often higher than average. None of these farmers own large farms, and thus their children who seek to continue in farming face the same hurdles of high land and equipment costs. African American farm families meet with additional obstacles in obtaining fair treatment from some businesses they deal with and in supporting the farm with off-farm work. As is true nationally, black women are the lowest-paid group in the county, and they are more limited in the work opportunities open to them. This pattern prevented many black women from making the same contribution as white women to family survival during the crisis. The numbers of black farms in the county have declined greatly over the years, and the outlook for the future is not good. Although there are FmHA programs targeted to aid minority farmers, at the time of this study there were no young African Americans in Dodge County entering the occupation.

Signals are mixed on the future dominance of large scale farms. In the future, average farm size can be expected to grow. The long-term trend over the last half-century toward ever-larger farms peaked with the stagnation during the crisis. But even if the economy does not improve, the mean can be expected to rise somewhat in the future as older farmers who operate smaller farms die or retire. Their children are less likely to keep up the farming tradition than are the children of more affluent farmers because of the higher costs of equipment and inputs today and the desire for a more comfortable standard of living. In addition, if the new trend toward in-migration of Hispanic farm workers accelerates in the Southeast, increasing the supply of low-cost labor, large scale farming may become cheaper and more attractive.

Technological pressures toward larger farm scale (the technology treadmill) were lessened by the crisis because investments in facilities and new equipment generally added to farmers' financial vulnerability. Irrigation systems were the major exception to the stagnation in capital investments. Though expensive to buy and operate, irrigation systems have become attractive to an increasing number of farmers of all sizes who desire the security of crop yield that irrigation brings. It remains to be seen what impact this reduction of risk will have on farm structure. Predictable yields and the lowered risk of raising vegetables, fruits, poultry, and eggs are important components of the success of agribusiness corporations in displacing family farms in certain areas of the country. However, the cable-tow and center-pivot irrigation systems in use in the Southeast are not as effective in reducing environmental risk as California and Arizona irrigation because weather is less consistent, and crop losses and fluctuating yields still occur. Nevertheless, this latest step on the technology treadmill may have more long-lasting effects on farm scale than Dodge County farmers generally realize. In addition, there seems to be a trend for some medium scale operators to enlarge their farms to support irrigation. It is not clear if this expansion will be substantial enough to require the use of hired hands and to push these operations into the large scale group.

Some medium scale farms have been able, however, to survive the crisis and prosper with less than three hundred acres. For families who are comfortable with the lifestyle supported by such a farm, there is no necessity to expand. Some larger farms have grown over the crisis years, but others have cut back on rentals. Especially if government payment ceilings are enforced, large farms may well stabilize in acreage.

Farmers' Views of Critical Issues

It is interesting to step back from an outsider's perspective of the crisis and its lessons to review the disaster years from the standpoint of the farmers themselves. In 1982 and 1983, farmers at the peak of the droughts and the cost-price squeeze spoke with me about their concerns and their views of the threats to their operations. Many of these issues have been substantially affected since then by changing national and international government policies and economic conditions. The farmers' top ten concerns and their current status are as follows:

1. Rising costs, especially for inputs, machinery, and diesel. Cost increases have moderated as inflation has been brought under control and oil prices have generally stabilized. Farmers have not received much relief in terms of lowered costs, however.

2. Droughts and the high cost of irrigation. Weather patterns remain irregular and it is still unclear whether the series of dry years is truly over. The summer of 1990 brought drought losses to many Dodge County farmers. Irrigation costs continue to be a problem, though larger farmers have received enough benefit from federal commodity programs to pay off their investments and reduce these complaints.

3. Low prices for crops and livestock, especially grains. Competition with more fertile regions continues to hamper the Southeast, but the set-aside program and the Conservation Reserve Program have lowered surpluses and raised prices to some extent.

4. High interest rates. Interest rates have also moderated as inflation has dropped.

5. High land values and rental costs. Land values crashed and have moderated somewhat. Land rental is no longer seen as inappropriately high, though the Conservation Reserve Program has led to debilitating loss of rentals for some operators.

6. Special advantages received by wealthy farmers from government programs. Such inequities still exist and are seen to an increasing degree in the impact of the 1985 Food Security Act.

7. Competition from part-time farmers whose hog production lowers the prices that full-time farmers receive. Hogs continue to show price cycles,

but droughts have discouraged many part-time farmers from substantial hog production, and full-time farmers complain much less about their impact.

8. Byzantine regulations governing federally controlled crops (especially peanuts and tobacco) and other programs. Such regulations have not been simplified, and this complaint is still heard among farmers.

9. Competition with Florida in vegetable and watermelon production and with Brazil and other countries in soybeans and other crops. This competition still exists.

10. Dealing with middlemen who take large cuts of farmers' profits and give special benefits to wealthy farmers. Relations with middlemen show no change, though there are now fewer such businesses. Large farmers continue to have advantages, and bulk purchases are one common economy of scale.

Dodge County in Context: Comparable
Findings around the Country

Many studies of the impact of the crisis in other regions of the United States have reached conclusions similar to those expressed here. High debts and risky expansion were found to be the primary causes of vulnerability in a variety of family farm areas (Murdock and Leistritz 1988:124; Friedburger 1989:65; Almas 1989; Bultena, Lasley, and Geller 1986; Smale, Saupe, and Salant 1986:24). Beginning farmers, with high start-up costs, were at particular risk in Texas and North Dakota (Murdock and Leistritz 1988:26).

In determining threats to farm survival, many of these same studies emphasized the role of management style and desired consumption standards (Murdock et al. 1986). Studies in Iowa, Illinois, Wisconsin, and Minnesota—the heartland of the Midwest—have shown a similar tension between cautious and ambitious styles and a tendency for the ambitious farmer to be more at risk in the crisis (Almas 1988, 1989; Friedburger 1988, 1989; Mooney 1988; Salamon and Davis-Brown 1986; Salant and Saupe 1986). In Wisconsin, operators of larger farms were found to be more dissatisfied with farming and with its ability to provide satisfactory income (Wilkening and Gilbert 1987).

The effect of the boom years in encouraging a more ambitious style was not limited to the Southeast. In Iowa during the 1970s the promotion of specialization, sophisticated machinery, high-volume production, and perpetual debt "turned the heads of farm families and many followed this gospel enthusiastically" (Fried-burger 1988:7). Farm programs encouraged the "more accountant style" and the more "manipulative side" of farming (Friedburger 1989:151). By the next decade, the successful farm was considered conservative in the use of credit, di-versified, and oriented toward landownership, transmission to children, and family commitment (ibid.:2, 166; Rosenblatt 1990). The same was noted in Minnesota (Conzen 1985:284), and in North Dakota, Wisconsin, and Minnesota, Reidar Almas cites a new emphasis on cautious management, hard work, modesty, and reliability (1989).

In other parts of the country as well as Dodge County, the crisis reinforced a return to lower aspirations for family living standards and a reassessment of farm practices. In Iowa, "[wives] returned, if they had ever left it, to what one farmer called 'the non-consumptive life,' " reports Mark Friedburger (1989:165). The disillusionment seen in Dodge County with technological "progress" and doubts about future productivity gains were echoed in Iowa where "the downturn had shaken the faith of many farmers in the standard practices of production agricul-ture—the utilization of big machinery, the unrestricted use of chemicals, and the emphasis on grain monoculture" (ibid.:166).

Such reconsiderations of management style can be found as well in earlier peri-ods in the Midwest. Jan Flora and John Stitz (1985) found in Kansas that different ethnic groups in the 1800s supported more or less entrepreneurial management styles, and the more cautious operators were more likely to persist in operation. The same pattern emerged in Minnesota, where German farmers were more likely to maintain communities of owner-operators. The farmer there of British Isles stock showed more entrepreneurial willingness to sell out and move on; German neighbors felt the English-speaking farmer paid less attention to soil fertility and the care of machinery and "plowed too much of his profit back into an elegant dwelling and a genteel life for his womenfolk" (Conzen 1985:266).

Many studies also found that the crisis did not hit all farmers uniformly. Al-though definitions of a farmer "in trouble" vary from study to study (perhaps appropriately so, given the diversity of lenders' behavior and local conditions), many found that a core of farmers were making money throughout these difficult years. The "selectivity of the crisis gave failure all the more sting" (Friedburger 1989:104).

Larger farms have been found to face more financial trouble in the crisis in a number of studies in Iowa (Friedburger 1988; Bultena, Lasley, and Geller 1986) and in Wisconsin (Smale, Saupe, and Salant 1986). A national survey finds the highest relative levels of debt among the farmers in the top sales category of $500,000 and over (Harrington and Carlin 1987). However, studies in North Dakota, Wisconsin, and Texas suggest that the larger farms may have had an edge in farm survival if they managed to avoid high debts (Bentley et al. 1989). Eugene Wilkening and Jess Gilbert (1987) predict that medium-sized family farms will suffer from low sales and lower off-farm income and thus be at a disadvantage in the inflationary 1980s. Two Iowa studies, however, join the Dodge County study in finding medium scale farms less vulnerable over the last decade; though lower in sales, they were able to respond to the bad years with "a tighter belt." The experience of being forced out of business had similar dimensions as well, though communities varied in the extent to which struggling and displaced farmers were shunned. Many areas experienced the painful limbo of the drawn-out process of farm loss, including delays in settling accounts with lenders (Friedburger 1989:104; Rosenblatt 1990).

The adverse impact of the disaster years on small town life and on the agribusiness community is well documented for Texas and North Dakota (Murdock and Leistritz 1988). Larry Leistritz and Brenda Eckstrom (1988b) report that 27 percent of rural nonfarm residents in North Dakota lost a job during the crisis because of the agricultural downturn. Over 50 percent of those responding to their survey experienced some loss in pay, benefits, or working hours or lost a job altogether as a result of the farm crisis.

The patterns of women's involvement with farms and their experiences during the crisis are also not unique to Dodge County. Almas, in his study of Norwegian-American farms in North Dakota, Wisconsin, and Minnesota found that on the more entrepreneurial farms, wives were less involved and thought about the farm more like "any modern citizen" (1988, 1989). A similar pattern is reported by Deborah Fink (1986b) and Max Pfeffer and Jess Gilbert (1989:5) for women on larger, more mechanized farms. Women's off-farm work was found to be particularly crucial for medium scale farm survival on Nevada ranches (Darby 1986:18) and supported farms through the crisis in Iowa (Pfeffer and Gilbert 1989).

The diversity of moral economies noted among Dodge County families is not reported in other studies. In Iowa, Friedburger relates that increased off-farm work among farm women was generally not enjoyed and questions whether women will continue such jobs once farming conditions improve (1989:165). For Dodge County, the phrase "it takes two nowadays" seems to express an acceptance of the two-earner family. Jill Darby writes that on Nevada ranches women accept and accommodate to "a simple and frugal lifestyle . . . and widely support ranch goals"

(1986:21). They see their interests "as synonymous with enterprise well-being and preservation" (ibid.) and thus seem to be less involved in an industrial marital model. The Dodge County situation, with massive opportunities for off-farm work, may promote greater ideological diversity in gender roles.

In several other ways, Dodge County may not be typical of other farming regions, and thus some of the findings of this study cannot be generalized. The decline in its land values was sharp but may have been less critical than in the Midwest, where the collapse forced more drastic loan renegotiations. On the other hand, midwestern land values remained high enough that they attracted nonfarm investors and complicated farm transmission. Several authors have studied areas in which contract vegetable production and closer linkages between farms and agribusinesses are typical (Gilbert and Barnes 1988; Mooney 1988). These challenges to farmers' ability to maneuver and adapt have not yet become common in Dodge County.

Lenders in Dodge County seem to be more concerned with finding ways to support farmers than lenders in other areas; even compared with banks in some other regions of Georgia, Dodge County banks have tended to give farmers time to make up delinquent loans and have not pushed otherwise viable farms out of business. FmHA loans were more complex, but here too, the agency did not create as adverse a climate for continuing in operation as reported in some areas of the Midwest (Friedburger 1989; Heffernan and Heffernan 1986; Rosenblatt 1990). Friedburger reports for Iowa farmers that credit from individuals and neighbors—seller mortgages and contracts—was central to farm purchases. In Georgia, financing from institutions such as the Federal Land Bank was more commonly obtained. The Iowa study also suggests a more widespread pattern of financial and labor contributions from the extended family and even in-laws in order to help farms survive (1989:107–8).

Public Policy, Self-Interest, and the Future

In this review of the problems facing farmers, it is clear that the role of the state, as the controller of monetary and agricultural policy, is primary in determining the lives of Dodge County farmers. From the issues of broad national impact such as inflation and interest rates, to the detailed congressional negotiations over the peanut program or the Soil Bank, the "invisible hand of the market" is manipulated by the interests and powers that affect these national and international decisions

(Mann 1990). It is clear that medium scale farms, in spite of their cautious management style and ability to survive adverse conditions, can be slowly strangled by benefits provided disproportionately to large farmers. A nation of large scale factories-in-the-field can be created, and some agribusinesses and other firms may benefit in the short run. In the long run, the resultant displacement of many previously prosperous farm families and a rising level of rural poverty and declining public services may generate substantial social costs. If the nation's concern is to maintain a diverse structure of agricultural units with the ability to provide healthful food, survive good and bad times, and contribute to a vital rural economy, then policies aimed at these goals must be favored. For example, as the Office of Technology Assessment concluded in 1986, "Income supports, in particular, provide significant benefits to moderate farms, and the targetting of income supports to moderate farms is an effective policy tool in prolonging these farms' survival" (1986:25). Likewise, farm lenders such as the Farmers Home Administration can prevent the takeover of farmland by nonfarm investors and pursue efforts to keep our best lands in the hands of farm families.

Woven throughout the Dodge County story is the natural environment, the ecological interaction that sustains agricultural production. Stewardship of the land is not part of the southern tradition, and in 1936 Arthur Raper described the plantation economy as resting "on a reckless exploitation of natural resources unknown to European feudalism" (1936:4). In studying agriculture within an industrial society, anthropologists' concepts of ecological adaptation and feedback with the environment are overwhelmed by the short-term pressures of the market and other powerful forces outside of agriculture (Barlett 1980:6, 1987b). Although Americans are becoming more concerned about the long-term impact of the nation's chemical- and capital-dependent farming system, they suffer both from the difficulty of assessing such costs and from the immediacy of financial pressures on farm operators to maintain production in predictable ways.

Roy Rappaport has shown that societies through the centuries have had to find ways to constrain self-interest in order to serve the broader adaptive demands of the survival of the majority. As modern bureaucratic societies become ever more complex and cultural diversity hampers the consensus of "right" and "wrong," individualistic action comes to play a more central role. "For the world is first broken and then dissolved by the apotheosis of self-interest, ever more destructive as special interests ramify with the elaboration of the division of labor, as technology becomes increasingly powerful, as money penetrates into ever more areas of life, and as knowledge itself is fragmented" (Rappaport 1979:312). The nation's struggles, in agricultural sustainability and other ecological dilemmas, reflect a secular society coping with the need to control self-interest—by regulating the use of DDT or Freon or toxic wastes—without the traditional cultural mechanisms of religious damnation or taboo.

As Dodge County farm families struggle with the tensions between agrarian values and the individualism of an industrial world, the nation as a whole is moving toward a late-industrial economy in which the interests of farmers are challenged by consumers and environmental concerns. In such a world, agricultural production is no longer seen as the isolated province of the individual or family, protected by traditional rights of privacy and private property. Agriculture, like all productive processes, is reinterpreted as a component of a complex global economy whose inputs and outputs have wide effects on nonfarmers. This awareness has penetrated public policy most noticeably in the countries of the European Economic Community. Increasingly, their agricultural policies reflect this postmodern sense of interconnections among societal groups and limits to individualism, through legislation concerning farmers' chemical and fertilizer use, soil and water contamination, product purity, and overall production levels. European consumer groups are highly vocal in articulating a mix of ecological as well as economic interests.

In addition, many European countries have come to value agriculture as a vital component of rural economic development and recognize the need to sustain small and medium farms in order to support vibrant rural communities. They also acknowledge that farms produce "landscape." The beauty of fields, pastures, animals, and crops is affirmed by legislators and taxpayers, who support incentives to use lands to enhance "landscape." Such countries consider the presence of farming not only an asset in attracting tourism but also as a way to enhance the overall national quality of life. These values represent a third path, an ideological orientation distinct from the agrarian and industrial perspectives. These values emerge in a context where even though farming remains very much a minority way of life, its interconnections with nonfarm sectors are powerfully recognized. Agriculture is supported and at the same time constrained, as it fulfills important roles in providing food, preserving desirable ways of life, and sustaining a healthy natural environment.

In the Dodge County story, we can see some glimpses of this emerging third path. The farmers who have survived the crisis exhibit a somewhat chastened attitude that might be considered a postmodern sense of limits. Their emerging doubts about unbridled individualism, consumerism, and unsustainable growth echo a disquiet found in many sectors of American life. Within the family, changes in work, marriage, and personal goals bring uncertainties about what is really best for family members. The dilemmas that farmers face in the devaluation of intergenerational cooperation, traditional skills, and conservative frugality and the glorification of short-term profit seeking over long-term productivity and stability mirror similar pressures in many aspects of American culture.

It is through these doubts and anxieties, this sense of loss of agrarian values and limits to industrial values, that a different future may emerge. The U.S. economy is changing, as is the nation's role in the global polity, and Americans can expect to see new orienting values arise and find acceptance. As intractable problems within local communities lead to the rejection of old solutions, the desire to construct more satisfying ways of life will point out new directions. Writers who dismiss the national homage to the family farm as romantic nostalgia for a simpler, preindustrial past fail to acknowledge its roots in frustrations with the industrial life. As Harriet Friedmann has pointed out, family farms represent a kind of human cooperation and commitment to neighborly principles that evokes for many a vision "of democratic ways to work together making useful products for ourselves and others" (1980:55). As the glorious greed of the 1980s gives way to the unknown rhythms of the 1990s, the lessons of the farm crisis provide both caution and inspiration in the quest for a future that combines work, family, and dreams of success.

ONE

Measures of Variables

Measurement of Farming Skill

Although a system of measurement of a farm operator's skill would seem to be relatively easy to develop, it is extremely difficult. In determining an appropriate rating procedure, I received invaluable advice from Gene Rogers, the county cooperative extension agent, and from several highly skilled farmers in the county. In the end, ten different variables were used, and farmers were given a rating of −1, +1, or 0 on each variable, for a possible score of +10 to −10. All of the following ten variables were used in the overall skill score, discussed in chapter 4, and the four pertaining to crop production were used for the crop skill score.

Peanut Yields. Since the most valuable crop for most farmers is peanuts, operators tend to put their maximum effort into that crop. Because peanuts are grown under the federal peanut program, careful records are maintained on each farm's production over the years. With the help of Marc Brooks and with the permission of the Agricultural Stabilization and Conservation Service in Dodge County, we averaged each farmer's recorded peanut yields for the previous five years, 1982–86. Yields for irrigated and nonirrigated acreages were separated and averaged independently. The mean five-year yields for all operators were ranked into quartiles; the top quartile was given +1 point, and the bottom quartile, −1. The middle two quartiles received 0 points.

One problem with this measure is that it cannot account for weather fluctuations within the county. Yields to some highly able farmers may thus have been depressed by low rainfall, while other less-skilled farmers may be given a higher score for having benefited from erratic showers in the county. Some farmers I talked with felt that these difficulties seriously compromised the measure; others felt it would nevertheless be generally accurate. To cope with this problem, I decided to combine this measure of farming skill with production levels in three other crops and with ratings in seven other activities.

Grain Yields. Though no other crop has the reliable recording system of peanuts, operators were asked to report their 1986 yields for corn, soybeans, and wheat. Many had losses from poor weather, so only the top quartiles were used. The cutoff points for high skill (+1 score) were 30 bushels for wheat, 22 bushels for soybeans, 150 bushels for irrigated corn, and 80 bushels for nonirrigated corn.

Hog Production. Another important area of productivity is the survival rate of weaned pigs per sow. Skilled farmers, especially those who are energetic in their attention to their animals, can average a significantly higher number of pigs. Farmers who produced hogs were asked their average pig production, and the top quartile was given +1 point. The lowest quartile received −1. This measure suffers from some weakness because farmers' reports may be inaccurate unless careful records are kept. On the other hand, the figures given and the resulting quartile assignments fit my own perceptions (based on conversations and observation) of the more careful and less careful hog producers.

Marketing Skill. Since farmers sell their crops at different times and under different circumstances, it is difficult to find a valid measure that captures a farmer's skill in watching the market and capturing the best price for a harvest. One simple measure was used to approximate this skill. In 1986, peanut prices soared because of the severe drought in the Southeast that year. Harvests were lower, and contracts to sell peanuts at extraordinarily high prices became available. Eight operators who received $900 or more per ton for their peanuts were given +1 point, and those who received $600 or more for peanuts not sold through the program were also given a point. No low rating was given for this variable.

Government Program Participation. "Farming the programs" is an important part of agricultural success for most operators in Dodge County. Several farmers, young and old alike, felt that these benefits were not worth the substantial demands in time and effort. Comparison between farms of similar size and type that did and did not use government programs extensively, however, did not support this assertion. Farmers were asked whether in 1986 they had participated in peanut or cotton programs; wheat, corn, or other crop set-aside programs (which pay the farmer to take land out of production); the Conservation Reserve Program (through which farmers offer land for tree planting or other conservation use); or the disaster payments program. Those who bid to have land accepted into the Conservation Reserve Program were considered to have participated, even if they were rejected. Operators who participated in no programs or only the minimum peanut program were given −1 point. Those who had set-asides in two or more crops and had received some disaster payments as well as participating in the peanut program or some other combination of four or five programs were coded as highly skilled in government program use and were given +1 point.

Information Gathering. Another important skill in farming is keeping up with technological changes and sharing information with other operators. Farmers were asked, "How do you keep up with the changes in farming?" The wording of the question was suggested independently by the county agent and by a capable farmer, and it yielded quite useful answers. A number of farmers said, "I don't keep up," or, "There aren't any changes nowadays," and these cases were given a −1 score. Those who attended extension service meetings and subscribed to several agricultural magazines were given +1 point.

Conservation Measures. Another arena of farming skill is an operator's attention to soil erosion and application of conservation measures. Though I gathered information on terracing of farmlands, it became clear it was not a valid indicator of concern or skill with regard to conservation matters. Some operators inherited land that was terraced and claimed to put some effort into keeping it up, but inspection of the fields suggested little effort in this regard. Other farmers operate only rented land and were unwilling to undertake the cost of terracing it without greater security of tenure. Three other activities proved more useful as measures of this skill: planting waterways on the fields, plowing on the contour, and leaving residue on the field to protect it from erosion in winter. Farmers who carried out none of these conservation activities were given −1 point; energetic activities in all or most of these areas were rated +1.

Soil Testing. The final dimension of farming skill was based on the use of soil nutrient tests, which are provided free of charge by the University of Georgia College of Agriculture. Those who said they tested their fields every year or every other year and who followed the recommendations on fertilizer and lime use were given +1 point. Those who tested their soil every three years or less and who reported that they did not use the amounts of fertilizer and lime recommended by the test results but rather used the amounts they could afford were given −1.

Measurement of Soil Quality

The ratings of soil quality for each farm in the study were carried out with the advice of Jesse Bearden of the Soil Conservation Service in Dodge County. Once farmers' permission had been obtained during the 1987 interviews, my assistant, Paul Patterson, located individual farm soil maps in the Soil Conservation Service office. Using transparent plastic grid overlays to measure acreage, he determined the number of acres per farm corresponding to each soil type. For a few farms in the county, no soil mapping had been carried out. In these cases, information from the operator combined with the knowledge of the Soil Conservation Service agent was sufficient to make a satisfactory calculation of soil types. Farm maps generally included acreage rented as well as acreage owned, since operators often wanted this information for rented land as well as for their own property.

Soil mapping in Dodge County used 45 different soil codes. These soils were divided into three categories: excellent/good, good/fair, and the remainder. The first two soil types were measured using the grids, and then the total acres of these two categories was subtracted from the total acreage of the farm, giving the "remainder" total. These remainder acres included swamps, roads, ponds, and areas that were for some reason not coded for soil type.

In general, the three scientifically based soil categories corresponded to farmers' informal labels. In the Georgia Coastal Plain, the sandy-loamy soils are the most fertile and have the best soil texture for most crops (rated excellent/good). Sandy soils are the next most desirable category (good/fair). With proper care, good rain or irrigation, and adequate fertilization, sandy soils can generally produce as well as loamy soils, but they often require a bit more work and perhaps more inputs. Most topsoils in Dodge County have a clay subsoil; no red clay topsoil existed prior to deforestation and erosion. Some farmers today say they have "loamy-clay" or "sandy-clay" soils. These eroded farms, in which the subsoil has been plowed up into the thin remaining topsoil, were coded as having "remainder" soils in this analysis.

For the final calculation of the variable called good soil deficit, the total acres needed for all rowcropping in 1986 (or 1981 for farmers who had gone out of business) was compared with the total acres of excellent/good land available to that farmer. If half or more of the land used for crop production was not top quality, it was hypothesized that the farm was at a disadvantage in productivity. A second measure—poor soil—was calculated, in which a farm that could not meet 75 percent of its rowcropping needs with either excellent/good or good/fair soil was coded as having "poor soil" (or more accurately, a higher percentage of poor soil). Comparison of these two measures showed that they identified mostly the same farms; the good soil deficit measure was chosen for statistical analysis because it coded slightly fewer farms as having poorer soil.

Measurement of Debt-to-Asset Ratio

The calculation of the debt-to-asset ratio used in chapter 8 was based on farmers' responses to a series of questions about debts, farmland, facilities, equipment, and animals.

Debts. The figure used for total farm debt makes no distinction between long-term and short-term debt. The cost of houses when purchased or financed separately from the farm was not included. In these cases, the farm family either financed the home based on the wife's income or mortgaged the home for some nonfarm purpose and did not consider this debt to be part of the farm. Though they may have chosen to differentiate types of debt because of a psychological need for less burdensome debt levels on the farm, such a division does have some validity, particularly in the eyes of lenders. This method of calculation was judged appropriate, and although this circumstance was rare, total debt levels were lowered in a few cases.

Assets. The value of land was assessed very carefully because, more than any other variable, it affects the total value of assets. This fact is well understood by borrowers and lenders alike, and during the early drought years, several farmers persuaded lenders to raise the assessed value of their land, thereby increasing their eligibility for further loans. At the time research began in 1982, the top land values were quoted to be $700–800 an acre. An average figure of $400–500 was commonly used. By 1983, bankers and other local experts claimed that land values were beginning to fall. In an attempt to document that decline, I investigated every 1983 sale of farmland in the county that I could find, but prices were all in the $500 range for good farmland. In fact, an examination of sales of farmland, with the value of timber and other farm assets taken into account, revealed no prices that were below 1981–82 levels.

By 1987, however, land values had definitely fallen. Land sales had been extremely rare in the early 1980s, but by the second half of the decade they had begun to pick up again. To begin the process of assigning a value to a farm, I asked each farmer, "What is your best guess as to the value of your farmland?" The average of the values reported was $330 per acre. In making their estimates, farmers took into account the timber resources on the land, fencing, permanent irrigation installations, slope, and soil quality. Interviews with real estate experts, bankers, and the county agricultural extension agent revealed that these farmer assessments were accurate. Farmland was selling for an average of $300–350 an acre.

In identifying a specific land value for each farm, I used the farmer's estimate, as long as it fit my own objective measures of the farm's assets, soil quality, and other factors. In only a few cases, high estimates were lowered or low figures raised, based on these asset indicators. The highest acreage value used was $800 and the lowest was $300; values between $500 and $330 per acre were most common. It should be noted that in the few cases of very high asset values, farm debts were usually so low that debt-to-asset ratios would not have changed significantly had a lower land value been used.

Equipment assets were valued at the 1987 estimated sale price. This determination was accomplished with the help of Danny Bennett, a Dodge Countian who made farm equipment assessments for lenders. From an anonymous master list of equipment compiled from farmer questionnaires, he rated each type of equipment as to estimated sale value, assuming fair condition. The same procedure was used to value irrigation pumps and pipe, equipment shelters, hog facilities, and other investments. Since the equipment of several farms in the area that had gone out of business had been sold at auction that year, the accuracy of his estimates was verified by those sale prices. Through examination of several detailed equipment listings from farms of different sizes, it was discovered that expensive items such as combines, tractors, trucks, and feed mills made up two-thirds of all equipment investments. Farmers were asked to list these high-priced items only, and the total value of such items was then multiplied by 1.33 to give the total estimated value of all equipment.

Livestock values were somewhat difficult to assess because farmers were not asked the weight or age of each animal, only the number of head of each type (number of sows, feeder pigs, etc.). Prices also fluctuate greatly. With the advice of lenders who were foreclosing farms in the area, brood cows were assigned an average value of $450 and sows $110. For other animals, the five-year average price per head as reported by the Georgia Crop Reporting Service was used: $318 for cattle and $71 for hogs.

TWO

Statistical Analysis of Farm Survival

The independent variables used in the statistical analyses were designed to test a range of farm survival determinants that are discussed both by other researchers and by Dodge Countians. The dependent variable is the dichotomous debt-to-asset ratio indicator described in chapter 8. The independent variables fall under four general headings: farming skill (including experience), resource access, standard of living, and management style. Coding to achieve a useful measure of each of these elements was carried out in an interactive process. With observational and open-ended interview data as well as survey data, the anthropologist can visualize each case; because I had seen the equipment, walked the land, visited the homes, and talked at length with each farm family, I could assess each coding of the data for its usefulness. If, for example, a diverse range of farms were identified as having "high use of hired labor," I first verified the data and then considered other, perhaps more accurate, ways to capture this aspect of an entrepreneurial management style.

Table A-1 reports the results of univariate analysis for the association of 22 independent variables with farm survival. The first two farming skill variables are described in chapter 4 and in appendix 1. The overall skill coding dichotomized the cases into two groups (higher skill versus lower skill) based on the combined ten variables discussed in appendix 1. The crop skill measure coded as "lower skill" any farm with low peanut yield in its five-year average of production, so long as it had no high yields in any of the other 3 crops. Experience (years of farming) was also dichotomized at the midpoint (13.5 years in 1982).

Measurements of the resource access variables were described in chapter 4. The good soil deficit variable (see appendix 1) was used to measure land quality.

Table A-1. Univariate Analysis of High Debt-to-Asset Ratio:
Lambda Coefficients by Farm Scale

Variable	Whole Sample (n = 58)	Large Scale (n = 21)	Medium Scale (n = 37)
Farming skill			
Overall farming skill	.08	.10	.21
Crop production skill	.10	.63**	.00
Years experience	.31***	.00	.56***
Resource access			
Good quality soil	.24*	.30	.17
Family land	.03	.00	.00
Low education	.13*	.00	.28*
Family background	.14	.30	.00
Wives' contribution:			
Production activities	.00	.08	.00
Helper activities	.00	.00	.00
Family equipment	.03	.10	.00
Off-farm income	.16	.00	.28*
Federal program rights	.14	.30	.00
Resource disadvantage	.28**	.60**	.06
Standard of living			
High consumption standards	.22*	.29	.17
Management style			
High acreage	.14	.00	.17
High capital investment	.14	.10	.11
Irrigation	.03	.10	.00
Hired labor	.24	.20	.22
1970s farm expansion	.41***	.30	.44***
Crisis debt acceptance	.59***	.50**	.61***
Expansion and crisis debt	.66***	.60	.67***
Expansion, crisis debt, and high consumption	.38***	.60***	.22*
Marital model	.29**	.11	.40**

*Significant by chi-square test (or Fisher exact test) at .10 level.
**Significant by chi-square test (or Fisher exact test) at .05 level.
***Significant by chi-square test (or Fisher exact test) at .01 level.

Access to low-cost family land and access to family equipment were also tested for their role in survival. Education was coded by years of completed schooling; operators who had not completed high school were categorized as more at risk for this lower education. I also checked whether farmers with some college education had an advantage in the crisis, but they are evenly split between good and poor financial situations. Family background is another dimension of privilege, and I used the codings described in chapter 2 for large and medium scale farm background versus small farm or landless backgrounds. In terms of labor resources, women's contributions in production activities and helper activities were tested. Another area of advantage for some farmers is off-farm income. I measured all sources of off-farm income, including pensions and interest, and divided the sample into higher and lower off-farm incomes. Federal program rights, described in chapter 4, constitute another type of advantage. The resource disadvantage variable is a combination variable that codes for either good soil deficit or low federal program rights.

The remaining categories of variables, standard of living and management style, are discussed in chapters 4 and 5. The high consumption standards measures are explained in chapter 8 and combine information about houses, appliances, and cars. The management style indicators break down dimensions of large scale operations—high acreage, high capital investment, use of irrigation, and use of hired labor—to explore their independent roles in farm survival. The first two variables were dichotomized. Irrigation was measured in two ways: presence of irrigation (which should lower risk) and presence of high-cost irrigation (which should raise risk). Neither measure has an association with the outcome variable, farm survival, and table A-1 presents the results of the first measurement (presence of irrigation). Expansion, disaster loan acceptance, and the combination of the two are described in chapter 8. I also assessed the impact on farm debt loads of these two variables combined with high household consumption. The marital model codings are discussed in chapter 6, and an agrarian model is assumed to confer an advantage.

For each of the variables presented, two statistical tests have been used. First, the chi-square test measures the extent to which the data diverge from a random distribution, that is, one that could have occurred completely by chance. A significance level of 1.00 means that the pattern with respect to farm financial situation is random. In much social science research, a significance level of .05 or .01 is chosen as a marker of a sufficiently nonrandom distribution as to be probable that the independent variable affects the dependent variable. As Michael Chibnik

Table A-2. Univariate Logistic Regression
for High Debt-to-Asset Ratio

Variable	Odds Ratio	Confidence Intervals (95%)
Years experience	0.96	(.920, .997)
Good soil deficit	3.11	(.953, 10.2)
Federal program rights	1.75	(.602, 5.10)
Resource disadvantage (good soil deficit or lower federal program rights)	4.41	(1.18, 16.5)
High consumption standards	2.81	(.921, 8.59)
Use of hired labor	2.68	(.906, 7.92)
1970s farm expansion	7.69	(2.07, 28.6)
Disaster loan acceptance	14.70	(4.01, 53.8)
1970s expansion and disaster loan acceptance	35.40	(6.55, 192)
Expansion, disaster loan acceptance, and high consumption standards	19.80	(2.25, 174)
Industrial marital model	1.64	(.372, 7.20)

(1985:140–41) has shown, however, with the smaller sample sizes (20–60 cases) characteristic of much anthropological research, a .05 significance level may be overly conservative and lead to the inappropriate failure to reject the null hypothesis. I have therefore chosen the significance level of .10 as a useful indicator of a nonrandom relationship. The Fisher exact probability test has been used in cases where the chi-square is inappropriate.

The second statistical measure employed evaluates the degree of association between financial situation and the independent variable in question, using the asymmetric measure lambda. A lambda coefficient of .37 for a particular variable, for instance, means that 37 percent of the errors in estimating the financial situation of a farm can be eliminated by knowing whether the farm is high or low on this variable.

Logistic regression analysis, both univariate and multivariate, was carried out with the assistance of the Emory University School of Public Health Department

Table A-3. Multiple Logistic Regression Model of Variables
Correlated with High Debt-to-Asset Ratio

Variable	Estimated Beta Coefficients	Estimated Standard Error
Disaster loan acceptance	2.792	0.788
1970s farm expansion	2.178	0.845
Federal program rights	1.655	0.830
Good soil deficit	1.329	0.814
Constant	−4.147	1.13

Note: Goodness-of-fit chi-square = 45.75, d.f. = 52, p = 0.72.

of Biostatistics. The univariate logistic analysis was performed with only those variables from table A-1 that showed some evidence of association with the outcome variable. The odds ratio and 95 percent confidence intervals are presented in table A-2. This analysis indicates how much each variable contributes to the unadjusted odds of being in poor financial condition. A multivariate model was built using stepwise logistic regression for choosing variables from those listed in table A-2. The final model is shown in table A-3. Multivariate logistic regression adjusts the coefficients of each variable in the model for the other independent variables in the model.

An analysis of table A-3 supports the general conclusion from the univariate analysis: expansion, disaster loan acceptance, soil quality, and federal program rights are the most useful variables in predicting good or bad financial condition. The other variables in table A-2 were offered but were not selected for the model. The chi-square goodness-of-fit value indicates, however, a poor fit of the logistic model to the data.

Analysis using continuous values for both the dependent and independent variables was tried, but the sample is too small for it to show any significant results.

NOTES

Introduction

1. Though I have found Bennett's concept of management style essential in understanding the fortunes of Dodge County farmers, I have modified and narrowed his use of the term. His assessment of style (Bennett 1980:218) includes analysis of expansion and development decisions, debt, "planfulness, carefulness," and "support load" (the consumer-worker ratio). I have omitted issues of the family cycle in support load and have focused more narrowly on farmers' preferences with regard to scale, use of hired labor, the work ethic, debt, social status, and lifestyle. My data cannot trace long-term shifts in management style that occur in response to changes in household composition, market conditions, or inheritance, however, in conversations with farmers it seems that for many there is great continuity in the attitudes I do measure in the ambitious and cautious orientations. It seems that the more massive economic flux and historical revolutions in southern agriculture have, paradoxically, created less visible life cycle shifts in management, though certainly farm operations tend to be developed and become stagnant in cycles. As his Canadian work was drawing to a close, Bennett was beginning to find his farmers responding to the highly favorable economic conditions of the early 1970s. I suspect that the time period during which Bennett undertook his study was less turbulent than the period I studied, and thus life cycle variation was more easily measured.

2. More information about the origins of Dodge County families might reveal diverse backgrounds within the British Isles. Fischer (1989) argues that successive waves of English immigrants to the United States were drawn from such different classes, regions, and agrarian traditions in England and Scotland that these origins alone could account for the diversity of farming styles in Dodge County.

3. Rodefeld (1979) has presented a persuasive typology of the changing structure of U.S. agriculture based on landownership/rental and family labor/hired labor, which I utilized in my early analysis of Dodge County (Barlett 1984). As my understanding of the individual Dodge County cases grew, however, this typology became inadequate. I found in Dodge County that family farm *renters* (Rodefeld's "tenants") and family farm *owners* were too similar in many important respects to be separated into different classes. Rented land was often secure and in many cases was family land that would one day be inherited or purchased. In the crisis years, landownership was actually a disadvantage for those still making

payments; renters might actually be better off (according to both farm experts and Dodge County farmers). As for the group Rodefeld calls "industrial farms," composed of renters who use hired labor, this group was found in Dodge County to be essentially identical to farms categorized as the larger-than-family-farms, who own their land and also use hired labor. Thus, only the Rodefeld distinction based on the use of hired labor remained useful.

4. Georgia's fifty-seven Coastal Plain counties make up the primary agricultural region of the state; the former cotton areas of the Piedmont region have largely declined in importance, except where contract poultry production has become dominant.

5. This comparison was also made based on the 1987 census, and again Dodge County farm characteristics resemble the U.S. and Coastal Plain figures. The average farm size in the study sample was 478 acres, nationally it was 462 acres, and in the Coastal Plain it was 429 acres. Mean sales were $71,183, $65,165, and $78,170, respectively. The proportion of farms over 1,000 acres was 7 percent in Dodge County, 8 percent nationally, and 9 percent in the Coastal Plain. Part-time farms made up 30 percent, 38 percent, and 35 percent of the three respective samples.

6. The ASCS list in 1982 was organized not by operator or by actual operating units but by farm number; all farms applying for benefits since the 1930s have received a number. Farms were identified by owner and operator (who might be a renter), the total number of acres, and the number of acres in cultivation. Many operating units consisted of several different numbered "farms." To obtain a sample of operating units, I consolidated this ASCS list into a master list of operators and all their farms (owned and rented), from which the 50 percent sample was selected. Farms whose operators listed addresses outside Dodge County were excluded (these were usually absentee owners of timberland who lived in Atlanta, Florida, or other states). The 503 operators identified by this procedure were numbered, and the 251 even-numbered farmers (and their farms) were selected for the study.

In choosing farms for the sample, I did not establish a minimum level of farm sales, a departure from the procedure of the Census of Agriculture. I found that, for a few farmers, crop failures had been so severe in 1981 that sales were far below normal. Some operations normally sold hogs but had cut back because of loss of feed or poor livestock prices. Thus, I decided a sales cutoff was inappropriate. In the end, this aspect of the sample definition affects only a few small part-time and retirement farms.

7. All through this analysis of the Dodge County data, the reader will note that at times the focus is *farms* and at other times, *operators*. Depending on whether the issue to be addressed is the agricultural production unit, the individual farm operator, or the farm family, calculations are carried out accordingly. The study sample is random with respect to farms, single family and multifamily. Because most Dodge County partnerships list only one operator with ASCS, this list cannot be used to select a random group of operators. In our surveys, we tried to talk to all the operators on each farm that fell into the study sample, and these data comprise our universe of operators. Because large scale farms are more likely to be partnerships than medium or small scale farms, figures based on *operators* in this study tend to overemphasize large farms. For this reason, whenever appropriate, data are presented by *farm*.

In the chapters that follow, there is some variation in references to sample totals, which stems from two causes. First, for certain analyses, cases with no data or inadequate data are omitted; in discussing marital expectations of farm women, for instance, farms operated by single men are not included. Second, depending on the data used, the sample actually changes size from life course shifts over the five years between the two surveys. Fathers died, partners split, and partners joined; where there was one farm in 1982, there may have been two in 1987. In certain situations, a father or son in financial trouble may have recruited a father or son to help, thereby increasing the number of operators on the same farm. In general, farms were coded for most analyses according to their form in 1987. For instance, if in 1982 a son worked with his ailing father, but by 1987 the son was the primary operator and the father had retired, the farm is coded Generation 3 (farms begun after 1972) because the son had begun his independent farm operation at that time. In 1987, I intended to expand the sample by including a randomly drawn group of beginning farmers from the ASCS list, to balance the loss of older farmers who had died or retired. Unfortunately, computerization of the ASCS records made it impossible to obtain a comparable list. Instead, I canvassed operators in all parts of the county about new farmers in their neighborhoods who had begun operating since 1982. I contacted those named, but most were found to have, in fact, been in business prior to 1982. Only two genuinely new farmers were identified in the county, one part-time and one full-time, and the full-time case was added to the sample. In addition to these two new farmers, two sons joined family partnerships, though one left soon after. These new partners affected the number of operators in the study but not the number of farms.

8. "Farmer" can be a political word; it may be used, particularly by some high-status people, to claim a more egalitarian family background. One woman whose father was a wealthy merchant, landowner, and bankroller of dozens of sharecroppers prior to World War II claims to have "grown up on a farm," though neither of her parents ever did farm work. Along with others in the county, her identification of her father as a farmer is based on the sale of crops and livestock, not the work necessary to produce them. People who own farms and rent them out also sometimes insist they are farmers, though they are only very remotely involved in making farm decisions. In a different context, these same people will denigrate the hard work and low return of farming and will distance themselves from this label. Some who claim to be farmers desire to assert a continuity with parental or grandparental farm lives. When asked to identify large scale farming families in the county, many name large landowners who have no connection to crop or livestock production, but who own land planted in timber. The ambiguity of the meaning of "farmer" is illustrated by the complaints of several large scale farmers that there is little support for farming among town elites in Eastman, while others say, "Eastman is a farming town anyway." The definitions in this study must therefore inevitably violate some Dodge Countians' identities with regard to farm ownership, operation, or background.

Chapter One

1. Though Numan Bartley (1990) puts Dodge County in the plantation belt and not the wiregrass region, the evidence presented in this chapter supports Ann Malone (1986), Mark

Wetherington (1985), and others who see it as more culturally and economically linked with the wiregrass.

2. The needles of longleaf pines (*Pinus palustris*) are commonly a foot in length, and needle growth is concentrated in a crest at the top of the tree (Wetherington 1985:57). These pine forests were described by early travelers as "quiet cathedrals" because of the cool shade and open understory created by trees 75–100 feet tall (Cobb [1932] 1983). Wiregrass is believed by some experts to have been encouraged by deliberate Native American burning to hold back the pine forest's natural succession to oak. Fires from lightening or from slash-and-burn agriculture may also have played a role in sustaining the ecosystem. Other experts believe that the more acidic parent material of these soils allowed pines to thrive and enabled them to shade out oaks.

3. In the process of this historical research, an interesting coincidence was discovered linking Emory University to Dodge County. When the final litigation over titles between settlers and the Dodge Land and Lumber Company was ended, the remaining acres were sold to Judge John S. Candler of Atlanta, who in turn sold or donated parts but retained an estate in Dodge County. In 1982, the Candler estate was the only absentee-owned corporate rowcrop and livestock farm in the county. Members of the Candler family were the founders and benefactors of Emory University. I did not learn of the family's landowner role in Dodge County until after my research began, and the Candler farm did not fall into the 50 percent random sample of the study.

4. The lack of hostile race relations in Dodge County is attributed by both Malone (1986) and Wetherington (1985) to the high rate of landownership, the numerical predominance of whites, and the milder impact of Reconstruction. Wetherington recounts the observations of one northern manager of the Uplands Hotel in Eastman: " 'The Southern prejudice, the blood thirsty ku klux and the insurrectionary negro' that friends back home warned that he would encounter were rare in the piney woods" (1985:418).

5. Total expenses for a year's farming before World War II are said to have been as little as $50–$60. One small landowner feels he lived better in the 1940s than he does now; "at least *easier*," he said. He remembers expenses of only $35 a month: $10 to pay off his furniture, $5 for his light bill, and $20 for groceries. His wife sold eggs regularly and used the money to buy groceries; once or twice a year, he paid off his remaining grocery bill by butchering a calf and giving the appropriate weight to the storekeeper.

6. One part-time farming woman remembers her mother driving a tractor and harrowing, as well as contributing to the more common labor of harvesting cotton and peanuts. This probably took place in the late 1940s.

7. It is possible that because other studies have attended more to the gender hierarchies within farm families, they have found more evidence for a gendered financial division of labor than I have. On the other hand, the class-based diversity I have described here may also be true elsewhere, but the tendency for more affluent farm families (and their children) to stay in farming may have biased our reconstructions of women's roles.

8. Tenants normally paid an annual cash rent and provided their own mules and agricultural equipment. Sharecroppers used the animals and plows of the landowner, though expenses for fertilizer were sometimes shared. Reports of individual sharecropping con-

tracts in Dodge County were diverse, however, and revealed considerable tailoring of land, capital, and labor exchanges between the two families involved.

9. Determining the number of tenants/sharecroppers and small farm owners is a bit more difficult than determining the number of owners of farms over 260 acres because census tables do not include all three groups in one table. Multiplying the proportion of tenant and sharecropper farms (versus owner-operated farms) by the total number of farm operations yields an estimated number of these combined types of landless operators.

10. Rootlessness and its effects on collective memory are probably more noticeable in plantation counties; Gavin Wright finds that in Jasper County, Georgia, 60 percent of the 1850 slaveholders no longer lived in the county ten years later (1986:25). But interviews with Dodge Countians about family background revealed that they commonly knew relatively little about their parents or grandparents and often expressed scant interest in the facts of their families' past history. A few did not know whether their grandparents were farmers, and others had no certainty as to their grandparents' farm size. Parents' education was not commonly known for sure, unless they had finished high school or gone to college. Ethnic heritage was even more rarely known. "I never heard anyone say anything about that," was a common response to inquiries about ethnic background. Occasionally a distant family member who was reputed to know genealogy and other family lore was mentioned. The majority of families had no knowledge of where the family migrated from or where distant relatives might live. Relatives close by, especially those belonging to the same church, are a vital part of everyday life, but families in Dodge County who share the same surname often say there is some kin link but they are unable to trace it.

11. The heirs of those storekeepers, on the other hand, laud the generosity of their parents, who "carried people for years."

12. It is hypothesized that African Americans in the South were not as susceptible to malaria as Anglo-Americans because the Duffy negative antigen in their blood chemistry protected them from the vivax form of malaria (Livingstone 1984).

13. Local Baptist churches have grown considerably wealthier in recent decades. In 1947, the total revenues of all Dodge County Baptist churches was $47,000. By the 1980s, the Baptist Association records $1,660,000 in local expenditures alone, and contributions for foreign missions and national projects matched that amount. There were 100 Baptist churches in the county in the 1980s, but there are no records of the number of Baptist churches in the county in the pre–World War II era.

14. Arthur Raper's work in Greene and Macon counties in the mid-1930s documented that between six and sixty times more money was spent on white education (1936:5).

Chapter Two

1. Dodge Countians' recollections of free-ranging hogs and cattle in the 1940s contrast with Steven Hahn's analysis of the imposition of stock laws as part of an earlier clash of class interests in upcountry Georgia (1983). Wetherington's study of the late nineteenth century recounts that wiregrass settlers successfully resisted fencing laws and interprets this

as a victory of indigenous agricultural practices over outside interests (1985:163–64).

2. In this fifty-year period, even though the total population of the county fell by 22 percent, as table 2-1 shows, the number of households actually rose. Though comparison of different census years is difficult because definitions change and data are not strictly comparable, these figures support the evidence of Dodge County genealogies that family size and household size declined. The recent rise in household numbers (in 1980) reflects some in-migration as well as a trend away from extended families and an increase in single-person households.

The trend toward off-farm work is true for other farming regions as well. Even in Iowa, farmers make up less than 30 percent of the employed population in the majority of counties.

3. In the Depression years, shopping "in town" was a status symbol that set off more fortunate rural families from those who had to rely on local stores.

4. Raper's upbeat analysis has been questioned by Kirby (1987), who argues that although automobiles broke down some patterns of deference and distance, they also generated resentments by whites. The role of cars as status markers that separate those families with cars from those without is echoed by a Dodge County farmer who said that in pre-automobile days "we were all on the same level then—no cars." This sentiment reflects the ideology of shared poverty and community cooperation discussed in chapter 1. Both views seem to me to be correct; stratification in this period shifted from being a more rigid lumping of large groups to a more fine-grained, but flexible, ranking among households.

5. The data for different years presented in figure 2-1 are not precisely comparable because the Bureau of the Census, which carries out a Census of Agriculture approximately every five years, changed the definition of a "farm" in 1959 and 1974. These changes, however, affect only the smallest and least active farm units. Economist Nora Brooks of the U.S. Department of Agriculture Economic Research Service has found, by comparing other agricultural surveys to the farm census, that these shifting definitions, in fact, do not make a big difference in the kinds of farms being measured in Dodge County (personal communication). Her research suggests that a mathematical adjustment of the Dodge County figures would probably distort the result more than simply using the unadjusted figures.

6. These figures and the ones in table 2-2 are not adjusted for inflation. Deflators reflecting national price trends are available, but since Dodge County undoubtedly has somewhat different patterns of inflation—as reflected in its much lower than average cost of living—I have been reluctant to apply these calculations to the county data.

7. At the same time, land in agriculture declined by 37 percent statewide, the same proportion as in Dodge County.

8. Though it might seem that winter wheat simply "grows" in the winter, farmers report that the necessity to double-crop fields (usually with soybeans) puts substantial pressure on them. Soybean harvests in the fall usually are delayed until after peanut and cotton harvests, and for many farmers this means that the turnaround time to plow and plant wheat is very short. Wheat plantings are often staggered through the late fall, leaving little of the short winter season for the plowing and harrowing of corn, peanuts, and other crops. A cool or wet spring and a late wheat harvest can force hurried field preparation for the replacement soybean crop, which often conflicts with other late spring and early summer tasks.

9. Table 2-2 was constructed by combining different tables from the Census of Agriculture. Numbers of tenant farms and farms that reported hiring workers 150 days or more per year are subtracted from the total number of farms, to give the number of owner-operated farm units. Unfortunately, it is not possible to compare the rise of total family labor farms with the overall decline of black farms in these years since farms using hired labor are not presented in the census by racial classification.

10. Table 2-2 shows a rise in farms with full-time workers in 1978 (from 61 to 106), but table 2-3 shows no corresponding rise in full-time farm workers counted by the census. This anomaly either reflects a desire on the part of farm workers to underreport their days of employment—from fear of possible tax repercussions—or a trend on the largest farms to cut back their total of full-time hands, while other medium-sized farms added a full-time helper for the first time. Data from conversations with Dodge County farmers suggest the latter trend may have occurred as older hands died or retired and mechanization made their replacement less necessary on very large farms. The decline in turpentine operations in the county may also be a part of this trend.

11. It would be interesting to understand better who these temporary farm laborers are and how this work fits into their annual survival. Though some are neighbors and kin of farm owners, others are from poor families, living in rural rental housing or in small towns. The availability of such workers seems to be part of the southern sharecropper past. For some workers, welfare, social security, and other programs provide support for most of the year; others have full-time jobs and temporary farm work is a form of moonlighting. It may be that the seasonal availability of such work is an important component of survival strategies for families who cannot find steady work and, conversely, a key to the perpetuation of an impoverished sector of the rural population.

12. Influences from grandparental farms were taken into account where they were dominant in operators' upbringing. Since the ages of the full-time operators in the study range across forty years, the figures in this section combine parents from several eras. Statistical analysis, however, shows no significant variation by generational cohort in family class background.

13. It is significant that the data for the 1950s and 1960s in figure 2-6, which is based on my sample, shows similar patterns to the data presented in table 2-5, which is based on census figures, because my sample is potentially biased by the fact that it is based on operators who survived to be studied in 1982, while the census presumably measured all those who were trying to farm at each point. The parallel patterns suggest that most restructuring occurred at the entry point into agriculture, not as a result of mid-career attrition. In other words, the decline in small farms in the county over this period was the result of young men choosing nonfarm jobs and not mid-career farmers being forced out. When discussing agricultural structure, social scientists often refer to groups as being "forced out," which is true in the sense that the group does not continue farming as a group but is not true in the sense that *individuals* try to farm but fail and must seek other jobs.

Chapter Three

1. Table 3-1 does not present data on women because definitions and categories of women's employment vary too much from census to census. Changing definitions of occupational categories affect the census figures on men as well, and therefore the figures in the table for different years are not strictly comparable but are useful to illustrate shifts in occupational structure.

2. I found three patterns with regard to children's farm labor in families with children at home old enough to contribute to the farm. Roughly equal numbers of parents either required no regular farm work, expected regular chores without remuneration, or hired their children as if they were regular wage laborers. Most children who were expected to do regular work were boys; in general, girls were asked to do minimal work on the farm. Around half a dozen farmers, the majority of whom grow small amounts of tobacco, referred to their daughters as important assets on the farm. This finding supports Daniel's argument that tobacco as a commodity system encourages pooled family labor, to an extent not found with peanut or cotton production (1985).

3. This man probably lived in town, since farmers did not usually have lawns until after the imposition of stock-fencing laws.

4. AT&T, for example, considered a proposal in 1928 to persuade the public away from the utilitarian view of a telephone toward a consumerist orientation: "AT&T, suggested a vice president, might even wish to entice the public to buy colored hand sets as 'outward and visible signs of an inward and spiritual grace' " (Marchand 1985:117).

5. The definition of a part-time farm differs in the literature (Barlett 1991). Two general approaches exist: one emphasizes the amount of off-farm work done by the farm family and the other focuses on who is doing the off-farm work. The pattern found by Van Es et al. (1982), Salant (1984), and Kada (1980) that if farm operators took jobs, they usually obtained full-time jobs was found in Dodge County as well. Very few operators managed a medium or large farm in addition to a full-time job; most who did attempt this balance were forced into the job by high debts. I found it was easiest to use the census definition of 200 or more days worked off the farm per year to define a part-time farm. Some authors such as Kada (1980) and Gladwin (1991) argue that women's work off the farm must be taken into account equally with men's. The Dodge County data conformed to the pattern found by Salant (1984), Bokemeier and Coughenour (1980), Coughenour and Swanson (1983), and Cawley (1983) that the operator's off-farm work had a strong impact on farm size, commodities produced, and sales, while the wife's off-farm work had a much less significant impact (see chapter 6).

6. Though part-time farming in Dodge County does not provide a reserve of labor for capital (Bonanno 1987; Davis 1980), it is true that it serves the interests of industry by ameliorating some of the onerous aspects of proletarianization. The number of families involved in such pluriactivity, however, when compared to the total who left the farm over the last fifty years, is small. The data show, however, that Dodge County part-time farmers are not a sector of downwardly mobile full-time farmers (Barlett 1986a).

Chapter Four

1. The few farms in which a farmer over sixty-five continues to farm without cutting back the operation and does not receive social security have been included in my category of full-time farms. Most retired farmers are in their sixties; one-third are in their seventies and eighties.

2. Though it is theoretically possible for farm parents to consider partnership with a daughter (or a brother with a sister), in fact, daughters and sisters are not seen as potential farm partners in Dodge County. Women rarely define themselves as "farm operators," nor are they seen as such by men, reflecting strong gender segregation in socialization and in skills (see chapter 6).

3. The absence of a norm in parental support for farm transmission may reflect an adaptation to Depression hardships or a desire to allow children free choice of occupation. I explored the possibility that each ethnic heritage in Dodge County—English, Scottish, Irish, German, and African American—might include patterns in the types of farms operated or the ways parents deal with issues of inheritance, partnership, or farm transmission but found no such pattern.

4. Much black farmland has already been lost in Dodge County, as is true throughout the South. Families have sold property in order to divide inheritances or to provide needed resources. Especially for children who have migrated to other states, interest in the family patrimony can be weak. Some African American parents express little attachment to the land and say they will be content if children choose to sell it. Others feel it is very important for land to remain within the group and have taken steps to reduce legal entanglements when they die.

5. Figure 4-1 shows total acres in each operation, including rental land. Partnership farms are divided by the number of operators to give a more accurate sense of acreage per operator.

6. Mooney (1988) uses a four-part scheme to identify farms on the basis of rationality (substantive versus formal) and privilege. The scale distinction I use here captures much of his dichotomy based on privilege, since medium scale farms have less property and often have less education and other marketable skills. Mooney's concern with tenancy and debt as aspects of privilege are inappropriate for Dodge County. Debt is not so much a measure of low resources as an orientation toward one's resources in Dodge County and is also, as discussed in chapter 5, a part of management style that can be found in both more and less privileged groups. The distinction Mooney calls "rationality" is not acceptable to economic anthropologists (Frank Cancian 1987; Plattner 1989) but is useful when translated into different *goals*, which I do in chapter 5, in my concept of management style (see also Barlett 1990). When the management style groups are mapped onto my scale groups, the resulting four types bear many similarities to Mooney's conceptualizations. His "economists' model farmer" and "successful family farmer" are essentially the same as my ambitious/large scale and cautious/large scale groups. His ranking of lower-resource farmers as "poor" or "marginal" does not correspond to my grouping of medium scale farmers, however. The cautious medium scale farmers are marginal neither in number nor survival, and some am-

bitious medium scale farmers are highly productive and efficient and have been upwardly mobile. Though many, as we shall see, are out of business and some were in fact poor producers, a pejorative label such as "poor" or "marginal" is not accurate for the group.

7. For this analysis of class background, those with blue collar nonfarm occupations were incorporated into the landless and small landowner groups, as described in chapter 2. Those with white collar and professional occupations were classified with the medium and large landowner groups.

Chapter Five

1. Most couples build their own houses or buy a house or mobile home; younger farm families rarely take over an older farmhouse. This pattern, unlike the midwestern tradition of inheriting the old farmhouse as well as the farm, is due to the rapid rise in living standards and incomes in the South and also to the decay of older houses in "the termite belt."

2. It is interesting to note that the microwave oven has made it possible for farm families to maintain a more traditional diet. The typical farm midday meal consists of a wide array of dishes—meats, vegetables, salads, and breads. In Dodge County, many farm women with jobs prepare such meals in advance and leave a plate for their husbands to heat in the microwave.

3. An important possible influence on lifestyle aspirations might be the economic conditions faced by each generational cohort, as noted by Easterlin (1980). From a statistical analysis of population censuses in Dodge County, I find no evidence of a postwar baby boom. Instead, family sizes continued to be small and county population dropped between 1940 and 1950, presumably in part from out-migration. It seems, therefore, that the Generation 1 farmers entering adult life between 1940 and 1950 experienced a small and declining cohort and relatively easier access to opportunities to exceed the earnings potential of their parents. They did not, however, respond with higher fertility rates. The Generation 2 cohort saw a leveling off of numbers of young workers in the county, but because more chose off-farm work, they again experienced less competition. Generation 3 farmers were part of a rising number of young people interested in farming. Though earnings potential in the economy generally was slowing down, the possibilities in farming during the boom years looked good. These contradictory pressures make it hard to apply Easterlin's generational analysis to the rising lifestyle aspirations of Generation 3 operators.

Chapter Six

1. This analysis of marital models does not address the issue of hierarchy within the family or the extent to which women are better off in one kind of marriage or another. Issues of status and power within the family are largely beyond the scope of this study. My concern is with changing definitions of success and personal ideals over time among generations of women and on different kinds of farms. I have used the term *agrarian* here

not to evoke the complex layers of agrarianist ideology that are of concern to some scholars but simply to label this rural marital ideology in a way that links it to anthropological work found in other parts of the world.

Since this study focused on farms, my information about women is necessarily biased toward women in the context of marriage and farm and cannot be a comprehensive account of the full range of women. I use the term "family" here to mean the nuclear family, living in one household. By this definition, several families can be in partnership on one farm.

2. Though some recent writers have emphasized gendered arenas of conflict on family farms (Adams 1988; Fink 1986a, 1992; Haney and Knowles 1988; Sachs 1983), other observers have reported a joint commitment to the farm and joint responsibility for family welfare (Hagood 1939; Hahn 1985:181; L. Jones 1985). Obviously, both dimensions of marriage are true and valuable, but they reflect different emphases. It may be that systematic interviewing of a cross-section of farm families tends to contextualize the stories of conflict and strife that women recount, which may for various reasons be biased toward more extreme cases. It may also be that an analysis focused on patriarchy and gender dominance reflects a theoretical orientation that emerges from an industrial context of individual rights.

3. Some women with a more agrarian model also use this language at times and will say, "My husband is the provider." This statement reflects both the decline in their productive role and the pressures of mainstream cultural norms. The husband has become the farm manager and the earner of cash for the family. At the same time, these women express a sense of partnership with their husbands and an expectation of cooperation in meeting family goals. This partnership contrasts with the "separate spheres" ideal of most women with an industrial marital model.

4. Out of ninety-seven cases, seven were too mixed in their marital orientations to be coded as one or the other. Numbers vary in subsequent tables because not all information is available for all women.

5. Class background was defined as described in chapter 1, so that women from pre–World War II large- and medium-sized farms were categorized as elite. For nonfarm backgrounds, business owners, professionals, and other white collar occupations were categorized with this elite farm group. The women from small family farms and sharecropper farm backgrounds were categorized as non-elite, together with children of skilled and unskilled laborers. There is some tendency for the agrarian perspective to be linked to the non-elite farm backgrounds (73% of non-elite cases are agrarian), but elite families are evenly split (48% agrarian and 52% industrial). Even when only those women with a combination of elite class background and a farm background are taken into account, considerable diversity still exists: only 67 percent are industrial in their orientation.

6. Farm background correlates with marital model at the .05 level of significance, but there is much variation (chi-square = 3.94).

7. Complaints about the availability and quality of child care are rare, however. Older Dodge County women usually stayed home with their young children and returned to employment only later in the family cycle. Younger women today are more likely to return to work soon after childbirth, taking advantage of private daycare centers or nearby home care.

8. The eight farm production tasks used to measure women's work included the regular performance of major animal care, minor animal care, field labor, and truck driving at harvest and the regular or occasional performance of field work with machinery, government program management, making farm purchases, and marketing farm production. The seven tasks used to measure farm helper work included the occasional or regular performance of bookkeeping, going for parts and running errands, and coordination of deliveries and workers and the occasional performance of field labor, major or minor animal care, and driving trucks at harvest.

Questions concerning these items were adapted from the National Farm Women's Survey by changing the language to sound more colloquial. With information from pretests, several items were expanded or contracted, such as changing the item "harvesting crops or other products, including running machinery or trucks" to "driving trucks at harvest." "Taking care of farm animals" was divided into "major" and "minor," a distinction that separated regular feed grinding and pen cleaning from occasional vaccination or doctoring. Work with federal programs—widely known as "ASCS office business"—was added, as was the task of coordinating farm deliveries and workers, an important role on some large scale farms. Pretests also revealed that the work of supervising other family members and hired hands was so rare that it was omitted. Questions were also asked about garden labor, domestic tasks, and farm and household decision making. These results are reported elsewhere (Barlett forthcoming).

Women's participation in farm production tasks did not vary significantly by marital model (chi-square = 2.47; p = .12). Likewise, women's participation in farm helper tasks showed no significant variation by marital model (chi-square = 2.22; p = .14).

9. I considered the possibility that the agrarian marital model is more common among families that historically produced tobacco, a commodity system linkage supported by Daniel's work on southern agriculture (1985). The evidence from Dodge County, however, suggests that small cotton and peanut farms may have been equally oriented toward the agrarian model. It is possible that such families migrated from tobacco-growing areas in North Carolina and that industrially oriented families reflect a different origin. However, since most Dodge County families do not even know for certain which state their ancestors migrated from, it was not possible to test such a hypothesis.

Chapter Seven

1. El Niño, the periodic warming of equatorial Pacific Ocean waters, occurs irregularly every two to ten years. It is given the name "El Niño," the Spanish expression for the Christ Child, because the warm current is usually felt in South America around Christmas time. The 1982–83 El Niño was the largest ever recorded; a stretch of warm water extending 8,000 miles along the equator changed weather patterns around the world and caused severe droughts, forest fires, and floods. Weather in the southern United States in 1983 and subsequent years was thought to be affected by this global phenomenon and by a shifting of the normal location of the jet stream.

2. Part-time farms generally have had to make fewer changes to cope with the drought. Off-farm income made up for annual losses, and only a few part-time farmers attempted to handle large debts. Several rented out their land—or left it fallow—and planned to resume rowcropping when weather became more predictable. A few part-time farmers planted portions of their farms to trees, either on their own or as part of the Conservation Reserve Program. Some operators scaled back livestock production to levels that they could feed even in dry weather, preparing the farm throughout the crisis to become a stable source of retirement income. By 1989, fully one-quarter of part-time operators were raising cattle and fodder only—a minimal farm that seemed the only prudent way to wait out the drought years.

3. Leistritz et al. (1987) point out that, in the early years of the crisis, farm real estate continued to rise in value, thus generating a declining debt-to-asset ratio in spite of poor profits and high debts. This changing net asset value often encouraged farmers and lenders to be optimistic and delayed the development of strategies in response to the crisis.

4. A majority of readers surveyed by *Farm Futures* magazine in 1990 agreed that farmers' ethical standards had declined in the last decade. Associated Press reported that economic pressures, government bureaucracy, and "bad examples from Washington" were components of increasingly difficult ethical choices for farmers (*Daily Corinthian*, Corinth, Mississippi, May 3, 1991).

Chapter Eight

1. As noted in several chapters, some farms forced out of business have been able to buy back part of the operation and stay in business. These farms remain highly indebted, and several were later foreclosed. It was unclear as this research ended how often farms that tried to get back into business would be successful.

2. Large scale farmers can be seen as having more to lose, and thus they resist giving up the operation more strongly than the medium scale farmers with lower assets and less local power. The opposite can also be argued, however, that medium scale farm operators have fewer satisfying job options to move to and thus may resist downward mobility more fiercely. It seems clear, however, that lenders are more hopeful of someday recouping their losses on the large farms.

3. The farm crisis also affected families by forcing lowered consumption levels, but such changes in spending patterns were not possible to document after the fact. Another measure of the crisis is "net worth change," which takes account of declining land values and savings or investment levels, regardless of debt. If the goal of this analysis were to measure the severity of the financial crisis in terms of net worth or some other financial measure, such a measure would be essential. However, this analysis is focused instead on the continuing ability of a particular production unit to stay in operation, with all the implications that survival has for the farm family and the farm community. In this chapter, farmers forced out of business before the 1987 survey were included to the extent possible. In a few cases, operators were not asked to reconstruct their equipment inventories or to answer

farming skill questions retrospectively, but assessments for these measures were possible from records, from past interviews and observations, or from other data.

4. The three full-time farmers in the Dodge County sample who quit farming voluntarily because of low income due to the droughts are included in this analysis as cases of good financial situation, but they are also out of business. Four farms surveyed in 1982 were not included in this analysis: three had gone out of business and the variables coded here could not be reconstructed, and the fourth was not willing to share all the information needed. These cases have been included in other chapters, when appropriate.

5. In this way, I have tried to balance the actual level of consumption and the level of resources that can safely sustain it. It is hard to say how big a farm must be in order for a family to be able to afford a new car, or how large a peanut allotment is required to pay for a 3,000 square foot brick house. I recognize that the purchase of consumer durables is a one-time expense, while an affluent lifestyle is more a risk to farm survival if it involves high continuing expenditures. Though it is unusual to measure a stream of expenditures by a stock of durables owned, it is nevertheless more accurate in this situation for two reasons. First, data on household consumption expenditures are nearly impossible to obtain from interviews in Dodge County. Few families keep the kinds of records needed, estimations would be unreliable, and annual fluctuations are hard to take into account. Second, the purchase of houses, cars, and appliances seems to be, in fact, a good marker of general expenditure levels because it represents a certain orientation to consumption and status ranking in the community. Confirmation of this linkage comes from the several farms in which operators pay themselves a fixed monthly income, which is entirely for household expenses. The families of those operators who take markedly higher monthly incomes from "the farm account" have higher consumer standards in terms of durables.

6. In addition to the variables described here and in appendix 2, three other issues can be considered with regard to farm survival. One is addictions. As in all walks of life, alcohol and drug use play a role in Dodge County, and a few of the financially strained farmers struggled with addiction problems, some successfully and some less so. In most cases, drug and alcohol problems do not seem to account for farm difficulties because the level of debt incurred and the type of ambitious farming style employed are sufficient alone to predict farm failure. In fact, one medium scale farmer with a drinking problem has been able to keep the farm alive with moderate but not threatening debt levels. There are undoubtedly some other cases of substance abuse problems that did not come to light in the study, but among the handful of known cases, it cannot be concluded that these problems play a major role in farm loss.

Drug dealing or marijuana production is another possible variable affecting survival and was laughingly discussed by many in Dodge County as the only way to make any money. Though no effort was made to investigate these issues, rumors about particular farms were taken into account in the analysis. Among the small number of farms accused of these illegal activities, no relationship between such activities and farm survival was shown in the county because these farms fall into both good and bad financial situation groups.

Luck is another matter. Though this analysis looks at the intentional activities of farmers, as well as certain advantageous characteristics of their backgrounds and families, chance happenings that bring good or bad fortune play a role as well. Luck determines a range of vital conditions for farm success, such as whether conveniently located land becomes available at an opportune time and at an affordable price, whether adequate rain falls on the farm, or whether farm prices provide good profits in critical years of farm establishment and expansion. Though some farmers certainly have more marketing savvy than others (and good grain storage bins plus no pressing debtors make smart sales possible), luck plays a role in explaining high sales in some years.

Many Dodge Countians say, "You make your own luck," and to some extent this is true. Nurturing relationships with a neighbor (who may sell land) and careful monitoring of livestock (which can reduce disease outbreaks) are two examples. There are nevertheless a few young farmers with the odds stacked against them who are going to make it in part because of luck and some established farmers who should have been able to get through the crisis years without problems who are victims of the same vagaries of nature and the economy.

Chapter Nine

1. The calculations in table 9-1 use data from the sample collected in 1982 and 1987. Operators who had taken full-time jobs off the farm just prior to 1982 are omitted because their farm sizes and activity changed in some cases.

2. In carrying out the analysis of farm survival in chapter 8, I tested whether farms cooperating in equipment use and purchase had an advantage. Although individual farms have benefited greatly from reduced costs, overall the group of operators sharing equipment was split evenly into good and poor financial situation.

3. The total excludes the farm operators who died or retired from farming between 1982 and 1989. It also omits the disabled and retirement farmers as described in chapter 4. The latter group can be expected to have a high attrition rate regardless of economic conditions.

4. The Dodge County experiences with extended family are quite different from those found by Rosenblatt in Minnesota. I found no cases in which pressure to maintain land payments to retired parents contributed to farm loss. Nor did I see the intrusion of former farmers, who "cared intensely about how the farm was being managed by the people who had taken it over" (Rosenblatt 1990:72). These Minnesota families seem to exhibit a greater commitment to family continuity in farming (as evidenced by parents' timing their retirement to facilitate farm entry for their children) and to property. This yeoman tradition (Salamon 1985) contrasts with the more independent decisions of Dodge County farm parents and children, reflecting their British Isles/entrepreneur heritage.

BIBLIOGRAPHY

Adams, H. C.
1885   Making Money. Transactions of the Wisconsin State Agricultural Society
            23:386–93.
Adams, Jane H.
1988   The Decoupling of Farm and Household: Differential Consequences of
            Capitalist Development on Southern Illinois and Third World Family
            Farms. Comparative Studies in Society and History 30 (3): 453–82.
Almas, Reidar
1988   Norwegian Farmers in the U.S.A.: A Contemporary Report Based on the
            Stories of 36 Midwestern Families. Santa Cruz: University of California.
1989   Ethnic Values and Survival Strategies among Norwegian-American
            Farmers. Paper presented at the Rural Sociological Society annual meeting,
            Seattle, August 5–8.
Archibold, Annie
1989   Reorganizing the Household: The Cooperative Extension Service and the
            New Deal. Paper presented at the Southeast Women's Studies Association
            annual meeting, Emory University, Atlanta, Ga., February 24–26.
Baritz, Loren
1989   The Good Life: The Meaning of Success for the American Middle Class.
            New York: Knopf.
Barlett, Peggy F.
1980   Agricultural Decision Making: Anthropological Contributions to Rural
            Development. New York: Academic Press.
1984   Microdynamics of Debt, Drought, and Default in South Georgia. American
            Journal of Agricultural Economics 66 (5): 836–43.
1986a   Part-Time Farming: Saving the Farm or Saving the Lifestyle? Rural Soci-
            ology 51 (3): 289–313.
1986b   Profile of Full-Time Farm Workers in a Georgia County. Rural Sociology
            51 (1): 78–96.
1987a   The Crisis in Family Farming: Who Will Survive? In Farm Work and Field-

work: American Agriculture in Anthropological Perspective. Michael
Chibnik, ed. Pp. 29–57. Ithaca, N.Y.: Cornell University Press.

1987b   Industrial Agriculture in Evolutionary Perspective. Cultural Anthropology
               2 (1): 132–49.

1989   Industrial Agriculture. *In* Economic Anthropology. Stuart Plattner, ed. Pp.
               253–91. Stanford, Calif.: Stanford University Press.

1990   Capitalist Penetration and Family Farming in Georgia and Wisconsin.
               Paper presented at the American Anthropological Association annual meet-
               ing, New Orleans, November 28–December 2.

1991   Motivations of Part-Time Farmers. *In* Multiple Job Holding among Farm
               Families in North America. M. C. Hallberg and Jill Findeis, eds. Pp. 45–
               70. Ames: Iowa State University Press.

forthcoming   Women, Work, and Power on Dodge County Farms. Typescript.

Barnett, Steve, and JoAnn Magdoff

1986   Beyond Narcissism in American Culture of the 1980s. Cultural Anthro-
               pology 1 (4): 413–24.

Barron, Hal S.

1990   Listening to the Silent Majority: Change and Continuity in the Nineteenth-
               Century Rural North. *In* Agricultural and National Development: Views
               on the Nineteenth Century. Lou Ferleger, ed. Pp. 3–23. Ames: Iowa State
               University Press.

Barth, Fredrik

1967   On the Study of Social Change. American Anthropologist 69 (6): 661–69.

Bartley, Numan V.

1990   The Creation of Modern Georgia. 2d ed. Athens: University of Geor-
               gia Press.

Bauer, Douglas

1979   Prairie City, Iowa. Ames: Iowa State University Press.

Bennett, John W.

1980   Management Style: A Concept and Method for the Analysis of Family-
               operated Agricultural Enterprise. *In* Agricultural Decision Making. Peggy
               F. Barlett, ed. Pp. 203–36. New York: Academic Press.

1982   Of Time and the Enterprise: North American Family Farm Management
               in a Context of Resource Marginality. Minneapolis: University of Minne-
               sota Press.

Bentley, Susan E., Peggy F. Barlett, F. Larry Leistritz, Steve H. Murdock, William E.
               Saupe, Don E. Albrecht, Brenda L. Ekstrom, Rita R. Hamm, Arlen G.
               Leholm, Richard W. Rathge, and Janet Wanzek

1989   Involuntary Exits from Farming: Evidence from Four Studies. U.S. Depart-
               ment of Agriculture, Economic Research Service, Agricultural Economic
               Report, no. 625. Washington, D.C.: U.S. Government Printing Office.

Billings, Dwight B., Jr.

1979   Planters and the Making of a "New South": Class, Politics, and Devel-

opment in North Carolina, 1865–1900. Chapel Hill: University of North
Carolina Press.

Bokemeier, Janet, and C. Milton Coughenour
1980   Men and Women in Four Types of Farm Families: Work and Attitudes.
              Paper presented at the Rural Sociological Society annual meeting, Ithaca,
              N.Y., August.

Bonanno, Alessandro
1987   Small Farms: Persistence with Legitimation. Boulder, Colo.: Westview.

Brooks, Nora L., Thomas A. Stucker, and Jennifer A. Bailey
1986   Income and Well-being of Farmers and the Farm Financial Crisis. Rural
              Sociology 51 (4): 391–405.

Bultena, Gordon, Paul Lasley, and J. Geller
1986   The Farm Crisis: Patterns and Impacts of Financial Distress among Iowa
              Farm Families. Rural Sociology 51 (4): 436–48.

Busch, Lawrence, and William B. Lacy
1983   Science, Agriculture, and the Politics of Research. Boulder, Colo.: West-
              view.

Buttel, Frederick H.
1983   Beyond the Family Farm. In Technology and Social Change in Rural Areas.
              Gene F. Summers, ed. Pp. 87–107. Boulder, Colo.: Westview.

Buttel, Frederick H., and Howard Newby, eds.
1980   The Rural Sociology of the Advanced Societies. Montclair, N.J.: Allan-
              held, Osmun.

Cancian, Francesca M.
1987   Love in America. New York: Cambridge University Press.

Cancian, Frank
1987   Economic Behavior in Peasant Communities. In Economic Anthropology.
              Stuart Plattner, ed. Pp. 127–70. Stanford, Calif.: Stanford University Press.

Cawley, Mary
1983   Part-Time Farming in Rural Development: Evidence from Western Ireland.
              Sociologia Ruralis 23 (1): 63–75.

Chayanov, A. V.
[1925] 1966   The Theory of Peasant Economy. D. Thomas, R. E. F. Smith, and B. Ker-
              blay, eds. Reprint. Homewood, Ill.: Irwin.

Chibnik, Michael
1985   The Use of Statistics in Sociocultural Anthropology. Annual Review of
              Anthropology 14:135–57.

Cobb, James C.
1984   Industrialization and Southern Society, 1877–1984. Lexington: University
              Press of Kentucky.
1990   "Somebody Done Nailed Us on the Cross": Federal Farm and Welfare
              Policy and the Civil Rights Movement in the Mississippi Delta. Journal of
              American History 77 (3): 912–36.

Cobb, Mrs. Wilton Philip
[1932] 1983   History of Dodge County. Reprint. Spartanburg, S.C.: The Reprint Co.
Cochrane, Willard W.
1979   The Development of American Agriculture: A Historical Analysis. Minne-
              apolis: University of Minnesota Press.
Collier, Jane F.
1986   From Mary to Modern Woman: The Material Basis of Marianismo and Its
              Transformation in a Spanish Village. American Ethnologist 13 (1): 100–
              107.
1989   From Co-owners to Co-workers: Changing Marital Relations in a Spanish
              Village. Bunting Institute Working Paper. Cambridge, Mass.: Radcliffe
              Research and Study Center.
Collins, Jane L.
1986   The Household and Relations of Production in Southern Peru. Comparative
              Studies in Society and History 28 (4): 651–71.
Conzen, Kathleen Neils
1985   Peasant Pioneers: Generational Succession among German Farmers in
              Frontier Minnesota. In The Countryside in the Age of Capitalist Trans-
              formation: Essays in the Social History of Rural America. Steven Hahn
              and Jonathan Prude, eds. Pp.259–92. Chapel Hill: University of North
              Carolina Press.
Coughenour, C. Milton, and Louis Swanson
1983   Work Statuses and Occupations of Men and Women in Farm Families and
              the Structure of Farms. Rural Sociology 48 (1): 24–43.
Council for Agricultural Science and Technology
1988   Long-Term Viability of U.S. Agriculture. Report no. 114. Ames, Iowa.
Danbom, David B.
1979   The Resisted Revolution: Urban America and the Industrialization of Agri-
              culture, 1900–1930. Ames: Iowa State University Press.
Daniel, Pete
1985   Breaking the Land: The Transformation of Cotton, Tobacco, and Rice
              Cultures since 1880. Urbana: University of Illinois Press.
Darby, Jill
1986   Survival Strategies of Economically Depressed Nevada Ranchers: The Role
              of Women. Paper presented at the Society for Economic Anthropology
              annual meeting, Riverside, Calif., April 3–4.
Davis, John Emmeus
1980   Capitalist Agricultural Development and the Exploitation of the Proper-
              tied Laborer. In The Rural Sociology of the Advanced Societies. Fred-
              erick H. Buttel and Howard Newby, eds. Pp. 133–53. Montclair, N.J.:
              Allanheld, Osmun.
DeCanio, Stephen J.
1974   Agriculture in the Postbellum South: The Economics of Production and
              Supply. Cambridge: MIT Press.

Donham, Donald L.
1990   History, Power, Ideology. New York: Cambridge University Press.
Easterlin, Richard
1980   Birth and Fortune: The Impact of Numbers on Personal Welfare. New York:
              Basic Books.
Eller, Ronald D.
1982   Miners, Millhands, and Mountaineers: Industrialization of the Appalachian
              South, 1880–1930. Knoxville: University of Tennessee Press.
Everett, William Johnson, and Sheila Johnson Everett
forthcoming   Couples at Work: A Study in Patterns of Work, Family, and Faith. *In* Work,
              Family, and Faith: Changing Patterns among Old Institutions. Nancy Tatom
              Ammerman and Wade Clark Roof, eds.
Fink, Deborah
1986a   Constructing Rural Culture: Family and Land in Iowa. Agriculture and
              Human Values 3 (4): 43–53.
1986b   Open Country, Iowa: Rural Women, Tradition, and Change. Albany: State
              University of New York Press.
1992   Agrarian Women: Wives and Mothers in Rural Nebraska, 1880–1940.
              Chapel Hill: University of North Carolina Press.
Fischer, David Hackett
1989   Albion's Seed: Four British Folkways in America. New York: Oxford
              University Press.
Fite, Gilbert
1981   Cotton Fields No More: Southern Agriculture, 1865–1980. Lexington:
              University Press of Kentucky.
Flora, Jan L., and John M. Stitz
1985   Ethnicity, Persistence, and Capitalization of Agriculture in the Great Plains
              during the Settlement Period: Wheat Production and Risk Avoidance. Rural
              Sociology 50 (3): 341–60.
Flynt, Wayne
1989   Poor but Proud: Alabama's Poor Whites. Tuscaloosa: University of Ala-
              bama Press.
Ford, Arthur M.
1973   Political Economics of Rural Poverty in the South. Cambridge, Mass.:
              Ballinger.
Foster, Gary, Richard Hummel, and Robert Whittenbarger
1987   Ethnic Echoes through One Hundred Years of Midwestern Agriculture.
              Rural Sociology 52 (3): 365–78.
Fox-Genovese, Elizabeth
1988   Within the Plantation Household: Black and White Women of the Old
              South. Chapel Hill: University of North Carolina Press.
Friedburger, Mark
1988   Farm Families and Change in Twentieth Century America. Lexington:
              University Press of Kentucky.

1989   Shake-out: Iowa Farm Families in the 1980s. Lexington: University Press of Kentucky.

Friedland, Roger, and A. F. Robertson, eds.
1990   Beyond the Marketplace: Rethinking Economy and Society. New York: Aldine de Gruyter.

Friedland, William H.
1984   The Labor Force in U.S. Agriculture. *In* Food Security in the United States. Lawrence Busch and William B. Lacy, eds. Pp. 143–81. Boulder, Colo.: Westview.

Friedmann, Harriet
1978   Simple Commodity Production and Wage Labor in the American Plains. Journal of Peasant Studies 6 (1): 71–100.
1980   Household Production and the National Economy: Concepts for the Analysis of Agrarian Formation. Journal of Peasant Studies 7 (2): 158–84.

Fujimoto, Asao
1977   The Communities in the San Joaquin Valley: The Relation between Scale of Farming, Water Use, and the Quality of Life. *In* Hearings on Obstacles to Strengthen the Family Farm System. U.S. House of Representatives, Subcommittee on Family Farms, Rural Development, and Special Studies. 95th Congress, first session. Washington, D.C.: U.S. Government Printing Office.

Gallaher, Art, Jr.
1961   Plainville: Fifteen Years Later. New York: Columbia University Press.

Garrett, Patricia, and Michael D. Schulman
1989   Family Division of Labor and Decision-making among Smallholders. Sociology and Social Research 74 (1): 16–21.

Gartman, David
1986   Reification of Consumer Products: A General History Illustrated by the Case of the American Automobile. *In* Sociological Theory 4 (Fall): 167–85.

Gilbert, Jess, and Raymond Akor
1988   Increasing Structural Divergence in U.S. Dairying: California and Wisconsin since 1950. Rural Sociology 53 (1): 56–72.

Gilbert, Jess, and Roy Barnes
1988   Reproduction or Transformation of Family Farming?: An Empirical Analysis of Wisconsin Farms, 1950–1975. Paper presented at the Rural Sociological Society annual meeting, Athens, Ga., August 19–23.

Gladwin, Christina H.
1991   Multiple Job-holding among Farm Families and the Increase in Women's Farming. *In* Multiple Job-holding among Farm Families. M. C. Halberg, Jill L. Findeis, and Daniel A. Lass, eds. Pp. 213–28. Ames: Iowa State University Press.

Goldschmidt, Walter
1978a   As You Sow: Three Studies in the Social Consequences of Agribusiness.
            Montclair, N.J.: Allanheld, Osmun.
1978b   Large Scale Farming and the Rural Social Structure. Rural Sociology 43
            (3): 362–66.
Goodman, David, and Michael Redclift
1982   From Peasant to Proletarian: Capitalist Development and Agrarian Transi-
            tions. New York: St. Martin's Press.
Goodman, David, Bernardo Sorj, and John Wilkinson
1987   From Farming to Biotechnology. London: Basil Blackwell.
Goss, Kevin F., Richard D. Rodefeld, and Frederick H. Buttel
1980   The Political Economy of Class Structure in U.S. Agriculture: A Theo-
            retical Outline. In The Rural Sociology of the Advanced Societies. Fred-
            erick H. Buttel and Howard Newby, eds. Pp. 3–32. Montclair, N.J.: Allan-
            held, Osmun.
Hagood, Margaret Jarman
1939   Mothers of the South: Portraiture of the White Tenant Farm Women. New
            York: Norton.
Hahn, Steven
1983   The Roots of Southern Populism: Yeoman Farmers and the Transformation
            of the Georgia Upcountry, 1850–1890. New York: Oxford University Press.
1985   The "Unmaking" of the Southern Yeomanry: The Transformation of the
            Georgia Upcountry, 1860–1890. In The Countryside in the Age of Capital-
            ist Transformation: Essays in the Social History of Rural America. Stephen
            Hahn and Jonathan Prude, eds. Pp. 179–203. Chapel Hill: University of
            North Carolina Press.
Hamilton, Gary G.
1977   Chinese Consumption of Foreign Commodities: A Comparative Perspec-
            tive. In American Sociological Review 42:877–91.
Handwerker, W. Penn
1986   Culture and Reproduction: Exploring Micro/Macro Linkages. In Culture
            and Reproduction. W. Penn Handwerker, ed. Pp. 1–28. Boulder, Colo.:
            Westview.
Haney, Wava G., and Jane B. Knowles, eds.
1988   Women and Farming: Changing Roles, Changing Structure. Boulder,
            Colo.: Westview.
Harding, Susan F.
1984   Remaking Ibieca: Rural Life in Aragon under Franco. Chapel Hill: Univer-
            sity of North Carolina Press.
Harper, Douglas A.
1987   Working Knowledge: Skill and Community in a Small Shop. Chicago:
            University of Chicago Press.
Harrington, David, and Thomas A. Carlin

1987   The U.S. Farm Sector: How Is It Weathering the 1980s? U.S. Department
                of Agriculture, Economic Research Service, Agricultural Information
                Bulletin, no. 506. Washington, D.C.: U.S. Government Printing Office.

Heffernan, William D., and Judith Bortner Heffernan
1986   Impact of the Farm Crisis on Rural Families and Communities. Rural Soci-
                ologist 6 (3): 160–70.

Hightower, Jim
1973   Hard Tomatoes, Hard Times: The Failure of the Land Grant College Com-
                plex. New York: Schenkman.

Hochschild, Arlie
1989   The Second Shift: Working Parents and the Revolution at Home. New York:
                Viking.

Innes, Robert, Edward Keller, and Hoy Carman
1989   Chapter 12 and Farm Bankruptcy in California. California Agriculture 43
                (6): 28–31.

James, David R.
1986   Local State Structure and the Transformation of Southern Agriculture. *In*
                Studies in the Transformation of U.S. Agriculture. A. Eugene Havens, ed.
                Pp. 150–78. Boulder, Colo.: Westview.

Jolly, Robert W., Arnold Paulsen, James D. Johnson, Kenneth H. Baum, and Richard
                Prescott
1985   Incidence, Intensity, and Duration of Financial Stress among Farm Firms.
                American Journal of Agricultural Economics 67 (5): 1108–15.

Jones, Jacqueline
1985   Labor of Love, Labor of Sorrow. New York: Basic Books.

Jones, Lu Ann
1985   "The Task That Is Ours": White North Carolina Farm Women and Agrarian
                Reform, 1886–1914. Institute News: Newsletter of the North Carolina
                Institute of Applied History 4:3–8.

Kada, Ryohei
1980   Part-Time Farming: Off-Farm Employment and Farm Adjustments in the
                United States and Japan. Tokyo: Center for Academic Publications.

Keller, Bill
1987   Gorbachev Calls for Family Farming. New York Times, July 1, p. 4.

Kirby, Jack Temple
1983   The Transformation of Southern Plantations, 1920–1960. Agricultural
                History 57 (3): 257–76.
1987   Rural Worlds Lost: The American South, 1920–1960. Baton Rouge: Louisi-
                ana State University Press.

Leistritz, F. Larry, and Brenda L. Ekstrom
1988a   The Financial Characteristics of Production Units and Producers Experi-
                encing Financial Stress. *In* The Farm Financial Crisis: Socioeconomic
                Dimensions and Implications for Producers and Rural Areas. Steve H.
                Murdock and F. Larry Leistritz, eds. Pp.73–95. Boulder, Colo.: Westview.

1988b   Selected Socioeconomic Characteristics of North Dakota Rural Residents.
               Fargo: North Dakota State University, Department of Agricultural Eco-
               nomics.
Leistritz, F. Larry, Brenda L. Ekstrom, Arlen G. Leholm, and Janet Wanzek
1987   Families Displaced from Farming in North Dakota: Characteristics and
               Adjustment Experience. Agricultural Economics Report, no. 220. Fargo:
               North Dakota State University, Department of Agricultural Economics.
Livingstone, Frank B.
1984   Duffy Blood Groups, Vivax Malaria, and Malaria Selection in Human
               Populations: A Review. Human Biology 56:413–25.
Lobao, Linda M.
1990   Locality and Inequality: Farm and Industry Structure and Socioeconomic
               Conditions. Albany: State University of New York Press.
McKendrick, Neil, John Brewer, and J. H. Plumb
1982   The Birth of a Consumer Society: The Commercialization of Eighteenth
               Century England. London: Europa Publications.
McMath, Robert C., Jr.
1985   Sandy Land and Hogs in the Timber: (Agri)cultural Origins of the Farmer's
               Alliance in Texas. In The Countryside in the Age of Capitalist Transfor-
               mation: Essays in the Social History of Rural America. Stephen Hahn and
               Jonathan Prude, eds. Pp. 205–29. Chapel Hill: University of North Caro-
               lina Press.
McNall, Scott G., and Sally Ann McNall
1983   Plains Families: Exploring Sociology through Social History. New York:
               St. Martin's Press.
Malone, Ann Patton
1981   Changes and Continuities in Wiregrass, Georgia, 1870–1900: Overview of
               the Wiregrass, Georgia, Rural History Project. Tifton, Ga.: Agrirama.
1986   Piney Woods Farmers of South Georgia, 1850–1900: Jeffersonian Yeo-
               men in an Age of Expanding Commercialism. Agricultural History 60 (4):
               51–84.
Mann, Susan Archer
1990   Agrarian Capitalism in Theory and Practice. Chapel Hill: University of
               North Carolina Press.
Mann, Susan A., and James M. Dickinson
1978   Obstacles to the Development of a Capitalist Agriculture. Journal of Peas-
               ant Studies 5:466–79.
Marchand, Roland
1985   Advertising the American Dream: Making Way for Modernity, 1920–1940.
               Berkeley: University of California Press.
Matthaei, Julie A.
1982   An Economic History of Women in America: Women's Work, the Sexual
               Division of Labor, and the Development of Capitalism. New York:
               Schocken.

Mooney, Patrick H.
1986   Farming, Rationality, and Craftsmanship: Beyond X-Efficiency. Agriculture
                and Human Values 3 (4): 54–58.
1988   My Own Boss?: Class, Rationality, and the Family Farm. Boulder, Colo.:
                Westview.
Moore, Henrietta
1988   Feminism and Anthropology. Minneapolis: University of Minnesota Press.
Murdock, Steve H., and F. Larry Leistritz, eds.
1988   The Farm Financial Crisis: Socioeconomic Dimensions and Implications
                for Producers and Rural Areas. Boulder, Colo.: Westview.
Murdock, Steve H., Don E. Albrecht, Rita R. Hamm, F. Larry Leistritz, and Arlen G.
                Leholm
1986   The Farm Crisis in the Great Plains: Implications for Theory and Policy
                Development. Rural Sociology 51 (4): 406–35.
National Issues Forum
1987   On Second Thought: A Report on the 1986–1987 Forums. Dayton, Ohio:
                Domestic Policy Association.
Nikolitch, Radoje
1969   Family-operated Farms: Their Compatibility with Technological Advance.
                American Journal of Agricultural Economics 51 (3): 530–45.
Odum, Eugene P., and Monica C. Turner
1988   The Georgia Landscape: A Changing Resource. Athens: University of
                Georgia, Kellogg Interdisciplinary Task Force on Physical Resources.
Office of Technology Assessment, Congress of the United States
1986   Technology, Public Policy, and the Changing Structure of American Agri-
                culture. Washington, D.C.: U.S. Government Printing Office.
Owsley, Frank L.
1980   The Farmers Possess the Land. In The Southern Common People: Studies
                in Nineteenth Century Social History. Edward Magdol and Jon L. Wakelyn,
                eds. Pp. 21–36. Westport, Conn.: Greenwood Press.
Paarlberg, Don
1980   Farm and Food Policy: Issues of the 1980s. Lincoln: University of Nebraska
                Press.
Padfield, Harland, and William E. Martin
1965   Farmers, Workers, and Machines: Technological Social Change in Farm
                Industries of Arizona. Tucson: University of Arizona Press.
Peterson, Willis
1980   The Farm Size Issue: A New Perspective. Staff Paper, no. P80-6. St. Paul:
                University of Minnesota, Department of Agriculture and Applied Eco-
                nomics.
Pfeffer, Max, and Jess Gilbert
1989   Gender and Off-Farm Employment in Two Farming Systems: Responses to
                Farm Crisis in the Cornbelt and Mississippi Delta. Sociological Quarterly
                32 (4): 593–610.

Pimentel, David, E. C. Terhune, R. Dyson-Hudson, S. Rochereau, R. Samis, E. Smith,
      D. Denman, D. Rufschneider, and M. Shepard
1976   Land Degradation: Effects on Food and Energy Resources. Science 194:
              149–55.
Plattner, Stuart
1989   Economic Anthropology. Stanford, Calif.: Stanford University Press.
Raper, Arthur F.
1936   Preface to Peasantry: A Tale of Two Black Belt Counties. Chapel Hill:
              University of North Carolina Press.
Rappaport, Roy A.
1979   Ecology, Meaning, and Religion. Richmond, Calif.: North Atlantic Books.
Reinhardt, Nola
1988   Our Daily Bread: Family Farming in the Colombian Andes. Berkeley:
              University of California Press.
Reinhardt, Nola, and Peggy Barlett
1989   The Persistence of Family Farms in United States Agriculture. Sociologia
              Ruralis 29 (3/4): 203–25.
Rodefeld, Richard D.
1979   The Family-Type Farm and Structural Differentiation: Trends, Causes,
              and Consequences of Change, Research Needs. Staff Paper, no. 24. Uni-
              versity Park: Pennsylvania State University, Department of Agricultural
              Economics and Rural Sociology.
Rogers, Susan Carol
1985   Owners and Operators of Farmland: Structural Changes in U.S. Agricul-
              ture. Human Organization 44 (3): 206–21.
1987   Mixing Paradigms on Mixed Farming: Anthropological and Economic
              Views of Specialization in Illinois Agriculture. In Farm Work and Field-
              work: American Agriculture in Anthropological Perspective. Michael
              Chibnik, ed. Pp. 58–89. Ithaca, N.Y.: Cornell University Press.
Roseberry, William
1989   Peasants and the World. In Economic Anthropology. Stuart Plattner, ed.
              Stanford, Calif.: Stanford University Press.
Rosenblatt, Paul C.
1990   Farming Is in Our Blood: Farm Families in Economic Crisis. Ames: Iowa
              State University Press.
Rosenfeld, Rachel
1985   Farm Women: Work, Farm, and Family in the United States. Chapel Hill:
              University of North Carolina Press.
Rubin, Lillian Breslow
1976   Worlds of Pain: Life in the Working Class Family. New York: Basic Books.
Rutz, Henry J., and Benjamin S. Orlove, eds.
1989   The Social Economy of Consumption. Society for Economic Anthro-
              pology, Monographs in Economic Anthropology, no. 6. Lanham, Md.:
              University Press of America.

Ryan, Mary
1981   Cradle of the Middle Class: The Family in Oneida County, New York,
               1790–1865. New York: Cambridge University Press.
Sachs, Carolyn E.
1983   The Invisible Farmers: Women in Agricultural Production. Totowa, N.J.:
               Rowmun and Allanheld.
Salamon, Sonya
1985   Ethnic Communities and the Structure of Agriculture. Rural Sociology 50
               (3): 323–40.
1992   Prairie Patrimony: Family, Farming, and Community in the Midwest.
               Chapel Hill: University of North Carolina Press.
Salamon, Sonya, and Karen Davis-Brown
1986   Middle-Range Farmers Persisting through the Agricultural Crisis. Rural
               Sociology 51 (4): 503–12.
Salamon, Sonya, Kathleen M. Gengenbacher, and Dwight J. Penas
1986   Family Factors Affecting the Intergenerational Succession to Farming.
               Human Organization 45 (1): 24–33.
Salant, Priscilla
1984   Farm Households and the Off-Farm Sector: Results from Mississippi and
               Tennessee. U.S. Department of Agriculture, Economic Research Service,
               Agricultural Economic Report, no. 143. Washington, D.C.: U.S. Govern-
               ment Printing Office.
Salant, Priscilla, and William Saupe
1986   Farm Household Viability: Policy Implications from the Wisconsin Family
               Farm Survey. Economic Issues, no. 97. Madison: University of Wisconsin–
               Madison, Department of Agricultural Economics, College of Agricultural
               and Life Sciences.
Schaub, James
1990   The Peanut Program and Its Effects. National Food Review 13 (1): 37–40.
Schertz, Lyle P., and Others
1979   Another Revolution in United States Farming?: U.S. Department of Agri-
               culture, Economic Research Service, Agricultural Economic Report,
               no. 441. Washington, D.C.: U.S. Government Printing Office.
Schneider, Jane
1987   Review of the Rise of Market Culture by William M. Reddy. American
               Ethnologist 14 (4): 752–55.
Schroeder, Emily H., Frederick C. Fliegel, and J. C. van Es
1985   Measurement of the Lifestyle Dimensions of Farming for Small-Scale
               Farmers. Rural Sociology 50 (3): 305–22.
Simpson, Ida Harper, John Wilson, and Kristina Young
1988   The Sexual Division of Farm Household Labor: A Replication and Exten-
               sion. Rural Sociology 53 (2): 145–65.
Skinner, Robert, and Scott Sanford
1990   U.S. Cotton Programs. National Food Review 13 (1): 27–31.

Smale, Melinda, William E. Saupe, and Priscilla Salant
1986   Farm Family Characteristics and the Viability of Farm Households in Wis-
            consin, Mississippi, and Tennessee. Agricultural Economics Research 38
            (2): 11–27.
Sonka, Steven, and Earl O. Heady
1974   American Farm-Size Structure in Relation to Income and Employment
            Opportunities of Farms, Rural Communities, and Other Sectors. Center
            for Agricultural and Rural Development, Report no. 48. Ames: Iowa State
            University.
Starr, Paul
1982   The Social Transformation of American Medicine. New York: Basic
            Books.
Strange, Marty, ed.
1984   It's Not All Sunshine and Fresh Air: Chronic Health Effects of Modern
            Farming Practices. Walthill, Nebr.: Center for Rural Affairs.
Thomas, Robert J.
1985   Citizenship, Gender, and Work: Social Organization of Industrial Agricul-
            ture. Berkeley: University of California Press.
Tindall, George B.
1967   The Emergence of the New South, 1913–45. Baton Rouge: Louisiana State
            University Press.
Tocqueville, Alexis de
[1840] 1958   Democracy in America. 3 vols. Reprint. New York: Knopf.
Tweeten, Luther
1984   Causes and Consequences of Structural Change in the Farming Industry.
            Washington, D.C.: National Policy Association, Food and Agriculture
            Committee.
Tweeten, Luther, and Wallace Huffman
1980   Structural Change. In Structure of Agriculture and Information Needs Re-
            garding Small Farms. Small Farms Project, Paper no. 7. Washington, D.C.:
            National Rural Center.
U.S. Bureau of the Census
1929–87   Census of Agriculture. Washington D.C.: U.S. Government Printing Office.
1930–80   Census of Population. Washington D.C.: U.S. Government Printing Office.
U.S. Department of Agriculture
1938   Dodge County Home Demonstration Report and Agricultural Extension
            Agent Annual Report. RG33, T855. National Archives, Washington, D.C.
1983   Handbook of Agricultural Charts. Agricultural Handbook No. 619. Wash-
            ington, D.C.: U.S. Government Printing Office.
1989   Agricultural Resources: Outlook and Situation Summary. Economic Re-
            search Service. Washington, D.C.: U.S. Government Printing Office.
Van Es, J. C., F. C. Fliegel, C. Erickson, H. Backus, and E. Harper
1982   Choosing the Best of Two Worlds: Small, Part-Time Farms in Illinois.

            Agricultural Economics Research Report, no. 185. Urbana: University of
            Illinois, College of Agriculture.

Veblen, Thorstein
1934   The Theory of the Leisure Class. New York: Macmillan.

Vogeler, Ingolf
1981   The Myth of the Family Farm: Agribusiness Dominance of U.S. Agricul-
            ture. Boulder, Colo.: Westview.

Weber, Max
1968   Economy and Society: An Outline of Interpretive Sociology. New York:
            Bedminster Press.

Wessel, James
1983   Trading the Future: Farm Exports and the Concentration of Economic
            Power in Our Food System. San Francisco: Institute for Food and Develop-
            ment Policy.

Wetherington, Mark Vicker
1985   The New South Comes to Wiregrass Georgia, 1865–1910. Ann Arbor,
            Mich.: University Microfilms International.

Wilkening, Eugene, and Jess Gilbert
1987   Family Farming in the United States. *In* Family Farming in Europe and
            America. Boguslaw Galeski and Eugene Wilkening, eds. Pp. 271–301.
            Boulder, Colo.: Westview.

Williams, Rosalind H.
1982   Dream Worlds: Mass Consumption in Late Nineteenth Century France.
            Berkeley: University of California Press.

Wolf, Eric R.
1982   Europe and the People without History. Berkeley: University of Califor-
            nia Press.

Woofter, T. J., Jr.
1936   Landlord and Tenant on the Cotton Plantation. Works Progress Administra-
            tion, Division of Social Research, Research Monograph, no. 5. Washing-
            ton, D.C.: U.S. Government Printing Office.

Wright, Gavin
1986   Old South, New South: Revolutions in the Southern Economy since the
            Civil War. New York: Basic Books.

Wynne, Walter
1943   Culture of a Contemporary Rural Community: Harmony, Georgia. U.S.
            Department of Agriculture, Bureau of Agricultural Economics, Rural Life
            Studies, no. 6. Washington, D.C.: U.S. Government Printing Office.

Young, John A., and Jan M. Newton
1980   Capitalism and Human Obsolescence: Corporate Control versus Individual
            Survival in Rural America. Montclair, N.J.: Allanheld, Osmun.

INDEX